THE LIFE OF METRICA
IN TWENTIETH-CE

ENr

 COLᵛᵀ

The Life of Metrical and Free Verse in Twentieth-Century Poetry

Jon Silkin

First published in Great Britain 1997 by
MACMILLAN PRESS LTD
Houndmills, Basingstoke, Hampshire RG21 6XS and London
Companies and representatives throughout the world

A catalogue record for this book is available from the British Library.

ISBN 0–333–59320–0 hardcover
ISBN 0–333–59321–9 paperback

First published in the United States of America 1997 by
ST. MARTIN'S PRESS, INC.,
Scholarly and Reference Division,
175 Fifth Avenue, New York, N.Y. 10010

ISBN 0–312–17239–7

Library of Congress Cataloging-in-Publication Data
Silkin, Jon.
The life of metrical and free verse in twentieth-century poetry / Jon
Silkin
p.   cm.
Includes bibliographical references and index.
ISBN 0–312–17239–7 (cloth)
1. English poetry—20th century—History and criticism.
2. American poetry—20th century—History and criticism.   3. English
language—20th century—Versification.   4. Free verse—History and
criticism.   I. Title.
PR605.V4S55   1997
821'.9109—dc20   96–44850
                                                                          CIP

This book is printed on paper suitable for recycling and made from fully managed and
sustained forest sources.

10   9   8   7   6   5   4   3   2   1
06   05   04   03   02   01   00   99   98   97

Printed and bound in Great Britain by
Antony Rowe Ltd, Chippenham, Wiltshire

Contents

Acknowledgements   vii

Note on the scansion marks   ix

Note on the text   xi

1   The Healing Process – Metrical and Free Verse   1

2   Imagism, Lawrence, Pound, Read and Eliot   30

3   Ezra Pound   108

4   D.H. Lawrence, Poet   179

5   Dylan Thomas   242

6   Basil Bunting and his *Briggflatts*   271

7   Some Poets Now   300

Appendix: Poets on Poetry   367

Free verse; verse free? *Jon Glover*   369
Mixed modes *Dennis Silk*   372
Syllabics *Thom Gunn*   374
Forms and inspirations *Jon Silkin*   377
Free and metrical verse *Rodney Pybus*   378
On the practice of free verse *Marvin Bell*   381
Poetry as discovery and potential *Anne Cluysenaar*   384
The prose poem   389
Basil Bunting 1900–85: a personal memoir *Connie Pickard*   390

References   397

Bibliography   403

Index   415

Acknowledgements

Writers and books must thank people who wittingly or not have helped them. The first four chapters of this book were written while I was teaching English and American literature in Japan at Tsukuba University. I thank my students and colleagues there who offered that reciprocity without which a writer's insight, where it exists, remains egotism and guesswork.

In the last stages of the work, Linda Goldsmith and Michelle Laing, who typed it, gave the kind of encouragement one needs when the thing is becoming visible and whole.

My gratitude to Rodney Pybus and Lorna Tracy, who read parts of the first four chapters, cannot be fully expressed, but it needs to be attempted. Theirs was the comprehensive response that encouraged me in the detailed discussion of poems which forms the substance of this book.

I am likewise more than grateful to my fellow-poet and critic, Jon Glover, with whom not dialogue but a constant exchange took place. This was because of the continuing mutual concern which ensured that, whatever the subject of our discussion, it fed the underlying concerns of this book. I believe this was over a seven-year period, when this work was actively in my mind.

I sincerely thank my editors Margaret Bartley and Charmian Hearne, both of whom assiduously read and provided crucial criticism of the text, the deficiencies of which, however, remain mine. And I thank those at Macmillan, and Ruth Willats, who have had patience with a long book. Without their tolerance, the writing and completion of the work would have been harder to accomplish.

And finally, I thank all my adult students, those in Continuing Education with whom, in conversation and debate, the idea of such a book of discussion and argument grew. It seems especially important to say this when Adult Education, as an activity and a concept, is presently in jeopardy. Governments come and go, but being adult and in need of reciprocal nourishment remains. Such reciprocity in my experience takes place more often than one has the right to expect.

I wish to thank the Arts Council of England for its major bursary, which greatly assisted me in the writing of this work.

The publishers and I would like to thank the following for their kind permission to use copyright material:

Carcanet Press and New Directions Publishing Corporation for 'Oread' by H.D., in *Collected Poems* (Carcanet Press, 1988) and *Collected Poems 1912–44* (New Directions, 1988); and also for 'Sitalkas' by HD, reproduced in Peter Jones, *Imagist Poetry* (Penguin, 1972).

Faber and Faber and Harcourt Brace and Company (HBT) for extracts from 'The Waste Land' by T.S. Eliot, from *Collected Poems 1909–1962* (1963).

Oxford University Press for extracts from 'Briggflatts', Basil Bunting, *Collected Poems* (1977).

Connie Pickard and *Stand Magazine* for 'Basil Bunting 1900–1985: A Personal Memoir', *Stand Magazine*, Vol. 26, No. 3, Summer 1985.

Penguin Books and Dufour Editions for extracts from 'Funeral Music' and 'September Song' by Geoffrey Hill, *Collected Poems* (1985).

Note on the Scansion Marks

/ stands for a stressed syllable, but I have avoided using u for an unstressed one. First, it would have cluttered the verse quotations even more, and second, the mark stands in the way of questions concerning the gradations of stress and unstress. Additionally, I wanted to avoid confusion with the sign ×, which I have used to denote, not a weaker stress in a system of weaker and stronger syllables, but a situation in which I perceived an as much as possible no-stress situation, usually one in which rapid movement occurs. I have also used a bar − over the top of a syllable to indicate duration more than stress, and a combination of bar and accent when I felt both to be operating. I have used ⌒, a bridge, to suggest that sometimes a stress is distributed over a cluster of syllables; and finally, I have used a bar under pairs or groups of syllables to indicate alliteration or assonance.

Generalizations are frequently out of place, and, worse still, misleading. So I'll offer just the one, which stems from what I believe I have noticed in reading my contemporaries. I believe I have detected in poets who began writing in the post-Second World War period a tendency to modify the weak/strong system of syllables in their work. There is not only an apparent tropism towards anapaestic/dactyllic rhythms, but also a moderating of the contrasting syllables of stress and weak stress, a greater deliquescence in the rhythms. Here again, in some of his work, Lawrence anticipates this, as I briefly suggested in contrasting his rhythms with Rosenberg's, the poet killed in the First World War. Clearly it is a matter of degree, but in Fisher's case there is a noticeable flowing fluid movement in his rhythms in contrast with those of, say, Larkin, who inherits an earlier ethos and its tone. I have made related comments on the work of Tomlinson and Redgrove, so it's superfluous to repeat those here. But it is worth remarking of Geoffrey Hill, who writes both free and metrical verse, that, in some of his metrical poetry, there tends to be a subtle avoidance of the earlier version of metricality I have indicated. Readers will notice, each in his or her own way, but if I have picked up something that seems, currently, to be the case, then it is possible to suggest that this modification of metrical verse is the result of the practice of free verse, and may thus indicate the way things are presently tracking.

Note on the Text

The sources of quotations in the text are invariably cited within the text itself, by means of the title of the work and the page numbers concerned. Fuller references are made in the listing at the end of the book, and, wherever possible, the main works are cited in the order of their appearance in the relevant chapter.

1

The Healing Process – Metrical and Free Verse

The verse of the poem is a delicate thing. It has almost ceased to beat, and seems maintained only by the flutter of tenuous hopes and sickening fears.

> the unlooked-for claim
> At the first hearing for a moment took
> More hope out of his life than he supposed
> That any old man ever could have lost.

Wordsworth, who was so often an imitator, here speaks with his own voice; and the verse is the contribution he makes to prosody.

Of 'Michael': James Smith, 'Wordsworth: A Preliminary Survey', *Scrutiny*, no. 7, 1938.[1]

No doubt this widespread metrical ignorance is itself a symptom of some deeper change: and I am far from suggesting that the appearance of *vers libre* is simply a result of ignorance. More probably the ignorance, and the deliberate abandonment, of accentual metres are correlative phenomena, and both the results of some revolution in our whole sense of rhythm – a revolution of great importance reaching deep down into the unconscious and even perhaps into the blood.

C.S. Lewis, 'Donne and Love Poetry in the Seventeenth Century' (from *Seventeenth Century Studies Presented to Sir Herbert Grierson*, 1938)[2]

1.   Reprinted in *William Wordsworth: Penguin Critical Anthologies*, ed. Graham McMaster, 1972, p. 347.
2.   Reprinted in *Seventeenth Century English Poetry*, ed. William R. Keast, 1962 pp. 99–100.

The second characteristic excellence of Mr Wordsworth's
works is: a correspondent weight and sanity of the thoughts
and sentiments – won, not from books, but – from the
poet's own meditative observation. They are *fresh* and have
the dew upon them.

S.T. Coleridge, *Biographia Literaria*, Everyman
Edition, p. 265 (my emphasis)

I group these three analyses in two heads. James Smith's feeling
for the prosodic and living motion of Wordsworth's lines intimates a concern for movement that can be realized without distorting metre. If iambic pentameter is ten syllables with a norm of
five emphasized and five unemphasized syllables (or a mixture of
emphasis and length/duration), Smith indicates what is achieved
in collaboration with the reader, whose mind can keep the met-
ronomic frame in 'active suspension' *and* play into it an extreme
version of the metre that 'has almost ceased to beat'. His feeling is
beautifully put, and it is this combination in prosodic counterpoint
enacting a delicate pulse of feeling that makes Wordsworth's lines
so fine. It constitutes one of the poet's many contributions to the
development of prosody.

I group C.S. Lewis's comment with James Smith's. The 'ignorance' and 'abandonment, of accentual metres are correlative phenomena, and both the results of some revolution in our whole sense
of rhythm – a revolution of great importance reaching deep down
into the unconscious and even perhaps into the blood'.

Interesting as this assertion is, what strikes one more is that
it appears to presume that rhythm is basic, that it cannot be got
'beyond' or 'under' – and it is atomic and primary. Yet I wonder
if beneath rhythmic impulse something springs which might be
referred to as the processes of active imagination.

What if a poet has no *active* choices? If s/he can write only in
free verse because s/he has not tried or cannot write metred verse,
or if the poet cannot put aside metre and try free verse, s/he is, I
believe, limited, because so much of recent creative flow, with all its
imperfections, has realized itself in the improvisation of free verse.

Without options, the conceiving of the poem in its primitive early
stages of creation is hardly provisional, not conceived but put forth
half-born in the poet's limitations. Evidently all human creation has
limitation, but I mean to identify some form of making which is
pre-made. What matters in such a case is that what has been made

has been denied the creative modesty, which the provisional endows. It is the difference, again, between a bird with a fixed song engineered in the brain through a conjunction of particular synapses enabling only an invariable route, and a composer able to explore some options. Or the plant that assembles its car(s) on an established matrix, as against a designer exploring the possibilities of locomotion without consideration for the oil companies.

Wordsworth is Coleridge's equal as a critic, but it is the latter's incisive insight that is crucial in his positive judgements of his friend's poetry. I put his comment in a second heading; Wordsworth's poetry of whom he wrote in his *Biographia Literaria*:

> thoughts and sentiments – won, not from books, but – from the poet's own meditative observation. They are *fresh* and have the dew upon them.
>
> (my emphasis)

Such freshness is 'won' through Wordsworth's being determined to have feeling engage with and invigorate its eventual form. Metricists will assert that Wordsworth's poetry works metrically, which is almost true. Yet the range within his metrical working is not an argument for our having to use metre to the exclusion of free verse, but more properly an indication as to how much Wordsworth wishes to draw the utmost variation into the limitations of metre, and how metre was submitted to the needs of his 'fresh' shaping impulse.

Moreover, although the 'Immortality' Ode is made of various metrical units, Wordsworth's composition (in the musical sense) comes within sight and hearing, syntactically and rhythmically, of free verse, in the very disparateness of its metrical parts, and the swift unexpected modulations between each metre. Hopkins puts his apprehension of this music in a letter to his friend R.W. Dixon (23 October 1886):

> The rhymes are so musically interlaced, the rhythms so happily succeed (surely it is a magical change 'O joy! that in our embers').

But in any case the argument between metricists and free verse writers is wasteful, since it is not a question of feeling, or of being, compelled to choose between either but of using, if the poet wishes, both:

It seems to me we have reached an impasse right now, and there IS an urgent need to reconcile meter and free verse, if that is possible, because meter is getting starved without the improvisational powers, and free verse simply turns to very dull prose without any connections to song.

(Letter from Thom Gunn, 19 April 1991)

Probably Coleridge's 'fresh' is such an attribute, without which we don't have poetry, but a simulation, whether in metre or free verse. The origination of either mode is in its primitive provisional shaping, and this is as a rule fresh only when it can choose its enablement. In a discussion with the American poet Marvin Bell (Spring 1991), he suggested that imagination, and not free verse, metre and lineation, was now the presentiment of form. If this is so, then it is imaginative energy in its provisional magmatic condition that is the poet's recourse.

True or not, poets must feel free, even in the West, to write in metre, free verse, or a mixture of both. To argue it the other way round, if much of Wordsworth's best poetry *is* fresh, it is also true that Whitman's free verse – it is free verse – is fresh through its discovery that rhythm and nuance shall be fresh and delicately alive as the form is riven back from metricality onto the modified principles of (Hebrew) parallelism, without the original Hebrew metricality. This constituted a rediscovery of the form compacted by thought, in the Psalms for instance, as it appears in the English *prose* translations; for, paradoxically, the existence of the form translated into prose without the original verse lineation had the result of bringing out the essential form of the presented thought. I hope it will be seen by fair-minded readers that I am not advocating a formless poetry, but arguing for conditions that ensure freshness. And from the reader's viewpoint I am, to quote Coleridge again, arguing for poetry in 'its *untranslatableness* in words of the same language [otherwise suffering] injury to the meaning' (*Biographia Literaria*, p. 263, my emphasis).

Such resistance, to paraphrase, is true for good prose also, but one notices that this instrinsic 'untranslatableness' is applicable not only to the words as they finally make up the poem, but to the initial, provisional state of conception in which the feelings, meanings and sensibility are not to be transgressed by the application of pre-made form, but enabled by the finding of, in the end, the only form. This finding puts greater stress on the imagination as its initial moves are plucked from the insistence of set lineation and the immediately demanded requisite words. This kind of 'thinking' should not find itself pressed to translate itself positivistically into final words, in the first stages of composition. What matters more is the wholeness of the initial creation. Quite apart from those who think in images and pictures, many, I believe, have experienced that *something* breaking into the mind's surface in the course of which it forms into some assemblage of meaning for which language may be the expression, but for which language isn't or may not be instantly desirable. It may be that the processes of language must start early, so that the language partake of what is in the process of formation; but to insist that these feelings 'be wracked to fit' (as Denys Harding denied it occurred in Isaac Rosenberg's poetry) is wrong, reductive of what I have suggested is creative.

If part of this be provisionally accepted, then perhaps some of the difficulties between metricists and free-versers may give way to prior and more important questions of imaginative energy.

Once again, this is not a plea for formlessness. On the contrary, because the energies are to be allowed to emerge, the most careful (I don't mean 'brutal'), sensitive and vigilant controls need to be brought into the complete shaping. It may also happen that the work comes out well first time, or nearly so, but writers have also to be prepared to work, as Owen did with 'Strange Meeting', work over and over the emerging poem without harassing or bullying it into shape, but on the contrary working with patience and often perhaps with despair, hoping that the work will open up its best possibilities and resolutions – if such exist. Sometimes, we must walk away from the poem so as to discover whether what one has made is 'right'. Such a discovery is indeed as blessed as it is rare. Is all this a plea for the organic form to which Coleridge was apparently committed? I believe not, though it clearly shares certain attributes. It is different in as much as Coleridge knew or at least recognized only the options of metre for his poetry, and in the event was prosodically less adventurous than Wordsworth. I am asking for the imagination to shape its substance within the full recognition of known but more diverse parameters than Coleridge seemed prepared to do, and, if needed, to disclose new limits. I am asking for something less vague *and* more flexible.

This sketch of a difficult situation might seem to imply that writers and readers are puzzling over the same territory, but this is probably not the case. It is the disjunction between writer and reader over what was, earlier, common territory, which may now constitute much of the reading problem. If, for instance, readers who may have been bored with poetry at school are even so now buyers of new verse and of literary magazines, they may still be trying to read free verse as if they imagined it to be metrical poetry, or a version of it. For those whose education included poetry (schools do not always provide it), the teachers themselves may have begun with modern poetry which often (though by no means invariably) means free verse. They therefore have little experience of metrical poetry. Thus their students may not, without a great deal of effort and independent-mindedness, find themselves able to feel on their pulses the structures and therefore the intricate variables metrical verse entails. How, for instance, might such readers perceive the stress and stretching of form in Hopkins' 'The Windhover', when the nature of the framework is unknown, unfamiliar or unfelt?

And if poets themselves were not instructed, and have not felt their way into *both* modes, and are not encouraged by their readers to do so, how can poets and readers hope to explore together these fuller possibilities? What we need now is not only the study of Metaphysical or Romantic poetry, but the thoroughgoing establishment of an inclusive territory of understanding and an informed mutual respect, so that our response to poetry (and other forms) is not compartmentalized into 'then' and 'now', but becomes, instead, an interacting whole. Such an inspection would have to look on metrical poetry and free verse as part of one understanding, each aspect of which modifies the perception of the other. They are different, if interrelated modes.

Not only is the argument between metricists and free-versers wasteful: it excludes mutually beneficent sources of enrichment, understanding and possible development. The problem is much more serious than an argument over forms, rhetoric and prosody, crucial though such an argument is; because *common* understanding would enable us to feel the apprehension of earlier poets – Wordsworth's felt life, for instance, in his best work slowly and deeply engaging with the suffering of others. Such a reciprocity of understanding might show us how to find fresh ways of mediating between life and our responses to it, recreated in writing. So that although this ought not to be thought of as a rhetorical problem, yet our ways of engaging it will involve us in looking at rhetoric and prosody.

Metrical verse uses the four components of which free verse

uses three only. Some (measured) metrical verse counts both emphases (or duration) *and* syllables. Iambic pentameter, for instance, the central measure for Shakespeare, Milton, Pope and much of Wordsworth, is, to the metronome, ten syllables, of which five are weak(er) and which alternate with five that receive stress, emphasis or duration. Additionally, metrical and free verse are each composed in lines, but they relate differently to the praxis and principle of *lineation*.

So here I want to look at the third and fourth components which might be seen to relate like the two sides of Saussure's 'sheet of paper'. In my picture, on one side is syntax or the energy of a sentence, and on the other the sentence's meaning. Of course, in one sense one cannot speak of the energy, or syntax, of a sentence without also experiencing its meaning. Yet if one looks at the way the energy of a sentence, its syntax, is deployed, we will be able to see the finely tuned meaning, and what tunes it. The frontal approach that asks simply, of a quite complex verse sentence, 'what is its meaning?' will receive an inadequate answer.

Supposing metre to be formalized rhythm, it may be possible to say that while metrical lines of verse have both metre and rhythm, free verse either mixes in, or has no, metrical lines, and is rhythmic only.

For poet and reader the question also involves the way in which the energy-and-meaning of syntax intersects with lineation. The position of the line-unit, and its intersection with the energy of the sentence, will reinforce and often create meanings additional to the sentence in its prose, scrolled-out form. Where metre intersects with syntax, a more distributed spread of the various components occurs than in free verse, where, by definition, it is rhythm alone that intersects with syntax in lineation.

Yet it's not a question that in one diagram we get metre and in the other, of free verse, we do not. The relationship between the components of free verse is different from the interconnection of the components in metred verse. In free verse not only does the rhythm have to bear the weight of itself *and* the absence (as a rule) of metre; it has also to relate in a more – I almost said dynamic way. Rhythm in free verse must relate, in its lineation, to syntax as a partner, with even greater interdependence than in metred verse. Thus in free verse in the interaction between them, rhythm is either more dynamic or more subtle (as Charles O. Hartman has shown) than it usually is in metrical verse. In this latter the danger comes from the round of metrical structures taking the strain in such a way as to risk weakening rhythm's quick and essential relationship with the energy of the syntax. On the other hand, free verse risks losing the *buoyant* lyric shaping of metrical verse. Consider in this respect Wordsworth's 'Resolution and Independence' and 'The Solitary Reaper'.

Look at two metrical examples from Lawrence and Eliot. The example from Lawrence is the opening of 'Bavarian Gentians' from the posthumously published 'Last Poems'; from Eliot, the opening of the *unrhymed* 'terza rima' section from the first movement of *Little Gidding* (*Four Quartets*). It may be objected that Lawrence's lines are more grounded 'in life' than Eliot's, which come more from the intellect. This, too, is the point I would make. Taking Lawrence's lines first:

> Not every man has gentians in his house
> in soft September, at slow, sad Michaelmas.

Lawrence starts this free verse poem with two iambic pentameters which, however, have in them much of the felt nature of his previous free verse practice. The two metrical lines quickly establish the context and orientation of the poem with its components 'gentians', 'his house', 'September'. Instigating these in his 'new' metrical verse, Lawrence operates his capacity as fiction-writer working with an economy Eliot lacks; with the contrasting result that whatever virtues there are in Eliot's deliberate restating, at the end of five metrical lines we find we are no further into an understanding of the context or subject:

> In the uncertain hour before the morning
>   Near the ending of interminable night
>   At the recurrent end of the unending
> After the dark dove with the flickering tongue
>   Had passed below the horizon of his homing.
>   (80–4)

Despite the defining words 'uncertain', 'interminable', 'recurrent' (markers of Eliot's restating process), 'unending' and 'dove', what have we understood, and where are we? (London's bombed streets during the Second World War, perhaps with Yeats, perhaps with Dante?) This part of the section is narration and colloquy, and would benefit, therefore, from helpful contextualization so as to free the reader to concentrate on those areas of 'meaning' which deserve the greater attention.

In Lawrence one notices that the most important realization of the two lines is made through enjambment, which serves to define the condition of 'his house' (body and being). And we are 'given' September with its inevitable movement to winter (and death). The reason we can concentrate on these meanings, and even become aware of the enabling enjambment, is because Lawrence has the capacity to contextualize and to quicken this with attributes of improvisation. It is in this quickly established context that the gentian-torch will acquire full significance. The enjambment (unpunctuated movement of syntax from one verse-line to the next) enables the first half of the second line to occur as if it came as an afterthought, yet which thinking subsequently supersedes in importance what was ostensibly the more important statement offered in the first line of the poem. The lesser voice pierces the greater with its 'lesser' condition. It is not merely that the enjambment enacts this but that without it, and its assistance in fusing the conversational voice with the formal metre, there would be no subtle enabling of the lesser voice to emerge as the important one. Adjectivally, Lawrence gets in a great deal with 'soft', 'slow', 'sad' in its slow realization of, not death, but dying. Thus 'sad', in its 'slow' disclosure, enables a marking-time that works by apposition, itself enabled by the enjambment process. With the help of the prosodic syntax, 'sad' is made to qualify the half- 'good' half-'not good' possession of such a flower (of death) in one's house. So that the opening phrase, 'Not every man', which ostensibly confers privilege, turns out to bestow a *partly* negative condition. All this is part of the central meaning of the poem.

In contrast, I get little but intellection from Eliot's adjectives. They entail a sense of something to come, but only within the rhetoric of grammar. The life by which we might (selfishly perhaps) include ourselves as readers and participants does not 'flicker' enough. There are lovely movements in Eliot's *terza rima*. Yet to enter another objection, why is it unrhymed? Eliot would know, in his admiration for both Dante and Shelley's *The Triumph of Life*, that rhyme is an integral constituent of this interlinked form.

The steady metred pulse in Eliot's first line is finely and retroactively disturbed by the athwart movement in the latter half of the second line, in which 'Near the ending of' almost replicates the movement of the previous line; but in the last phrase, 'interminable night', beautifully flutters, hastens, almost but never fully frenzies the shivering apprehension of a (theological?) night that does not end. It is finely done, but at a distance, not only perhaps from the author but from the reader also. The syntax, in its repetition, has no life-engaging context to offer the reader – though it might be objected that that is its purpose.

Essentially, a writer's relationship with his/her readers is achieved through having a spectrum of concerns, which is in its turn the product of being engaged with the distress and pleasure of the creaturely life of this earth. It requires considerable courage not to have such a concern, but still more to possess and use it, sensuously enacting the pleasurable and moral vision. This needs to be done in a conscious mode, modern, yet not solipsistic, neither courting despair nor avoiding happiness. For the great defect of modernism is that it has forgotten how to realize happiness, taking despair, as of supposed common consent, as humanity's Yiddish, or *lingua franca*. As Roy Fuller in 'The Barbarians' suggested, 'anyone happy in this age, is daft or corrupt'.

Yet to think this way, grounding one's faith in a supposed axiom, is self-fulfilling prophecy. And on the other hand, the ethics of modernism require its practitioners not only to be concerned with language, but concerned in a particular and intellectual way. Its attitude towards those who do not work within its canon is concessive – that is, they may or may not be 'admitted'. Thus the issue for some modernist poets is not whether they have a theme – 'the theme is indeed important' – but whether modernism will permit him/her use of the humanly discursive language of 'and' and 'but'. In fact, nothing is wrong with such compunction and its reluctance to be discursive, but everything is wrong when the style inhibits substance, subject and theme. Additionally, the breadth of human sympathy as well as its fascination with degradation seems limited by that censorship of what is acceptable to the sardonic and ironic modes; or by the operation of the mode of intensity. But mostly, in Anglo-Saxon culture, it is irony that is thought to be perspicuous. And self-consciousness is its preoccupation, but in a mode different from Wordsworth's. In 'The Solitary Reaper', Wordsworth is concerned with recording his supposed (not actual) responses to the voice and music of a girl singing in a language he cannot understand. Its 'effect' on him is not, as one critic suggested, consolatory, but exultation and gratitude ('And, as I mounted up the hill' being the physical analogue to exultation). Contemporary poets use the self-conscious mode as a theme rather than a response to 'something'. There is a difference. What drives a contemporary writer into re-creation is extreme experience (not necessarily his/her own) and it is often violent experience that achieves this. With Primo Levi, in his controlled re-creation of his camp experience in *If this be a man*, the narrative blends inner and outer experience, mutually and reflectively dramatized into unitary narrative. This is not offered as a criticism of Levi, but to suggest what it takes writers to set reality in narrative that can be shared with a reader.

But the question that deserves to be asked, even if it cannot be answered, is why writers should feel so driven away from narrative. Perhaps it is the surfeit of nineteenth-century fiction that has achieved this alienation. But it may also be that the world has successfully made the writer feel that his/her experience, real or imagined, is not worth setting before a reader. Thus the literary writer feels 'reality-reticence', and the popular writer forbidden to explore the values of a life otherwise paste-boarded into supposed re-creation. It may be objected that such polarities have always existed, yet what I think is new is the domination of the literary not simply by itself, but in combination with an uncreative scepticism, prized in English culture, which possesses not intelligence but intellect. Not the firefly, but its image. To offer intimate reality one must be ironic, or brutal. Clearly the limitation of two such not unrelated modes prolongs the uncreative condition.

The poets I have chosen to consider have in their different ways, but not without a price, managed to bridge with self-conscious artifice the modes of psycho-physical and aesthetic integrity, purity and authenticity. Theirs is the sensuously enacted moral vision which has contrived to retain a world exterior to themselves which they share with readers.

I might have started with Blake, or more readily with Wordsworth, both of whom are modern poets. They, for instance, often offer experience, without explanation. Consider as an example the unexplained vital connection between the first and second stanzas of Wordsworth's 'She Dwelt Among the Untrodden Ways'. But since I am concerned with the tensions between free and metrical verse as the locus of inner and outer worlds struggling for expressive re-creation, I chose, wrongly perhaps, to begin with the paired writers Whitman and Hopkins. What they do and do not share is part of the concern in this chapter; but one sees that their poetry takes on aesthetically a vision of an inwardly realized exterior world, in the way that Owen's, Rosenberg's and Lawrence's poetry also did, doing so without diminution of their poetic. In achieving this, they, in their different ways, advanced or modified the condition of prosody, to the ultimate benefit of the reader. The same holds true for Dylan Thomas, and for Bunting in his *Briggflatts*.

WHITMAN AND HOPKINS, THE DISSIMILAR PAIR IN THE DESIGN OF THE SACRED

If Newton's work in optics disturbed those whose faith in God was partly vested in the divine attribution of light, Bishop Robert Lowth, in his *Lectures on the Sacred Poetry of the Hebrews* (1753), first published in Latin and later translated into our vernacular, but especially in the chapter skilfully analysing the varieties of Hebrew parallelism, might similarly have disturbed his believers. For how could the sacred *voice* of God be schematized through analysis? Apparently it could.

At any rate we have little difficulty in recognizing the parallelism Bishop Lowth made evident, the structure that delivers the thinking in the Psalms designed to glorify God. What we may find more difficult to remember is that the clarity of this thinking design – what Hopkins called 'a figure of grammar' – moved, in the Hebrew original, in lines of three or four as a rule regularly recurring stresses. Hebrew metre was part of the parallelism of the original poetry, which in all the English Biblical translations, including the King James recension, reappeared in non-lineated syntax; sentences without the traditional form of poetry, the lines of which had beginning, end and recurrence. But with Whitman and Hopkins, who in their different ways responded to the design and energy of parallelism, what they discovered in the English Bible was, in a sense, the *un-*clothed energy of parallelism, a form, without the clothing of lineation. It was *this* nakedness they found apt to their particular faiths, or nakednesses, which they proceeded to clothe, each after his own fashion, in separate yet related versions of lineation – interrelations of structure, syntax and energy with lineation. This combination is, after all, of the essence of free verse, which, in denying metre, may sometimes bring the tension of that interrelationship closer to the reader.

So the how-to, that spiritual engineering, was of crucial importance to the pioneers of verse-form, in the West, in the nineteenth century, and it was this that these two poets, one in comparative the other in total obscurity, redesigned. To the invisible advantage of both, each stood at the wayside of their century's main traffic, of poetry. Whitman's poetry had more in common with the *prose* of Melville and Emerson than with their verse. Though the base of his work, Timothy Steele's assertion notwithstanding, is not prose structure, but prose idiom, the prose-concerns of our daily living as part of a comprehensive vision. Consider the moving part in SoM of the rescued but dying fireman, as one of so many instances of that actuality which comprises Whitman's vision. Whitman broadened the base of poetry just as we English-speaking writers today (especially perhaps in America) have shrunk it; and free verse was the enabling instrument with which he enlarged the base; as Smart earlier discovered for himself in his omnivorous poem, *Jubilate Agno*. (It was composed 'over a period of four years during Smart's incarceration in a private madhouse from 1758/9 to the end of January 1763'.)

Hopkins widened the *linguistic* base – broadening it to include vernacular, and the native 'thew' of an older English (must one say Anglo-Saxon?) – claiming in effect that metrical verse had become too refined, too narrow and poetic (consider his none too flattering responses to Tennyson's verse which, in the main, contrasts with Hopkins' verse as much as it does with the work of Whitman – who also cared little for Tennyson). To complete this part of the comparison between two dissimilar poets, each in his different way engaged in parallelism, and each also concerned with the designs of the sacred upon the soul. Thus in Hopkins' journals and poems shows forth the benign aspect of God through His handiwork Nature, though dichotomy exists. It was not enough for Hopkins to say that while God created us and the beauty of Nature (and natural catastrophe?), humanity created it own misery. Such a plausible perspective was too simple for Hopkins' intelligence.

What then? In the poetry, at least, he must try to account for the demanding personal God ('Deutschland'), God's predatory love ('Windhover') and the dichotomy of good and evil ('Spelt from Sibyl's Leaves'), which latter perhaps comes nearer to investigating the bifurcated vision I am hypothesizing. 'God's better beauty, grace.' Hopkins could not redesign the world as Whitman did in his poetry. His theology went against that. But he could praise his

God and His creation of *beauty*, and subscribe to such a God with the intensity of his being. At any rate all this seems to me to support my idea of Hopkins' use of adjectives. That is, they describe the existing world. Unlike freshly selected nouns they do not, or rather, cannot, postulate a new world. Adjectives praise God's world as it is perceived and appreciated, and so through Hopkins' adjectives, parts of the actual and theological worlds are brought into coincidence.

Whereas Whitman's sacred remaking is comprised of a world of nouns. The world as phenomena reminted. Yet in word-order and syntax, for instance, he is more traditional than Hopkins and, in his sense of working machinery, less dynamic. Whitman's 'To a Locomotive in Winter', which one might expect to convey the power of machinery, leans back upon a supposed creatureliness:

> Thy great protruding head-light fix'd in front.

More telling still in the same poem is 'Type of the modern', where the position from which the 'creature' is viewed is, in that phrase, not contemporary with it. One does not say 'modern' in that way if one feels part of the age and its productions.

Consider three portions from very different poems by Hopkins:

> O then, weary then why should we tread? O why are we so
> haggard at the heart, so care-coiled, care-killed, so fagged,
> so fashed, so cogged, so cumbered
>
> ('The Golden Echo')

The intricacy and extending dynamism of the vernacular adjectives coming after 'haggard at the heart' suggest the energy of vision derived not only from an understanding of the power of machinery, but also from a perceiving of the fatigue in those who operate but are outpaced by it. In 'The Blessed Virgin Compared to the Air We Breathe', the industrial, chemical nature surrounding the sun and stars makes aspects of Whitman (and neither is the worse for it) appear jovially prelapsarian:

> the sun would shake,
> A blear and blinding ball
> With blackness bound, and all
> The thick stars round him roll
> Flashing like flecks of coal,

Quartz-fret, or sparks of salt,
In grimy vasty vault.

And in 'Spelt from Sibyl's Leaves' the sewing-machine or spinning-jenny imagery has, again, the energy of working parts (and that of the unfeeling intelligence that devised them). That is, the moral processes of human beings have been translated into the alliterative assonantal energy of working parts:

> Lét life, wáned, ah lét life wind
> Off hér once skéined stained veined variety'upon, áll on twó
> spools; párt, pen, páck...
> (Hopkins' prosodic marks)

Here, Hopkins' adjectives transmit a version of energy that reflects the dynamics of Victorian machinery and engineering – to work against the point I made earlier. Whitman by comparison never bifurcates the world of evil, violence, the pitiful condition of the suicide, the 'veneralee', the victim of war or the 'bedraggled' prostitute whom men taunt from their position as 'the good'. The new society, in its democratic condition, is ultimately for him benign and strong; and the nouns which express a consonance of the human with the natural world conspire, despite the 'cross-hatchings', to manifest a benign order. Indeed, a sacred one. By contrast, the Jesuit's picture is fraught and questioning, its dynamism notwithstanding.

With respect to adjectives, Whitman's do not so much define as buttress the nouns, being aspects rather than independent or imperious qualifications of them. Thus in the last Chant of SoM,

> I depart as air, I shake my white locks at the runaway sun,
> I effuse my flesh in eddies, and drift it in lacy jags...

– that mysterious 'jags' (air? clouds? light?) is made both more particular *and* more complex by 'lacy', yet the adjective would have no real meaning without its noun. Again, a half-way independence is achieved in the phrase that reflects Whitman's experience as a carpenter

> the plane's ascending lisp.

One feels at first that 'lisp' is auditory and that 'ascending' is adjunct to the sound. But 'ascending' also includes the visual recognition of the shaving, planed and rising off the wood. 'Lisp' is nevertheless the crucial word, determining the sensuous realization of the whole activity and its reception by both carpenter-poet and reader. Instances of the noun being the crucial determinant in the experience-cluster may be multiplied, and indeed I am soon to instance more, indirectly, in examining part of Chant 24. Yet the ultimate point towards which I am working is that Whitman's nouns are neither evidence of his commitment to a materialist apprehension of a cosmos, nor a spiritual one (it need not be exclusively either), but instead form a sacred sense of unity in which the material and spiritual inhere in each other. But because our existence is incarnated in the physical, our praise (Hopkins) or our redesigning (Whitman) are both implicated in the material. Thus nouns and adjectives are different aspects of one world and our experience of it.

The next offers to understand the adjectives and nouns of both poets in relation to the flow and pace of their syntax. Whitman's lists (nouns), whether 'enveloped' in a design as in Chant 24 (below), or more free-standing, nevertheless, despite the repetitions in syntax, move – or rather, the syntax and flow move them. Within the marking-time of the repetitions, the syntax is even so 'driven with loosened reins'. Loosened, yes, but driven; there is a quite gentle but 'irremissive' impulsion, the sense-connections appearing to be made within, and from, that energy.

Hopkins' energy is similarly 'pressing', but its formations are closer-knit. This may be an expression of the priest feeling his religious obligations as much as the poet acknowledging his to metricality. For even when we (readers) may not perceive the metre, Hopkins can still account for it; in the most extended (tenuous?) count and calculation, he can measure it. The energy arises, but, in the process, the obligations of metricality intervene to cooperate with a prosody essentialized from adjectives that repeat their insistent apprehension of God's earth. This is visible in a great deal of Hopkins, very beautifully in those stress-bearing adjectives phalanged in the opening of 'Spelt from Sibyl's Leaves':

ÉARNEST, éarthless, équal, attúneable,ˈváulty, volúminous, . .
  ⁔stupéndous
Évening stráins tọ be tíme's vást,ˈwómb-of-all, hóme-of-all,
  héarse-of-all night.

(my stress marks)

The adjectives set up their rhythm and prosody. The old world is prosodically seen afresh.

But the new vision! That is Whitman's case, although, with his Quaker background in mind, it is an older light that effects the new outer human world. Even so, this inner light is also 'democratic' where praise is accorded not only for what is useful, but for what is beautiful and has life. Not slaves useful to a despotic centripetal world hubbed on the axle of centralized power, but, on the contrary, the investing of each creature from the 'dung-beetle' to the 'sea-captain', 'veneralee', the 'lilac' and the 'vitreous pour of the moon' (it is 'pour' not 'pouring') with a worthy, valued life.

It is tempting to suggest that for Whitman it was a fairly simple, short step from the sacred to what Hopkins called parallelism, the 'figure of grammar', with which Biblical poetry is constructed. I suggest that when Whitman's psyche was ready, somewhat in the way that Lawrence, through Imagism, became ready for Whitman's influence, then the forms of sacred poetry made themselves over to him as the likeliest forms. That is, when Whitman had done with metrical verse. And if this is so, wholly or in part, then we are doubly induced to consider the relationship between his use of parallelism and his rhythmical free verse. And finally, though parallelism is involved in value-making (since it institutes comparisons), it is not intrinsically a hierarchical mode.

Before considering however the portion from Chant 24, I want to try to identify a feature of Whitman's verse that is both self-evident and difficult to describe. It is most easily identified as a mode of simultaneity whereby the ongoing movement and sense of the syntax are delayed or even temporarily worked against by other elements in the verse. It is, for instance, apparent to this reader that although parallelism reinforces the progress of sense (the general drift of the ongoing theme), together with the overall meanings, it delays the *completion* of these as well as of the syntax itself.

Indeed, in his 'aerial' spaces and parallelism, in his maximization of sensuousness and the scented nuance, in his conversational drama, in his operatic form (*Out of the Cradle*) and enactment of 'life-scenes', Whitman finds various ways of delaying but not avoiding completion. The delay would have no meaning were there no completion. At any rate, this delay is part of what I mean by simultaneity, the direction the poem is travelling in conjunction with the delays.

I should also consider delay in Hopkins. In his essay 'Redeeming the Time', Geoffrey Hill speaks of the 'cross-hatching' in Hopkins, meaning, presumably, the capacity to implicate more than one voice and rhythm in his discourse. This will involve the two in dialogue and perhaps in partial disagreement. Thus voices and rhythms, that may, in certain respects, come athwart each other. But an equally radical and probably much wider-spread practice in Hopkins with respect to delay comes from the piling-up of adjectives. Thus the wonderful assemblage of these in 'Spelt from Sibyl's Leaves' does not merely delay but in some sense thoughtfully qualifies the onwardness of the fairly uncomplicated syntax of the opening sentence which, notwithstanding the comma and continuity dots after 'voluminous', could be simplified to: 'Earnest evening strains to be time's vast night'. It is the ruffling sensuously chequering adjectives that slow, and save, the simple sentence from sententiousness. And what adjectives!

Spelt from Sibyl's Leaves

EARNEST, earthless, équal, attúneable,⎮váulty, volúminous, ..
   ⸝stupéndous
Evening stráins to be time's vást,⎮wómb-of-all, hóme-of-all,
   héarse-of-all night.
Her fond yellow hornlight wound to the west,⎮her wild hollow
   hoarlight hung to the height
Waste; her earliest stars, earl-stars,⎮stárs principal, overbend us,
Firé-féaturing heaven. For earth⎮her being has unbound, her
   dapple is at an end, as-
tray or aswarm, all throughther, in throngs;⎮self ín self steepèd
   and páshed – qúite
Disremembering, dismémbering⎮all now. Heart, you round me
   right⸝
With: Óur évening is over us; óur night⎮whélms, whélms, ánd
   will end us.
Only the beak-leaved boughs dragonish⎮damask the tool-smooth
   bleak light; black, ⸝
Ever so black on it. Óur tale, O óur oracle!⎮Lét life, wáned,
   ah lét life wind
Off hér once skéined stained véined variety⎮upon, áll on twó
   spools; párt, pen, páck
Now her all in twó flocks, twó folds – black, white;⎮right,
   wrong; reckon but, reck but, mind
But thése two; wáre of a world where bút these⎮twó tell, each
   off the óther; of a rack

Where, selfwrung, selfstrung, sheathe- and shelterless,⸍thoughts
against thoughts in groans grind.

                                        (prosodic marks mainly mine)

Here the imaginative capacity lies in the application of such adjectives to 'evening'. They are inventive, apt; they uplift and are awe-
some. If the surprising 'EARNEST' belongs to the character of, say,
a young novitiate, 'vaulty' suggests mortality (vault), while at the
same time upholding the idea of size (vaulting), which is awe-
inspiring, yet approachable, being both 'earnest' and 'equal'; so that
despite the intrinsic size there is an approachability to time's (God's)
evening as it strains to become night. 'Strains' is surprising, not so
much because of the question as to why evening should so have
to strain for what is inevitable, as in the almost jovial, friendly
(approachable), amiable feeling conveyed by the swaying adjectives:

EARNEST, earthless, equal, attuneable,⸍vaulty, voluminous, ..
stupendous

the stresses fall where one might expect; though the one that falls
on 'voluminous' (my stress mark) stretches out, through rhythm,
the word's meaning, striking itself much later, in that word, than
the emphases on the other words in the line have so far accustomed
us to expect – a fine piece of footwork, which varies the line's pace.
By emphasizing this word and its essential meaning, Hopkins pre-
pares us for the principal sense of the next line, which is 'womb'
and 'home' 'of all'. 'Womb' and 'home' should be friendly, but
the night that is voluminous associates death. In the next line the
adjective 'fond', with its lovely human attribute, cross-hatches the
'wild hollow hoarlight' into some version of friendly presence, yet
the syntax, though its meaning isn't entirely clear to me, concludes
the idea in 'Waste', which again suggests the emptiness of death.
Yet this again gives way to the stars watching over (caring for) us,
as in 'God's Grandeur':

the Holy Ghost over the bent
World broods with warm breast and with ah! bright wings.

The stars 'Fire-featuring heaven' are here ambiguous, but probably
friendly. Yet the 'For' that follows this, meaning perhaps both 'because' and, reflexively, 'on behalf of', leads on to Hopkins' favourite and positive nature word 'dapple'. 'Fire-featuring' seems to do

double duty, positively and negatively, as if to suggest that death's presence here (and worse) is qualifying everything. In the disintegration that follows on the self being 'pashed', that self loses its capacity for remembering, which for us all, and for Hopkins more than for some, is the essential attribute of being alive. This represents Hopkins in one of his best modes, and at his best in it, though at the opposite end of the long continuous 'reeve' of the syntax and rhythms in WoD. Another triumph.

The devastation of all this ought to be enough, but more follows: 'our night whelms . . . us'. And in the sestet of this non-iambic but rhymed, and argued, sonnet, line 9 is noticeable in that Nature, so often seen as a manifestation of God's love (beauty), is here hostile. The trees are 'beakleaved boughs dragonish', whose imprint on the 'bleak' light implants a double negativity. The hostile leaves become, then, part of the prophesying implicated in the title. In line 10 the almost childish 'Ever so' takes a risk in the way it chooses to add pathos; but it is kept in balance and so adds the right note to that which life winds onto. It is not only life's winding away, as the cotton winds from our spool of life onto that of used-up life. It is the essentially mixed character of the lives we live, as Leavis indicates in *New Bearings* (p. 138) – 'two flocks, two folds' with the stress on 'two'. These are 'black, white'; 'right, wrong'. Yes, but isn't Hopkins at it once again? One of Leavis's strengths, which is also a weakness, is to 'strike' the right meaning but leave little room for ambiguity. Yes, but what if ambiguity exists, as I believe it does here. Yes, the human character is 'black, white', and so we live and thus we die. Yet in the previous line the good nature-like (positive) life with which we started

hér once skéined stained véined varíety

in facts winds

upon, áll on twó spools;

why 'two'? Why not just one spool of mortality? The answer I think is in that

párt, pen, páck

which suggests that the two spools are those of judgment, separating sheep from goats. So that in the end, and despite God's loving-kindness, He will also act as a God of justice. Thus some will go 'to a fry below' and some will ascend. 'Part, pen, pack.' 'Part' means here to separate and divide as we are each separated from our fellow-mortals in death's (God's) judgment. The pessimism of that 'pen, pack' comes from the seeming likelihood that most of us will end up in hell. That is, the poem Sibyls – prophesies in a loose yet menacing gesture what will happen to us. 'Pen' and 'pack' suggest that like animals we are packed onto the spools. Yes, but two spools, and 'pack' holds also the suggestion of being closely packed in hell. My memory of space-references to hell invariably packs the tormented beings close together, so that, as a subsidiary torment, they cannot escape hearing and witnessing each other's torments. Heaven, quite the contrary, is an Elysium of openness. Space is a commodity of goodness. Hopkins might have reason to harbour this idea since in his pastoral work he could observe, feel and despair on the condition of the penned-up poor who comprised his flock (like Wilfred Owen and his despair). The poem may contemplate some of us safely housed in hell – 'there are too many of us'. Our ultimate fate is to be sorted, promises the Sibyl. 'Rack', on the penultimate line, may suggest 'shelf' but in context it is more likely to signify 'torture'. But for 'this last pain' we have self-torture; we may not ('shelterless') shelter from our own judgement. Conscience makes adults of us, and we have no right, in our adulthood, to expect from God anything but what we deserve.

RHYTHM

In these and other such long lines the interlinking rhyme helps to sustain, of course, a whole flight of lines. Thus including alliteration (head-rhyme) the first three words in the first half of the first line are echoed by the first two in the second half – and then the 'ous' 'earse' enter rhymes, some of them ingenious: 'voluminous/stupendous/hearse/overbend us/end us' – the reader may pick out more. They help to sustain, but surely do not always succeed in holding together, the rhythm. The first four lines have four stresses either side of a marked caesura ('), which one hears, feels, sees. Thereafter, with line 5, the rhythm begins to founder, even in places to disintegrate, and with it, to a lesser extent, depart sense and syntax. The sentence beginning in line 5 with 'For earth' and ending in line 7 with 'Disremembering . . . all now' is only just held together in its meaning by the fine, strong ending just quoted. Without that the sense and rhythm would be harder still to follow. The meaning is accomplished here by rhetorical cadence. It is significant (for me) that Hopkins feels he must distribute an increasing number of stress-marks, some of which do not occur in their natural, spoken places; and their apparent wilfulness appears sometimes to be part of Hopkins' instigating a metrical pattern alien to the speech patterns. Sometimes the result is thronged syntax and alliteration – not much more. Yet I do not mean to indicate failure, but difficulties, with respect to this poem. It is a fine achievement; and with respect to 'failure' I had rather read and ponder Hopkins' failures than the successes of some other poets.

WHITMAN

Whitman's capacity to 'contain multitudes', to be one and simul-taneously many, is in democratic fashion, cognate with the aerial character he requested for verse. 'I resist any thing better than my own diversity' (349) and 'I am the man, I suffer'd, I was there' (832). This is not masochism but a proliferation of grass-like energy, avid and delicate. Sandburg in his poem 'Grass' gets the avid part, but Whitman, like other great poets (America's only one, so far) has that interacting of opposites which makes, not a simulation of energy, but a living tissue of strength and delicacy. And so it per-mits Whitman one of his greatest gifts, modesty. Consider Chant 24, that part devoted to praise of the male body – his and/or an-other's. And to press the crux, in making the body interconnect with the benign aspects of Nature, the handiwork of the Creator, Whitman reveals his commitment to the sacred. In this Whitman and Hopkins are one, as the priest probably understood. Here is that part of Chant 24:

> If I worship one thing more than another it shall be the
>   spread of my own body, or any part of it,
> Translucent mould of me it shall be you!
> Shaded ledges and rests it shall be you!
> Firm masculine colter it shall be you!
> Whatever goes to the tilth of me it shall be you!
> You my rich blood! your milky stream pale strippings of
>   my life!

Breast that presses against other breasts it shall be you!
My brain it shall be your occult convolutions!
Root of wash'd sweet-flag! timorous pond-snipe! nest of
    guarded duplicate eggs! it shall be you!
Mix'd tussled hay of head, beard, brawn, it shall be you!
Trickling sap of maple, fibre of manly wheat, it shall be you!
Sun so generous it shall be you!
Vapors lighting and shading my face it shall be you!
You sweaty brooks and dews it shall be you!
Winds whose soft-tickling genitals rub against me it shall
    be you!
Broad muscular fields, branches of live oak, loving lounger
    in my winding paths, it shall be you!
Hands I have taken, face I have kiss'd, mortal I have ever
    touch'd, it shall be you.

I quote at length, partly because the poetry being out of copyright
need not be licensed with a fee, but of course because it is fine,
delighting one with its directness *and* complexity, and its modest
praise for the human body. It does not presume so little for the
human as not to place him (her) on comparable terms with Nature,
though it positions the human as the focus of our attention.

The flight consists of an 'envelope' whose evident rhetorical
feature is parallel sequential repetition (though the accumulating
repetitions interconnect). Thus, indeed, 'it is you' – the male body,
mine perhaps, and, perhaps, some other one, some particular one.
The unegotistical character of the passage consists in the personal
being instantial and representative, but remaining an actual living
being, designed by God.

Rhetorically, Whitman gets to act his diversity by enabling the
body–Nature metaphor within the accumulating unity-through-
metaphor repetition. Consider, for instance, the subtle and tender
making-over of the arrogant penis into a 'timorous pond-snipe', and
the testicles as vulnerable, fertile, 'duplicate' nest-eggs. Please note,
sexists, of either gender. As I have suggested he interchanges the
male with Nature's attributes, disturbing one's certainty as to which
is being re-created:

Winds whose soft-tickling genitals rub against me it shall be
    you!
Broad muscular fields, branches of live oak, loving lounger in
    my winding paths, it shall be you!

The *fluctuations* of interconnected-with-nature formation, between one line and the next offer subtlety. The variety of Nature-correspondences – colter, tilth, sweet-flag, dews, fields, live-oak – ensure diversity.

In each of the non-enjambed start–stop lines exists a statement complete with specificity. Finally, in this envelope of accumulations, the concluding line makes itself into a list of lists, citing parts of the body in a quickening completion that compounds into the form the rhetorical structure of all the previous lines: '. . . – it is you'. By tripling the statement and switching its possible prior self-reference to that of the beloved, Whitman transforms all those previous lines' loving into a modesty that praises the loved one:

> Hands I have taken, face I have kiss'd, mortal I have ever
> touch'd, it shall be you.
>
> (543)

As for *Rhythm-sense*, this device in Whitman, inhering in parallelism, is in English not metrical but a structure made of collocations of thought.

'Reconciliation' first appeared in 1865. Coming at the end of America's Civil War, it presents attitudes that had probably accumulated in Whitman's activity as an unofficial volunteer nurse in Washington's hospitals. Unlike many of the poems from *Drum-Taps*, it, and its companion, 'Look Down Fair Moon', shows no enthusiasm for combat. Instead, each poem, in its own way, makes the dead into sacred presences. Those who speak of Whitman as garrulous do so unfairly, because they do not attend to what is ample rather than verbose in his work. 'Reconciliation' is concise, not in the linear mode of logically successive meanings, but as a fundamentally organized whole. The poem is comprised in one long sentence, the principal agents of which are 'Beautiful/for/I look/I bend down and touch':

Reconciliation

> Word over all, beautiful as the sky,
> Beautiful that war and all its deeds of carnage must in time
>   be utterly lost,
> That the hands of the sisters Death and Night incessantly
>   softly wash again, and ever again, this soil'd word;

For my enemy is dead, a man divine as myself is dead,
I look where he lies white-faced and still in the coffin – I
  draw near,
Bend down and touch lightly with my lips the white face
  in the coffin.

On first inspection 'For' seems a contradiction; although that semi-colon round which the poem is halted and organized requires us to look closely at what the word is modifying. 'For' in the sense of 'because' seems to modify either nothing, or to mean 'it is beautiful that (because) my enemy is dead'. Yet such is clearly a mistake, since no work of reconciliation can either say or mean that.

The key is to be found in the poem's consisting of one sentence, with a 'reeve' of sense that culminates in the lightly touched kiss of reconciliation. In that sense 'For' means something like 'Beautiful/softly wash again/For (since he who is dead) I touch with my lips'. Thus it is beautiful that the 'soil'd world' can be redeemed (we might hardly be as sure of it these days) and (since) in the same sort we may, as enemies, be reconciled. Renewal of the world does not mean individual renewal of life, which is perhaps why 'For' does not lend equivalent signification to the two parts of the poem either side of the semi-colon (line 4). But the two actions, that of earth slowly cleansing itself (it will take time) and the human act of reconciliation, unequally performed between the living and dead, form some balance in the fulcrum 'For'. Thus the syntax, enacts *dynamic* parallelism – 'beautiful/that/That/For' – jointed through the poem's open-faced urgency; additionally, there is an over-arching parallelism of the *sentence's* two halves.

One might say that the structure gives the lie to the metricists' accusation that free verse fails to enact a form.

Last, a remark about the rhythm in relation to the line-endings. Like Dryden's lines, in this respect, the rhythm pushes beyond the formally stopped lines, considerable energy being needed to achieve this. The sense in 'Reconciliation' is of undulant, mixed dactyllic and anapaestic lines that seem to want to overcome the end-stopped impositions and reach that moment of reconciliation.

Hopkins wrote to Bridges on 18 October 1882,

> though [I have read] very little, [it] is quite enough to give a
> strong impression of his marked and original manner and way

of thought and in particular of his rhythm ... I may as well say what I should not otherwise have said, that I always knew in my heart Walt Whitman's mind to be more like my own than any other man's living. As he is a very great scoundrel this is not a pleasant confession. And this also makes me the more desirous to read him and the more determined I will not.

(*Letters of Gerard Manley Hopkins to Robert Bridges*, pp. 154–5)

That little convolution of desire and its denial throws some light on the mechanism of Hopkins' impulsion. He then goes on to deny Bridges' assertion that a resemblance between his and Whitman's rhythm exists; and then, to analyse a line from SoM (which he misquotes) and so, reverts to his own 'sprung rhythm'. Near the end of this long letter, which needs consulting in full, he says:

The above remarks are not meant to run down Whitman. His 'savage' style has advantages. . . . Neither do I deny all resemblance. In particular I noticed in 'Spirit that formed this Scene' a preference for the alexandrine. I have the same preference: I came to it by degrees, I did not take it from him.

(*Letters to Bridges*, p. 157)

The whole letter makes interesting reading. (For George Saintsbury's review of Whitman, see *Letters*, pp. 311–16.)

POSTSCRIPT

Strictly speaking the following note on Hopkins' prosody belongs above, but it would have formed such an impediment to the reader wherever it came that I offer it separately. Writing to R.W. Dixon on 5 October 1878 Hopkins had a number of things to say about Milton's 'rhythm . . . metrical system (and) verse-structure', which in turn led him to:

I had long had haunting my ear the echo of a new rhythm which now I realised on paper. To speak shortly, it consists in scanning by accents or stresses alone, without any account of the number of syllables, so that a foot may be one strong syllable or it may be many light and one strong . . . there are hints of it in music, in nursery rhymes and popular jingles, in the poets themselves.

... Here are instances – 'Díng, dóng, béll; Pússy's ín the wéll' ...
For if each line has three stresses or three feet it follows that some
of the feet are of one syllable only. So too 'One, twó, Búckle my
shóe.' ... it appears ... to be a better and more natural principle
than the ordinary system [of counting both stresses and syllables]
... and my rhymes carried on from one line into another and
certain chimes suggested by the Welsh poetry ...

This accounts for much of Hopkins' rhythm and its 'chimes', and
moreover discloses something he does not make explicit – the 'reeve'
and tension of his verse, especially as we experience this on WoD.
The problem comes with Hopkins' phrase 'without any account
of the number of syllables'. It seems harmless enough, but the difficulty, as Charles O. Hartman has well observed, is that Hopkins
brought the structure of music into his prosodic calculations. Music
has tempted a number of prosodists into analogizing or even ac-
counting for verse-structure in musical terms. For example (they
analogize), the *length* (duration) of musical notes which are put into
a given bar of music determines how *many* notes are placed within
a bar. So if two crotchets have the (time) value of one minim, two
weak syllables in verse may, they analogize, be the equivalent of
one stressed syllable. However, syllabic value is much more complex than notes in music. Yet this notwithstanding, the analogy so-
called appears to correspond to Hopkins' account where he says
'scanning by accents or stresses alone, without any account of the
number of syllables ... there are hints of it in music'. Yet as I suggest, any given syllable cannot be measured as can a note of music
with respect to the length of time it occupies in relation to other
syllables. Whatever account Hopkins may make of weak syllables,
those without stress do have varying duration, and to treat them as
if they did not shows a wilful even (surprisingly) tyrannical approach
to language. And, a partial objection, syllables within words will,
with crucial minute importance, vary in duration according to their
context within the overall meaning of the sentence.
   Hopkins offers three prosodies, which he regularly works:

1. ordinary or running rhythm where stresses *and* syllables are
    both counted;
2. counterpointed rhythm where a stress falls upon a normally
    unstressed syllable –

$$\text{Háil } \overline{\text{hó}}\text{ly líght, ófspring of Héav'n fírst-}\overline{\text{bórn}}$$

where 'ofspring' (offspring) has two stresses, the first of which occurs where expectations in the iambic metre prepare the ear for a weak or *unaccented* syllable. But instead the ear gets a stressed syllable. The other, weak stress falls metrically on the second syllable, which is indeed intrinsically weak but which must bear the metre's ghostly habitual demand of a stress. The first three words of the line stray into

3. 'sprung rhythm' (accentual), where, as Hopkins says, a stress may be used without counting syllables or, indeed, having any unstressed syllables to accompany the stressed (see above with his examples taken from nursery rhymes). Sprung rhythm excludes counterpointing.

I have also to say that (see letter to Bridges, 21 August 1877) there is also in English verse prosody – though often barely accounted for – the phenomenon of duration or length of time a syllable takes. When duration is applied to either a strong or weak or unstressed syllable a very complex rhythm is felt. Duration (as distinct from stress) was what Greek and Roman poetries used in their prosodies; and attempts (Bridges', for example) to substitute duration for stress in any systematic way have so far failed in English. Duration as a prosodic system seems likely to prove unviable for as long as spoken English remains a stressed language. But this is not to say that duration may not be used in conjunction with stress. Milton, for instance, uses both stress and duration.

So, I believe, does Hopkins, though I am not aware of his having made any formal recognition of it in his prosodic accounts. Rather, his prosodic theory is based on stress and syllable counting. As he says, paeons may have a movable stress syllable occurring anywhere within or beside three unstressed syllables.

The problem with Hopkins' metrical theory may, however, be put more positively. If we try to apply Hopkins' accounts of prosody to his verse we may find ourselves in difficulties, even where the rhythms are legible. In as much as his verse offers difficulties, we need not incorporate Hopkins' anxieties concerning the prosodic orthodoxy of his procedures into our reading of his poetry.

To take a last instance of all this, the stanzas of WoD claim to

approximate to each other. Their visual arrangement, insetting, and numbers of lines offer an appearance of stanzaic congruence.
    Here is stanza 11:

PART THE SECOND

11

'Some find me a sword; some
The flange and the rail; flame,
Fang, or flood' goes Death on drum,
And storms bugle his fame.
But we dream we are rooted in earth – Dust!
Flesh falls within sight of us, we, though our flower
    the same,
        Wave with the meadow, forget that there must
The sour scythe cringe, and the blear share come.

And here are the last two lines of the next stanza:

Yet did the dark side of the bay of thy blessing
Not vault them, the millions of rounds of thy mercy not reeve
    even them in?

Theory would make the concluding two lines of the two stanzas rhythmically consonant with each other, but the ear and the pulse cannot hear it.

2
Imagism, Lawrence, Pound, Read and Eliot

The components antecedent in the quarrel between morality and beauty ('Beauty is truth, truth beauty') do not appear to be in *open* conflict in Keats, nor were they always at loggerheads. Before him, the poet Sidney 'praises poetry not only for its "teaching" but for . . . its special power to penetrate, where the soberer precepts of the philosopher merely bounce off'. Thus 'it is able to "move men to take that goodness in hand, which without delight they would fly as from a stranger." The idea derives from Horace's ("movere aut docere", "to move or teach") about mixing the useful with the pleasing, and is a commonplace of Renaissance literary theory' (Sidney, *Arcadia*, Maurice Evans, p. 40). If this conjunction implies a cynical view of human nature which can be bribed by pleasure into accepting the preceptual, it is nevertheless presented without any seeming strain. But Keats's formulation suggests some strain. The neatness of the soldering indicates the pressure of that necessity under which he feels obliged to formulate the unity of beauty with truth. Moreover it is eighteenth-century Augustan, rather than post-Johnson, where the terms are obliged to lock together, like mortice and tenon, rather than interact in a continually re-forming unity, as with Blake and Coleridge.

In the latter half of the nineteenth century little of this will hold anyhow. If Hopkins' version of God's beauty is inscaped in Nature, his moral God is often the source and provider of affliction. In this double sense God not only creates but reflects the world.

The disagreement between Ruskin and Pater is in the open. For Ruskin art subserves morality, although it is worth noting that for him morality roots in art's beauty. For Pater it is beauty that justifies existence, such as that which inheres in art:

> To burn always with this hard, gemlike flame, to maintain this ecstasy, is success in life. . . . For our one chance lies in expanding that interval, in getting as many pulsations as possible into the

30

given time. Great passions may give us this quickened sense of life, ecstasy and sorrow of love, the various forms of enthusiastic activity.... Only be sure it is passion – .... Of such wisdom, the poetic passion, the desire of beauty, the love of art for its own sake, has most. For art comes to you proposing frankly to give nothing but the highest quality to your moments as they pass, and simply for those moments' sake.

(from 'Conclusion' to *The Renaissance*)

Pound's definition of the 'image' as 'that which presents an intellectual and emotional complex in an instant of time' reads as though it derives from Pater's 'the focus where the greatest number of vital forces unite in their purest energy'. The tone is Pater's; and 'To burn always with this hard, gemlike flame' offers the text not only for Pound's poetics, as it does for the other Imagists, but for a part of Eliot's also. We notice Pound's insistence on the aesthetic constitution of Imagism, and Eliot's questionable paradox:

The chief use of the 'meaning' of a poem ... may be ... to satisfy one habit of the reader, to keep his mind diverted and quiet, while the poem does its work upon him: much as the imaginary burglar is always provided with a bit of nice meat for the house-dog.

(*Selected Prose*, 93)

Each is rooted in the Paterean half of the proposition 'beauty and truth', 'delight and instruction'. In bifurcating the terms, beauty, its hard clear image, is made to evacuate meaning and morality, as though beauty and morality were, or had become, antithetical, which of course they can be made to be; and to appear irreconcilable, which they are not unless they are first polarized into some figure of opposition. In the 'hard, gemlike' nature of such a position with respect to art's beauty, no Blakean or Coleridgean interaction of discrete opposites, if such they be, is possible.

For Pound and Eliot, beauty and truth are not *per se* mutually exclusive modes; and any attempt to enforce this dichotomy may entail a further fragmentation, which of course is the cliché character of modernism. Yet fragmentation is part of a mode used in opposition to discourse and discursiveness and of that tendency to grandiloquence, to a lyricism combining itself with an easy-flowing confidence uninterrupted by any suspicion of the defects in human activity, including those of the writer. Fragmentation, therefore, as a function of self-doubt. Discourse, continuous and flowing, completed syntax and naturalistic, linear narrative – these are in modernist aesthetics rejected in favour of an attempt to render, mimetically and sensuously, the experience itself, what the experience *feels* like in all the self-doubt of the writer as it is mediated through the evaluative layers of a mind's conscious and underlying faculties. And this preamble must serve as a way into a look at Imagism, a glimpse at Lawrence, Read, Pound and finally Eliot.

H.D. conscripted Lawrence into contributing to *Some Imagist Poets* (1915 and 1916), and his consent may indicate a recognition that Imagism may have helped him in his decision to use parallelism as the thinking and expressive form for his free verse. Not that he relinquished metricality, as we see in his *Last Poems* (1932); and what he did in his fusing the fresh improvisatory nature of free verse with metricality I discuss in chapter 4. But it should be added that the Imagist perception that Hebrew parallelism might provide an alternative form to metricality was not only a discovery made by Whitman, but was also something that might have occurred to Lawrence. For he was grounded in both the Bible and 'the Nonconformist hymns' (see 'Hymns in a Man's Life', 1928). Lawrence's use of parallelism in his free verse is obvious enough, and it serves, as a method of composition, to indicate that Pound, with the magnificent exception of his stepped lines and their rhythmic redesigning, never got much beyond the method of juxtaposition. It is only a partly flexible instrument, designed to keep out discursive explanation and authorial interference, yet all it succeeded in doing for Pound was to frustrate and intensify his didacticism, and so produce tangles of information. For his obsession with economics as a moral instrument necessitated his imparting this 'knowledge'.

This blockage in composition which stood in the way of Pound's developing expressive emotional strengths, was not something from which Lawrence suffered. In his 'creature poems', and many of his *Last Poems*, Lawrence develops and essentializes his sense of the *quick* that is life itself.

And humour for humour, *The Pisan Cantos* (1948) not excepted, we find unpleasing rightist and partisan wit in

> Pétain defénded Verdún while Blúm
>   was defénding a bidet

(80, 494)

compared with

> A tíny, frágile, half-ánimate béan. . . .
> All ánimate creátion on yōur shóulder,
> Sét fórth, little Títan, únder your báttle-shīeld.
> ('Baby Tortoise', *CP*, pp. 352–3)

The rhythms, of course, are different. With Pound, the rhythm, though less realized in this instance, is finely wavered over two stepped halves where, with Lawrence, the rhythms, like those of Whitman, are sub-joined within the contour of a single line. For Whitman and Lawrence the line remains the basic unit.

If, as seems possible, Imagism arrested some part of Pound's development, when he develops his prosody it is therefore by a route he had not propagandized on behalf of Imagism, but which he had quietly practised quite early on:

> With them the silyer hóunds,
>   sniffing the trace of áir!
> ('The Return', *CSP*, p. 85)

This was, I believe, Pound's discovery. Whereas the 'image' as 'that which presents an intellectual and emotional complex in an instant of time', in 'A Few Don'ts By An Imagiste', though finely redesigned, is ultimately unworkable, not susceptible to development in the medium of syntax. For syntax is sequential, even if simultaneity may be simulated in the reader's mind by mosaic or a cyclical recurrence of particular images.

Thus, whatever vision of modernism Pound may have had as he worked on the complex of poems that became Eliot's *The Waste Land* (1922), some of Pound's finest achievements were in his sequential, fully syntactic *and* metrical mode. *Successful* disjunction is more Eliot's than Pound's achievement, though it may be that Pound helped Eliot to achieve this, for both men's impulsions often worked best in short bursts of energy. Yet it is Pound's most substantial achievement to have produced, in *The Pisan Cantos*, stretches of sustained poetry which, despite the traditional mode they use, *feel* modern in their synoptic power (see 'The ant's a centaur' passage in Canto 81, pp. 521–2).

My additional conjecture is that Pound's want of fuller growth (and integration) is partly due to his having an obsession with 'money', in the absence of any real theme or subject, and, as I suggest, that he fixed on the juxtaposition of images and statements as his method of communicating those meanings in lieu of finding a way of transcribing such intractable information.

It is the failure in prosody and structure that impedes a fruitful development of responses and ideas. A considerable proportion of the Cantos involves a juxtaposition of untransmuted obsessions. Again, there is the wonderful exception to this, for when Pound is put into the position of a suffering creature having to reflect on his actions and their results, though not repentant of his affiliations, he is able, in *The Pisan Cantos*, to make a more but by no means entirely coherent set of structures. But when he achieves wonderful coherence, in passages of humility, mythic and natural splendour, as much as in synoptic moral perspective, the result is major poetry, much of it working in traditional structures of sequential and completed syntax in metrical form. This is the achievement, so that when he wrote of Whitman (and himself) 'I make a pact with you' ('A Pact'), it is Whitman's free verse that looks new, rather than Pound's poetry, though the best of Pound is 'fresh'. Yet Whitman remains the great poet, untouched by Pound, and it needs to be said that Pound's syntax is traditional, in those sustained passages constructed along the ley-lines of continuity and completion of syntax with meaning. So we frequently find consonance between traditional metricality and traditionally formed syntax in much of Pound's finest poetry. Whereas with Lawrence's 'The Ship of Death', especially its opening phases, we find elements of disturbing discontinuous syntax running athwart the traditional metricality. Such complexity probably comes with an upsurge of feeling from, and a religious response to, being close to death, and provides a feeling of immediacy and imminence lacking in much of Pound's verse, though not in Eliot's *The Waste Land*. At any rate, I discuss this question of metricality with discontinuous syntax in chapter 4. All I would repeat here is that Lawrence is in certain respects the more modern, less trammelled *prosodist* and, despite his poetry being ignored by academic studies at university level, has, with respect to prosody alone, at least as much to offer as Pound.

> Nów it is áutumn a̅n̅d the fálling frúit
> and the lóng jóurney towárds obliviō̅n̅.
>
> The ápples fálling like gréat dróps of déw
> to brúise themsélves an éxit from thémsélves.

And ít is tíme to gó, to bíd farewéll
to óne's ōwn sélf, and find an éxit
from the fállen sélf . . .

('The Ship of Death')

in relation to

The ánt's a céntaur in his drágon wórld.
Pūll dōwn thy vánity, it is nót mán
Made courage, or made order, or made grace,
    Pūll dōwn thy vánity, I sáy pull dówn.
Léarn of the gréen wórld what can bé thy pláce
In scáled invéntion ōr trúe ártistrý,
Púll dówn thy vánity,
            Páquin pūll dōwn!
The gréen cásque has óutdóne your élegance.

(81, 521)

In attitude, these are comparable passages, and I examine them in detail later.

The most evident difference is that where Lawrence's syntax runs athwart the metre, as if to emphasize 'The apples falling like great drops of dew', dropping in both fruitfulness and mortality, Pound's comparable richness of moral complexity arises with the scale. The verse structures together the different-sized ant, centaur and warrior's helmet, the latter being unfavourably compared to the 'casque' (carapace) of the insect. Pound's continuous syntax here enacts a synoptic morality, though we tend to think of Lawrence as the didact.

IMAGISM AND FREE VERSE

Imagism and free verse are not interchangeable modes. Imagism is part of free verse, but most free verse is not Imagism; and if we count Whitman's non-metrical poetry as free verse, as we ought, then Imagism is not, as Timothy Steele in *Missing Measures* asserts it is, the 'originator' of free verse. It is precisely because Whitman was there before [him] that he elicited fierce disclaimers. In his 'Ezra Pound: His Metric and His Poetry' (before 1918), Eliot wrote:

The metres and the use of language are unfamiliar. There
are certain traces of modern influence. We cannot agree with
Mr Scott James that among these are 'W.E. Henley, Kipling,
Chatterton, and especially Walt Whitman' – least of all Walt
Whitman.

It is not in the ideas so much as the vehemence and even the contempt of that 'least of all', which suggests very complex responses
in the face of Whitman. One of them may be the desire to erase
paternity, but it is clear that the aesthetics of Imagism, which is the
most substantial gift the movement made, have antecedents in prior
critical writing. For instance the item below resembles Pater's 'To
burn always with this hard, gemlike flame'.

1. To use the language of common speech, but to employ
   always the *exact* word, not the nearly-exact, nor the merely
   decorative word.
2. To create new rhythms – as the expression of new moods . . .
3. To allow absolute freedom in choice of subject . . .
4. To present an image. . . . We are not a school of painters, but
   we believe that poetry should render particulars exactly and
   not deal in vague generalities . . .
5. To produce poetry that is hard and clear, never blurred nor
   indefinite.
6. Finally, most of us believe that concentration is of the very
   essence of poetry.

                    (Preface to *Some Imagist Poets*, 1915)

Imagism's aesthetics, however, differ significantly from Pater's in
one respect, for where Pater asserts 'Not the fruit of experience, but
experience *itself*, is the end' (my emphasis), Imagism lays stress –
on the image – 'To present an image'. It could be argued that Pater
is contrasting the wisdom derived from experience (if that is what
is obtained) with the experience itself; but my point is that in any
case the difference between Pater's aesthetics and Imagism is that
where Pater is concerned with experience, Imagism is concerned
with literature. And if we consider that first principle which Wordsworth lays down in his 1815 Preface, 'the ability to observe with
accuracy things as they are in themselves' (907), we can see how
limited were the aspirations of Imagism and how, if it constituted
some kind of revolution, it was of a kind limited to literary expression rather than being a new way of understanding exterior reality.

Wordsworth's 'to observe with accuracy things as they are in them-selves' does not confine itself to visual observation; but in the event the principles of Imagism seek to limit. Perhaps this is in part responsible for the politics of some of those constellated round Imagism. Certainly, we find Herbert Read recording in *The Contrary Experience* (1963) that he, himself an Imagist, became dissatisfied with the movement:

> I criticized them because 'in their manifestoes they had renounced the decorative word, but their sea-violets and wild hyacinths tend to become as decorative as the beryls and jades of Oscar Wilde'.
> ... We were trying to maintain an abstract aesthetic ideal in the midst of terrorful and inhuman events. In my own case I am certain that this devotion to abstract notions and intellectual reveries saved me from a raw reaction to these events. But as the war went on, year after year ... some compromise between dream and reality became necessary. The only worthy compromise, I even then dimly realized, was a synthesis – some higher reality in which the freedom of the mind and the necessity of experience became reconciled.
>
> (pp. 176–7)

That last sentence, 'some higher reality in which the freedom of the mind and the necessity of experience became reconciled', provides a profound criticism of Imagism and its limitations. It is more as a catalyst than for its intrinsic productions that Imagism has proved valuable.

Pound quarrelled with Flint who, with T.E. Hulme, could fairly be claimed to have originated Imagism in 1909. Pound felt that if Imagism was to retain its value, its practice needed constant scrutiny and its nature must be essentialized. Yes, and ponder Pound's confession thirty or more years later, in *The Pisan Cantos* (80, 513), 'I have been hard as youth sixty years.' Yet consider the diverse poets in the four Imagist anthologies which included H.D., Pound, H.D.'s husband Richard Aldington, and Lawrence, this last also being represented in Edward Marsh's collections – five between 1911 and 1922 (Eliot's *The Waste Land* appeared in 1922, completed 1921). Imagism and the Georgians were seen to represent different impulsions. Indeed, we still think of Imagism as helping to instigate modernism, and of Georgianism, thought of as revolutionary in its time, as continuing the traditional native English verse. Thus although Lawrence published with Imagists and Georgians, it was with *Marsh* and his preference for 'smooth verse' that Lawrence clashed. 'It is the hidden *emotional* pattern that makes poetry, not the obvious form', he wrote to Marsh (19 November 1913, in *Selected Literary Criticism*, p. 80).

Yet the clash seems to imply that Lawrence felt greater kinship with the native tradition. Moreover 'hidden *emotional* pattern . . . not the obvious form' defines a positive never admitted into Imagism which, in such omission, prognosticates attenuation. I do not imply that writing can be made from feeling alone, but I believe that language without feeling (and positioned only or mainly in other literature) leads to extinction. Thus C.K. Stead's assertion that 'Imagism was essentially a free verse movement – a cutting down as close to the bare bone of poetic statement' (whose?) – seems more closely related to Imagism's professed principles than its practice. It is in any case a limited view of free verse, not all of which, or even the best, is 'close to the bone'.

With these reservations concerning Imagism made, it might be useful to compare Whitman's free verse 'Look Down Fair Moon' with H.D.'s poem 'Oread'. This latter was first published in *Blast*, No. 1, 191, under the instigation of Pound, where it featured within the splinter-group of Imagism named *Vorticism*. Here are both poems:

Oread

Whírl up, séa –
Whírl your póinted pínes,
Splásh your gréat pines
On our rócks,
Húrl your gréen óver us,
Cóver us with your póols of fír.
        (*Selected Poems*, p. 17; Louis Martz prints all
        but the first line with lower-case first letters)

And Whitman:

Look Down Fair Moon

Look dówn fair móon and báthe this scéne,
    Póur sóftly down night's nimbus flóods on fáces ghástly,
        swóllen, púrple,

On the déad on their bácks with árms toss'd wíde,
Pour dówn your unstinted nímbus sácred móon.
                              (*The Complete Poems*, p. 344)

Each is non-metrical. Neither poem arouses those traditional expectations in the reader by placing a regular recurrence of stressed and unstressed syllables in a pattern that repeats itself over a number of lines. Though if a poem in free verse may be defined as a form in which the lines differ rhythmically from each other, then Whitman's poem is more 'free verse' than H.D.'s. Whitman's poem precedes H.D.'s by some sixty years.

Each poem has strong pictorial qualities, though unlike Whitman's poem, H.D.'s initiates external reality, only to subvert it. Whitman's focuses on suffering, imploration, death, by infusing pictorialization with feeling. If it is an elegy, which perhaps it is, H.D.'s poem confounds external reality. Whitman's dead soldiers are present; the poem fulfils the essential requirement of 'war' poetry, presenting violent death, humanly inflicted. In 'Oread' (= 'mountain nymph') we see no human life, though some profound human disturbance is implied. Whitman's poem sees and feels the prior agonies of the dead in 'arms toss'd wide', while H.D.'s dissolves what she initially presented in nature 'out there'. The referents end up as neither pine nor sea but 'pools of fir', while the syntax treats this dissolution as though it were nothing strange. Part of the mysterious dissolving process, itself contributory to the elegiac possibility, is dependent, like a surrealist poem, on the left hand of syntactical normality behaving as though the right hand, subverting external reality, were doing nothing extraordinary. The deeper feeling is dependent not only on this subversion but on the poker-faced collusion between both. If this is Imagism it is noticeable that the claims of 4 and 5 (above) are subverted by this poem; though as Louis Martz indicates in his 'Introduction' (p. vii) to the *Selected Poems* (1988), Pound's presentation of the image as 'a radiant node or cluster . . . a VORTEX, from which, and through which, and into which, ideas are constantly rushing' fits the poem better. Though 'rushing' would hardly apply here.

SYNTAX AND LINEATION IN BOTH POEMS

Whitman's habitual practice is to make each line of verse coincident with a syntactical unit, and this holds true for his American Civil

War poem. 'Look/Pour/On the dead/Pour' instigate both the rhetoric of a pattern, and a syntax of which there is unchecked progression across only lines 2 and 3. Such an inching movement could stultify, but the diversifying rhythms prevent this. It is further prevented by there being no repeated congruence between rhythmic impulsion and syntactical formation. Further, the images of reality are rich *and* horrifying, a version of sensuous verse that much nineteenth-century poetry in English eschewed. Though this horrific character is itself in contrast with the 'fair moon' that is asked to annoint the 'ghastly', violently made dead. In this perhaps there is a correspondence between the moon's function in the poem and Whitman's activity as an unofficial nurse in the Washington hospitals that served the wounded of both sides.

This coincidence of verse-*line* with syntactic sense-units is a strategy H.D. also uses in 'Oread', and raises the question as to whether the poet who lived her first twenty-five years in America was perhaps influenced by Whitman: 'Whirl/Whirl/Splash/On our rock/Cover'. The rhetorical strategy is remarkably similar to Whitman's 'Look Down Fair Moon'. Her poem's sensuous density is also comparable with Whitman's. Both poems are of course brief, but the similarity consists in that both finally bring together an interpenetration of sensuous opposites. Yet there is an important difference. In Whitman's poem the moon is the unifying agent of an externally realized scene, whereas in H.D.'s the reader habituated to a poem presenting literal referents is likely to be confounded, while at the same time feeling that the poem constitutes some kind of unity. Thus the two most contrasting images, sea and pine, are worked together to produce the impossible actuality of 'pools of fir'. I suggest that this erasing of the literal in the final composite induces that sense of exultation and desolation, which is the grieving and celebrating secret heart of the poem.

If this is the high point in Imagist achievement, what then were the costs to an art of which this poem is in certain senses representative? Quoting again that phrase of Wordsworth's, 'the ability to observe with accuracy things as they are in themselves', I imply not a slavish mimetic compulsion but a respect for external reality. For that little 'as they are in themselves' is not tautological, but denotes respect. In dissolving that reality the costs are very high, not only for the art but also for readers. However, in the 'Essay, Supplementary to the Preface' (1815), Wordsworth wrote:

the medium through which, in poetry, the heart is to be affected – is language; a thing subject to endless fluctuations and arbitrary associations. The genius of the Poet melts these down for his purpose.

(*William Wordsworth*, Vol. II, p. 947)

It is this 'melting down' and unification that H.D. achieves in 'Oread'. Imagist theory, and some of its practice, has its roots in Wordsworth's critical theory. In the third edition of *Lyrical Ballads* (1802) he had declared:

a large portion of the language of every good poem can in no respect differ from that of good Prose. I will go further. I do not doubt that it may be safely affirmed, that there neither is, nor can be, any essential difference between the language of prose and metrical composition.

(*William Wordsworth*, Vol. I, p. 875)

Coleridge did not agree, yet it seems that Pound's 'a poem should be at least as well-written as good prose' (see also letter to Harriet Monroe of January 1915, No. 60) and Eliot's 'anything that can be said as well in prose can be said better in prose' (*SP*, 93) are each in ambiguous concurrence with Wordsworth's idea; for Wordsworth's assertion claims that one *language* does for both verse and prose. By pointing to prose Wordsworth identifies the common source from which poetry must renew itself. And as Wordsworth indicates in the same Preface, poetry must not weaken itself by reducing language to (poetic) diction.

Yet my objection to a number of H.D.'s earlier poems is not that they use the language of prose but that, syntactically and prosodically, the form of prose uses them. The poems do not melt down the language to produce something new. Dispensing with metricality, it is not enough to make a non-metrical poem. Such poetry must redesign the resources released in non-metricality so as to produce something vital. Nor should the poem be a non-metrical version of a metrical one, but an exploratory regrouping and reutilizing of the remaining resources, which may be renewed and felt differently in their re-formed relationship. A prose merely broken into lines at its intermediate syntactic joins is a form of metricality.

In his Introduction to H.D.'s *Selected Poems*, Martz writes (p. vii) of this early poetry with 'its swirling, dynamic power: the sort of turbulent force', and so on. This cannot be, and its 'swirling' exaggeration serves to obscure the tough stilled power that some of her later verse does have. For my purposes, however, two of H.D.'s early poems I want to select indicate what Imagism, as a form of free verse, did not achieve.

Read objected to the (bogus) 'classicism' of Imagist poetry. In H.D.'s case the real subject, though it does not feel as if it has been obtained, is purity. Classicism is its coded analogue. The objects, gods, flowers, exist in this artificial paradise. But this construction is an error, for to suppose that such metaphors can, for whole poems at a time, sustain the poetry is an evasion of the requirement that all art register and evaluate 'felt experience', of which very little underpins these early poems:

> The light passes . . .
> the blue tips bend
> toward the bluer heart
> and the flowers are lost.
> ('Evening', *Selected Poems*, pp. 4–5)

Nothing eventuates, except evening. Unlike 'Oread', though more like 'Storm' (p. 12), the syntax crosses the line-endings at those points where the syntactical breaks occur, thus making the prose syntax responsible for the lineation. The lineation concurs with the syntax rather than having an identity of its own, and then working cooperatively with the syntax. Thus:

> Thou art come at length
> More beautiful
> Than any cool god
> In a chamber under
> Lycia's far coast . . .
> ('Sitalkas', *Imagist Poetry*, p. 63)

'Cool' is, I think, a coded word for 'purity' but the deity is never seen; the word, contrary to desiderated Imagist practice, asserts rather than presents the attribute. No rhythmic energy exists, and there is little active intersection of the syntax with verse lines. This may be because there is no rhythmic energy. For where that doesn't exist, what else would initiate a meeting of the other impulsions?

These lines take the least form of resistance. They are the obedient ciphers of prose syntax.

We are at the impasse where Imagism must be catalyst to something other than its proclaimed intentions, something inherent in language and syntax. With verse sheared of its metricality, it must develop different limbs, and this seems to involve working rhythm and lineation with syntax in such a way that all three actively cooperate.

That this happened at all is partly due to the talent that was there to enable it; but development also took place because the life of verse over a long period had acquired enough energy to ensure its continuation. Tradition as a whole impelled the creation of new forms. For there must also have been forms of creation that arose and died for want of a long and sustaining prior life. At any rate I suggest that having posited the hard, clear image, Imagism found the mode incapable of intrinsic development. Interested readers may consult the work of the German poet August Stramm, which represents the beginning and end of verse posited upon the image as its principal constituent. It is fine, but leads nowhere.

The positive development arising from Imagist practice reconciled 'the freedom of the mind' with the 'necessity of experience'. Herbert Read's unjustly neglected longer poem 'The End of a War' (1933) is a sustained achievement, which Yeats, to his credit, included in his (old-fashioned) *The Oxford Book of Modern Verse* (1936), though he excluded Rosenberg and Owen.

READ

In the poem's first section, 'Meditation of a Dying German Officer', we read,

> This failing light
> is the world's light: it dies like a lamp
> flickering for want of oil. When the last jump comes
> and the axe-head blackness slips through flesh,
> that welcomes it with open but unquivering lips
> then I shall be one with the Unknown . . .
> (*Selected Poetry*, p. 101)

Read lineates effectively, having learned from Wordsworth, whom he described as a most marvellous 'fashioner', something which he did not discard. By having the syntax and rhythm cooperate with and design the line, the line becomes the rhetorical equivalent of a visual element. A nice answer to Imagism. 'Failing light' and 'world's light' are lineated into parallel figures and by doing this the meaning of the former is made to create the fate of the latter, itself 'flickering for want of oil'. But this is the life of the dying German officer too, whose ebbing life connects with the defeated and dying German Empire. For him the world *is* or seems to be dying, and we may compare this sense of failing existence with that 'dying' in Owen's 'Exposure'.

> For love of God seems dying.

'Like a lamp' suggests the condition of common mortality, but the enacting line-break anticipates something different. Because of the long, continuous, rhythmic flow of the syntax over eight lines, the poet is justified in thinking we will be waiting in anticipation for something. This something anticipated is not only death but *violent* perishing, and it is this, by the very nature of war, that qualifies 'like a lamp'. Death is 'the last jump', but like the executing bayonet of the British soldier, death as 'the axe-head blackness', is a violently inflicted death. This physiological response of the body's dying is reflected in the flickering quickening rhythms of the line beginning 'that welcomes it', such a quickening being akin to the quickening flame of a dying lamp (the living lamp burns with a steady easeful flame). All this is no mere mimesis, but, to meet the exigencies of meaning, is beautifully controlled by the intersection of a varying rhythm with lineation, and, with the sustained syntax that is analogue to the long dying of the executed soldier. A little more remains to be said which is to do with the wider purpose of the poem. The work falls into three parts, each of which embodies typified national types representing the essence of three different nations. Thus the idealism of the German, the purity of the French and the quotidian sacred values of the English incarnated in a genuine humility.

The line that 'welcomes [death] with open and unquivering lips' has a quickening rhythm which contrasts with the heavy ones that precede it. Where before the body is labouring to live, while the mind of that body is working to articulate for itself its dying thoughts, this line expresses the body's physiological response to its own death, in those actions of the dying flicker of the lamp 'for want of oil': a religious symbol of some unspecified kind. Yet this expression of an accelerated dying, achieved through an extra number of weak syllables which makes the line move faster, is slowed at its end with the use of strong compacted stresses, which fall on 'unquivering lips'. And this heavy stressing expresses the stoic idealism and courage of the German soldier who has no regret, either for his death, or, as the enemy British see it, for his human treachery. For the German sees such treachery as an act done for the fatherland in the interests of idealistic duty. Thus the rhythm is made to enact locally one constituent meaning of the whole, and is enabled to do so because Read has understood the necessity of intersecting the three components, rhythm, syntax and lineation in active (free verse) cooperation. Not but that the last line (above) is not pentameter, its ease expressing, perhaps, a flicker of ironic anticipation at becoming part of his friend's 'Unknown'. It is wonderfully done, major poetry awaiting the recognition it deserves.

ELIOT'S ROUTE

In *Free Verse: An Essay on Prosody* (1980), Charles O. Hartman elucidates Carlos Williams' poem 'Exercise' (pp. 93–8). By examining the cooperative working of syntax with lineation he offers a close reading of the poem's meaning; an informative experience, suggesting that when the direct method of trying to understand a poem's meaning has failed, this other may be useful (I'm not saying Williams' poem has baffled its readers). However, the opening three lines of Eliot's 'The Love Song of J. Alfred Prufrock' have, on the evidence of (mis)readings, presented difficulties of comprehension:

> Lét us gó then, yóu and Í,
> When the évening is spréad out against the ský
> Like a pátient étherised upón a táble; . . .
>
> (*CP*, 13)

The first thing to be said is that out of the total of 131 lines, these are not, as Richard Ellman asserts, free verse, 'the vers libre of "Prufrock"' ('The First *Waste Land*', in Litz, p. 58). But he is not really *listening*. In 'An Anatomy of Melancholy' (*T.S. Eliot, The Waste Land*, p. 91), speaking of the poem's 'wonderfully varied use of rhythmed free verse', Conrad Aiken seems to be making a similar

claim, and neither reading is accurate. A number of the lines are
vers libéré, that is, they are verse lines hovering within the ambit of
metricality. But of the 131 lines only some 25 lines are probably, in
some cases ambiguously, free verse. And there is the further effect
that where the greater proportion of lines are metrical, this will mag-
netize the lines of ambiguous rhythmic status towards metricality.
Nevertheless there are alternative ways of reading stresses, and for
these first three lines of the poem I offer an alternative scansion:

> Let us go then, you and I,
> When the evening is spread out against the sky
> Like a patient etherised upon a table.

Reading the poem on record, Eliot, I believe, gives metricality to
these and other lines, but in any case the problem with the above
scansion is that the third line gets stowed away as if it were an
afterthought, while the voice-emphases fall with cheerful and banal
confidence upon the first two lines. Yet even were this the right
rhythmic reading to give the lines, we still need to understand the
relationship between the kind of evening being presented and the
patient 'etherised'. Perhaps, we say, it doesn't matter, for we might
subordinate the 'patient etherised' to the sentimental evening, somewhat in the way that the alternative second scansion absorbs the
third line without giving it much further thought. That's adequate,
one supposes. But if the poem invites further readings, which has
I think been the experience of many, one comes again against the
crux of the relationship between the evening 'spread' like 'a patient
etherised'. 'Spread out' certainly requires one, but not everyone, to
reflect on the patient 'etherised'. Angus Calder says that 'we must
infer that the image's main function is not to describe but to shock'
(p. 26). That reading adds, if anything, a minus quantity to our
understanding. The Norton Anthology (third edition, 1974) explains
that 'A contrast is perhaps here implied between "ether" as the free
sky or the heavens and the word's medical connotations – help-
lessness, disease, the elimination of consciousness and personality'
(p. 2164). We must, it seems, find some other, more patient, way of
reading. For surely 'ether' as even a part-reading for sky is permissible only if one ignores the patient anaesthetized. I have no wish
to be rude, merely to indicate what maladroit criticism and 'explanation' is driven to without recourse to a gentler, alternative route.
  Eliot's syntax moves in these first two lines with parallel increment,

'Let us go/When', the third line asymmetrically disrupting the congruence; which is how Eliot quite frequently works, first lulling the reader by establishing a pattern only to break it by veering in some unpredictable direction. This would seem to suggest that I am after all supporting Mr Calder's 'designed to shock', but my understanding is that in this mode Eliot is, on the contrary, expressing a partly open, vulnerable, wayward aspect of his responses. The syntax's pressure culminates, in the third line, in particular on 'etherised'; I am saying nothing but that which many have experienced in their reading.

We tend to let it go at that. It is a startling image, we say. It is intended to shock, Mr Calder tells us. We remember it for that reason, we tell ourselves. But the syntax with its irremissive emphasis on 'etherised' requires us to respond to this pressure built up in combination with the lineation and its metricality, which creates two effects.

One is the evident passivity of the patient, and the other is the predatory action of the ether upon the patient. That is, the grammatically passive form is, underlyingly, charged with an active predatory one. The passive voice declares one meaning, but releases both, the substance *etherizing* the patient as much as the patient is etherized by it.

The OD supplies a verb-form of the word, though readers might in any case easily elucidate Eliot's verb-form. Indeed, in some ways it is fortunate that he is obliged to use a rare word, for the easily comprehensible but unusual formation here assists in the sly functioning of both levels of meaning. And by having the verb in its passive form this allows the active and predatory meaning to communicate simultaneously with the passive – with greater sinister effect than it would have done had the verb been in the active voice. The form in which the word exists obliquely inserts this double sense into the mind. The passive voice is not subsumed by the active effect, when the grammar is this way round, and we thus enter into a one-word drama in which we are, or feel ourselves to be, both the passive patient and the predatory ether; this condition is sporadically continued by the ether's covert association with the sometimes playful sometimes less than playful ubiquitous fog.

The ether, though, is ominously bullying. Thus, without logical explanation, we sympathize with the seemingly shy man, and suffer etherization with the patient who is the concealed analogue for Prufrock. We are thoroughly dramatized. Therefore the smiling tincture of terror. This figure of aggressive passivity recurs in lines 58–9, but less subtly suggestive, in

> And whén I am fórmulated, spráwling ón a pín,
> Whén I am pínned and wríggling ón the wáll...
>   (*CP*, 15)

Unless we apprehend this interacting doubleness, established by the syntactical working of 'etherized', we may not properly obtain the crucial strand in the poem, which is the drama between the would-be amorist and intelligent ironic observant, whose irony and aggression are deflected, or even abruptly reversed in, for instance,

> I shóuld have béen a páir of rágged cláws...
>   (*CP*, 15)

This example, to take a phrase from Herbert Read's *Phases of English Poetry*, is intelligent, not civilized; our involvement in the poem depends on our complicity in playing either or both roles, of civilized mocker and intelligent sufferer – one who is creaturely, wounded, reduced. And at times aggressive.

In this area of pendularity, consider the effect of the jingling rhythms and rhyme that recur in the famous couplet, of 'go/ Michelangelo'. And the additional mockery in the reductive rhyme 'ices/crisis'.

But a complete reading depends on our understanding that his self-deprecation alternates with these sadder and aggressive moments; the poem is a continuing drama of perpetuating/perpetuated pair of feelings. For a man who is so self-deprecating, for instance, he is resiliently assiduous in his failure. The subject of the poem is neither partly submerged aggression nor deprivation entailing irony, but an interaction between persistent effort only half brought-off, and self-examining, rueful, sometimes aggressively registered failure. I offer nothing which readers haven't felt; but I do suggest how crucial an understanding of the doubleness in 'etherised' is in leading to an apprehension of this interaction which supplies the poem's momentum.

In this sense of momentum, Prufrock is not a modernist poem, not fragmentary, but a merry-go-round of continuous self-doubting effort and failure. It is modernist only in its allusive, elusive character, and in its overtly psychological examination. The syntax is continuous and provides the meaning through the shuttling back and forth of mainly metrical forms of *vers libéré*, and, in that sense, the oscillating rhythmic effects are like those of Prufrock's character, patiently enacting a persistent failure of a yet hoping mind.

A detail

A note on line 64:

(But in the lámplight, dówned with líght brówn háir!)
(*CP*, 15)

What a difference plural 'hairs' on enticing arms would produce in discommoding both levels of gentility. There exists the level of deliberate gentility – to observe hair even on naked arms is permissible; to register 'hairs' impolite, indelicate, pubic. So the code goes. So thus far 'hair' is deliberate in fitting the code. But Prufrock-the-character apart, Eliot may not feel it (is) permissible to break the code, though the 'Bolovo' poems he was writing are, according to Ackroyd, his biographer, 'unpublishable'. Is this the point at which the poem falters, hiding the conceivably impolite behind the determinedly polite register? As they exist, the responses are 'what lovely arms, the hair is like down, etc.' An almost pre-pubic response. Are we meant to see this limitation? Or does Eliot not see it? Or are we supposed to incorporate the limitation into our reading?

The question of gentility re-emerged with the redrafting of the 'typist/clerk' episode in 'The Fire Sermon' of *The Waste Land*.

PROSODY

I should make a point about the collaborative role of syntax and metre in 'Prufrock', for the formal nature of the syntax and the metricality give the poem a stability and urbanity both of which help to preserve the social code that holds Prufrock in its enterprise. But the metres also give a reassuring balm to Prufrock's failure to obtain sex within the society, helping us to feel he is secure in the very class-structure that denies him something equally essential. Even the jingling rhyme 'go/Michelangelo' attached to rhythms that are almost nursery-rhyme doggerel give a certain reassurance. It is partial, as it must be for Prufrock, because, as I suggest, its reassurance also constitutes denial. Nor are the women entirely reassuring in their culture, for the sense is that they speak of Michelangelo as if he were contemporary. Such familiarity is strange, off-kilter, and the rhymes provide not merely a sense of mockery and boredom but a feeling of entrapment within some activity that has gone wrong – like a record with a scratch that will not release the player's arm to continue. Yet culture is the women's domain and in endowing security they also confirm their unattainability. In this sense they function like erotic *mothers*, and the pain in the poem may in part derive from this crossing of the desirable with the forbidden.

If I can I must make good my claim that some three-quarters of the poem is metrical. So I offer lines which look the least metrical in the poem, and am counting on some to approach these lines as if they were 'vers libre':

> The yéllow fóg that rúbs its báck upón the wíndow-pánes,
> The yéllow smóke that rúbs its múzzle ón the
>   wíndow-pánes, . . .
>
>   (CP, 13)

These are 'fourteeners', the number of syllables giving a cantering effect nicely out of sync with the fog rubbing its back on the glass. We can, as usual, count on Eliot to vary with great subtlety the metrical balance. In the first line the caesura, as if to signal the reader that this is metrical verse, falls between, and neatly divides, 'back' from 'upon'; but the next line, though having the same metricality, would, if one tried to place the caesura in the same position, so as to give it congruence with the preceding line, fall within 'muzzle'. We might place the break after 'muzzle', but the effect is messy, and the break, which a long line needs, falls better after the repeated word 'rubs', imparting an added feline, tactile quality that is approximately friendly. Line 105 may look like a puzzle –

> But as if a mágic lántern thréw / the nérves in pátterns
>   ón a scréen . . .
>
>   (CP, 17)

But this too is susceptible to a metrical reading.

This approach to metricality, notwithstanding Eliot's playfulness, is in some respects similar to Wordsworth's strategy in 'Immortality', where the latter moves in and out of the reader's expectations, one metre barely being established before it changes, as if to the poet's astonishment, into another. If Wordsworth's metricality is more flexible and various, to express his theme of response and renewal, Eliot's almost staid movements (his or Prufrock's?) are the suitable outer garment Prufrock uses to contain his more volatile feelings, including those of aggression. Despite the staid nature of some of the rhythmical transitions, what Eliot creates is a rhythmical teasing, paradigmatic of the poem's rhythmic-and-sense strategies.

The climaxes occur in a metricality that, however teasing the general strategy of the poem, emphasizes feeling, and which metricality bursts into conflagration – the 'sea-girls', the psychosexual intimacy, but taking place only in a vision that might readily change from sexuality to religion (see 'Ash-Wednesday', III, stanza 3 (1930)). Yet Prufrock retains *this* vision even though he is denied actual fulfilment. In holding on to such a vision he partly refutes the stereotypical image of a man wounded by self-consciousness and defeated by diffidence. Unfulfilled perhaps, yet he holds to some kind of visionary centre. The Hyacinth-girl episode of *The Waste Land* shows a similar shielding retention of a vision of love.

A PLEA FOR INCLUSIVITY

The potential inclusiveness of literary criticism contrasts with the narrowness in which most of it is practised. Critical theory is like words on one side of a sheet of paper backed on the other with the poem. Moreover criticism habitually exists in a condition of argument with others in the literary community, though the limitations which it most of the time suffers with regard to its numbers of readers does not always limit its hubris. This writer is vulnerable to his commentary, but without positing a need for tendentious work, a criticism that aspired to address a wider spectrum of readers would be valuable. In which case, it would have to write in all seriousness not for another aspect of academy, but have in mind those issues which are the concern of those not specially, if at all, interested in writing, or literature. Such criticism would engage the writer in acts that are tentative, yet needing courage, and it would entail the writer taking seriously not only the character of the writing but its intrinsic matter, together with the prejudices and politics of the work it was addressing. It would need to behave as if the work it was considering had not only 'as if' or metaphoric application, as most writing has, but as though it had literal application, which I think literature must also have.

This is important because we continue to live (survive) in a period when totalitarian regimes have exerted unprecedented power. The machinery of our times has enabled it; science has equipped it. It is within this framework that Eliot, even more than Pound, has insisted that the poetry matters more than its meanings (*SP*, 93), and has then made assertions including those of racist commentary which critics, if they have noticed, have assimilated into their prose, as if such assertions had only metaphoric, figurative or academic relevance. Yet this is of no value for other writers, or readers, and is dualistic in its application. Moreover, if we claim that *The Waste Land* is to do with the spiritual crisis in the twentieth century, we cannot then, while offering an important reading of the poem, absorb and neutralize the anti-Semitism, in his other work, attributing the racism to some kind of fashionable reflex, or an authorial 'grumpiness' (Stead).

This needs looking at in a little detail. I had better say now that I am a Jew, though not a religious, orthodox one; but neither Hitler nor Stalin was fastidious in this respect: any Jew would do.

Professor Stead manages to analyse Eliot's rightism, as it may be found in his contributions to his own magazine *Criterion*, for instance, and his presentation is unflinching. For others, racism appears to be a cause of self-approbating mirth. Richard Ellman (in Litz, p. 55) speaks with a modest chuckling humour of 'poor Bleistein, drowned now but still haplessly Jewish'. Yes indeed. And the light-hearted tone seems to suggest that he may share his mirth with others.

Peter Ackroyd, Eliot's biographer, does not examine Eliot's rightism by providing as extensive scrupulous detail as Stead manages, and he limits the citation of anti-Semitism in Eliot's work. He refers (pp. 303–4) to (1) *After Strange Gods* (1934) and (2) quotes one line from 'Burbank with a Baedeker'. He cites certain references in Eliot's letters, and leaves the racism there. Yet the most egregious of all occurs in the opening verse paragraph of 'Gerontion', one of Eliot's best poems:

And the Jew squats on the window sill, the owner . . .

The first publication of the poem (1920) used lower case for 'jew'. Eliot it seems may have been sensitive to what others thought of this line even if Ackroyd may not be, for in the *Collected Poems, 1909–1962* (1963) he capitalized 'J' for the word 'Jew'. There is nothing arcane in Eliot's line, as the lower case of the original version makes clear. The intention is pejorative in its resuming the Jew as the traditional enemy, 'the owner'. The Jews are said to own property and rack-rent the gentiles. The slander is too well known to need elaboration, although Mr Ackroyd's oversight needs identifying. Moreover, that implication in combination with the word 'squats', with its multiple overtones of 'immovable', toad-like, shitting and possessing, is aggressive in its reinforcing of the stereotype.

In 'Sweeney among the Nightingales',

> Rachel *née* Rabinovitch
> Tears at the grapes with murderous paws ...
> (*CP*, 59)

'Paws' is brutalizing. Because the family name is Semitic, the complication is that Rachel is no ordinary Christian name but precedes a Jewish patronymic which Rachel has either changed by deed-poll or 'lost' in marriage. Moreover, in citing individual lines one should be aware that this is not the complete tale, for the whole portrait of 'Bleistein' ('poor Bleistein') is repellant, whose 'protrusive eye'

> Stares from the protozoic slime.
> (*CP*, 42)

And in 'A Cooking Egg',

> The red-eyed scavengers are creeping
> From Kentish Town and Golder's Green[1]
> (*CP*, 47)

1. The verbal nature of Eliot's anti-Semitism *may* be revealed in the following. Consulting the Bartholomew's *Atlas of Greater London* (1954) I find there are nine topographical citations for *Golders Green*, the London suburb containing a Jewish community, and only one of them, 'Golder's Green Crematorium', uses the apostrophe. Is it possible Eliot made a mistake? Of course it is, for in his lines

   > The red-eyed scavengers are creeping
   > From Kentish Town and Golder's Green

   he uses an apostrophe, thereby forming, either deliberately, or inadvertently, a pun on the first name for a Jewish woman, Golda or Golder. It is the Saxon genitive that makes the pun, intended or not, into a joke with an edge.

this latter, then as now, is a middle-class Jewish suburb. Additionally, Ackroyd *does* refer to unpublished (unpublishable?) 'Bolovian' stanzas of an obscene character, 'in which words like "pricks", "fucking", "penis", "bunghole" and "Jewboy" were used for light relief' (Ackroyd, p. 165). We are, it seems, in good company. It is the insensitivity of 'for light relief' (whose?) which surprises, for if Mr Ackroyd senses light relief, what are we 'Jewboys' (and 'Jewgirls') to feel? Mr Ackroyd, as if to extenuate Eliot, quotes Leonard Woolf ('himself a Jew', he tells us):

> I think Eliot was slightly anti-semitic in the sort of vague way which is not uncommon . . .
>
> (quoted by Ackroyd, p. 304)

Ackroyd more frankly says:

> distrust of Jews and women was the sign of an uneasy and vulnerable temperament in which aggression and insecurity were compounded. This is an explanation, however, and not a justification.
>
> (Ackroyd, p. 304)

As if to further extenuate Eliot, Ackroyd (p. 303) speaks of 'fashionably anti-semitic remarks' (before the Second War).[1] Which was probably true. But we can easily appreciate that such a climate permitted and encouraged the rise of a destructive racism, for anti-Semitism rarely arrives on its own. I say 'rise' when I should speak of anti-Semitic resurgence, since what culminated in the Reich, Poland and Stalin's Russia was the consummation of centuries of persecution. Charles Maurras, and his *Action Française*, a writer whom Eliot thought highly of and praised in his magazine *Criterion*, also contributed to the health of pre-war anti-Semitism. It is the subtly disarming 'fashionably' that dismays. I need to make clear that although I see Ackroyd as having mislaid both the virulence and persistence, over a considerable period, of Eliot's rightism and anti-Semitism, I in no way imagine Ackroyd to be anti-Semitic. Rather, I feel that his understanding of this, and perhaps other forms of racism, is naive and untutored. It is as though there has

---

1.   But see *Imagination at War*, Adam Piette, especially 'Rationalizations of Prejudice', pp. 190–7.

been for him neither a supervening history during the Second World War and after, nor any preceding history, any soil in which Eliot's anti-Semitism was nurtured. For in that narrow sense it is a culture, dangerous intrinsically for the example it sets. It licenses others and is permissive in the work of a poet who has written extraordinarily fine poetry, as this chapter attempts to show. And this inattention is all the more disturbing in the biographer whose position, in modern times, is that of a version of social historian. This inadequacy underscores the point I made at the start of this section of the chapter, which is that literary criticism needs to be inclusive in such a way as to take a writer's responses and his/her contribution to society, with proper seriousness, not within literary criticism or biography alone, but more widely in a criticism that is responsive to the effects of literature within its society. It may be hard to determine this kind of bell-jar effect – we should not therefore exclude consideration of it. (Stead's account of Pound's anti-Semitism is, in respect of the full spectrum of Nazism, uninformed; see Brambert, *TLS* (5 June 1992), p. 12.)

These remarks on a critic's position in society are offered between accounts of 'Prufrock' and *The Waste Land*, suppositional and actual poem, because I want to indicate that all but one instance of Eliot's anti-Semitism occur outside *The Waste Land*, notwithstanding Stead's speculation that Eliot's racism was a function of his grumpiness, as it were on an off-day:

> And wretches hang that jurymen may dine

although Eliot's rightist attitudes, as Stead himself shows, were sustained over a decade or more. Yet the composition of *The Waste Land* occurred during what many note as having been an extremely disturbed period in Eliot's life, and yet which occasioned minimal anti-Semitic offering either within or without the received version. It would seem that deep *disturbance* did not lend itself to racism, in Eliot's case. The source for his infection is otherwise, its execution being deliberate and exploitative, perhaps, rather than responsive.

A FINAL NOTE, ON ACADEMIC READING

With respect to the copies of *After Strange Gods* (lecture of 1933, published in 1934) in the regular lending part of a British University

Library I report the following. The books appear to have to been in the library since the academic year 1969–70 and have thus over a period of twenty-five years to date drawn marginalia from academic readers to those parts considered of literary critical interest. For this reader it is noteworthy that where Eliot anathematizes Lawrence; and for 'reasons of race and religion' does not want 'any large number of free-thinking Jews' ('undesirable') (p. 20) in a Christian society, the margins are free of 'glossolalia'. One edition bears the question 'what?', the other a blank. Few apparently thought it worth their attention, or worse, some may have concurred. Isn't this a form of ethnic cleansing?

In conclusion I would like to reverse the roles of predator and victim, or rather, I should like to change the *design*, so that Eliot and Pound, each afflicted with the pathogen of racism, become the object of this inquiry. Of all the words that Eliot uses in his racism, the one that is most informative is the one that though it carries overtones of abuse is largely factual:

'The red-eyed *scavengers*' of Kentish Town and Golders Green. I have already suggested the racist character of Eliot's topography, but the interesting word here is 'scavengers'. The SOD has several definitions, but most centre on the keeping clean (of streets) by the removal of dirt. An occupation that is not only useful but attracts the opprobrium of those whose dirt is removed, this being, one imagines, a function of their guilt. It also implies levels of social superiority, where we whose dirt is removed look down on those who do the removing. This relationship has not changed and is today endemic in western and eastern societies alike.

Eliot appears to be making use of the security provided by such an unearned sense of superiority, and in all but his best poetry, and writing, it is as if he needed that reassurance. It was only when he was so wounded that he could no longer claim any feeling of superiority that he turned to the basic materials which engendered his poetry, *The Waste Land*. Though even there, we read the note concerning the 'eastern hordes' (85), notwithstanding that the poetry dictated itself to him and he experienced its full flow.

But to return. In its other sense, 'scavengers' implies *one* who makes money out of others' waste material, scrap-iron and broken machinery – sold to scrap merchants. Eliot's vision of the streets seems, on the basis of his poetry, to have been limited, almost entirely, to those quarters housing brothels and the corruption of *money* that surrounds the manipulation of sexuality. The nature of Eliot's understanding of working life was simplified, of necessity. Had it been otherwise he might, perhaps, have given a little quantum of that humility with which he was not well equipped – he might have refrained from using the term 'scavenger', inseparable as it is from overtones of contempt and superiority. To scavenge, for anyone who has done it, or has observed people doing it closely, is hard work. The men who remove scrap metal from the back lanes using a laden hand-cart, or the women of Singapore who drag a small cart loaded with collapsed cardboard boxes behind their cycle, these scavenge. So in a sense do most of us scavenge, and are none the worse for it, unless we think we are. Those who are forced more plainly into the open with their activities cannot bother to think well or ill of themselves. They must work. Ackroyd's biography reveals Eliot's strong pride over being helped with money, but helped he was, and the comic story of the loss and recovery of the bundle of Tss and Mss from which *The Waste Land* was constructed, and from which money issued, out of Quinn's generous hand, can be found in the Facsimile. Quinn's niece, Mrs T.F. Conroy (Facsimile, XXIX) changes it, apparently, for cash.

Eliot's wife joined the British Union of Fascists in 1934. Vivien was, of course, fully adult, but the life that Ackroyd lays before us is that of an unhappy woman for whom we feel sympathy. She was not as strong as her husband, and in the unequal struggle that ensued (I do not think that marriages invariably become struggles for dominance) Vivien became dependent on her husband and his attitudes. We will probably never be able to assess how much of her husband's personality enabled or inclined her in the decision to join that Union of Fascists, but the work done both by the more benignly disposed biographer Ackroyd, as well as the more motivated C.K. Stead, suggests that Eliot's rightism and its related pathogen of racism were something that communicated itself to his wife, supposing she had not previously become infected. Eliot himself remained more canny. His signed and unsigned notices and commentary in *Criterion* (old and new) gave him the means with which to express his views. He did not need to join the Fascist Party, and probably native caution prevented him from taking a step he himself may not in any case have wished to take. But the orientation, the direction of the magnetism, and its energy, went in that political and psychological direction.

With Pound we have a more fanatic personality, and in certain respects, adjoined to this a more courageous one. Of the racism, there is no reason to reproduce Pound's anti-Semitism. But with respect to its virulence we may question the authenticity of the refined cultural utterances because of the existence of the former. For it is not a matter of someone losing control when provoked. What is different about Pound's political conduct is that he worked overtly for the Fascists. Apparently he also *hated* the Jews, but there appears to have been no attempt to use his anti-Semitism to *ingratiate* himself with the regime. The 'torrential' anti-Semitism was sustained over a number of years. And as I will show later, he remained, according to his declarations in *The Pisan Cantos*, an unreconstituted fascist, though his anti-Semitism became partly concealed.

On the other hand, Black people are not even, it would seem, regarded on the same scale of comparison. Pound uses the word 'nigger' (p. 455, for instance) throughout. And where in Canto 89 we come across the beautiful sustained passage of Lynx and vineyard (see below) in lines 40–1 (p. 485) we find:

> whereas the sight of a good nigger is cheering
> the bad'uns wont look you straight . . .

We are hardly talking of people, if we can discuss them in this unregarding plurality and generalization. And one remembers that this occurs in those Cantos in which Pound is supposed to have shown himself to be at his most sensitive. This is not a speck on the window pane, but an outcrop of something constant that continually emerges. With respect to his courage, one is obliged to acknowledge that Pound did not desert the regime, though his attitudes are more covertly expressed. Which is natural. What is less acceptable is

> Nor can who has passed a month in the death cells
> believe in capital punishment
>
> (83, 530)

for surely Pound is forgetting those millions of Jews, and other minorities, Gypsies, homosexuals, communists, Jehovah's Witnesses, who did perish, under the worst conditions in the world, and for whom no Black man provided a table so that the poet (as he tells us) might write. The final picture is of a human being enclosed in his own prejudices who betrayed no impulse to compassion, though it appears that he may, towards the end of his life, have suffered a period of remorse. Nevertheless, it is in spite of all this that one must admit those wonderful passages in *The Pisan Cantos*. And it is in this apparently dualistic situation that we, as readers, must try to offer a firm and compassionate evaluation of his work, if we are to be of use to other readers. We must do no less for Eliot's work.

THE WASTE LAND: MODERNIST POEM BY DEFAULT

The Suppositional Poem

Raj Nath's article '"The Waste Land" in the Facsimile edition' offers Professor Bergonzi's assertion, in *Encounter* (April 1972, p. 80), that 'most of the material that was cut out, whether by Eliot himself or Pound, deserved to go'. That is shutting the stable after the horse has been pushed out. I am less certain, for reasons all of which are hard to disentangle. So I had better try and schematize my reservations:

1. Some interesting, partly formed fine poetry was cut; mostly, it seems, at Pound's instigation. Stead notes this as he strengthens his case for Pound the man *against* Eliot.
2. The poem as we have it may not have benefited from what amounts to a reduction in the variety of modes.
3. Because poets make verse, they have, perhaps, earned their right to be less certain than critics about the quality and constitution of a poem. There are questions one may want to ask concerning the narrowing effects of the cuts upon
    (a) the remaining verse,
    (b) the structure and constitution of the poem,
    (c) the nice question of by how much Eliot's talent was reduced to fewer modes in this work and subsequent poems. I do not accept the theory that to focus necessitates the cutting of diverse material,
    (d) what effect this altered (in my belief, reduced) poem had on others' work and the subsequent critical opinion of others' work.

My feeling is that Eliot's poetry worked in two strands, at least, and that the continuing vitality of the whole depended on the interaction between two different modes of verse. I describe them as 'Prufrock' and 'Gerontion'. Thus Eliot's is a rich, double, perhaps multiple, talent, one of whose modes Pound successfully helped to suppress. So that not only did the one not fully recover its energy and health, but the other, of 'Gerontion' – a harder, more authoritative and confident mode, developed in 'Ash-Wednesday' (1930) – was given greater scope than was good for it, or for Eliot's verse as a whole. Further, that as it strengthened so his verse atrophied, until that vitality, directness with subtlety, all those capacities most readers of Eliot encounter with gratitude and delight, declined. Thus there ceased to be a fruitful interaction of modes, in as much as Pound helped Eliot to etherize and remove a whole area of Eliot's sensibility. I am aware that these surmises, intimations, feelings will meet with hostility, but before they are blown away, critics of this might ponder the insistence, sometimes the bullying character, of Pound's 'margin' remarks reproduced in the Facsimile.

Under the 'Prufrock' mode I put delicacy, flexibility, playfulness – as exhibited, for instance, in the 'go/Michelangelo', 'ices/crisis' rhymes – freshness, a deftly managed impulsiveness, and the practice of ambiguity of feeling, self-effacement *and* aggression, comparative openness with respect to sexuality, and finally, the practice of uncertainty within the practice of *un*fragmentary, completed syntax.

Within the 'Gerontion' mode, despite its practice of fragmentation of meaning, I put unity, and something hard to characterize but which I call the rhythm of will and determination. For where 'Prufrock' assiduously professes wavering uncertainty, a kind of half-defeated underdoggedness, what one might term side-lined behaviour, although in that condition, sensitivity, 'Gerontion', both the character and the poem, advance a sense of authority, even authoritativeness, of which I say more later. 'Gerontion' (= little old man) struggles towards order, control, surprises us with the controlling epiphany of 'Christ the tiger'. The poem *qua* poem attempts the confident face of the adult achiever. Much more important, because rhythms articulate instinct, 'Gerontion' uses heavy rhythms reinforced by repetition

The word within a word, unable to speak a word . . .

which Henry Reed, in 'Chard Witlow', parodied so wickedly with 'The wind within a wind, unable to speak for wind'. As with

'Prufrock' the rhythmic practice is part of both the character and the poem. Prufrock is subservient to, if fitfully defiant of, the fate that society with his unwilling collusion appears to have devised for him ('To spit out all the butt-ends of my days'). Whereas Gerontion, though less 'passive' than the Tiresias witness-figure in *The Waste Land*, is, nevertheless, an evaluating witness. Tiresias shores up knowledge; Gerontion judges. Though I suggest that Tiresias, the narrator of the typist/clerk episode in 'The Fire Sermon', becomes the hidden narrator of the morally active concluding section, 'What the Thunder said'.

The point I am attempting is that however painful it may be, for the poet a continuing vitality seems to depend, as it has with Geoffrey Hill, on the conflict between irreconcilables or opposites being retained in interplay. It is not good for the poet to reconcile these oppositions. The meaning of unity is not singleness and homogeneity, but heterogeneous elements momentarily unified in interaction. A state of continuous active tension. Reconciliation in singleness and homogeneity brings entropy.

Eliot may also have subscribed to this, albeit at a half-conscious level. Certainly, the Facsimile reveals a number of very different styles, in this sense resembling the Joyce of *Ulysses*, of which Eliot had written admiringly. (But see also 'Ulysses, Order and Myth' (1923), *SP*, 174–8.) Though with Eliot these are not simply different styles but different modes of expression and being. And though it can't be proved, I do not think Eliot was hurling into the smelter all the scrap metal he had in and by him. My 'interpretation' of the Facsimile is that the instinctual Eliot was tentatively attempting to fit together very different components into a richer wholeness than Pound had realized, but which attempt Eliot with Pound's assistance relinquished.

It is often said that Eliot was ill, having perhaps something akin to a breakdown, and had in any case great trouble within his marriage, which finally collapsed. Were all this the case, there is more reason for not wishing to enroll such a nexus of factors with which to help us evaluate the poem, or accept uncritically Pound's sympathetic, if insistent, role. We need not invoke Eliot's difficulties in helping us to evaluate Pound's intervention in the poem's ultimate constitution; for this we have the drafts to place beside the received versions, we have Pound's comments, and our intuition and tact. Each interested reader may evaluate what was omitted against the published version, and compare what was published against what might have been, including for instance such significant rejections as 'He do the police in different voices' Part 1 (p. 5); one, or a conflation of, the Fresca episode(s), those for instance on pp. 39 and 41; and the extensive first part of 'Death by Water' (pp. 55, 57 and 61).

Coleridge was right in invoking freshness as one of the touchstones by which he judged Wordsworth's poetry; and the poetry itself may have helped Coleridge to form this touchstone. Thus despite the repellant nature of a significant amount of the drafted material, in substance and underpinning treatment, the work is fresh, an essential living part of Eliot. It is alert and feels motivated, some of it different in this respect from what the two poets permitted to survive. Perhaps Pound, though maybe Eliot as well, excluded the work on the basis that it was prurient, or not respectable. Though since Eliot was its creator, that judgement is more likely to have been Pound's. I have already touched on this ambiguous question of what is or is not respectable in the image of 'Arms/downed with light brown hair'.

It might be argued that the effects in the poem depend upon the preservation of a restricted social code and register; Patrick Kavanagh's magnificent poem *The Great Hunger* (1942) deals with a comparable subject to that of 'Prufrock', within a similarly restricted social register. Only in Kavanagh's case, it is a constrained rural community. Prufrock is a figure in a different order of respectability, yet in considering the candour of the Irish poem one is reminded of the limitations of Eliot's. That it is not true of Eliot the *poet* is borne out by the material rejected from the received version of *The Waste Land*. The two poets (Eliot and Pound) excluded vigorous if differently limited material that Eliot had already broached on a less ambitious scale in 'Preludes' and 'Rhapsody on a Windy Night'. The scope of *The Waste Land* permitted him to explore the polarities of his poetic social register, 'Prufrock' as against 'Preludes' and the 'Rhapsody': the powerful genteel as opposed to the *demi-monde*. And in certain respects he explored sexuality with more depth and intimacy, in *The Waste Land* though with no greater sympathy. Yet that is not the question. With Pound's likely approval, Eliot substituted symbolic material and figures for the rough life of the streets and the ship. I deplore the contraction.

The division between the 'Prufrock' and 'Gerontion' modes is not absolute, but even so, a significant part of what Pound cut was in the 'Prufrock' mode. If I argue that the quality of the material is not relevant to this part of the question, I shall no doubt be accused of ignoring the true question, namely exclusion on the basis of quality. Yet that is what I dispute, since the kinds of cutting and exclusion entailed a corresponding working up of certain material, apparently without consideration of the actualities and potentialities of the excluded matter. It is likely that for his own reasons Pound wanted to see Eliot develop a poem that featured free verse more significantly – he liked the 'Highbury bore me' passage – 'OK' Pound wrote, three times, against this. Or again, where the seduced woman says 'I made no comment', it had been more poignantly 'I made no outcry'. For it is surely permitted to give the character emotion while denying the author direct access to it. Again, against the moving Hyacinth-girl passage, Pound placed two wavy lines and a question mark as if to question the worth of the passage. If this is the case, then the universal approbation for Pound's critical judgement is itself open to question (pp. 6 and 7). 'I have been hard as youth sixty years,' Pound confessed in Canto 80. Pound may have liked not too much reality and perhaps even less feeling.

I would not argue over exclusion of the lyric 'Dirge' (p. 121) as it was then formed, or the Gautier remodelled rhyming tetrameter quatrains of 'Elegy' (p. 117). Also, it would have been difficult to admit such diverse material when the mode of allusion was being explored. Two diverse difficulties would have made unification even harder to achieve.

Some delicate passages survive in a *new* form, even if they seem to derive from the 'Prufrock' and 'the sea girls' mode, one of them being the Hyacinth-girl passage, which Stead, I think, seriously misreads (see below). Other passages of more brittle response, but light in touch and tone, that derive from the 'Prufrock' sensibility are the 'Fresca' sections and, more obviously, 'The Death of the Duchess' (pp. 105 and 107). The latter is so grounded in Eliot's earlier poem ('Prufrock') that reworking would have proved difficult, although there are passages that deserve to have survived, which did not, as there are those Eliot plundered, and that survive in 'A Game of Chess'.

Pound appears to have disliked what I call Eliot's street-freshness, such as the first part of 'The Burial of the Dead', which Gardner described as a 'bold but unsuccessful experiment' 'in loose blank verse' ('*The Waste Land*, Paris 1922', in Litz, p. 78). Stead thinks Eliot probably got rid of this on his own, yet consider the climate in which Eliot was working. Pound's heavy deletions of the voyage section of 'Death by Water' (pp. 63, 65, 67 and 69) indicate not only his dislike of actuality-based narrative but his preference for symbolic, synecdoche-like passages, as we can see from his 'OK from here on I think' (p. 71), referring to the opening of 'What the Thunder said', beginning 'After the torch light'.

We can infer that Eliot's judgement of what to retain and exclude was working in the strong laser-light of Pound's and, further, that Pound's objection to the Fresca passage may not have been based solely on aesthetic considerations.

'Pope has done this so well', Pound had written of Eliot's Fresca section(s), 'that you cannot do it better; and if you mean this as a burlesque, you had better suppress it, for you cannot parody Pope unless you can write better verse than Pope – and you can't' (Pound, *Selected Poems* (ed. Eliot), 1928, p. 18). (Fresca, a name, appears in 'Gerontion', p. 41.)

Yet it is not entirely Pope; 'Disguise the good old hearty female stench' (*Facsimile* p. 23), though it hasn't Fielding's geniality, has something of his thorough-going bodiliness, which Eliot needed. He had it, that is, and he needed to retain it. Moreover in these Fresca passages is a lightness of touch, curiously metallic in its persiflage, being teasing and intimate. These two tones would have added a quality lost to the poem, and, losing this section, we lose also freshness and composure, which is an unlikely and valuable combination. The poem needs any unlikely alloy of responses in what has been made over into a fine but monolithic creation, so as to give it, not merely a composite character, but what Whitman wrote in the *Preface* to the 'Centennial' edition of *Leaves of Grass*:

> poetry or melody, must leave dim escapes and outlets – must possess a certain fluid, aerial character, akin to space itself, obscure to those of little or no imagination, but indispensable to the highest purposes.
>
> (*The Complete Poems*, p. 788)

Perhaps in the sense that Whitman defines it, Pound was then wanting in imagination. For in the larger sense of it, in the overall constitution and accessibility of the poem, somesuch failure of imagination (in Pound) occurred. Since though it is still possible to read *The Waste Land* as if it were a new poem because it gives that shock of recognition which is the sign of authentic poetry, yet still the reader is forced to supply certain suppositional links in order to thread the blocks of emotional understanding which the poem offers. In the 1959 interview, Eliot, disingenuously perhaps, claimed that after Pound's work on the poem it 'was just as structureless, only in a more futile way, in the longer version' (*T.S. Eliot: The Waste Land*, p. 26). 'Longer version' may be just a form of words, yet the suggestion that Eliot considered that an earlier 'version' in theory existed is tantalizing. But the other suggestion is that Eliot is not being disingenuous in still feeling after some thirty-eight years that the poem is 'structureless'. Even the most practised of Eliot's readers, and of modernist literature as a whole, would not deny that the poem is difficult. That it is accessible at all is miraculous, though not perhaps in the sense that those who endorse Pound's work on the poem would suppose; but rather, that it has survived Pound's surgery. For what Pound did was to suppress the possibility of links in favour of juxtaposition (which was always Pound's more than Eliot's strategy). Pound also suppressed a possible accessibility through interrelating mosaic, for in reading the Facsimile that is what this reader feels Eliot to have been working towards. Instinctively, and with great self-doubt, he was working towards a different, more subtle yet legible form of juxtaposition than it had been in Pound to create, which Pound did not use in the huge disruption of the Cantos, *The Pisan Cantos* notwithstanding. Indeed, it is part of my argument that in his finest passages Pound is traditional and sequential in a way that he inhibited Eliot from being, and partly being, in his poem. In *The Waste Land* we not only have sections of differing social register and responsiveness, but also the possibility of coherence through mosaic where extended narrative parts might have cross-referenced each other, and so have provided not only a more comprehensible whole than presently exists, but one with a richer if less determinedly modernist and monolithic structure. By making the poem more singular in mode, Pound made it unnecessarily more difficult, more wilful *and* less rich. That, too, is an achievement, and it was perhaps in lieu of writing his own poem that he performed on Eliot's. Certainly, the evidence is there for others to disagree with or ignore. I say this acknowledging that Pound's tact as a poet-critic helped Eliot; Pound's failure was in the architecture of the imagination.

Consider the evidence in a little detail. The 'wicked', mischievous, funny and telling picture of the corrupted and innocent that opened 'The Burial of the Dead' is better verse than critics have allowed. There is tacit agreement that we must endorse what has become published history. Though in that case was the Facsimile published simply to vindicate Pound as critic? Are his and Eliot's judgements not to be questioned? At any rate despite the sensitive, just essay by Helen Gardner, 'The Waste Land: Paris 1992', and her judicious mourning for certain losses owing to Pound's surgery, she describes (again) that opening discarded section as a 'bold but unsuccessful experiment' 'in loose blank verse' (Litz, p. 78). Nor does she invite the reader to question her 'unsuccessful'. Yet Eliot provides an insightful picture of police corruption and the inviolability of the Force culminating in Mr Donavan's (wantonly?) putting his foot through the cab's window. We have lost this particular, lively mode of Eliot, of which only the merest trace survives in *The Family Reunion.* (p. 95). It would have enriched *The Waste Land.* Additionally, Gardner's incorrect ascription of 'loose blank verse' suggests that she was not reading with her usual care, for a number of the lines do not approach (or recede) from pentameter but instead are lines of a poet interfusing new rhythms:

Gét me a wóman, I sáid; yóu're too drúnk, she sáid.

If the second section of 'A Game of Chess' is regarded as successful, I cannot see why this section, less of a set-piece, should be denied, with its lethal re-creation of the related underflow of police and civilian criminality. The mode is convincing with its subversive comic effects, in which an element of hilarious enjoyment is released through a careful re-creation of anarchic behaviour, of which Donovan is both symptom and catalyst.

Few would dispute that the opening of the poem, with its lyrical bitter-sweetness, is the right beginning, yet it would have formed a rich structure with the Donovan section, which would in its turn have formed a contrast with the Hyacinth girl, and her sexuality. 'I've kept a decent house,' said the respectable brothel-keeper (p. 5).

Pound's poetry, some twenty years later, it is true, is lyrical, metonymic, mythic in mould. Pound may have shrunk from looking at the *demi-monde* Eliot successfully re-created. Pound it seemed preferred the authoritative over the mode of actuality, preferred the government of mythology to the lived life of the street and the workplace. Perhaps the myth, a form of personification and synecdoche, fashions and *controls* an image of life. Perhaps Eliot's material taken from the real world scared a part of Pound's soul. In Eliot's earlier version, having fucked the typist, the bank clerk

'Delays only to urinate'. So much for the human body, with which Eliot may not have felt at ease. But the response he creates is honest, direct, dismaying. The acts of sex and urination are brought into proximity, reminding us that nature has made this double arrangement, which it is for humans to keep in two separate functions (we do not always do so). Pound's comment in the margin 'probably over the mark' seems to have prompted Eliot to cut. In doing this, Eliot made further significant changes to this episode, the rightness of which I question. My point is that this retreat from a telling if unpleasant episode not gratuitously offered, though perhaps maliciously made, meant that once Eliot had given way here, much more followed. Pound liked and perhaps felt more comfortable with the Tiresias 'figure', for against that stanza of Tiresias having foresuffered all he wrote his code word 'Echt' (= good/ true). Kenner's comment that in remodelling this section Eliot got rid of the Drydenic mode is interesting but not entirely germane, for it is more a question of what replaced the stanzaic verse ('The Urban Apocalypse', in Litz, pp. 30–2). Eliot de-stanza'd the section into continuous verse, which led imperceptibly into a different mode, where the debased lovers become copulars in Tiresias's witnessing. He becomes the important authoritative figure as against the human lives and their actions and autonomy. For they come very close to subserving Tiresias's 'moral' vision. This is not anything but loss, and leads to the authoritative mode that forms a greater part of Eliot's later verse. The removal of the bank-clerk's urination, and other actuality passages, elsewhere, may seem insignificant, but having done this its removal permitted the pressure stacked in the opposite direction. The mythologizing, abstract mode, which is a part of 'Gerontion' with its distasteful anti-Semitism, took the place of an actuality filled with life's 'fractured atoms'. The sustained portion of the voyage with its ending of shipwreck and death, which originally formed the major part of 'Death by Water' (pp. 63, 65, 67, 69), was almost entirely removed. Eliot may have felt some reluctance for he kept and used later in his beautiful 'Marina' 'The gardboard strake' ('planking nearest the boat's keel, hence its most vital spot'). I regret the cutting of this section, first for those reasons to do with variety within the whole that I have argued (above). Second, Eliot usually writes well about the sea (those parts in *Dry Salvages* are almost the most vital of *Four Quartets*). Third, like the sustained street scene that originally opened 'The Burial of the Dead', it is sequential sustained writing undisturbed

by knots of symbolism or disjunction of syntax, of which there are
sufficient in the existing poem. Stylistically, too, the reader would
have benefited from another mode, for it is 'the longest poem in the
English langwidge' (*Selected Letters* (Pound), p. 169). And last, it is
good narrating verse embodying a supervening voice that both
narrates and listens to the evaluating narrative. Ackroyd calls it a
'seaman's yarn' (p. 117), yet I am not sure a seaman would use the
term 'garboard strake' (he might), and I am less sure *he* would so
pointedly reproduce a shipmate's witty rough complaint:

> 'It aint the eating what there is to eat,
> For when you got through digging out the weevils
> From every biscuit, theres no time to eat.'
> (Facsimile, 65)

And feel even more sure that the line following (which Pound
'corrected')

> So this injurious race was sullen, and kicked;

is the narrator's kind of speech; the element of 'yarn' (= adventure
story) is only a strand in this rope of several strands. Moreover,
Eliot invariably writes pentameter very well, and so it is here, every
stroke of the ictus having due regard for its unemphasized fellow-
syllable. Eliot's capacity for laying down evaluation of human conduct, within the narrative itself, makes its welcome appearance:

> A spar split for nothing, bought
> And paid for as good Norwegian pine.
> (p. 65)

The premonitory figures of 'Three women leaning forward, with
white hair' is also well done, adding a touch of the supernatural
and a synecdoche-like shaping to the narrative. And surely shipwreck and death are essentially matter for the post-war waste land.
     Of those portions rejected I have left to last the Fresca section(s)
which, prior to Pound's criticism, Eliot had 'thought an excellent
set of couplets'. This is the hardest to deal with because Pound's
criticism (above) has real teeth: 'for you cannot parody Pope
unless you can write better verse than Pope – and you can't.' The
judgement may be right. Yet Virginia Woolf recorded part of a

conversation with Eliot in March 1921. He had already begun work proper on the poem, and when she had said to him 'We're not as good as Keats', he had apparently replied, 'Yes, we are. . . . We're trying something harder' (quoted by Ackroyd, p. 110). That too seems fair. And the impersonations, if that is what they are, not set in motion by Joyce's *Ulysses*, yet perhaps sanctioned by another's practice – these styles of another character's are filled with a lively narrative that is all Eliot's vitality. The chamber shit, the duplicitous reply that is probably understood to be that when it is received by the correspondent, the mode, not so very removed from 'The Death of the Duchess', give the reader a version of the body that, to repeat this, Eliot needed. Moreover, apart from the abnegation in the poignant 'Blown hair is sweet, brown hair over the mouth blown' ('Ash-Wednesday' III), with its fine rhythmic break which the slant rhyme 'Blown/brown' enacts, it is the nearest Eliot comes with respect to intimacy – with a woman – even if it is observed intimacy. Fresca is a more intimate figure than the 'typist' in 'The Fire Sermon'. Nor is she presented as entirely negative, or with bad humour; 'Unreal emotions, and real appetite' being, perhaps, a little envious more than it is judgemental.

The retention of Fresca and her adventures would have led with greater point to the retributive 'The rattle of the bones, and chuckle spread from ear to ear'. The Marvell reference in the previous line is sharp, but what now precedes it in the received version doesn't properly relate. Here is a case where retention of episodic narrative would have made the section much stronger, had Eliot had the fortitude to have rewritten the whole. The section needs that suspicious Flaubertian touch of a 'meek and lowly weeping Magdalene' thwarted, apparently, by her living in the wrong age. It is more merciful and insightful than the scoffing 'nymphs are departed'. Only Eliot is the loser in this rather easy – sarcasm. Thus it seems in close-up that Eliot is sometimes more sympathetic than when he achieves the synoptic compacted perspective. We should now consider the poem, not as its received version might have been, but as it is.

The Waste Land

In her chapter on *The Waste Land* (*The Art of T.S. Eliot*, 1949) Helen Gardner says, 'Like Mr Eliot, Langland gives us vivid pictures of contemporary society', but unlike Langland, '*The Waste Land* contains no such revelation' of spiritual power and triumph. The poem ends 'as the religious mind conceives it . . . the beginning of wisdom is fear' (pp. 97 and 98).

These comments need pondering. 'Vivid pictures' is what Eliot gives us and perhaps in these lies the poem's capacity to keep its readers. 'Vivid' is akin to Coleridge's 'freshness', a word with which he essentialized his recognition of Wordsworth's poetry. Whatever our intellectual aspirations, the appeal is not unworthy. We are that we are. And despite David Craig's 'The Defeatism of *The Waste Land!*' (*T.S. Eliot: The Waste Land*, pp. 200–13) though it lands smart blows, Gardner's 'the beginning of wisdom is fear' is so much more relevant, both for the poem, and for the vision of life to which it connects Eliot's work. For minatory though it is, it could be argued that the positive, creative, fruitful moments in our lives are like holes punched out of darkness, and that, moreover, a fear of the life *in* which we live our individual existences does not invariably entail our defeat. Such a vision is dark, but is often the reverse of 'Defeatism'. Certainly, in desiring to score his points, some of them reasonable, Craig has ignored, or deflected, what suffuses the poem with involuntary, ineluctable power: the fear. It is *in* the poem, a power Eliot shared with readers some of whom had managed to survive the horror of a European war. In

> The awful daring of a moment's surrender
> Which an age of prudence can never retract
> (CP, 78)

where the authoritativeness is beginning to sound, the confidence is prevented from assuming control because as it grows, so the fear grows with it. Ecstasy[1] and fear, to borrow a hint from the opening of the poem, may inhere in each other. The doubleness of feeling that I identified in 'Prufrock' recurs, as how could it not, in this poem, where, as Cleanth Brooks has observed, one may have the surface meaning pointing in one direction and the underflow moving in a contrary one. And to add to Brooks' perception, we sometimes obtain some third figure resulting from the contrast between the counter-directions of the first two:

1.   Consider Wilfred Owen's 'an ecstasy of fumbling' in his 'gas attack' poem 'Dulce et Decorum Est'.

The basic method used in *The Waste Land* may be described as the application of the principle of complexity. The poet works in terms of surface parallelisms which in reality make ironical contrasts, and in terms of surface contrasts which in reality constitute parallelisms. (The second group sets up effects which may be described as the obverse of irony.) The two aspects taken together give the effect of chaotic experience ordered into a new whole, though the realistic surface of experience is faithfully retained. The complexity of the experience is not violated by the apparent forcing upon it of a predetermined scheme.

(T.S. Eliot: The Waste Land, pp. 156–7)

Fine. Though Brooks' attempt to hammer the poem into a Christian figure, which the poem itself stops short of, is finally irritating and distorting. The strand is there, at least in 'What the Thunder said', but, and I hope Christians will forgive this, something finer lives in the poem. This exists in the courage to be both open to religious possibilities and necessities and the need for spiritual regeneration, but in combination with responses that are secular, humanly unpleasant and powerful; it is these together, over which Eliot cannot have the control he may wish to exert, that give the poem its strength and power. For it needs strength to give these things the life wherewith to exist, like some kind of heresy, but it is surely the only thing worth doing. As Milton understood. And it may be that Eliot saw this, was afraid, and sought protection within Christianity, which, in its doctrine of love, though less often in its practice, seeks to protect those who come in under its shelter. And if the poem in some ways seeks to convert, it is not by distorting human responses. Perhaps it is this openness that prompted Eliot to say in 'The Use of Poetry':

It is the half-educated and ill-educated, rather than the uneducated, who stand in (the poet's) way: I myself should like an audience which could neither read nor write.

(Selected Prose, p. 94)

To read a poem without cultural prejudices is a very great achievement, but to read as if the principal attribute of a poem were its music, at the expense of its meaning, is finally to attenuate both. *The Waste Land* is difficult, not because it hasn't meaning, but because its meanings exist in their inter-qualification of each other. I shall try what others have tried, to understand the meanings in the poem; but following the hint that Eliot drops with respect to an uneducated audience, I shall try to make use of the rhythms – that which is basic to all of us, for rhythms are expressed instincts – to help me understand and explain the meanings.

We respond to the presence in the poem of 'vivid life', yet it seems to me that in respect of that characterization Helen Gardner does the poem less good service when she says, 'there are no characters in the strict sense, no persons' – though it is thronged with people and we hear many and varied voices (*The Art of T.S. Eliot*, p. 88). For that little equivocation 'strict sense' denies what seems to this reader evident: that from Eliot's interest in Jacobean and Elizabethan drama, whatever symbolic value the individual characters and their web of relations expressed, it is in the freshness of their lives that they live. As they do in this poem. 'I am the resurrection and the life' has symbolic value (I say this as a Jew and an outsider) because of the sense it conveys, among many things, of actual, lived life, which is the only *experience* we have, though we may infer something other. I imagine that Gardner when she says 'characters' means those we encounter in drama and fiction, creations endowed with a life, some of whom develop over the span of the work. But this may be to confuse realism with essentialized presence. And when she joins 'persons' to 'characters' we may feel that the insistence cloaks confusion. Joyce's Bloom is no less a person because he in some senses refers us to the character Ulysses.

This question needs a little more examination. Poetry compacts and evaluates life and a sensuous experience of it, the 'felt life' as Leavis calls it. The strength of fiction is to double a part of this by making its characters perform synecdoche; they are themselves, yet at the same time a representation of the whole by being a *vivid* essentialized part of it.

However illusory, fragmentary, episodic or momentary the persons in Eliot's poem are, they exist, their poignancy being all the more so because they are momentary, within the parentheses of a moment, contracted yet essentialized. To overload them with intellectual abstraction, and to deny them the life they have, or so this reader feels, is to distance further a difficult poem from readers, while – as it seems to me – to enact a heresy, if not a blasphemy, by reducing these lives to symbols. The extreme version of this occurs in Brooks' manipulation of Madame Sosostris, who does not realize 'any more than do the other inhabitants of the modern waste land that the way into life may be by death itself' (*T.S. Eliot: Waste Land*, p. 133). The 'out' in that, if I may criticize the words of a dead man, is in the 'may be'. And that it needs such qualifications arouses my suspicion of the nature of the claim and the guardedness with which it is asserted.

The Waste Land oscillates, sometimes quivers, between actuality and representation in the form of myth, religion, anthropological figuration. Herein the strength of Brooks' doubleness, where the vivid presence may have an underflow that sometimes confirms, sometimes contradicts and sometimes ambiguously qualifies the vivid presence of the life. An example of this last is the Hyacinth-girl where if we read hyacinth as fertility, yet the nature of love, in its very pure intensity, cannot express itself (see below).

No one has the same interpretation of a poem the method of which allows for such width of speculation, and this even applies to the scansion of, for instance, the opening:

> April is the cruellest month, breeding
> Lilacs out of the dead land, mixing
> Memory and desire, stirring
> Dull roots with spring rain.
> Winter kept us warm, covering
> Earth in forgetful snow, feeding
> A little life with dried tubers.
>
> (*CP*, 63)

My sense is that lines 1 and 2 are five-beat; lines 3, 4 and 5 four-beat; line 6 five-beat (though one might contract it to four-beat, yet why do so?); and line 7, which concludes this opening phase, four-beat.

To some, such analysis may seem pedantic, but by reading the rhetorical structure with care, of which metre is its essential partner, important features emerge. First, this metrical verse works closely with an *almost* symmetrical but subtly varied rhetorical structure. The participles that draw enjambments of run-over syntax across line-endings – lines 1, 2, 3, 5 and 6 are all simple present-participles forming participial clauses that express nature's nurture.

Lines 1 and 2 do not match metrically with 3; and where lines 3 and 5 have matching metrical and rhetorical structure, the OVER-ALL metrical *sequence* as a pattern is reversed. Thus in respect of emphases or stresses we may read 5, 5, 4 + statement (4 beats); then 4, 5 + statement (4 beats), where lines 5 and 6 have symmetrical rhetoric but are asymmetrical to each other metrically.

'So!' readers may say. I would reply that this is yet another form of Eliot's doubleness, where a sense of congruity is set up between rhetoric and metre, but that sense is given simple variation through a partly asymmetrical pattern. The result of all this is an essential part of the meaning of the poem's opening: unease. Moreover, it provides a good working example, but in reverse, of Eliot's proposition that the reader is given a sop so that the poetry can get to work on him/her. Here it seems that it is the rhetorical structure that engages the reader so that evocation and meaning may work on the mind. Here evocation is the dominant element of the meaning, for it tells us that though nature and spring continue their work, the human being is not happy in his arousal.

A little inspection of how the rhetorical and metrical patterns work together will suggest that the word which receives most emphasis is 'cruellest'. If we consider rhetoric and metre as aspects of each other we may more readily see that 'cruellest' receives an emphasis from both, plumb on its root part 'cruel' which, with its double syllable made into three by the superlative 'est', has the additional effect of giving *duration* to a stressed syllable (see also Gardner, *The Art*, p. 29). The most emphasized word turns the key to the meaning of the whole passage which, by the way, turns out to be one of the most popular lines of the poem. It is of course a turn of the key but not a complete unlocking. For this prolonging of an important word 'cruellest' is linked, rhythmically, and thus in associated meaning, with two other tri-syllabic words, the second of which may be read as a dipthong; 'memory' and 'desire'. And the three words, to atomize them further, each have in their three syllables a weak syllable, which in ordinary speech tends to get elided but which because of the demands of the metre require full articulation; thus not 'desyr' but 'des-i-er'. Further, by bringing out the strong vowels in these words through the metres, the links between 'cruellest', 'memory' and 'desire' are confirmed, thus reminding us that to be stirred by desire from lethargy, custom, habitude, is painful. The resemblance here between Lawrence, whom Eliot anathematized in *After Strange Gods*, and Eliot himself, is ironic. Compare this passage with Mellors in *Lady Chatterley's Lover*:

> And he stood up, and stood away, moving to the other coop. For suddenly he was aware of the old flame shooting and leaping up in his loins, that he had hoped was quiescent for ever. He fought against it, turning his back to her. But it leapt, and leapt downwards, circling in his knees. . . .
>
> 'In a way!' he replied, looking up at the sky. 'I thought I'd done with it all. Now I've begun again.'
> 'Begun what?'
> 'Life.'

(pp. 119–22)

But this is an old grudge, and the resemblance need only be noted rather than a score evened.

The desire is positive within the total designs of the poem and in its pain leads immediately to a block of contrasted meaning.

Set in Vienna, this picture is of the enervated upper class, without real activity and lacking convictions. Though the conviction with which Austria embraced the entrance of Hitler in 1938 should give us pause before we decide that convictions are invariably a good possession. But nor, to argue this differently, is it clear that such enervation led inevitably to an enthusiasm for Nazism – notwithstanding Eliot's strong liking for Maurras and his *Action Française*.

Of the line 'I read, much of the night, and go south in the winter' Helen Gardner remarks, 'before she gives herself away by her summary of the routine of her life now'. The remark's lack of charity surprises, and prompts one to suspect that this is an instance of where the academic mind overcomes the ordinarily human. For which one of us would care to be pilloried, or feel it justified to be so, because of midnight reading? 'Go south'; well, yes, she evades winter. I think rather than condemnation ('gives herself away') we might feel pity for the stultified condition: the childish mixture of delight and fear, which appears to lead to no adult sequel or development in her life. Yet that is cause for commiseration rather than condemnation, and as such ought further to qualify Craig's ascription of 'defeatism'. (Eliot's is, incidentally, criticism of a moneyed class.) Eliot's achievement here is in his re-creation of the voice of childhood:

My cóusin's, he tóok me óut on a sléd,
And I was frightened. He sáid, Marie,
Marie, hóld on tight. And dówn we went.
(*CP*, 63)

This is mimesis, where the childish double renegotiation of the syntax, 'my cousin's, he took me', is an excitement of anticipation abridged by the swift plunge in the sleigh, 'And down we went'. Which carries fear. It is harmless, after all, and if that were the sum of human folly our world would not be what it is, or has been. But beyond that remembered moment – in which inheres neither in the experience or its memory any sin – nothing develops. There exists neither ecstasy nor even tentative relationship. Yet before we (or we with Eliot) apply adjectives such as shallow or limited, we may remember this is the experience of a child ('we were children'). The judgement is made by an adult, of another who has not developed.

Significantly (transitions in the poem are often of much importance) this passage leads into one of fear, perhaps the dominant response of the poem. Of course, the childish fear during the sleigh ride is in the greatest possible contrast to the biblical fear which in this passage culminates in

I will show you fear in a handful of dust.
(*CP*, 64)

The burial of the dead. Here again is doubleness, for this is not merely the burial service of the dead with its accepting (?) 'I commende . . . thy body to the grounde . . . asshes to asshes, dust to dust', but an evocation of failure, of those whose lives have never properly come to life. It is almost a communication. 'A heap of broken images' is a summation of no life. One remembers E.M. Forster's epigram 'Only connect', and the imploration in that. Certainly the fiction of the period seems more merciful than the poetry. Eliot points to Ezekiel and Ecclesiastes (in his notes) and Gardner (p. 91n) adds Isaiah ii, 10, 'Hide thee in the dust, for fear of the Lord'. This instigates fear through guilt and spiritual inadequacy – poor humans have enough to contend with without a fear of their inadequacy in the sight of God. Yet this is justifiably *identified* because Eliot is blending his sense of spiritual failure with an image of life reduced to nothing – a fear of being answerable to God for having done so little with the life He originated. It does not seem to me impertinent to suggest that Eliot presses this sense of inadequacy into the service of a poem that also makes use of a failure to engage a meaningful sexuality.

In contradistinction to this failure there follows the Hyacinth-girl episode. 'It is a moment of failure that is recalled but is also a moment of mystical revelation' (p. 97), Stead informs the reader. We all read love differently, and for Stead's confident 'failure' I read this as Eliot's delicate filiation of a love so intense and so imbued with idealistic goodness as to render it incapable of expression. It is a key passage, one that creates directly a positive human relationship incarnating love. If, as Gardner suggests, the close of the poem is darker than the beginning, there is the more reason for seeing the positive where it may exist, especially in love, and as it exists in contrast to the 'handful of dust'. Stead could only make this assertion of failure by leaving unexamined the actual passage in its rhythmic life. It is a love the very intensity of which precludes a total consummation of the physical and spiritual in reciprocal realization.

Though Eliot's essay 'Dante' (1929) follows *The Waste Land* by eight years, we know from the quotation from the *Purgatorio* (Eliot's line 427), for instance, that he had read the poet. We find this in his essay:

> *Beatrice mi guardò con gli occhi pieni*
> *di faville d'amor così divini,*
> *che, vinta, mia virtù diede le reni,*
> *e quasi mi perdei con gli occhi chini.*

Beatrice looked on me with eyes so divine filled with sparks of love, that my vanquished power turned away, and I became as lost, with downcast eyes.

The whole difficulty is in admitting that this is something that we are meant to feel, not merely decorative verbiage.

(*Selected Essays*, p. 266)

Eliot's admonition in 'meant to feel', reapplied, might give us pause. Presumably the prose translation is Eliot's; the emotion that transfigures this – Dante, and the Eliot Hyacinth-girl and her lover (husband) are noticeably similar:

'You gáve me hýacinths first a yéar agó;
'They cálled me the hýacinth girl.'

> – Yet whén we cáme back, láte, from the hýacinth gárden,
> Your árms fúll, and your haịr wét, I cóuld not
> Spéak, and my éyes fáiled, Í was néither
> Líving nor déad, and I knéw nóthing,
> Lóoking ínto the héart of líght, the sílence.
> 'The sea waste and empty'
>
> (CP, 64)

I have translated the last line, from which Stead concludes that this signals inadequate love; but the case is as subtle as Dante's, for it is the spiritual intensity of the love which renders its total completion so hard. And a reading of the rising, positive rhythms in

> Your árms fúll, and your haịr wét, I cóuld not
> Spéak, and my éyes fáiled, Í was néither
> Líving nor déad . . .
> Lóoking ínto the héart of líght . . .
>
> (CP, 64)

should not yield a negative response, leading to a negative reading of the whole passage. Only an intellectual imposition of that last line upon the whole could wrench this whole into 'failure'. In any case the last line, 'waste and empty', may register the consequence of not fully realizing love; for the love is there, in the poem, and correlatively in the marriage, at this point. The enjambment of 'I could not/Speak' enacts the difficulty arising out of *positive* feeling, where the verbal level denies communication. Yet the enjambment places great emphasis on 'Speak', where the line-break interposes itself in mid-syntax. The feeling produced works against the negative interpretation as much as against 'could not speak'. Speechlessness does not necessarily mean failure of love. It might be expressed thus: 'positive emotional response is entailed in the negative inability to speak to that other'. We have surely, many of us, experienced that. Here is no mystery, on that level, and the rhythms and enjambment with the lineation beautifully enact it.

The Hyacinth-girl episode gives a sense of individual, as well as representative and symbolic, experience, all of which we may share because the character is so experientially realized.

I am describing that doubleness which ensures the distinctiveness of *The Waste Land*, which in many of its sections imparts the experiential and its symbolic representativeness, yet in such a way

that we often feel a simultaneity of effect. Like a borrowed frag-
ment of the whole, somesuch moment succeeds in touching a larger
aggregated, collective power. Yet at the same time the experience in
its tenacity is kept fresh, as it is with the hermit-thrush and the cock
crowing before the damp gust of rain in 'What the Thunder said'.
Where *some* of Eliot's later poetry is *about* experience, circumspectly
or authoritatively generalizing its nature, this poem seems to arise,
directly, out of a number of experiences, whether simulated or not.
So that although the Hyacinth-girl has symbolic value, we ought
not to shroud a living episode in symbolism, making it safe in its
intellectual value for ourselves and others; for this being alive is the
very condition we are in danger of overloading with intellection.
We should value the doubleness of the achievement. In this, only
Lawrence in this period, with his *Birds, Beasts and Flowers* (1923),
compares with Eliot and *The Waste Land* (1922) and gives us, perhaps, an even more precious achievement.

A contemporary poet recently explained to an audience he
took to be incapable of appreciating imaginative leaping in poetry
that the modern differed from the earlier poetry precisely in this
activity. In Eliot's poem however, it is true that in some mysterious way juxtaposition is often the means of releasing the poem's
energy. So here, between the Hyacinth-girl and Madame Sosostris,
the fortune-teller, and the 'Unreal city' where 'A crowd flowed
over London Bridge', commerce and church close-packed, we meet
Stetson. Yet the kind of geometry we are asked to undertake in linking up bursts of meaning and experience feels right – I hope this is
not said out of specious familiarity with the words. For if the under-
flowing motif of the Hyacinth-girl, as it was with the lilacs 'breeding
. . . out of the dead land', is fertility, here with Stetson is a fertility
in the feared sprouting of 'That corpse you planted last year'. If it
is a growth it is, for Stetson, as for the next man, 'undesirable'. And
here the reliance on the fake apparatus with which Madame Sosostris
manipulates her clients solicits the magic in the Tarot pack to some
purpose. For here, anthropologically, in the Stetson episode, the
meaning rather than the experience is uppermost, conveyed with
both wit and fear. Though the realistic figure of Stetson *and* the
casually impudent question is perfectly realized.

Yet here, or rather, just before it, it seems to me that critics and
readers have their hardest job. 'Fear death by water' (line 55) is
what the fortune-teller instructs her client. But that, despite her
bogus activity, is what we are to fear. Yet death by water, we are

told, is rebirth into a fertile life (Brooks). This may be the meaning here, but it is not experience we can verify. If we are to understand new life through destruction by salt water, which is *not* fertile, though the ritual entailed throwing the drowned (Phoenician) sailor into the sea, each year, to ensure fertility, we are forced to function as readers on a single level of response. We must deny or suspend understanding based on experience, so as to permit meaning transmitted only through anthropological and symbolic figuration. It is this disjunction of levels with which readers may still experience difficulties. Though in overcoming them they may be rewarded.

An easier mixture of modes occurs in the Stetson passage which, set beside the Hyacinth-girl and those double levels of experience and symbolism, works in inverted fashion. Thus where with the Hyacinth-girl episode the experiential worked above and over the anthropological, and from that construction the meaning was obtained, in the Stetson passage the literal experience communicates some nameless but 'understood' crime, the symbolic meaning of which dominates the literalization of the episode. Landmarked by London Bridge and the church of Saint Mary Woolnoth, these are all but 'buried' in one's sense of symbolic and anthropological meanings. Yet, as with Madame Sosostris, it is by 'vivid pictures' that the communication is effected – in the Stetson passage buoyed up by five- and six-beat lines that work powerfully:

> There I sáw óne I knéw, and stópped him, crýing: 'Stétson!
> 'Yóu who were wíth mé in the shíps at Mýlae!
> 'That córpse you plánted lást yéar in your gárden,
> 'Hás it begún to spróut? Will it blóom this yéar?

> (CP, 65)

With Eliot, as it is with some of the best of Pound, it is the metre that keeps the verse going. Though to take a phrase from 'Gerontion', it is the 'impudent' inquiry that sauces this passage. Gardner (*The Art*, 92) has glossed very well the dog that unearths and presents to us our crime that for all the world we wish had remained under the earth. I would extend her insight by adding that the dog that innocently exposes and presents us with our crime also lays our hypocrisy before us; we keep buried what we are frightened of having revealed, together with our fear of detection itself. And in saying this of another I am revealed in my hypocrisy because, like my neighbour, I, too, am afraid of these things. By *nature* I am congruent

with him, 'mon frère'. Confederates in guilt, and hypocrisy. Only
the dog is no hypocrite. The final question, 'Will it [the corpse] bloom
this year?' reflects back, ironically, upon this first section's title:
'The Burial of the Dead'. For with that we might be thought to be
referring to the honouring of the dead with burial and thus paying
our respects, whereas the meaning here imparts the opposite. Such
burial will bloom our crime. Yet of course, to complete the ironies
we are tacitly complicit with others in our misdeeds.

Irony often needs the reader's reflection for its full operation.
In this instance the final irony inheres in the compression of the
historical reference of Mylae; history itself repeats its acts and
consequences. But then, all the more reason to be grateful for the
'literal' component of the chat with Stetson.

In section II, 'A Game of Chess', the analysis of the ambiguity
expressed in the fluid syntax, has been done by Empson in *Seven
Types of Ambiguity* (1930) (pp. 77–8): I can add nothing to it. But
it is worth stressing that this ambiguity is supported by two con-
stants that, by definition, work athwart the deliquescent syntax. The
first Shakespearean Cleopatra reference is that device by which epic
meaning is compassed into a small space.

So that allusion here functions as a norm whereby we are asked
to test, assess, evaluate our conduct in relation to a (famous) instance of human conduct. The norm (please forgive this contradiction) may not 'stay still' but is there as an instance against which
we form a judgement. Its existence is constant, even though interpretation may vary.

The other norm in this passage is metre. It is important because
it serves to define the two other parts which are in free verse –
a mode which Eliot uses much less frequently than critics (and
readers) suppose.

The effect of this iambic pentameter is various. First it sets in the
reader's mind not only the substance of the comparison and norm
(Cleopatra), but the Shakespearean mode –

> The barge she sat in, like a burnished throne,
> Burned on the water; the poop was beaten gold . . .
>
> (II, ii, 190–1)

One remembers what Pound said about the 'Fresca' drafts in
relation to Pope – 'you cannot do it better'. Which is applicable
here, for Shakespeare's rich metaphor in its paradox 'Burned on the

water' is not matched by Eliot's adaptation. But the setting of his Cleopatra figure in pentameter, which is, of course, the verse norm of Elizabethan and Jacobean drama, will remind us that, unlike Wordsworth's democratized figures, those in Shakespeare's pentameter are mostly kings, queens, princes and lords. The working people often speak in prose to which in *A Midsummer Night's Dream* the kings and nobles condescend (V, i). Or, to which they temporarily conform.

So here, in 'A Game of Chess', are three modes: pentameter, then pentameter in the process of disintegration, then that which finally does eventuate – free verse. Of these the first two are reserved for the upper-middle-class 'Cleopatra', 'a closed car at four'. The third mode, of free verse, is used by the working class and their set of victimizations and treacheries.

The metre, then, serves at least two functions. It is literally as well as allusively a mode of class stabilization. So that while the syntax is ambiguous and deliquescent, the metre, the class, the social stratum and its conduct all remain intact (just). And though much is awry within this stratum (here), as the neurasthenia of this 'Cleopatra' and her irresponsive partner shows, yet the class-group holds even in its disintegration – into more *culture*, 'Shakespeare' and Jazz. Finally, the metre is still a norm in which moral judgements are implicitly formed. Even in the last section, 'What the Thunder said', where everything is starting to change, as it must if regeneration is to take place, the metrical norm of pentameter is an audible and legible ghost from which other prosodic forms issue.

Criticism has been preoccupied with whether or not the image of Cleopatra's love is one of love for love's sake, or is imperfect, inadequate, as human love is. If we say that Cleopatra's love was as nearly as possible perfect, then her image, and other images of past couples, such as Elizabeth and Leicester, or the nymphs in Spenser's 'Prolathamion', serve, by contrast, to point up the supposed inadequacy or nastiness of contemporary sexuality. But if we see Cleopatra and the other older examples of human couples, or of women (sic) as imperfect, then what becomes legible is the continuity of human imperfection. The arguments accumulate 'politically' either side of the divide. Those who read the former – that Eliot intends a contrast between then and now with the invariable denial of modern virtue because of the earlier model's virtue – such readers usually end up accusing Eliot, not merely of being facile,

but of rightist responses. The problem with this is that while Eliot
was, or became, rightist, it does not follow that he is invariably
operating such a simple contrast in his poetry. We cannot extrapolate from his politics to his poetry, or erect a two-way valve
of interpretation. On the other side are the more conservative, or
Christian, readers, who maintain that Eliot cites instances from the
past in order to emphasize the continuity of human imperfection,
though the problem here is that Eliot's contemporary nastinesses
are usually more visible than his past instances. To cite names,
Craig claims that Eliot is in the former position of being facile,
Matthiessen, Brooks and Gardner claim complexity for him. So these
latter all claim that Eliot's past-present instances are congruent not
contrasting parallels. Gardner argues, for instance, that the 'love' of
Elizabeth and Leicester was a 'barren flirtation' between the 'Virgin
Queen' and an 'astute and ambitious courtier' (*The Art*, pp. 94–5).
The sumptuousness of the royal barge would therefore only serve
to depreciate rather than enhance the conduct of the royal couple
and their supposed love. The problem is that, while this view is in
Eliot's note, I am not sure that it is in the poem.

I believe that in this dispute it is, in theory, possible to take the
instances case by case. And further, that if we see the poem composed, in part, of 'figures' then, to return to the beginning of this
section, the Cleopatra-woman may be viewed as another aspect of
the Hyacinth-girl.

'So all the women [in the poem] are one woman,' Eliot noted. Yet
his note collapses the possibilities that exist within the poem. Eliot
did more in *The Waste Land* than he realized.

For if we follow Eliot and call the woman in the second half of
'A Game of Chess' 'one woman', we will miss the terrible 'treachery' of Lou who, we are to believe, has or will have betrayed her
friend Lil. In a sense they are one because all human beings act in
a composite way, but this is too easily to collapse the distinction between predator and victim, of which latter the figure of Philomel is,
like Lil, an instance. The pathos of Philomel in the poem resembles
that of the Cumaean Sibyl imprisoned in the bottle (epigram to
poem). Philomel was 'forced', raped. As the Sibyl hangs in a jar, so
Philomel is, in a sense, suspended in a picture on the wall, an item
of pastoral decorating the modern bedroom, where love (not rape)
recurs. She hangs there as if no rape had been suffered. The ironies
are multiple for the decoration of the modern bedroom with a scene,
or image, of rape, or the raped, says little for contemporary sensitivity

to 'forced'. Or perhaps it says more than we would like, as if our sexual appetites are sauced by these scenes. Yet was it not ever thus? The intended moral ambiguity of this bedroom is not made clearer by the *social* contrast with the scene in the pub, though the latter involves nastiness, whereas the former 'Cleopatra' scene offers anxiety and emotional impotency. Even so there is continuity not between the upper-middle-class figure and Lil, but between the latter and Philomel. That is, Lil will continue to be a victim. She bears many children to Albert, whose lust rather than love is their progenitor. So that this sexuality is barely a step from rape.

That is not the fate of the modern 'Cleopatra', enriched with complicated cosmetics, the subtlety of which is duplicated in the room's decor

> Hūge séa-wōod féd with cópper
> Burned gréen and órange, frámed by the cóloured stóne . . .
>
> (*CP*, 66)

which is followed three lines later by the rape of Philomel. Readers may say that such a sequence is decisive and can only admit the meaning of immorality. Yet the case is subtler, for all of this is decor, Philomel included. It may be that this is Baudelaire's vision of *ennui*, the modern urban condition, but it seems likelier that the perplexity of this woman's responses differ in one important respect from Marie's, the woman who goes south in the winter. Both are upper-middle-class, but this woman's perplexity is unlike the satisfied emptiness of the adult Marie. This Cleopatra woman's responses are, or verge on, hysteria. We may read her condition as a *version* of the Hyacinth-girl's, for both suffer incomplete love. In this case we sympathize with her angst as much as with her partner's incapacity to alleviate it with love and sympathy, the lack of which may be the cause of the hysteria. People only wish to 'act', 'do', 'speak' when there is a fundamental inactivity between them. I do not wish to administer psychiatric care, but to repeat the suggestion that the Hyacinth-girl episode finds a corresponding, though inflamed, difficulty in this one. And that in both episodes is a level of actuality that deepens the overall symbolic meaning.

If we read the poem not only as myth and anthropology, ancient and modern, but also as drama of a kind, then Lil, her abortion, her drugs that 'brought it off' at a cost, her premature ageing, as Helen Gardner so movingly footnotes (*The Art*, p. 94n), makes her correspond by sympathetic contrast with the modern 'Cleopatra'. But she resembles Philomel and the Cumaean Sibyl not only by being a victim, but in one other respect. The Sibyl is contained in a jar, Philomel in a picture, and Lil within Lou's talk with May:

When Lil's husband got demobbed, I said –

(*CP*, 68)

so Lil never speaks for herself – she is framed by another, and soon she will be 'framed', that is, betrayed, by the one who tells her story. These are real figures indeed.

The 'hot gammon' that Lou is invited to share with Lil and her husband, the demobbed Albert, is the prelude to betrayal, or else the instance of it, where food and sex (appetite), here as elsewhere in literature, merge. It is made more ominous by the 'HURRY UP PLEASE ITS TIME', which is not only the barman's call for the supping up of drinks prior to closing but also suggests Lou's closing in on Albert for the 'kill'. We may remember that a 'game of chess' refers to Middleton's *Women beware Women*, where the daughter-in-law, her son's wife, is seduced, almost raped, by the Duke, while the mother-in-law is 'diverted' by 'a game of chess'. The poem has accelerated the Hyacinth-girl's love into sexual betrayal. Nor should we lose sight of the most obvious minatory layer which is the fear that our civilization decays.

The degrading of love, of which Eliot propounds an over-large share in his poem, continues in 'The Fire Sermon'. If it is the theme of Eliot's life then, it is the literal and symbolic meaning of the poem. A contrast is drawn between the modern 'nymphs' with their companions in sex, 'the loitering heirs of City directors', and the nymphs of Spenser's 'Prothalamion'. F.O. Matthiessen (*TSE*, pp. 121–2) presents the plausible argument that the repetition of 'The nymphs are departed' implies 'that this glimpse of present life along the river, depressingly sordid as it is, being human cannot be wholly different from human life in the past. And, concurrently, the idealized Elizabethan young men and women who appear as attendants in Spenser's marriage songs begin to be seen with new eyes. They cannot be wholly unlike the present idle young men about town and their nymphs.' This looks persuasive, but one might make two observations. First, that repetition may have the effect opposite to that which Matthiessen claims. That 'The nymphs are departed' may indeed mean that at one time there was chastity, etc.

Second, that Matthiessen is falling into the trap of imagining, with an element of prurience, that all sexual conduct is as *he* supposes; whereas that is a somewhat hot-blooded view of human nature. Third, that whether Eliot meant what Matthiessen supposes him to have meant, Spenser's image proves too strong for Eliot (and Matthiessen). Spenser's nymphs are what the poet claims them to be:

> 'And let fair Venus, that is queen of love,
> With her heart-quelling son upon you smile,
> Whose smile, they say, hath virtue to remove
> All love's dislike, and friendship's faulty guile
> For ever to assoil. . . .
> And let your bed with pleasures chaste abound,
> That fruitful issue may to you afford . . .'
> ('Prothalamion', lines 96–104)

Spenser's nymphs anticipate their marriage joys, whereas the modern nymphs have (had) theirs. Through Venus's presiding over them, they possess their chastity prior to their nuptials. 'Pleasures chaste' is emphatic about this. 'Pleasures' means sexuality, and these are chaste not only because not extreme, but because chastity is retained until marriage has made their bed. 'Fruitful issue' implies that sex may be a pleasure but it also reminds us that the purpose of sex is (also) procreation.

One may dissent from this earlier culture, but I do not think that Eliot intended to subvert it, or was capable of doing so had he wanted to.

So if we are *not* to read Spenser's and Eliot's 'nymphs' as representatives of a continuous depressingly loveless sexuality, we must probably read the conduct of the past and present nymphs as contrasting. Moreover, it would seem that were we only to read the instances of past and present as representing continuity of human conduct then we would lose the point of the poem, which is to do with a crisis in *our* morality and culture. If there is a depressing continuity to human conduct, why should there be crisis now? Yet it seems to be Eliot's recurring point in this poem that such a crisis does exist, and one may therefore assume that somewhere in this structure of pasts and presents some of these pairs of lovers are in opposition. These two sets of nymphs may offer one contrast, and the Elizabeth and Leicester axis one half of another:

Sweet Thames, run softly, till I end my song.
The river bears no empty bottles, sandwich papers, . . .
Or other testimony of summer nights. The nymphs are departed.
And their friends, the loitering heirs of City directors;
Departed, have left no addresses.
By the wáters of Léman I sát down and wépt . . .

(*CP*, 70)

Eliot makes three culture references. First, Elizabethan rural London, which is of course the setting for Spenser's 'Prothalamion', second is the re-creation of twentieth-century urban London, and the third, the exile of (sic) the Jews captive in Babylon. With the exception of the first two lines and their mysterious image of the 'river's tent' in its spreading rhythm,

The river's tent is broken; the last fingers of leaf . . .

(*CP*, 70)

this is not strong verse. Its easy gurgling superiority depends for its fix on the ironically used word 'testimony' which works to reassure the reader that the poet is making sober judgements, else why would he use such a word? At the same time it works to depreciate further promiscuous sex and its paraphernalia of feast and contraceptive. 'Nymphs' is sneering and plainly nasty, and only the tone of upper-class railery, not however as accomplished as the persiflage in Pound's 'Mauberley(s)', saves it from total crudity. The passage (see above) seems to rely upon its sufficient contrast with Spenser, not the least of it being that Spenser's nymphs wait for the joys that the modern nymphs have had already. The contrast, as this reader understands it, between Spenser and contemporary London (England?) is complete, and this might seem to suggest that here Eliot 'faltered somewhat'.

Yet there is a further term of comparison. Psalm CXXXVII begins:

By the rivers of Babylon, there we sat down, yea, we wept, when we remembered Zion.

Which says that the exiled Jews mourn not merely their captivity, but their absence from Zion, and the Temple. This has something in it of the action of 'atonement' which signifies through repentance a making of one's self at one with God, where exile from Him is misery. Often God punished the transgressions of the Jews with exile. Thus as the Jews mourn their absence from Zion, and so from God, we mourn our exile from the right and good conduct from which we have fallen. 'How shall we sing the Lord's song in a strange land?' (Eliot was indeed an exile.) As the Jews wept in their exile from Zion and God, so we weep in our spiritual contemporary exile from God's love, which we have forsaken – and languish by the 'waters of Leman' (Lac Leman in Switzerland, as one ingenious critic has suggested). We may remember Christ's aphoristic parallelism

The foxes have holes, and the birds of the air have nests; but the Son of man hath not where to lay his head.

(Matthew, 8:20)

The *human* animal is not at home in the universe. By our acts we exile ourselves from God's love.

Thus this third term represents a touch of compassion, and if it does erase Eliot's jejeune snigger at contemporary sexual conduct, yet the psalmic term qualifies his sneer. The merciful act, and there are not many of them in the poem, is like fertility. If we allow it to play back into the poem it bathes the Hyacinth-girl, the modern Cleopatra and Lil. But this is not how the poem continues. For the sexuality which opens 'The Fire Sermon' is followed by apparently unrelated images of disgust and predation. These, however, key in with the intellectual condemnation with which the section begins. Thus the softly creeping rat with its 'slimy belly', which we may contrast with the rat in Rosenberg's 'Break of Day in the Trenches', and its fanged superior intelligence (*The Collected Works*, pp. 103–4):

It seems you inwardly grin as you pass.

If 'the king my father's death' is to be taken as the death of the drowned Phoenician sailor, or of the Fisher King, whose decease is ritualized to bring fertility, then the sexuality that has provoked disgust is to be read as not the proper 'issue', not love's true activity. And should we be in doubt, the leitmotif of the 'forc'd' Philomel is brought on stage to put us in mind of her, and her earlier reappearance in the picture adorning the modern woman's bedroom in 'A Game of Chess'.

If this analysis seems to emphasize sex too much, we may notice that this is the section in which Mr Eugenides makes his proposal of 'homosexual debauch'. That this is immediately followed by the sadly dated audacity of the typist and the unfairly disadvantaged 'carbuncular' clerk (= boils, spots, pimples). Though this is poor realism, on a number of levels. For if the typist suffers 'assault' and is 'glad it's over', could she not have found herself a more attractive partner? Eliot seems to have selected the most unfavourable representatives in order to enforce his tendentious meaning, which is to berate the unfortunate with misfortune. Yet the paradox here is that the original version (Facsimile, pp. 42–7) is much more unpleasant, and it is in this that its earlier strength lived. It is the disgust, and perhaps the horror, that gave the episode its strength, overlong though it perhaps was. By giving Tiresias greater control as narrator and witness, the authoritative mode is strengthened and the unpleasant nature adulterated. We are left with a lesser couple (in the sense of their not possessing their own lives with power over themselves) and an enlarged Tiresias. Which is a poor exchange. As if one were to have a Greek Chorus without any characters on whom they were to squander their collective commentary. This making respectable, which seems to be the work of Pound, for Eliot wrote the original, proves decisive. Eliot never again attempts to give courageous licence to his disgust in his poetry. By 'licence' I mean what Coleridge calls 'laxis effertur habensis' – 'driven with loosened reins'.

Many critics have praised this passage, and perhaps my criticism is mistaken. Yet is it perhaps their disguised prurience, or is there virtue in the cut version? Does the received version 'keep [the reader's] mind diverted and quiet, while the poem does its work upon him'? (*Selected Prose*, p. 93). Does the verse tilt its product away from meaning onto its execution, verse for the sake of verse? For if we compare the uncut with the received version, the latter does not house all the meaning inherent in the former.

Most critics have praised Pound for his 'shaping' of the poem, by which is meant 'surgery'. Yet in this question of help Eliot needed the additional advice of someone alive to the concerns of fiction. A look at Pound's work, the Propertius and Mauberley poems notwithstanding, will show a deficiency in this department. The writer whom Eliot anathematized in *After Strange Gods* could have 'helped' him both in the example of his work, and preceptually, in his 'never put one's thumb in the scales'. That is, never 'interfere' with your characters. By coming out, subsequently, so strongly for Tiresias, as the Facsimile shows (pp. 46–7), Pound enables Eliot to flout this rudimentary conduct, and the result is both gentility and prejudice rather than the earlier strong disgust. 'Tiresias, although a mere spectator and not a "character", is yet the most important person-age in the poem, uniting all the rest.' The language of Eliot's note requires our attention, for the word 'mere' is disingenuous in its rhetoric. By putting the word 'character' between disowning quo-tation marks and by using the elevated and non-committal word 'personage' Eliot seems, indeed perhaps seeks, to disencumber the entire episode of its responsibility for creating fiction. The whole note proceeds in this tenor, and though it is offered as strategy for the whole poem, applied on the smaller scale of this episode, it atomizes its own substance.

Thus the phrase 'mere spectator' needs scrutinizing. Off-guard by what it professes, we may easily miss the point that although Tiresias takes no actual part in the sexual episode between the human couple, his role in this for the *reader* so subverts the couple's life, in the received version, that he becomes both a character and the hid-den narrator, arrogating to himself the role of the sophisticate in his déjà vu. For has he not 'foresuffered all' before? Yet though he is akin to Prufrock's 'For I have known them all already', Tiresias acquires the role of moral evaluator. 'I Tiresias, though blind . . . can see.'

That is greedy of Eliot, and the episode pays dearly for it, since the poet deprives his characters of their earlier and greater inde-pendence, making them subservient to his moral intentions. Which act is as tendentious as any to be found in a left-wing political poem by an English poet in the 1930s. The evidence that Eliot had better in him is in the material he omitted, or altered. It is evident in his drama where, of necessity, his characters have the autonomy denied them here. I emphasize this because *The Waste Land* may be seen as, not a dramatic poem, but a new form intermediate between a poem such as Prufrock, and drama itself. 'Sweeney Agonistes' (and the abandoned 'Bolovo' experiment) shows the form driven into the ground. Perhaps there could only be the one *The Waste Land*.

We may now look at the strengths of this 'seduction' passage which, if we take Eliot at his word, of preferring the poetry over the meaning, is what does survive.

The change from (Kenner, in Litz, pp. 30–2) rhymed quatrains of iambic pentameter to continuous verse that is almost rhymed 'blank' entails losses, some of which I have suggested. Some of the loss is of delicacy and modesty in the nature *of the poetry* (compare pp. 71–3 with *Facsimile*, pp. 42–7).

I have suggested that, in unDantesque fashion, undue emphasis has been put on symbolism and its typology. But it must be said that the episode has written power, wherein the images are brought to the surface of the discourse. There they ply their trade upon the reader, uncluttered, and with due breathing space, while the articulating voice is fitted to the section's rhythmic patterning. In this sense only, it has something in it of 'Prufrock', and it may be that this is why Pound advised Eliot not to place 'Gerontion' at the head of the poem (*Selected Letters*, p. 171):

> At the violet hour, when the eyes and back
> Turn upward from the desk, when the human engine waits
> Like a taxi throbbing waiting,
> I Tiresias, though blind, throbbing between two lives,
> Old man with wrinkled female breasts, can see . . .
>
> (*CP*, 71)

This has something of the interlinked intricacy of the rejected and despised Whitman ('Look down fair moon') and is all the better for it. The pacing of the stresses is sure and, since Tiresias is the controlling narrator, this helps to establish his supremacy in this preparatory scene, as well as in the ensuing sexual one. The change of footing and pace, where the second half of the line quickens with 'throbbing between two lives', is very fine. Yet if we are to take the poetry seriously, we cannot abandon meaning, especially when certain words receive rhythmic emphases. One of these is 'throbbing'. The 'violet hour' might be felt to be throbbing, and the 'human engine' waiting ('Like a taxi') is also throbbing – with expectation or weariness at day's end, or with both. Sufficient attention has been generated upon the word for its recurrence within the 'nature' of Tiresias to be felt to have meaning. Yet what? 'Throbbing' suggests excitement, anticipation, response of some kind, though it seems careless of Eliot to give Tiresias this, only to endow him subsequently with the tone of one who has seen it all before, and, moreover, one in whom such disdain, especially for the clerk, inheres. For Tiresias is the narrator who 'Perceived the scene, and foretold the rest' (line 229).

If the excitement is not bisexual, which I think is neither meant nor present (to deal with another's suggestion, negatively) perhaps it is that of one who reincarnates the desires of both sexes, as well as the anticipation of the witness. Yet of all the possible meanings of this 'throbbing', the passage vibrates (throbs) most to the exhilaration of active disdain and censorious judgement. It is that which works up the passage, if that can be said is what happens. Certainly, 'One of the low on whom assurance sits' (Pound wanted the quatrain containing this cut; Facsimile, pp. 44–5) is emphatic and powerful. The 'low' it seems are not permitted assurance; being 'low', it is an inappropriate possession, almost as unacceptable as the working-class Bradford *nouveau riche* who has 'only' earned his silk hat with money (compare this with Eliot's 'aristocraticizing' claim that he was a New Englander: *After Strange Gods*, p. 16). It may be retorted that Eliot does not mean 'low' socially but morally, yet although the moral objection is right and the clerk is 'low' in that sense, Eliot makes his moral character inseparable from his class. It is the class that stamps him, as the original, in such details as 'simple loiterers' (Facsimile, p. 45), shows. Moreover his partner is of the same class, with her 'false/Japanese print' – one who rooms in what Pound correctly identified as 'that lodging house' (Facsimile, p. 45).

Perhaps the most accurate verse in this passage is

> Endeavours to engage her in caresses
> Which still are unreproved, if undesired.
> Flushed and decided, he assaults at once . . .
>
> (*CP*, 72)

This catches the quick of the engagement. 'Endeavours' is the fastidiousness of Tiresias, not the human participants. Unseen, he watches the clerk who, failing to get the response he had wanted, takes what he desires anyhow, and leaves. His acts are 'unreproved/ undesired', a device which Geoffrey Hill echoes, perhaps, in his zeugmatic pair 'Undesirable/untouchable' in 'September Song' (see chapter 7, below). Reproved is to do with propriety but, much more, with morality. It is hard to decide what has been more violated (we may remember Philomel in 'A Game of Chess'); whether it is the normal code of conduct whereby sex is reserved for marriage, or if not that, then an assenting intimate relationship; or whether it is the woman, who suffers the man's mechanical ego-preening callousness. In her passive suffering later in 'The Fire Sermon', we may connect this woman with the one 'on the floor of a narrow canoe'.

Here, the image of male callousness is reinforced by 'decided/assaults' with the effective caesura acting to emphasize the two phrases that punctuation and syntax formally separate. The syntax in two parts is bound together by the flow of the metre mirroring the mental determination that precedes the physical assault. Stead tells us that the woman's 'and I'm glad it's over' is her 'post-coital sadness'. Sadness?

What follows is another of those several passages that anchor the poem by creating a visible reality, but which here simultaneously convokes a mystical summation of the city's complex life:

> 'This music crept by me upon the waters'
> And along the Strand, up Queen Victoria Street.
>
> (*CP*, 72–3)

(topographically inaccurate in its implied connections). Who speaks the first line? Is it Tiresias fading from the surface level of actuality? Is the music the typist's gramophone? Is it hers? It all transists beautifully into a demotic touch. Eliot, like many educated people, appears to detest the petit bourgeois, as represented by the clerk, and likes the 'uneducated'; thus the life in the pub, together with its 'pleasant whining of a mandoline'//'Where fishermen lounge at noon'. He liked music-hall. And so the popular culture, here juxtaposed with the splendour of the church of Magnus Martyr. I miss the line in Facsimile pp. 46–7, 'Fading at last, behind my flying feet', which Pound crossed through together with 'Michael Paternoster Royal', but this latter excision may have prompted Eliot to provide Magnus Martyr with its 'Inexplicable splendour'.

The passage which Stead appears to call 'free-verse' (p. 108) is in two stanzas of mainly two-beat accentual verse, reflecting the tug and sweep of oars being rowed. It begins with 'The river sweats', and repeats its metricality in 'Elizabeth and Leicester/Beating oars'. The point of both stanzas being rhythmically patterned is to compare the industrial Thames, which however has its own dignity, with the sumptuousness of the couple Elizabeth Queen and Leicester. It is the rhythm, in metre, of beating oars, the purpose of which we do not perceive until we reach the second stanza containing Elizabeth and her escort. Then we understand that the accentual verse of the first stanza is set up so as to resonate and chime with the same metre in the second. There is not the simple contrast (*TSE.*, p. 204) Craig asserts between the modern and the Elizabethan for

Craig misses the stinking dignity of the modern Thames (is perhaps unfamiliar with it); but in true doubleness there is a contrast of that with the Elizabethan *sumptuousness*, recalling and linking it with the Cleopatra in 'A Game of Chess', back beyond Shakespeare and his creation, his source in Plutarch, to the actual Cleopatra, her splendour, her power and love. Gardner refers us to the note of Eliot's concerning their amorous flirtation and comments, 'Of all the lovers of history these are the most preposterous: Elizabeth, the Virgin Queen, flirting with the astute and ambitious courtier'. Gardner's instinct, it seems, is to establish the modern dirty Thames as consonant with and not in contrast to the 'soiled' Elizabethan couple. I can only observe that what is in the note I cannot find in the poem, since I read both cultures in the poem to some degree *positively*. If we read the verse itself we are left with a contrast but which, directed back through the prior stanza with its corresponding accentual metricality, is with the sadly degraded sexual episode of clerk and woman (real figures), in which the latter is (just) felt as a victim. 'By the waters of Leman I sat down and wept.' Thus the clerk and typist are in some degree parallel with the degraded Thames, but in contrast with Elizabeth and Leicester, the note notwithstanding. From which conjunction we obtain the bonus of (river) symbolism.

Eliot's note tells us that from line 266, 'The river sweats', begins the Song of the three Thames-daughters, and that from 292 to 306 they speak in turn. The word-music refrain presumably constitutes Eliot's attempt to interlink or even make interchangeable (Europeanize) the song of the Thames-daughters with those of the daughters of the Rhine. But the principal effect of 'Weialala leia' is temporarily to suspend the speaking 'valved voice' in its mode of sense, and interpolate the music of, not poetry, but music itself. It has something of the 'electric' effect of *Sprachtmusik*, making one aware of what has momentarily ceased.

Indeed the sense of the passage beginning 'Trams and dusty trees' (evocative of my London childhood between the wars) on to 'la la', is not only one of songs, and singing, but of opera (not Wagner, but something less noisy). The echoing 'la la' links with the earlier music-interruption and has the same effect of getting us to listen more acutely to the words because the poet has temporarily suspended their operation with respect to meaning.

The effect of these *three* songs is of aggregated meanings, though the total testimony is overlapped since, individually, it comprises

the comparable histories of three women. All are probably victims of seduction, or some kind of betrayal, sexual, emotional, or
both. In the first song 'undid me' works like 'you have undone me'
('ruined') and all that such sexual morality implies. 'Raised my
knees' could mean the act facilitating sex or, more finely, might
suggest that the woman is reconstituting the act in her mind. In
joy, perhaps. Yet 'Supine' suggests passivity, compliance rather
than assent. The full weight of the rhythm falls on the first with
its intrinsically strong accented first syllable:

'Súpine on the flóor of a nárrow canóe'
(*CP*, 74)

she sings.
In the second song the man appears penitent: 'He wept.' But
Anglo-Saxon cultures distrust a man's weeping. The point is not
whether such distrust is reasonable, but that it exists in the culture
and is therefore a possible implication for the reader. I believe that
we are meant to doubt the sincerity of the promise. I miss on the
woman's part the passion of 'outcry' (Facsimile, 51), which Eliot
commuted to something much blander, though one sees how 'com
ment' tunes with the passivity and meekness:

'I máde no cómment. Whát shóuld I resént?'
(*CP*, 74)

Yet 'outcry' in the earlier draft gave the woman greater identity
without its impairing her 'humility' which is, one sees, the purpose of this passage. It is an opportunity possessed, then lost. A
rhythmical point worth noticing: I read the line above as iambic
pentameter, with a durational sign over 'should', meaning, in all
humility, 'for what good reason'? But the line could also be scanned
accentually:

'I made nó cómment. Whát should I resént?'

where 'outcry' would have been both a stronger and rhythmically
richer *and* more subtle word. The stresses in this reading form a
pattern closer to speech, perhaps. But the point is that the mind
reading to itself, which is the reading experience we have most of
the time, virtually merges the two rhythmical readings, so that the

mind, hesitating between both, subjoins them. And how finely rhythmical hesitation, hidden were the line read aloud, enacts the likely emotional confusion and hesitation the woman feels in relation to her lover.

The third song is partly in free verse:

> 'I can connéct
> Nóthing with nóthing
> The bróken fingernáils of dírty hánds.'

Though with characteristic indirection the maverick rhythmical line is metrical pentameter, as indeed is the one after embodying these 'humble people'. The effect, though not patronizing, is touched with paternalism; authority is beginning to speak. Yet more important is it that in the third song, which culminates the predicament of the previous two women with the third, despair speaks. 'I can connect/Nothing with nothing'. The enjambment enacts the effort made to articulate her condition. Nothing will come of nothing. Nothing *can* come of it. Also the reverse: that the only thing I can connect with is nothing. The humble people expect nothing, because they are humble; alas, that, precisely, is what they get. Or do they? The collocation from 'Buddha's Fire Sermon' ('Burning') with St Augustine's 'O Lord Thou pluckest me out', which Eliot abjures us to read together is very well as mysterious music, enticing in the reader a sense of religious mystery. Fire = 'refining'. Yet if quotations are to form allusions, on whom might Eliot fairly count on to have read Buddha (in what depth and with what understanding formed from prior acquaintance)? If we must go and read Buddha, some of the imaginative spontaneity is lost. Nevertheless the humble people receive the music and the rhythm, 'Burning'. Multiple meanings are possible. The burning lust Augustine relinquished for the refining fire he experienced, that is God's, as he was plucked burning by God.

Section IV, 'Death by Water', Eliot thought of cutting completely, perhaps because Pound had already cut so much (Facsimile, pp. 62–9). Pound advised not. 'In fact I more'n advise . . . (Phlebas) is needed ABSOlootly' (*Selected Letters*, January 1922, p. 171). Critics (almost) uniformly applaud Pound's editing, yet what remains of the section? It is difficult to answer. This short section reads in the mode of an epitaph. Bleistein, 'poor Bleistein', has been lost in 'Picked

his bones in whispers' or, perhaps, in 'Gentile or Jew'. And if we
read this whole section in the guise of the last line.

Consider Phlebas, who was once handsome and tall as you.

(*CP*, 75)

taking it as *memento mori*,

As you are now so once was I
As I am now so shall you be

it reads well. It accounts for the 'stages of his age and youth' in the
leisurely but sure-footed rhythms reaching their resolution in death.
But that in a sense is the problem, if we are going to consider
properly the section's place and function in the whole poem. For its
success in the mode of epitaph confirms its function as registering
the finality of death. 'Death', Wittgenstein tells us, 'is an event outside life', but its effect is that of taking life from within life. Critics
advise us to turn back to the Tarot and the minatory 'Fear death by
water', and thus to read into this section the renewal of life in
death, ours, or the (ritual) sacrifice of the drowned Phoenician sailor.
And perhaps trace in this a resemblance to Christ's sacrifice. But
with respect to the function of this section that is the problem. We
may certainly read it as instancing the generality of epitaphs, speaking for all life and its mortality. Yet reading it thus we may find it
difficult to understand this part on the symbolic level of *renewal*. It
may be that in the next life we are renewed, but in that case renewal does not appear to need the sacrifice of the sailor or Fisher
King. I am not being awkward, though it may seem as though I am.
I merely suggest that read on the symbolic level, which we must do
if we are to ensure the poem's total design, we may experience
disjunction between that and the *felt* level in the mode of epitaph,
in which this section is so successful. Again, ancient cultures may
posit sacrifice as necessary for renewal, but we don't properly feel
that, though in as much as we acknowledge the sacred feel of the
act of personal sacrifice something of that idea remains. But we
wouldn't accept the sacrifice of those we love or, at least in theory,
of anyone, as a means of renewal. Death is death, and nothing
results from it. So if we are led to continue reading the poem in
symbolic and anthropological terms, we may experience disjunction here between that and our experience.

Yet, as I suggest, Pound was right to insist on retaining this section. Without it, the poem loses its 'watery' cohesion, and the idea of fertility upon which the last section is predicated, 'V. What the Thunder said'.

The first note to this section informs the reader that the three themes employed are, respectively, 'the journey to Emmaus, the approach to the Chapel Perilous (see Miss Weston's book) and the present decay of Eastern Europe', the last of which is for lines 366–76 further glossed by a quotation from Herman Hesse's *Blick ins Chaos*.

I indicate here what I see as the emergence of an authoritarian character. If it is present in the note, it has no explicit presence in the text itself, though one may feel it beginning to creep into the poetry.

The power of the verse inheres in the energies working within spiritual conviction and a predominating metricality. Together they may make readers feel that this is the most powerful section. In this may be a problem. The 'falling towers' passage (lines 373–6), with the short one-word line, make this part seem willed and pretentious. See also line 207, 'Unreal city'. Perhaps this willed, even wilful sense results from a formal contradiction, for if these cities and their abominations were 'unreal', notwithstanding the philosophical meaning the word may have here, there would be no substance to a condemnation of them, or their destruction, and thus the entire design of the poem. 'Unreal' I take to mean without spiritual substance. Yet in terms of 'real' the truth seems otherwise. The cities are real, in their spiritual decay ('carious') and spiritual infertility.

There is thus a danger of the assured and strong character of the verse, together with this willed quality, imposing here a spiritual diagnosis (and remedy) for the most part so sensitively enacted in preceding sections. I say this notwithstanding my reservations concerning the opening 'The Fire Sermon' (see above). We may feel here how those precious threads of the poem, of myth and anthropology, seem in the main to get discarded in this section in favour of a religion grasping and battening onto the hapless life in the verse.

This can be indicated though not conclusively demonstrated, but then nor would I in that sense wish to be conclusive. Still, with Eliot's note to support this, the opening section seems principally to be speaking of Christ, the road to Emmaus and 'His' Garden of Agony. 'He who was living is now dead' provides Christian and historical references, and so this presence excludes that of the drowned Phoenician sailor. And, with one exception, the Fisher King is also excluded, he who had balanced such delicate roles, negotiating between symbolism and anthropology on the one, and belief on the other. For these performed such a precious metaphysical role in the poem that to discard them now seems ruthless. But no, this seems to be Christ – He who was dead is now risen. Though in what sense risen if the world has disregarded his redemption?

In stanzas 2 and 3 we have the mountains of rock without water; and in the beautiful free verse of stanza three, the 'hermit-thrush'. Stanza 4 recurs to Christ, and 5 is 'those hooded hordes' coupled with, eventually, the discarded, decayed civilization of 'empty cisterns and exhausted wells'. Stanza 6 repeats the unwatered condition in 'decayed hole among the mountains', perhaps not merely decayed through nature, but also from lack of human attention.

Here the grass is singing which, considering the almost automatic and thoughtless positive we habitually give to 'song' and 'singing', might seem to register a rejoicing sign; but the phrase ties in with stanza 3, line 354, where the singing is caused by the wind passing through 'dry grass'. So in recurring to this, Eliot beautifully consolidates his theme of dryness and infertility. The cock crows triumphantly when the rain comes in a 'damp gust' where four lines before 'There is the empty chapel, only the wind's home'; meaning, no spiritual care or observance. It might be worth recording that for this reader the freshness here indicates discovery by the poet rather than something imposed from without by religious belief or observant duty. The chapel is empty, windowless, unlatched, unbolted and the 'dry bones' that 'can harm no one' indicate not merely the absence of superstitious fear but an absence of the awe and reverence for the remains of the dead, which is itself matter for lamentation.

Yet in all this does the cock crow merely, and the rain follow it? Or does the rain, in its symbolic falling, bring regeneration? Or is the rain falling, preceptual? I cannot decide.

By the time we reach stanza 7 the *religion* of the east, that appeared briefly in the conclusion of 'The Fire Sermon', recurs. None of this is wrong, of course; but by replacing myth with religion the delicate spiritual tentativeness and imaginative resilience of myth has been replaced by the more authoritative structures of the west and its religion as well as the 'authority' of Buddhism in the east.

Hugh Kenner has said of the thunder's utterance in stanza 8:

There the activity of the protagonist ends. Some forty remaining lines in the past tense recapitulate the poem in terms of the oldest wisdom accessible to the West. The thunder's DA is one of those primordial Indo-European roots that recur in the *Oxford Dictionary*, a random leaf of the Sibyl's to which a thousand derivative words, now automatic currency, were in their origins so many explicit glosses. If the race's most permanent wisdom is its oldest, then DA, the voice of the thunder and of the Hindu sages, is the cosmic voice not yet dissociated into echoes. It underlies the Latin infinitive 'dare', and all its Romance derivatives; by a sound-change, the Germanic 'geben', the English 'give'. It is the root of 'datta', 'dayadhvam', 'damyata': give, sympathize, control: three sorts of giving. To sympathize is to give oneself; to control is to give governance.

(*TSE*, p. 192)

This is, perhaps, the most difficult moment in the poem. And what Kenner claims is clearly a challenge to the suggestion that religion has evacuated myth and anthropology, with the consequence of that authoritativeness I have indicated. But what is wisdom? The Christian Church has tried to reassure its adherents by claiming that various passages in the Old Testament are prophetic of the coming of Christ. This is to wrench utterance from its socket, which even were it remotely possible to establish would be prophetic of Christ, and not of the Church. Wisdom, in the Old Testament, was often associated with the prophets – 'I am no prophet' – and the prophets in their turn were often maverick perhaps, but dissident in their opposition to kings and their nations. Wisdom becomes the possession of the tribe but it is often compounded out of singleness of position, opposition to and dissent from, the worldly conduct of power. It is not the romantic position of deriving strength from opposition, though that is not the easy thing so many contemporary intellectuals claim it to be; were it so far fewer university professors would have supported Hitler, out of fear, presumably. The strength of the prophets lay in their moral singularity, which might or might not collide with the interests of power. Sometimes it did not, more often it did. And in this bracket we remember wisdom is also the attribute of folk understanding; indeed, we say 'folk wisdom', meaning some collective understanding enshrined in *sacred* power which only the rising of a new culture or cultures can shake.

It is true that myth and ritual embody the wisdom of the tribe, which may be far from beneficent in character. But in the myths we have seen operating in *The Waste Land*, and in their application, their 'character' is or arises from perplexity: the cruellest month, the Hyacinth-girl, the Cleopatra, Philomel, Lil (and her 'friend' Lou), Stetson and the crimes he and we have committed, the typist (and even the clerk), the three Thames maidens. And threading them the myths of required fertility, and impotence in need of regeneration. It is a vision of contemporary society but also of those who in the past have lived in as hapless a condition. So it is in its rare but unretractable moments of compassion that the poem, and its gifts, corresponds with those of the tribe's most valuable collective wisdom. The adroit tilting of that into the authority and power of religion and its institutions is a worldly wisdom that in effect undermines the lonely wisdom which, in its suffering, is that best grounding of *The Waste Land*. In the short story 'Thinking of Zenzo' by the Japanese fiction-writer Dazai Osamu, the narrator says: 'Only those who want to listen to my moronic obstinate music – only they should listen. Art cannot order people around. Art dies the moment it acquires authority' (quoted in *Printed Matter*, Spring 1991, p. 44). The stanza Kenner glosses wavers through this crux where wisdom is revised in a religion vested in authority and temporal power. See also Eliot's note to the effect that the juxtaposition of 'eastern and western asceticism' is not accidental (p. 84).

Yet the images of 'beneficient spider' and 'lean solicitor' whose sinister character belong to 'Gerontion' cannot destroy

> The áwful dáring óf a móment's surrénder
> Which an áge of prúdence can néver retráct . . .
> (*CP*, 78)

It has never been clear to me whether this surrender is 'in principle' a moment's unselfish surrender to something not belonging to the interests of self; or if perhaps it is, as seems possible, surrender to the demands of some religious belief. This nevertheless has been given. But as the verse moved through 'Datta, Dayadhvam, Damyata', 'Give, Sympathise, Control' into the paradigm half-composed of Christianity with which this section began, and against which are set the 'hooded hordes' of Eastern Europe, the poem chooses its ground; and shudders into place, in religion and with power. It cannot and does not do that overtly. The movement is more mixed, the result more dappled and more mottled.

The pattern of reference and of benediction, in which the thunder brings rain and thus an implied fertility, is part of the myth this poem uses. Gardner's suggestion that the poem ends more darkly than it began needs to be linked to the question of on what level the rain arrives, and what it brings. If it brings 'relief' and even fertility, has it come too late? Or does the rain taunt us, offering the analogue of physical moisture and spiritual fertility, but bringing only the former? It seems as though there is some dichotomy here between perplexity 'enshrined' in myth, and the possible solution incarnated in religion. For when we come to 'Damyata', 'Control', the meaning of which I am in no position to read within the original Buddhistic context, its relocation in western thinking has very definite connotations. Indeed in the analogue, who or what is controlling whom? If, as so much of the poem is, this is an analogue, for some larger social power, then it is hard to avoid the idea that the conclusion of the poem confronts the reader with Authority and the Church. *In that order.*

Moreover the presence of religion seems to destroy the life of myth, as the official organism destroys the unofficial or maverick. To bring in the latter seems to amount to the expulsion of myth. And though some anthropologists argue that the Judaeo-Christian religious inheritance is yet another myth, officially in place, for most of us in the West, including those whose belief is decayed, or who have lost what little faith they once had, this inheritance, if that is what it still is, constitutes for them, as for believers, the official, historical religion, canonical in status.

This brings with it the crux of the poem hesitating between myth and religion, both in its strategy and its *belief*, and, in its hesitation, undermining both Coleridge's 'willing suspension of disbelief for the moment' and Eliot's 'suspension of belief'. For a structure that hesitates between belief and imagination impales the disbeliever on its own dubiety. You cannot disbelieve what is neither one nor the other.

The poem, properly perhaps, will not commit itself. It appears to offer a belief system, but avoids subscribing itself to that. The question may be unresolvable, yet since I have raised it, I must try to indicate my reading, perhaps hardly different from that given by many others.

The desire for water (and a healed sexuality) that underflows this poem is most poignantly expressed in the third stanza, where the hermit-thrush 'sings in the pine trees'. One hears her song where there is no water. It is the hint which renews the desire for water and, at this point, all that water implies. In stanza 4 the hooded figure of Christ is perceived in contradistinction to the 'hooded hordes' in stanza 5. The juxtaposition of the latter with 'Murmur of maternal lamentation' works both politically and humanly, by which I mean that all catastrophe brings with it the connotative music of maternal lamentation, that seems closer, here, to the Judaeo-Christian tradition.

The abrupt unexplained transition from the falling towers to the woman drawing her hair out tight, as a figure of tension and angst, parallels the lamentation induced by catastrophe. The fiddled music, the upside-down bats with 'baby faces' implying a resemblance to what they have eaten, the recurrence of the now sinister and soiled 'violet hour' all bring specificity and a sense of actuality, which is Eliot's strength. And the decay of the mountain chapel, with these other creatures, actualizes negative bursts of life, against which is posited the clear performance of 'Give, Sympathize, Control'. It is true that the Fisher King makes a brief appearance, 'with the arid plain behind me', but the dominant mode is formularization; the mode that approaches injunction truly 'enshrined' in religious instruction.

It is against this that the Fisher King (?) feels that he may and can –

> Shall I at least set my lands in order?
>
> (*CP*, 79)

The religious power instructs myth. But perhaps this interpretation is premissed on this reader's misplaced anxiety.

The *signs* with which the poem closes enact ambiguity. The flashes of other languages, poems and cultures which briefly constellate the ending of the poem, in hesitant but persistent metricality, the breaking down of metricality, and then the building of it, here, as earlier on, suggest a mind labouring towards assurance. There is the peace that passeth all understanding in the repeated benediction of 'Shantih', that follows the religious injunction from the *Brihadaranyaka – Upanishad*, 5, 1: but we have also felt the conditional mood in 'your heart would have responded'. The tenuity is not reassuring even if the benediction is made. It is hope rather than an achieved condition. The achieved condition arrives, if it does come, through institutionalized wisdom. I see that the question implied in Gardner's observation that the poem ends more darkly than it began hasn't been answered.

Perhaps the question can be turned about by drawing on Coleridge, whom Eliot treated with a certain condescension in 'The Use of Poetry' (*SP*, p. 90), but whom in certain respects Eliot resembles.

With relief the Ancient Mariner returns home, and begs the hermit to shrive and render him absolution for crimes which he appears both to recognize and understand. This is Christianity. Yet though he has been shrived, it achieves nothing:

> a woful agony,
> Which forced me to begin my tale;
> And then it left me free.

This is what he tells the hapless wedding-guest, but that does not free him either:

> I pass, like night, from land to land;
> I have strange power of speech;
> That moment that his face I see,
> I know the man that must hear me:
> To him my tale I teach.

Eliot too passes from one land to another, having 'strange power of speech', and the diagrammatic substance of one poem bears certain resemblances to the other. But these are incidentals. What most stays with one is that the mariner, shrived and presumably forgiven, achieves no freedom from his acts, and the telling of his narrative bestows only momentary relief. His freedom is illusory, and the forgiveness has no meaning for him. Not even the belief he acquired, with 'The awful daring of a moment's surrender', is of consequence. There is no forgiveness. Like Eliot he has, however, 'strange power of speech', the Tongues, the story compelled through him. But no forgiveness is effectual. What does this mean? *Is* there no forgiveness? And even if it is not Coleridge but the poem saying this, isn't it unChristian? What concerns me is whether or not Coleridge knew that this 'figure' and its ensuing existence belonged, not to Christian thinking, but, if I dare say this, to something deeper; since the realization that one's crimes cannot be forgiven is perhaps the deepest realization of all.

I do not suppose Helen Gardner would have accepted this, and I am not sure that I find it acceptable either. But if Coleridge did not realize the windowless room into which he had led the mariner and himself, it is also possible that Eliot may not have realized that his question was not susceptible to Christian solution – not in those terms in which it was raised, and its solution hinted at. For perhaps the deepest of all those of God's attributes is that where no forgiveness exists love does.

POSTSCRIPT

I regret disagreeing yet again with Helen Gardner, though this may be the result of her delineating her position so clearly. *'The Waste Land* [she tells us] is a series of visions: it has neither plot nor hero' (*The Art*, p. 89). It is the word 'plot' I want to question, although considered from the position of the realistic novel this assertion is correct. And though I have suggested that the poem contains people making their transitory appearances, 'plot' is more difficult to argue, and thus it might be easier to accept 'a series of visions', and run. Yet one of a number of fascinating questions concerning modernism is this doubleness of structure and fracture. We all know (don't we?) that a novel coheres through its plot and because of a group of characters who retain their identity throughout. To take an extreme example. Though we know more about Bloom at the end of *Ulysses*, his identity remains the same. He undergoes no change such as that of *Orlando*. And in Lawrence's short story 'The Horse Dealer's Daughter', Mabel is an altogether integrated but separate person from the woman widowed in his 'Odour of Chrysanthemums', notwithstanding Lawrence's theory concerning the allotropic condition of his different characters.

The collection of short stories by Isaac Babel, *Red Cavalry*, constitutes a different condition. The stories are interlinked by a shared context, and through a number of recurring characters. They are set within the parenthetic experience of one Jewish soldier in a Cossack regiment that is fighting the White Russians and Poles during the latter part of the Russian Revolution (those whom Eliot would probably have included in his 'hooded hordes' on the 'Polish plains' (Facsimile, p. 75)). More importantly for my argument, the stories share a number of characters, so that while they do not endow the collection of stories with the unity of a novel they give the effect of someone keeping a diary in which, intermittently, some of the people recur.

We are approaching my sense of *The Waste Land*, not only as 'a series of visions' but more as something continuous. The Babel stories are like a sheet of glass that has been lightly tapped by a hammer; the sheet disintegrates, but the shape of the original is clearly visible. To present the crux in the theoretical terms of modernism; what is fragmented was once whole. The question then, for *The Waste Land*, as for other modernist works, is, what whole has been fragmented? Theologically, too, that is probably a sound question. Yet there is an additional factor to consider, for the plot involves the rise and fall of action(s). My belief is that the staying power of this poem for readers consists in there not only being persons who briefly flare across a stage, but also in there being for the reader some mysterious sense of a fragmented whole, which involves a drama, disjoined but, notwithstanding that, felt instinctively by its readers to exist. And I believe it would have been the same had the poem included those large sections which were finally omitted.

The plot cannot function realistically because though there are characters that resemble each other in their predicaments or fates, different persons appear. I certainly do not believe that Tiresias, Eliot's note notwithstanding, unites 'all the rest'. Instead, the poem has a more fundamental unity to do with the interacting rise and fall of energies, of which the different characters are the dramatis personae but who, however, change from time to time though the same action continues. The condition is somewhat akin to Aristotle's 'action' as a dramatic component. So. In *this* picture of the poem there is both unity of 'action' *and* a fragmentation of the whole. There are characters who are different in different parts of the poem, but they all perform grouped functions in relation to the complete action. Like a drama with its integrated acts and unity.

Which is, enquires the sceptic? It is the identity of wounded sexuality, infertility and healing, on both an intrinsic and instantial level. In a sense Eliot has transmuted his painful life, but, equally, the continuing pain ensures that the problem be sustained in terms of a complete action over a whole poem. Thus the action entails desire being stirred, and that desire being in turn frustrated distorted or perverted. It is (the poem) to do with that perversion, which registers the actual and symbolized immorality of a culture and its subsequent infertility. Or an infertility inhering in the perversion, where it is both intrinsic and symbolic. And withal, infertility, and sexual, emotional and spiritual crisis. Such crisis can be traced in its rising from cruel April, through the Hyacinth-girl, Cleopatra, Lil and Lou, into the infertile sexuality of the typist/clerk episode. And this culmination may in part account for Eliot's endowing this episode with such strong responses, which, I believe, it may have been a mistake to moderate. Such an episode was not merely important to him as an individual, though we oughtn't to underrate this possible factor; it was the high-point in the poem's graph of *action*, in which the poem's maximum energy encountered its dramatized maximum distortion and perversion. For illness is the rise, not only of the life of the pathogen, but also that of the suffering patient. Thereafter ensues 'Death by Water' as an alternative to infertility in life, with, in the last section, the possibility of renewal, not through sex, or sexuality, but through some spiritual vision.

3

Ezra Pound

PROPERTIUS – MAKE LOVE NOT WAR

Between

> Ánnalists will contínue to recórd Róman reputátions, . . .
> And expóund the disténtions of Émpire,
> Bŭt fŏr sómethĭng tŏ reăd ĭn nórmăl cĭrcŭmstăncĕs?
> For a féw páges brought down from the fórked híll unsúllied?
> I ásk a wréath that will not crúsh my heád.
>   And there is nó húrry about it . . .
>
> *(Collected Shorter Poems*, 225)

and

> And nów Propértius of Cýnthia, táking his stánd among
>   thēsē . . .
>
> *(Collected Shorter Poems*, 247)

is The Poem. For what passes between the opening and the poem's conclusion is a set of variations on what a poet should write about, and what avoid, but especially in time of war. These poems, it has been variously debated, are translations; equally, they are Pound's poems, taking (their) stand. Is it possible for them to be both?

Blackmur observed that Pound wrote at his most personal when he worked through the medium of another's poetry. Perhaps one could add that he had most to say when it was directed through the substance someone had written before him, but, and here (to use Blackmur's word) begins the 'surd' of qualifications, in having nothing to say, he makes that nothing say something. In any case, those who have read the early *Collected Shorter Poems* (1968) may concede that aside from the two Mauberleys, the Propertius and the translations of *Cathay* – and it is a considerable amount – Pound has, apart from a handful of short poems, very little to say. Whether poetry is obliged to say anything has been worked over by Eliot in 'The Use of Poetry and the Use of Criticism' (1933) and I discussed that crux in chapter 2. Nevertheless I had better say now that a poem saying little is, as I see it, a betrayal of language.

But as to the question of translation, it involves not only a consideration of what verse Pound has transposed from one to another language but what themes he has made over to *his* purposes, since that, too, could be thought of as a form of translation. As Blackmur has indicated, 'the Latin itself seems as much a version as either translation'. . . . 'the value, that is, in translation, of making a critical equivalent, rather than a duplicate, of the original'. With respect to his 'equivalent' Pound remodels not only the Latin, but the themes of Propertius. Pound's strategy is, in a sense, desperate. The themes have to become his own, since there is nothing there of Pound's unless this grows in that empty space.

Pound's set of variations is predicated on two themes. One is love, and the other a debate as to what might be the proper subject for poetry. It turns out that the proper subject for poetry is (also) love:

> And Phoebus looking upon me from the Castálian tree,
> Said then 'Yóu idiot! What are you doing with that water:
> 'Who has órdered a boók about héroes?
>   'You néed, Propértius, nót think
> 'About acquiring thát sort of a reputátion. . . .'
>   (*CSP*, 228)

This is very funny, the more because it is in earnest. It turns out that the kind of 'war poem' Pound is deploring (he seems a bit out of touch) is the patriotic verse he *appears* to imagine everyone was writing in 1917 – poetry praising military exploits, expressed with high-flown servility. The poem seems unaware of Sassoon, Rosenberg, Owen:

> And, 'It ís, I thínk, Índia which nów gives nécks to your
>   triumph,'
> And so forth, Augustus. 'Virgin Arabia shakes in her inmost
>   dwelling.'
>   (*CSP*, 233)

But

> ...I álso will sing wár *when this mátter of a gírl is exháusted*...
>   (*CSP*, 233; emphasis added)

And when he wants to rebuke his friend Lynceus for snatching a night with his girl Cynthia, the jealousy, if it can be called that, expresses itself through an identical criticism, but of *Lynceus's* verses aping Homer (*CSP*, 245). It is not merely that Lynceus's ambitions with respect to verse are ludicrous, misplaced and perhaps servile, but that the proper and modest, intimate subject of poetry is (he claims) love, Amor. So it is in this complex, if anywhere, that 'his' (Propertius/Pound) readers will spring up. His readers, if they exist, the poem argues, are like those of Catullus, to be found among the 'devirginated young ladies'. 'My genius is no more than a girl' (= inspiration) (*CSP*, 234).

What distracts one's attention from the oddity and bias of the theme is the rhythmic richness of the free verse, together with the sophisticated banter and persiflage. Though there is a moment when this is suspended, its place taken by a variation on the 'Ubi sunt' theme, of beauty in its mortality:

> There are enóugh wómen in héll,
>   qúite enough béautiful wómen...
> Déath has his tóoth in the lót...
>   (*CSP*, 240)

This brings out the evanescence of his relationship with Cynthia, though not of humanity killing itself in war. Much of the poem involves playfulness, notwithstanding that much modern verse (if this poem is modern) does not accommodate humour and laughter well. Perhaps poetry as a whole does not, though one thinks of Dryden and Pope, of Burns, Byron and Henryson (perhaps it is stronger in the Scottish tradition) and one sees immediately that there are too many exceptions to make a rule. But if the dire nature of experience, war for instance, finds verse such an apt instrument for its expression, this does not suggest that poetry will readily accommodate laughter. Nevertheless it is with salty delicate humour that the Propertius poems, though one may weary of the banter, are, in their range of invention, so successful.

And it is the complex strategy of the humour that concerns us. We looked (above) at the poet's interview with Phoebus; now the situations are reversed, and Propertius is receiving a report from his servant Lygdamus:

> You, you Lygdamus
> Saw her stretched on her bed, – ...
>
> Dámp wŏolly hañdkeřchiĕfs wĕre stúffed iñtŏ hĕr uñdrўable
> eyes,
> And a querulous nóise respónded to our solícitous reprobations.
> For which things you will get a reward from me, Lygdamus?
>
> ('IV/Difference of Opinion with Lygdamus', 231–2)

Complex strategy indeed. After we have read this section we see that the title itself contains the germ of a complexity which, despite what I have suggested with respect to Pound's inability to create character, indicates otherwise. This is a Conradian 'what A looks like from B's vantage-point if we hear what C thinks of B'.

With this section the poem is in the midst of its theme, 'And still a girl scorns the gods'. The implication is that love is the most important condition, more important than war, at least, as a subject for poetry, though we are, in 1917, in the midst of unremitting warfare in Europe. Lygdamus, the servant, has returned from the fact-finding mission on which he was sent by Propertius to discern Cynthia's state of play. 'Vast waters flowed from her eyes?' For the reader's benefit Propertius is evidently repeating an exaggerated item from the report Lygdamus has brought him concerning Cynthia's disposition. And when Propertius is told that 'a querulous noise' greeted Lygdamus's 'solicitous reprobations' on behalf of Propertius, he seems to promise, and withhold, a 'reward'. This means that he wants to believe that the grief is a mark of her love for him, and is sceptical of that. This is the reverse of 'shoot the messenger', even if it is not rewarding him either. And like almost everything else in this plotless plot it trademarks the ambiguity. Then follows a difficult part of the report concerning 'Cynthia's supposed abuse of her rival'. For despite John Speirs' fine essay ('*Mr Pound's Propertius*: Homage to Sextus Propertius' *Scrutiny*, Vol. III, 1935), his clarification does not entirely dispel the problem of who is saying what of whom, though the trademark of ambiguity is not here part of Pound's intentions. Thus Propertius is repeating what Lygdamus reports Cynthia as having said – that much is clear because of the convention already established. But then

And the óther woman 'has not entíced me
by her prétty mánners,

and

'Does he líke me to sleep here alóne,
Lygdāmus?'
(*CSP*, 232)

The 'other woman' is Cynthia's rival, and this part of the report
is in quotation marks because Propertius repeats Lygdamus's re-
laying of Cynthia's actual words. But 'has not enticed me'? 'Me'
might refer to Cynthia, but ought, I think, to indicate Propertius
towards whom Cynthia, *according to Lygdamus*, feels distrust. Yet,
as Cynthia says, does he (Propertius) expect 'me to sleep here
alone'. The final twist to the narrative, addressed both to Lygdamus
and the reader, is

And yóu expéct me to beliéve this
after twélve mōnths of discómfort?
(*CSP*, 232)

This is 'Propertius' speaking, and we must believe that he *has*
undergone twelve months of intermittent or continuous *enforced*
separation from Cynthia. Thus rival or no rival, this precarious
delight at what the messenger has relayed, this bringing to earth
with 'And you expect me to believe this' resolves the situation into
its actual unsatisfactoriness; someone is stalling, and under the circumstances it appears to be Cynthia. Yet we don't know whether
Propertius has a second lover or whether Cynthia is nurturing this
suspicion as a pretext to pursue her own purposes.

Put briefly, the problem is how we as readers are to apply the
ambiguity within the whole poem. The section establishes a complexity of motives and possible duplicities, which in a sense is
extended by an unequivocal infidelity on Cynthia's part with
Propertius's 'bosom' pal Lynceus.

And in a sense that does clarify the total matter of the poem. The
relationships are comic, and we are supposed to understand this
with the 'Damp woolly handkerchiefs ... stuffed into [Cynthia's]
undryable eyes'. We laugh, not at her, but at the wit that exagger-
ates the weeping with 'undryable', only to have the whole deflated

with 'woolly'. Even in classical literature dreams are not a cause for such excessive grief. And to recur to that last section XII where Lynceus has taken Cynthia to bed, for Propertius the wound is not mortal. Rather, to add a scandalous comic touch, it is, possibly, the exclusivity of Lynceus' and Cynthia's conduct that most offends Propertius:

> But in óne bed, in one bed alóne, my dear Lýnceus
> I déprecate your atténdance...
>
> (*CSP*, 245)

Yet having characterized one component of the poem as comic, the problem remains in that we do not know how seriously we are to read this amour; and the dissipation of any plot, even though some sections bloom into episodes, increases the difficulty.

This is one of the two aspects of the poem, that of love. The other, the proper subject for poetry, also receives light, sharp treatment throughout. To return briefly to the episode with Apollo, where Propertius is deflected from martial verse into writing love poetry.

Phoebus (Apollo) is, among many things, the god of *song and music* as well as *prophecy*. Such is the long tradition of classical Greek literature in English culture that we find it natural to over-hear a conversation between a man and a god. And despite Professor Stead's sense that the Judaeo-Christian religion has, unwisely perhaps, been 'pasted over the deeper Graeco-Roman traditions of European culture' (*Pound, Yeats, Eliot*, 279), a human conversation with a god is made further credible by the advent of Hebrew tradition into European culture, in which protagonists frequently speak with, and occasionally harangue, their god. At any rate here Phoebus condescends to deliver, in colloquial terms, mild abuse, and advice, in 'You idiot! What are you doing...'. The strategy increases its comic incongruity by striking across the expectation in which poets in their greatness are expected to sing of arms and courage, and then of love. For here, by comic reversal, we deprecate the former and elevate the latter. 'Who has ordered a book about heroes?' The idea of 'ordered' is comic, in its delicate conjunction of god with publisher, emperor and a commission. It is serious moral advice, the strategy of its humour for the instruction of the reader and for a culture engaged in war.

If we read the Propertius as the precursor to both Mauberleys we may with hindsight see the culmination of a self-examination of life-style, life-achievement, in the latter poem; the lifestyle of a poet in a society of loose, jovial, unreliable morals. Of the war-period in which the actual life of Pound was actually held, there is no direct hint. The retrograde praise of Augustus and Empire might be paralleled with the patriotism helping to actuate the 1914–18 war, but the literary criticism entailed in the idea that love not war was and is the proper subject for poetry, would be as effective, and limited, during a peace remote from war.

And yet, apart from these concerns, the poem has no theme except its lack of one; the love exists to supply and justify the poem in its preferred activity: love – not war – and poetry. 'Something to read in normal circumstances', that is, war or no war. In the last analysis the poetry has no other *serious* preoccupation than poetry. Is it presumptuous to inquire that if the poem chooses to turn its back on the prevailing human catastrophe of the war, what remains but poetry about the appropriateness of writing poetry?

Related to this is the tribal language Pound uses here, with such control, yet which is achieved through an act of ventriloquism, not of the voice of Propertius but of the educated and partly educated English upper class. Postmodernism? From *The Pisan Cantos* we know that Pound is capable of providing the fine instrument of sophisticated wit:

> ⟋ Fórd's conversation was bétter, . . .
> despite William's ánecdotes, in that Fórdie
> never dénted an idéa for a phrase's sake
>
> (82, p. 525)

This is writing of some thirty-five years later. The wit strikes in 'dented', where we are asked to feel the parallel between a physically wilful act and Yeats' rhetoric which, Pound records, had more regard for its *effect* than the *truth*, out of Ford's mouth. 'Dent' is wonderfully rich *and* unpresuming, the wit lying subservient to the virtue Pound is offering. The wit itself truthfully enacts its precept.

Whereas in section XII of the Propertius, when he is deploring the visit of his friend to his mistress's bed, he says

> I deprecate your attendance.

The humour is relaxed and amusing, its very pointedness arising from the discrepancy between the normal uses of 'attendance' and its present application. That is, the gap between the 'public' application of the word and its redeployment here for personal use. The difference between the neutral public presence and the unwanted personal one, causing, surely, a modicum of pain. It is a kind of reverse zeugma, though retaining its structure, and it is witty partly because it *implies* an unspecified pain. And finally, in its sophisticated understatement, 'attendance' standing for 'presence' and 'activity' – we all know the act for which the noun 'attendance' stands in.

We could read it as the perfect representation of a man seeking to shield his pain at his friend's act from that friend; yes, but for the fact that this sophisticated banter, and its metaphoric elaboration in persiflage, occurs throughout the poem. Though this recurrence does not detract from, or weaken, the finer touch of the wit here. Yet finally this recurrence tires readers, in its unflagging application of wit for its own sake, and contrasts with the later-told depthful anecdote concerning Yeats, and Pound's ascription 'dented'. Which contrast is one way of touching on the ventriloquism here, because, for all the poem's delicacy of language, the shielding of a class from direct abrasion, the application of that delicacy in its verbal wit *is* here unflagging. Ventriloquism is replication of a speech-style, a device; whereas language closer to natural speech would be the speech itself, speech therefore used with much greater awareness. One measure of Pound's development is the difference between the wit of the Propertius and that word 'dented'.

RHYTHM

The last set of comments on this poem concerns the route Pound chose, of rhythm, as against the 'image' which, as the governing agent, he had originally recommended (see chapter 2 above). 'Stultification' (Blackmur's word) is certainly inapplicable to the Propertius poems, which have both fluidity and contour. With F.S. Flint, Pound had formulated principles relating both to good writing in general and Imagism in particular. Under the heading of 'A Few Don'ts By An Imagiste' Pound had written 'An "Image" is that which presents an intellectual and emotional complex in an instant of time . . .'. I have already suggested in chapter 2 that the demands of the image as defined here presented Pound with a crux he could not resolve, because the nature of language would not permit it. Yet at the same time as he attempted to press his verse into this condition, the extension of which is his method of juxtaposition, he quietly went about developing his prosodic invention, of stepped lineation. I cited the line from 'The Return',

> With them the silver hounds,
>   sniffing the trace of air!
>   (*CSP*, 85)

where the two halves read as a broken continuity. In Δωρία (*CSP*, 80) he makes

> Have me in the stróng lóneliness
>   of súnless cliffs

where a more meaningful hesitation occurs between the two portions of the line. In terms of nuance, which in this line is a function of rhythm, the feeling would be different were the line continuous from 'Have' to 'cliffs' *and* laid out on one level. It is not only the insetting that won't let us merge the two. A clumsy rhythm would ensue rather than the present delicate articulated line in its doubleness. A second objection to making it unambiguously one line is that it is one syntax, broken in two by *enjambment*. And third, that this enjambment while enacting continuity also produces hesitation, making 'sunless cliffs' in the position it occupies more strongly interact with 'loneliness' than it would had the line been one. Equally, it is not two lines either because, first, the insetting insists on that; second, two lines would be rhythmically different; and third, 'of sunless cliffs' in a line on its own would stress the stoic implications of 'sunless' ('strong and silent') in such a way as to melodramatize the existing delicate balance between 'loneliness' and 'sunless'.

In all this we may notice that though the effect is transmuted in images, it is executed through rhythm. 'Loneliness' is half-transcribed into metaphor by 'sunless cliffs', just as that latter exists as an attribute of 'loneliness'. The executive of this reciprocal effect is rhythm working in stepped lineation.

I want to re-apply this understanding to the Propertius where the free verse is principally in two interacting modes. One is that of a long line with a fairly frequent spondaic ending. 'Ending', not 'cadence' which would imply a falling away, for the spondee does not fade, but, as it were, stamps its feet. The second mode is of course stepped lineation, interacting with syntax-rhythm, often to produce flow and interruption.

In section X after having been shoved along by the little priapic gods of love, Propertius finds himself at Cynthia's house,

> And it was morning, and I wanted to see if she was
>   alone and resting,
> And Cynthia was alone in her bed.
>   I was stupefied.
> I had never seen her looking so beautiful . . .
>   (*CSP*, 242)

He is surprised to find her bed bore 'No signs of a second incumbent'. The mind must travel a little distance to translate the implications of both 'second' and 'no', but once it has, the slight delay in the transmission of wit is not only worth the effort and delay but itself performs the kind of delay we experience, of his surprise and relief, in the stepped lineation above. The task is to convey meaning-impression almost as simultaneously as possible – 'an emotional and intellectual complex in an instant of time' – yet also to *enact* the mental processes of the speaker, Cynthia's lover. Thus 'alone' registers agreeable surprise, then relief, even gratitude. The second response is to her beauty, no doubt enhanced by his surprise and relief. But verse is not a photograph only, if at all, but an evaluation, perhaps an explaining of, experience. Pound is conveying not only 'Propertius's' reaction to Cynthia – 'I had never seen her looking so beautiful' – but also his, Pound's, evaluation of 'Propertius' (himself?) – 'I was stupefied'. All this may seem needlessly to complicate what we already feel, but I hope it is worth seeing how Pound's practice works. Theory is predicated on practice, and because there has been so little theory concerning free verse, in Britain at least, a shapeless retreat in the practice of free verse as well as from it has resulted.

Yet it is possible to analyse what Pound is doing, here, as it is to understand the workings of free verse in other poets. At any rate, to apply the same kind of understanding here to the divided line of stepped lineation:

> And Cynthia was alone in her bed.
>   I was stupefied.

If we run these as one line, we not only get the wrong kind of ambiguity by linking his stupefaction too closely to finding her 'alone'; we make the stupefaction too overwhelming, making it appear as naive inexperience, which is not part of his character. And in doing that, we would inject 'Propertius' with stupidity and, a step further, hint a character incapable of sensitivity and development. Whereas what I think Pound intends us to feel is a subtle separation and interfusion between delight at discovering her alone, and delight in her beauty; and a sophisticated yet quite overwhelmed response stemming from this interaction between the two.

The visualization of this double (stepped) line creates the right amount of rhythmical ambiguity, which is the equivalent of emotional hesitation and surprise, and it also ensures the necessary loose relationship between the half-lines. It is these things that enact the delicate meanings.

In a poem where banter, persiflage and a degree of ventriloquism overlay the emotional responses, we may again be prompted to ask what the poem is about. Too seldom perhaps do we have the (modest) coming together of meanings in that quiet 'My genius is no more than a girl', or the feeling of mortality but especially that of beauty's in 'There are enough women in hell . . . Death has his tooth in the lot.' Because of this life of intimacy, the delicate quiet emotion here is of great importance, not just because it meets the crucial needs, but also because in its enactment it indicates what kind of poet Pound is.

Unlike Eliot, Pound is, at his best, a delicate poet. Nevertheless the intimacy here is soon dispelled, and in a poem of almost 500 lines, the iteration of restraint, railery and polite ennui strains the reader. Even so, the poem's full effect is of rhythmic vitality and suppleness. It explores and develops stepped lineation, and elaborates the long line derived, almost certainly, from Whitman as much as from classical poets.

POUND AND MAUBERLEY

The profitable way to approach John Esprey's *Ezra Pound's Mauberley* (1955) is to take gratefully that hard work on the sources, and run, for he reads all kind of sexual reference into the verse. The 'red-beaked steeds of / The Cytheraean' are perhaps horses visualized as male organs, for Cytheraea is the island of Venus. Yet to read the

Mauberley poems (of 'life and contacts') as coded expressions of sex is to distort and limit poems already carrying limitations, notwithstanding the eulogistic weight they presently bear. If sex is what the Mauberley poems are about, Pound could, and on occasions did, express himself more plainly and as beautifully. Moreover, and this is the critic's failing, if, on close reading, the poems express the sexuality that he claims they do, how are we supposed to read them? Are they principally poems of sexuality, or are they helplessly permeated with a sexuality that neither poet nor reader is capable of making fully legible?

Pound and Eliot might, after all, be represented as sexual obsessives, purloining – ransacking culture to present sexuality in all its persistence and tyranny. 'Chained to a maniac' is how one man has described a lifetime's experience of his sexual drive. Good writing is often better than that.

I had at one time thought I might represent Eliot up to and including *The Waste Land* as a poet whose work is dominated by sex. That *The Waste Land*, for instance, was a poem about sexuality, thwarted by what our culture in its present state of taboos would licence. Certainly the hints Peter Ackroyd cautiously offers his readers concerning the fragments of the Bolovo drama (see chapter 2, above) go some way to supporting what may appear an extreme idea: that Eliot was thwarted from writing the sexual poem he wished to achieve, by the taboos of the culture he was serving.

Some dilemma concerning sex is also worth considering in relation to Pound, possibly a man with a frailer libido and more vulnerable emotional drive than his friend. For though the Mauberley poems cannot be transcribed into a simple reading of sexuality, achieved or denied, yet Esprey's indication of sexual presence implicated in various images is, after every criticism has been made, helpful, in as much as it additionally forces one's attention onto what the double-poem is not about.

Only contingently related to the question of the poem's sexuality is another preoccupation Esprey has with respect to the identity of the characters in the two Mauberleys:

the poems [he says] in the first section [are] dominated by Pound and the poems in the second section [are] dominated by Mauberley. . . .

(p. 76)

This conjecture is interesting, yet, to argue that, we need to know if the poems are autobiographical (or not) in order to suggest that the interpretation of them would be different if we could only identify who is 'who'.

Perhaps a more useful approach to the Mauberleys, as with the Propertius, is to consider Pound's use of other writers' ideas as a means of secreting his own feelings. In his translation of Remy de Gourmont's *Physique de l'amour* (1909) we find

> The emotions are equal before the aesthetic judgement. He does not grant the duality of body and soul, or at least suggests that this mediaeval duality is unsatisfactory; there is an interpenetration, an osmosis of body and soul, at least for hypothesis.
>
> 'My words are the unspoken words of my body'. . . .
>
> Sex, in so far as it is not a purely physiological reproductive mechanism, lies in the domain of aesthetics, the junction of tactile and magnetic senses; as some people have accurate ears both for rhythm and for pitch, and as some are tone deaf, some impervious to rhythmic subtlety and variety, so in this other field of the senses some desire the trivial, some the processional, the stately, the master-work.
>
> (*Esprey*, 68–9)

This passage, quoted by the thorough John Esprey, is valuable for an understanding of the condition of sexuality in the Mauberleys –

> The emotions are equal before the aesthetic judgement. . . . 'My words are the unspoken words of my body'. . . . Sex, in so far as it is not a purely physiological reproductive mechanism, lies in the domain of aesthetics, the junction of tactile and magnetic senses . . .

The syntax does not make clear if 'the junction of tactile and magnetic senses' is sex or aestheticism, or both, and from my point of view such ambiguity gives support to the idea I want to offer. Thus the preoccupation of the Mauberleys is not, as it is with Propertius, a debate of love as against martial exploits being the proper subject, but, instead, to do with the junction of tactile and magnetic senses instigating the true concern. Which is love *and* aesthetics. And as in the Propertius the denial of martial exploits (killing) as a theme for poetry was a moral act, so, in the Mauberleys, the purity of the aesthetic ideal, implicated with sex, is asserted against all other practices in poetry. Those other practices are in any case intrinsically corrupt, as with Mr Nixon and his manipulation of writing for wealth – 'In the cream gilded cabin of his steam yacht', or else the usefulness of poetry as social property, albeit of a lesser kind: Lady Valentine and 'Poetry, her border of ideas', like trimmings on the edge of her dress. If we remember that with Owen 'The Poetry is in the pity', for Pound in his Mauberleys the poetry here is in an intricate interfusion of sex with aesthetics. What follows is a working out of this, and it could be argued that the other questions of power and corruption that arise in the poems hinge on the retained purity of the aesthetic-sexual interconnection, where the one ensures the rightfulness of the other in a mutually fulfilling and purifying reciprocity.

But before looking at this, one more frame needs to be put in place.

Pound has presently displaced Eliot in scholarly and literary esteem. For though Pound is not popular in the sense, for instance, that Frost and Owen are, he is well considered in this narrower and in some senses self-interested band of readers. At any rate, his readers are not the 'common reader(s)' of Samuel Johnson ('Gray') 'uncorrupted with literary prejudices, after all the refinements of subtlety and the dogmatism of learning'. The purity of the aesthetics and the devotion to poetry impinge on, or are impinged upon by, the so-called pure language spoken by the middle-class tribe, of which the present writer is one member.

Thus unlike Eliot who, whatever his political persuasions, had always a broader-based language, Pound, whether out of social compliance, or because his upbringing in Idaho produced this, used an English with a more refined, even smoother code, except when he spilled over into racist obscenity (see below.) This 'refined' English is the coded language of middle- and upper-class diction. Diction is language restricted by the application of a particular sensibility, and results in what Wordsworth in his Preface to the 1802 edition of *Lyrical Ballads* objected to in Gray's sonnet.

Pound's diction in the Mauberleys can be checked, and may be identified in the caste-speech he devised, adopted, inherited – the antecedent causes probably cannot at this stage be distinguished; and I am suggesting that there may exist a coincidence between certain elements in the Mauberley speech (and to a lesser extent the

Propertius) and the interests of the class that has rated his Mauberley so highly, in Britain and America. Is it possible that the extremities of such praise arise partly from a fear lest one be thought out of step with one's caste and their way of speaking, and also from a desire to keep pre-eminent the diction of one's particular tribe?

Within this expression of my unease I would also indicate the inconsistency with which influential critics afford similar praise to *contrary* effects in Eliot and Pound. Thus in seeking to validate the question of Eliot's complexity and depth, Matthiessen, Kenner, Brooks and Gardner each point to Eliot's juxtaposition in *The Waste Land* of past and present as NOT being in contrast, but in some kind of complex extension the one of the other (see chapter 2, above). Each critic argues that Eliot does *not* present an idealized past in opposition to a degraded present. Whether Eliot does or does not perform this is another question. All I indicate is that these critics, different as they are in their approach to Eliot, nearly all concur in shoring up this particular wall of defence. Yet when critics praise the Mauberleys, and these are the poems of Pound's on the excellence of which there has been agreement for sixty years, no critic seems prepared to notice that what he praises in Eliot he or she chooses to ignore in Pound. That is, Pound *does* set out to praise the past culture, of *Greece*, at the same time using that touchstone as a means of denigrating the culture of the present and, in so doing, heap with contempt the theory and practice of democracy, which some would, not uncritically, regard as the cornerstone of our culture, its aggressions notwithstanding. Those who think Pound's fascism was an aberration occasioned by the Second World War should be prepared to enter this early 'critique' of democracy by Pound into their evaluation.

> All men, in law, are équals.
> Free of Pisistratus,
> We chóose a knáve or an éunuch
> To rule óver us.
>
> (*CSP*, 207)

Clearly, political knaves (though less often 'eunuchs') do, in democracy, sometimes rule over us; but the blatant unfairness in Pound's stanza operates within his application of the insouciant paradox. 'You claim that democracy ensures the rule of the best because you, the enfranchised electorate, have chosen such men (and women).'

Notice the tactics of educated *abuse* in the name-pun Pisistratus. 'I [Pound] suggest that in "choosing" such knaves as rulers you demonstrate the incapacity of the democratic system to turn up the best men as rulers as well as your incapacity to choose them. Indeed choice is what is wrong with your system.' It is the audacity of the paradox that has, perhaps, shut the mouths of critics – set as it is in the 'attic' elegance of the prose-like syntax. And disposed in metres forming a pattern of concise lineation.

With respect to the naive contrast between the supposed superiority of the 'attic' past and the degraded present, the concluding quatrain of section II from the Ode of Mauberley One will indicate this unequivocal opposition:

> The 'áge demánded' chíefly a móuld in pláster,
> Máde with no lóss of time,
> A próse kínema, nót, not assúredly, alabáster
> Or the 'scúlpture' of rhýme.

> (*CSP*, 206)

and in the next section (III), in case we have not yet accepted his judgement, he asserts (stanza 3) that our vulgarity will survive us.

If it is suggested that this is not 'really' Pound speaking, or even Mauberley, I reply that I can detect no gap between the speaker and the views repeatedly expressed (they occur elsewhere). And to set this perception more firmly in place I interpret the fate of the speaker, or his extended self in Mauberley, as something we are supposed to deplore if only because he alone in this gallery of fools (the 'stylist' excepted) keeps his aesthetics and thus his morals pure. This steadfastness is something the whole poem endorses. If 'the case presents / No adjunct to the Muses' diadem' this is because none has been so pure as Mauberley. (Flory sees these Mauberley poems as working in a mode of 'self-criticism'.)

Perhaps a momentary ironic shrug at the obstinate adherence of Pound/Mauberley to such pure values shows up, but that allowed, the reader is invited to deplore his death or else find ourselves aligned with the corrupt and the philistines – Brennbaum, the despised Jew who has abandoned a tradition hardly in any case, accorded much respect. Mr Nixon[1] (Arnold Bennett perhaps) who is

---

1. Bennett gave money (anonymously) to Lawrence. See *D.H. Lawrence* by Ronald P. Draper, p. 163.

the 'successful' novelist, and the society hostesses, Lady Valentine (Lady Ottoline Morrell perhaps) and Lady Jane. Surely such either/ or manoeuvres are designed to bully the middle-class scholars and intellectuals into subservience to a version of the position of the undistributed middle, where if you are not of one persuasion you must be of the other. Either you are a 'knave', or a Mauberley sympathizer. That this conduct has pressed such readers may be attested by how few if any have dissented from the either/or predicament, or suggested that there may be a morally and aesthetically honourable position which belongs to neither of the positions Pound has laid down. It is, for instance, perfectly decent to write the impure verse that Eliot did in *The Waste Land*, or the programmatic verse of Wilfred Owen's 'war' poems. It is also entirely honourable to do any of these things, and survive, and address society's ills in another style. The 'stylist's' position, inevitably entailing poverty, though to be sympathized with, is not the only one, heartless though it may be to say as much. In Rosenberg's case he had both a version of such 'impurity' and poverty.

As to survival itself, in the First World War Eliot attempted to enlist in the Services but his physical condition 'militated' against this. I have no information on Pound concerning his willingness to enlist or be conscripted, and there is no reason why he should have felt any such compunction. Yet we have the celebrated criticism of the war (and by implication all wars) in Mauberley One, sections IV and V, beginning with 'These fought in any case'. Both sections deplore the war with its 'wastage as never before' and offer moaning deploration in the second vowel of 'before'. But here we come up against a different perspective in as much as the culture in place seems not to justify the 'wastage', yet yields the contingent implication that there might be a culture that could justify such 'slaughter':

> For two gross of broken statues,
> For a few thousand battered books.
> (*CSP*, 208)

The 'two gross', like a merchandise item, depreciates the culture by substituting quantity for quality. Yes, it is sharp, but it is discouraging that the intellectual community of the Anglo-Saxon world should have accepted the cerebral depreciation of its culture (which?) in lieu of no felt reference to the death and the suffering. Thus it is not 'wastage', but 'wastage as never before'; as if it is not death we mourn but the amount of wastage, as if the whole business of perceiving the slaughter was itself a question of *competition* or merchandising. More death, larger death. Death as never before. There, I believe, we encounter Pound's perfect horrifying vulgarity. It is perhaps the audacity of the conclusion, 'statues/books', that has forced decent criticism into acquiescence, when in honesty it ought not to have stayed silent. For contrary to the ideas here expressed many thought that this culture was precisely what men fought for, however unwillingly, so as to preserve it (see especially Owen's 'Exposure', Silkin). And a comparison between the simplifying and extended anaphora of 'Some/Some from/Some from/Some from/Some for/Some in' and 'came home, home/home', with its Churchillian rhetoric, as against the complexity of Rosenberg's 'Daughters of War' and Owen's 'Strange Meeting', might suggest that Pound's is not only a different but lesser achievement, in certain respects inauthentic.

Moreover that 'wastage as never before' needs a marginal note:

Dear Mr Pound [Rosenberg wrote in 1915, the year of his enlistment] Thank you very much for sending my things to America. As to your suggestion about the army I think the world has been terribly damaged by certain poets (in fact any poet) being sacrificed in this stupid business. There is certainly a strong temptation to join when you are making no money.

(apparently unfinished letter to Ezra Pound, 1915, from his home, 87 Dempsey Street, Stepney E; *CW*, 214)

Thus on the one hand, Pound deplores the waste, yet this tactlessly surviving letter of Rosenberg's suggests that Pound may have advised Rosenberg to enlist. Between Pound's apparent advice and his 'wastage' exists a seemingly unbridgeable gap. Pound placed Rosenberg's 'Break of Day in the Trenches' and 'Marching' with Harriet Monroe who was the editor of *Poetry*, a magazine she had started in Chicago in 1912; but we also need to attend to his letter to get the full sense of what he felt he was about. The generosity has some alloy:

He has something in him, horribly rough but then 'Stepney, East.' . . . We ought to have a real burglar . . . ma che!!!

(Jean Moorcroft Wilson, in *Isaac Rosenberg/Poet and Painter*, 1975, p. 104)

In view of Pound's subsequent Italian 'connection' the resonance of that little phrase 'ma che' is disturbing. Pound endorsed Rosenberg's poems and apparently advised him in a course of action that put him (Pound) in a position comparable to a recruiting officer's. I am not making an *ad hominen* attack on Pound's verse, but am suggesting that the thinness of Pound's conduct, and of some of the views expressed in the verse, are consonant.

Given what I have suggested about the possible collusion between reader-critics, the present writer not excluded, whose roots, careers and livings are bedded in middle-class culture as they are in some of the diction of Mauberley; and at the same time bringing Pound's concern with purity forward, the achievement would be to distinguish and disengage this diction from the authentic purity. The task is probably impossible at the central gathering-place of the spectrum, and most readers would probably disagree on which element was which because of the finer shading of modes. But at the polar ends it might be possible to identify some of these. Even if readers still did not agree, such attempts might serve as the basis for finer discriminations.

The task is instructive in that this superior tone, syntax, style is a little more discernible on the wing, arising like a 'sussurus', to use Pound's word. It does not easily disclose itself under scrutiny. Even so the following is a selection of the more identifiable items. In the Ode prefacing Mauberley One

> trout for factitious bait

its tone 'emanates' – to use a word apt to the voice I am trying to describe – from the nature of the metaphor. On a certain level this is not a good example of the middle-class diction because the metaphor's *meaning* works so well. Capaneus was one of the seven against Thebes who was killed by Zeus for his impiety and presumption. 'Impiety' works well in the context of a poet striving to remain pure within the impure conduct of the age and society in which s/he lives; because although ironically it is presumptuous for the poet to remain pure in impure times, it is indeed 'impious' to offend against the truly false pieties of the age. All this works well, and the subtlety of the 'real' trout being supplied as artificial bait, appears to mean that the real poet is sacrificed not only for his purity but for some (impure) notion of poetry being valued by our culture. The real poet is the bait, and the impure culture survives. Capaneus was struck dead by Zeus's thunderbolt for declaring that not Jupiter himself should prevent him from scaling the city walls. Ambition, achievement and even purity of intention are all locked into the myth. Clearly, the 'Pound' or 'Mauberley' figure will not survive his Age.

Most of this is on the positive side, even if the 'equivalents' are hard to match up. My cavil, for I have almost talked myself out of my objection, is with the way the metaphor sequesters itself from readily available discourse. For even if the 'trout' is not taking the bait but is actually the bait, the invention is itself so rarefied, and appears to delight in its being so, that the final effect is of privileging literature for those few whose sensibilities are rare and refined enough to retrieve all the nuances. It is not the obscurity itself, but the sequestering superiority that I feel exists, which gives this reader pause. It is admittedly a long paragraph to make what may seem a small point, but there are others.

In the II (Mauberley One) there is

Nót, not cértainly, the óbscure réveries . . .

The repeated negative and so my slight objection to it arises from the tone. A repeated negative could not of itself be considered offensive. It is the calm assurance of the denial process which conveys more than anything the assurance of being right, and the certainty that brooks no challenge because it is sure it has the power and privilege with which to defend the speaker, which jars. Thus the tone, like a 'sussurus', arises from a large bulwark with an even greater fortification behind it. It is this that Pound makes use of. It is the power-principle inhering in these velvet-gloved phrases that is offensive.

In the same section we have:

A próse Kínema, nót, not assúredly, alabáster
Or the 'scúlpture' of rhýme.

(*CSP*, 206)

Most of us mightn't use 'assuredly', though we understand exactly its meaning. But in conjunction with the adjective 'prose' and the unusual slightly superior spelling for 'cinema' (Greek = culture) the effect is of belittling the culture for which this is a metaphor (not the cinema itself, we understand). Prose (cinema) here means both prosaic and utilitarian – possibly common, all of them in the poem's conspectus of positive values receiving here a negative sign in contrast with the solid and delicate 'alabaster'. To reinforce his point Pound places 'sculpture' in quotation marks, which makes the whole phrase seem more distinguished than it is.

In the next section (III) is

> The teá-róse tea-gówn, etć.
> Suppláñts the móusseline of Cós,
> The piánóla 'repláces'
> Sáppho's bárbitós.
>
> (*CSP*, 206)

'Supplants' means 'replaces' but with the added implication of something spurious or inferior, something in the nature of an impostor replacing the real thing, which, given that what is replaced is Greek silk, and precious, can hardly fail to be superior. (Tea, implying afternoon refreshment, 'the taking of the toast and tea', and chit-chat culture. At the back of this are the dames or donnas whose domain is culture, and who supervise the light-weight salons.) Clearly the pianola is an inferior instrument, as, again, how could it not be when set up against the poet Sappho (and the piano). The inverted commas, by a nifty piece of manoeuvring, echo 'replaces' back onto the preceding 'Supplants' so as to explain what supplants means. But, since the 'pianola' clearly cannot replace Sappho, this reinforces that what culture the tea-gown stands for cannot truly replace what the mousseline of Cos represents. All this is a quite shameless use of the noble past employed to denigrate the inferior present, but again the tone implies a confident sense that the speaker belongs with the favoured.

This, too, is a long note for a seemingly small point, but it is worth extending it to remind ourselves that just as Pound, one year later, told Eliot with reference to his 'Fresca' section in *The Waste Land* that he should remove it because this 'was' Pope, and he couldn't write better than him, so we may pick up on this. Pound's condemnation of his present age is imbued with a sense of superiority, and does not compare well with Pope's working a similar gallery in the concluding passage of *The Dunciad* beginning

> In vain, in vain – the all-composing Hour
> Resistless falls: the Muse obeys the Pow'r.

She comes! she comes! the sable Throne behold
Of *Night* primaeval and of *Chaos* old! . . .

The concluding passage establishes, for this reader, that Pope does
not impart a tone of superiority or discriminating fineness. No sense
of aristocratic selectivity adheres to the passage; instead Pope blends
depression and savage indignation in such a way as to express complete disinterestedness in his deploration of the state of things, in
a way that Pound does not. No attention is drawn to the person's
voice and identity (Pope's) within society, perhaps because Pope
may have felt more secure within it than Pound did in his context
– London.

In the same section (Pound's) other locutions of social affectation
occur: 'Faun's flesh is not to us' uses the preposition strangely, distancing the sexual identity/purity possibilities by avoiding the preposition 'for', and making the whole question of our flesh now seem
somehow distasteful. At any rate after all that Pound has abjured
us with respect to using the spoken language, this speech – if it is
speech – is of a restricted social register. The almost sighing register
of the inversion in the 'war' section IV in 'Died some, pro patria' is
what Pound might have called a poeticism, and the anaphora of
'some/some/some/some' achieves easily an effect of Churchillian
rhetoric – 'now that Winston's out' (*The Pisan Cantos*). 'Poetry must
be *as well written as prose*' (letter to Harriet Monroe, January 1915,
Selected Letters, 1907–41, p. 48). The effect of 'home/home/home' in
the next stanza has a hectoring politician-like quality. It gathers not
intensity, as in the structured, thinking repetition of Hebrew parallelism such as we read in the Psalms, but hostility. David, the King,
was here an infinitely better poet than Pound.

It might be objected that this despotic quality is precisely what
Pound wants to achieve; that he is forming a contrast out of what
a politician would not say, in the political cliché, syntax and language he would use. But I do not think so. No such ironic gap
appears to exist between the idea and the expressive mode.

If this seems over-critical, I should *like* to offer an instance of
where the self-conscious tone (for that is what superiority is, among
other things) – an instance of where it works to great (and grave)
advantage. Section X of Mauberley One, thought to be based on
Ford Madox Ford, 'Fordie' of *The Pisan Cantos*, draws a moving as
well as charming analogy between the man of the poem and the
vulnerable creature – as if he were the deer taking refuge –

> Beneath the sagging roof
> The stylist has taken shelter . . .
>
> (*CSP*, 212)

What a relief this is from what I have objected to. It is beautifully
tender, and belies the hardness of tone of much of this poem. Here
the gap between the word objectively uttered – 'sagging' – and the
speaker opens up to admit sympathy for the 'stylist', who is fugitive, and at a loss within his society as to know which way to turn
– as is the pursued hind. The tone reverts, with the 'placid and
uneducated mistress', as the woman receives the slight. It is delivered to restore 'perhaps' the hardness of tone required to continue that expression of contempt for the greater part of society,
which is the poem's burden. That too, here; for it is the combination of 'placid' with 'uneducated' that deprives the woman of her
worth. In the meanwhile the 'stylist' of pure talent shelters from
the society that has denied him more than a 'sagging roof' and an
'uneducated mistress', but the approval of which he would not wish
were it offered him. Yet once again the tone of defiance reverts to
tenderness and sympathy in

> He exercises his talents
> And the soil meets his distress.
>
> (*CSP*, 212)

This is the stuff of poetry, unparaphrasable, yet expressive *and*
communicating. For though we cannot readily say how 'the soil
meets his distress' (except in death), yet it is the very sympathy of
the earth with his condition, especially when human sympathy is
so evidently lacking, that moves one. 'Distress' is a word differently
used by different classes, but retaining a sufficiently broad base,
and written (uttered) with such evident sympathy as to cover the
spectrum from hunted hind to a 'gentle person in distress', which
means poverty. For poverty itself causes distress! So the two lines,
and this word in particular, ramify; and everything that is kind,
merciful and sensitive, to the person and to the language the poet
uses, issues from them.

We are now in the midst of the poems that comprise Mauberley
One, and some follow-through of the thought in them might be
helpful. Thus in noting that when Pound is sympathetic the wit
works to best advantage

> He offers succulent cooking;
> The door has a creaking latch . . .
> (*CSP*, 212)

we are reminded that poverty and excellence can and often do coexist in partial symbiosis, when nothing else assists the excellence or alleviates the poverty.

In the next section (XI), we are back with woman-slanging. Women are quite frequently the victims of Pound's 'wit' and the means to his self-elevation. They constitute another race, and suffer one unique form of his racism.

The dictionary glosses 'Milesian' as 'early Celtic people of Ireland said to have come from Spain'. A 'milesian tale' is of 'a class of short salacious tales current in Greek and Roman antiquity'. The word also refers to one 'belonging to the ancient city of Miletus . . . belonging or relating to a Milesian school of nature philosophers of the 6th century BC who were mainly concerned with the basal stuff of which the world is made'. Which should we choose? Aware of Pound's habits of 'thought' concerning race one might be tempted to suppose the reference is to the Irish, but Pound's superiority often, as in this poem, works by contrast; so that the Greek philosophy and its preoccupation with 'basal' and a possible dash of the 'salacious tales' seems more likely. The sad contempt is evident for the woman who lives in the petit bourgeois and middle-class area of London, in Ealing. Not unexpectedly, she lives with a bank-clerkly type of Englishman – the character rather than the profession being the allusion. And she has betrayed tradition, whatever it be, through the simple device of forgetting it. That little phrase of 'her station' is spoken as though, with all its resonances, Pound were at the top of the social scale. It is invariably directed by such upon those others who are required to 'know their place' and keep to it with a minimum of disruption.

In the last section before the concluding 'Envoi' we see that the women, like those in 'Prufrock', are the unworthy custodians of culture; thus the Lady Valentine (possibly Lady Ottoline Morrell) whose country-house gatherings Pound may have attended. (For another largely negative glimpse of Lady Ottoline Morrell consult Sassoon's *The Complete Memoirs of George Sherston* (pp. 464–7).) Thus with Pound the inevitable reduction of her takes place, while the poet of pure aesthetics probably consumes the substance and hospitality. At the same time he decries what is clearly considered to be uncultured, debased or owned culture, as in 'Poetry, her border of ideas'. Culture as social property. Evidently there are women (and men) of this sort, even if this is probably unfair on Lady Ottoline Morrell; though clearly culture possessed, or as it were, dispossessed, is a culture degraded. The other point to notice is that where, in Mauberley One, 'His true Penelope was Flaubert' occurs in one line, as if it were an assertion of some discovery concerning himself, the quotation marks round its second appearance, in Mauberley Two, mark a deliberate application of this discovery and formulation. Mauberley resuming Pound, or vice versa, it hardly seems to matter. The principal thing is the use of the pithy utterance for the purposes of aesthetics and purity. One further point to note in the lineation of Mauberley Two is that it is here more stringent, which perhaps suggests that the stringency is not merely aesthetic but the result of life pressing harder upon him. For though in Mauberley One his death and oblivion, more or less, are prefigured in 'He passed from men's memory', in Mauberley Two he dies after marooning himself, in his imagination, on the tropical island of the 'Scattered Moluccas' (Malay Spice Islands, therefore fragrance experienced in the imagination).

> Thén on an óar
> Réad this:
>
> 'I wás
> And I no móre exist;
> Hére drifted
> An hédonist.'
> (*CSP*, 221)

That is spareness indeed, where the double or even single stress of the line has 'almost ceased to pulse'. It is both nervous and almost extinct. And it is a species of self-mockery, with the tiny pedantic 'An' crossing the 't', as it were, before extinction.

The most difficult thing to read is the relation between the aesthetic and the sexual, yet since I have set myself to account for this I suggest the following. The poet's 'final/Exclusion from the world of letters' is *qua* poem the product of his uncompromising purity. We can read a movement beginning in sexuality and aesthetic purity and terminating in his exclusion and death. Whether this tendency implies that sexuality entails extinction, which is unlikely; or whether the true demands of sexuality entail a purity that in turn expresses an aesthetics unassailable but also unacceptable to the world, is not clear. But somesuch process, almost a progression, is visible. In section II he wishes time

> to designate
> His new found orchid . . .

where flower often stands for sexuality (his?) (his with hers?). Two stanzas further on, the failed task was

> To sift TO AGATHON from the chaff

so as to obtain the true and 'durable'. But then 'he found his sieve', that is, both his true preoccupation and his means of riddling the valuable from the unworthy, finding very little. The right act consisted in urging into language the exquisite visual and pure relation between parts of the face (*CSP*, 217).

It is probably right to censure this patronage of culture, though any sensible writer would either know how to use such 'patronage' (in both senses of the word) or, the more preferable conduct, stay away. Yet the objection to Pound's strictures remains. As with Eliot's stereotypical creation of the property-owning Jew in 'Gerontion' (see chapter 2, above) one suspects that Pound is manipulating an image to yield an effect. Lady Valentine (like the stereotyped Jew) has no option but to fulfil the 'racial' cliché.

This puts the reader in a bind for the writing is clear and delicate even though an element of the sentiments is coarse. But if we ignore the arrogance and inhumanity, and accept the proposition of the writer's representing in the poem a purity of action (the poetry s/he writes), the attack is on the values of Lady Valentine and Lady Jane, who dishonour culture because of their fundamental disrespect for it and failure to understand its value. Then we can grant the validity of the poet's criticism, and the purity of the writing that impugns these 'society' women.

It is at this point that the poem becomes complicated, as it invariably does when sexuality becomes part of the equation, albeit a failed sexuality. The poet's failure to achieve worldly success, and even success in terms of these powerful women who value poetry, that is to say who do not value poetry except as their 'border of ideas', is all part of his failure in sexual terms:

> To stimulate, in her,
> A durable passion...
> (*CSP*, 213)

It is not clear if he wants to stimulate any passion or strong feeling in her, but it is also clear that he does not reject the possibility of his desire (Ottoline Morrell had a husband). The situation is equivocal. He might desire her, but not her approbation because he despises her capacity to truly appreciate his (pure) work. She does not seem to have 'A durable passion' for him, perhaps because he is unsuccessful in respect of the worldly terms suggested above. Yet one could not say that sex is absent from the arrangements, such as they are, just as one would not say that it is actively present. It, too, is part of the 'border of her ideas' (I adapt the quotation) just as by implication it is also part of his. The honey-pot exists, and in the meanwhile sex has become a commodity, part of the transaction of esteem, self-esteem and success. How much of all this the poem registers is not clear but, I believe, most of it is there. In this complex, aesthetic-and-sexual purity is in a dubious condition, askew partly through an alignment with his failure, and, as I suggest, desired, if desired at all, as something separate from the woman's literary approbation of his work:

> The tea-rose tea-gown, etc.
> Supplants the mousseline of Cos.

Again it needs to be said that the verb 'Supplants' implies not only a replacing of, but also of an overthrowing and a succeeding, in exact proportion as it is unworthy to achieve this. Supplants implies not only imposition but also impostor. Fake. Pretender. Clearly Lady Valentine's values are with the rosy 'tea-gown' and in contrast to 'the mousseline of Cos'. (Mousseline is fine sheer clothing, often of silk.) And to recur to the foundations of the poem, the past is the repository of values of which the present is its betrayer (Ford is an exception to this and presumably the Pound/Mauberley figure is also.)

Vulgarity in the form of ordinary life is also deplored; in the Fleet Street where Dr Johnson 'grew', selling socks has

> Long since superseded the cultivation
> Of Pierian roses.
> (*CSP*, 214)

(Pierian is to do with learning, or poetry.) Here is a beautifully executed instance of Pound's intransigence, for there is no reason why the ordinary, represented by 'half-hose', should not coexist with 'Pierian roses'. If it is objected that this is symbolic in its application, one might still question why 'half-hose' is so unworthy. Or will only the 'mousseline of Cos' do? The objective part of the symbol vitiates the validity of the symbolic part.

In Mauberley Two we experience a tightening of the mode of Mauberley One, with an in general more stringent application of the expressiveness, which is reflected in a tendency to shorter lines. With Mauberley One we are advised of aesthetic purity in

His trúe Penélope wás Flaubért

Flaubert representing the devotion to concision of form and expression in relation to the substance of the work. In Mauberley Two he outdoes his discovery by making the original line now actively reflect this stringency, in its revised form:

'His trúe Penélope
Wás Flaubért,'

Is the tautology of 'true' meaningful? Penelope was faithful and true; that is her historical and mythologic meaning. Here the tautology is active in as much as it means not only true and faithful but real. The tautology reflects the *active* pursuit of the ideal.

Two differences may be noted in the reapplication (Mauberley Two) of the original line (Mauberley One). First, the lineation, which not only stresses 'true' in the rhythmic formation of the two lines, but now emphasizes the internal half-rhyme of 'true' and 'Flaubert', which is of course part of the essential meaning. But by dividing the syntax and shortening the movement in each of the two lines, we obtain a sharpness that conduces to, confirms and approves, the 'engraver's' art. This is the style and the aspiration; the profile-art which creates firmness yet avoids confrontation of subject, and blur. The limitation creates the 'virtù', although the virtue instigates its limitation.

We read here a frank and almost humanized version of Imagism; the visualized idea subserves the spareness which reciprocates its support, of the idea. Also, this idea supports the whole poem where value, spareness, authenticity are part of each other's natures. And in turn these are part of the aesthetic purity where 'strait', for instance, in the first stanza of 'Mauberley (1920)', means not only straight but, even more, strict (narrow). 'His tool', some readers suggest, has sexual connations. It may have, but in what respect we are to apply this beyond the slang word for penis the poem does not make clear.

Emphasizing the commitment to aesthetic and sexual purity, the rhythm is beautifully firm, right-paced and various. Rhythm here is a complex term, for whereas the first and third lines above are stress-lines, receiving metricality of an accentual character from the emphases, the middle line, by virtue of the two delicately placed hyphens that both join and separate 'eye-lid' and 'cheek-bone', formalizes the line by duration: the four syllables are isometric and have length rather than stress. Or so this reader hears it. The effect is to emphasize the delicate physical relationship perceived between parts of the body and thus allude to the sexual element. (See also with respect to 'eye-lid' Yeats's later 'News from the Delphic Oracle', stanza 3.) 'Manifestations' means to make evident, but to make evident in a mode in which aesthetic and sexual purity interact in reciprocal confirmation and reinforcement.

Yet ominously in the same stanza, this sexuality is set, hardened, 'in medallion'. I say sexuality, because in current usage is implied the whole female energy rather than the idea of sex available to men (and women). And this is what is presented here, 'in medallion'.

The 'Medallion' poem itself creates an image of the head comparable with the living insect set in coagulant amber. The sexuality, the life, is 'medallioned', valuable as a commemoration, but dead.

> For this agility chance found
> Him of all men, unfit
> As the red-beaked steeds of
> The Cytheraean for a chain bit.
> (*CSP*, 218)

The Cytheraean red-beaked steeds express sexual passion perhaps, but this 'as' instigates comparison. Thus just as the sexual steeds are not fitted for the restraint of the 'bit', so the poet is unfitted for the debased age with its consequent demands. Conform or die. Conform and die. Thus the dilemma, for the sensitive. No choice: hence death. For though the delicacy of 'The glow of porcelain' cannot be destroyed, his re-creation of it in verse is the last thing society wants of him. It ' "demanded" chiefly a mould in plaster' (Mauberley One, II). Yet

> Thús, if her cólour
> Cáme agáinst his gáze,
> Témpered as if
> It were thróugh a pérféct gláze . . .
> (*CSP*, 219)

Such is his attentuation through the unresponded-to, or even rejected, purity of his creation that, finally, he cannot respond to *her* delicacy, her porcelain, *and* cannot redeem his societal irrelevance. For in the social rejection of his aesthetic purity and delicacy lies the attentuation of his sexuality, leading to extinction. Thus, ironically, what causes this attentuation, a devotion to purity, ultimately renders him incapable of the sexuality that is a partner to it.

In a final twist the poet re-creates the woman in a medallion, out of his 'atrophied' desire for her. She (and his desires) are medallioned as a result of his insisted-on purity. The final ironic if uncommunicated act of love medallions the lover's feeling and beloved in the aesthetic purity of an artefact.

> Luíni in pórcelain!

The persistent image of delicate artefact is also a human being 'soprano', typically, living in art (music). I am indebted to Esprey for his indication that 'the gold-yellow frock' swathing the woman's body is a marriage-colour, and this information decodes the irony in which she who is presented is also, because of who and what he is, unobtainable. She is being removed and purified by art. 'Honey-red, closing the face-oval' is art, not a face but an object. The poet is probably aware of this final 'sexual' act, in isolation and self-purity. Sexuality is transformed into aesthetic re-creation.

It remains to say something about the metrical character of the two Mauberleys.

The most obvious difference between the *Propertius*, *The Cantos* and the Mauberleys is that of stanzas. This is immediately visible, but no less important for that obviousness. *The Cantos*, despite the root meaning of 'song', are not typically lyrical, though of course there are many lyrical passages that stand out from their context by their contrasting nature. The *Propertius* however is a spoken gracefulness. It would be what song would be if – I am aware of the difficulty of what I am attempting – song were spoken. That is, the Propertius poems are spoken lyrics, even when they are *discussing* the habitual subjects of love and what the fit subject for poetry is 'today'. The Mauberleys, with the significant exception of Section IV (Mauberley One), which is in strophe-paragraphs, are in stanzas. Section IV stands out from the rest of the poem as not only not being in regular stanzas but also in being in free verse *and* being unlyrical, the rhetorical device of the anaphora notwithstanding. Its rhetoric simulates argument, subdued to indignation and deploration.

The dominant impression of the poem connects with what Eliot wrote of Marvell's poetry: 'wit, a tough reasonableness beneath the slight lyric grace' (*Selected Essays*, 293). It does not fit entirely because the grace is more assertive than Marvell's; Pound's ideas are both less imaginative and more aggressive. The metaphors, such as

> We háve the préss for wáfer;
> Fránchise for circumcision

lurk on the illustrative side of comparison, like those in Bacon's *Advancement of Learning*. They are, in that sense, 'a prose Kinema'.

In comparing the *Propertius* with the Mauberleys we discover opposite processes. In the former the song tends to be prosed; in the Mauberleys the prose inches towards song despite the prose character of a number of the metaphors, as I have described this above. This 'song' character is created by the form in which it is made. Stanzas are lyric, and the fascination of the Mauberleys, for this reader, is to do with the diamorphic nature of the poetry, which is energy in both speech and song fluctuating between the two and defying any attempt to classify it permanently in one of these. The element that prevents the setting process is the imaginative part of the wit; and the character of the verse is fluid, partly because of this. The wit is the unsettling agent. It helps to stay the poem from simple characterization and single identity.

The syntax is simple and direct, even when it offers affectation – 'Not, at any rate, an Attic grace;/Not, not, certainly' – though affectation is far too strong to impugn what is going on here.

Many of the stanzas are quatrains, and in them lurks a partial simulation of the literary ballad. In that sense they are sired by Wordsworth's Lucy poems, though very different from them. If the foundation for both, as it is for Coleridge's *The Ancient Mariner*, is folk ballad, Wordsworth and Pound have radically altered the character though not the sophistication of the original. And that is their outstanding feature. They are not folk poems but literary stanzas. Most of Pound's lines vary, and hesitate, between three and four pulses. Sometimes five, and more frequently than this latter, two. Even one. The number of syllables clustering these pulses varies, so that sometimes we have sprung verse, where there are no weaker syllables. Though sometimes weaker syllables stand in place of stresses. The metricality – it is (mostly) metrical verse – is elusive in its pulsing and immensely supple in its firm engraved delicacy. The most conversational aspect of this 'song' is not so much in the language but that hovering metricality just referred to, which is the way our speech behaves, pulsing and various. (See also Ken Smith, chapter 7.)

Thus consider the quatrain that concludes the Mauberleys (*CSP*, 222). The last lines of many of these quatrains sometimes differ metrically and rhythmically from those preceding them in the stanza. One notices that as the lines contract, the rhyme becomes more pronounced. This effect due to contraction seems to be inevitable, but is probably calculated.

FASCIST ART AND (POETIC) ORDER

The question of structure, or its lack of it, is crucial in relation to our reading *The Cantos*, and Flory offers Pound's own gloomy assessment:

> His readiness to deny value to the whole poem when he realized that he could not conclude it to his satisfaction suggests that he may consider his ideogrammic method a kind of 'poetic licence' which is only allowable on the condition of a final, unequivocal assertion of significant order.

And then, offering her own (auto)biographical approach as the one likely to adduce the poem's shape and unity:

He cannot see, as the reader can, that as a 'record of struggle' his poem has a unity which is in no way compromised by his failure to arrive at the kind of conclusion which he has hoped for.

(*Ezra Pound and The Cantos: A Record of Struggle*, Flory, 285)

(Pound's comment to Daniel Cory in conversation, quoted in Stock's *Life*, pp. 457–8.) Yet the failure to conclude a very long poem may not be because the poem obtains no satisfactory terminus. It may indicate a want of structural coherence. In that case terminating would simply be the point at which transit had ceased. Flory compares *The Cantos* with *The Prelude*; yet as a 'record of struggle' this depends more on the reader's bringing Pound's life into the poem rather than the life being evident and intrinsic to it.

Seeds of such an objection are in fact offered by Flory herself when she comments:

In the meantime he hypothesized, from a distance, an ideal of 'Totalitarian art' which would be characterized by inevitability and perfect equilibrium and would show no trace of struggle. In *Guide to Kulchur* he describes the performance of a Boccherini piece as 'utterly beautiful' because 'no trace of effort remained', and contrasts this to Bartok's Fifth Quartet, to much of Beethoven, and to his own *Cantos*, which all contain defects because they are 'record(s) of a personal struggle' (*Guide to Kulchur*, p. 135). He prizes most highly moments of perfect repose and equilibrium at the center of the vortex of the whirl of 'facts'.

(Flory, 50)

There are insights to be obtained in that area Flory is reluctant to explore: Pound's conception of 'totalitarian' art, in which a sense of struggle has been removed, rather in the way in which totalitarian regimes themselves destroy opposition. In both the art and the political regime the world is seen as crystalline. And indeed much of Pound's paradisal imagery is predicated on the crystalline from which, yes, any sense of struggle has, by definition, been 'refined' out. It is not that the poet may not have had to struggle to refine, and produce 'hypostasis' (essence or foundation), another of Pound's recurring words. But by the time this one paradisal aspect of the poetry has reached the reader, no sense of struggle or contradiction is visible. Pound's alternative provision to this paradisal imagery seems to be the undigested history of, for instance, the Malatesta in Cantos 8–11, where the information is chopped into lineation. It is as though the imaginative energy has been unable to synthesize the history and its 'lessons'. If we attend to the implications of this failure to assimilate this history into art, we may sense that as we engage *The Cantos' total* vision that it is in some senses schizophrenic, both refined of conflict, full of conflict and of this unassimilated matter. As late as Canto 91 we find the anti-Semitic outburst:

> *and, in this, their kikery functioned, Marx, Freud*
> *and the American beaneries*
> (91, 614)

The unassimilated information is rhythmicized into the outward manifestation of verse, but isn't verse any more than those metrical and agricultural treatises are which used verse as a medium for conveying information.

Or is that so? Perhaps one of Pound's inadvertent substantial achievements is to have enlarged the frontiers and territory with respect to what verse can do, with what material it should be concerned, and not only turn it into verse but be turned into verse by it. Surely this is the very crux of the dilemma not only for a reading of Pound, but for the creation of verse now. It is that the means we have available for making verse are imaginatively predicated on not including some of the most important human experiences and understandings. At any rate some of Pound's best seems not to be a poetry that bears the marks of struggle within itself. And Flory's allegiances lie, it seems, with the paradisal poetry, where the struggle has been refined away – except in such crucial passages as the essay on vanity (81, 520–1), which in any case we value not only because of its formalized poetic declaration on the immemorial theme of humility (see below), but because it appears to bear the marks of what Pound contended in himself – arrogance and aggression. It is moving because while it hasn't evacuated a sense of struggle, it also provides some of this crystalline purity with which Pound's vision of poetry is nourished.

This latter aspect of the poetry is to do with love and of course visionary insight. It intersects our life under those normal circumstances alluded to in the Propertius with our experience of earthly paradise, incarnated in Pound's gods and goddesses, but the struggle has been taken away. The poetry has been conceived in a condition in which an evacuation of struggle was of the essence and precondition of its inception. So, this corresponds to Pound's desire for a Boccherini-like tranquility. It is a problem.

The significance of these contrasting opposed modes, of the life of customary difficulty and struggle, and of the crystalline, is that their existence as parameters helps to explain why, *pace* Flory, no overall structure, or integrated 'record of struggle', exists in *The Cantos*. And in terms of dislocation and discontinuity, which is perhaps a function of there being no overall structure, the modes, operated on a basis of mutual exclusivity, prohibit structure. There needs greater digestion into an overall scheme, rather than a furious indictment of usury, or the piecemeal incorporation of historical material, say, without its being rendered from its historical state into a poetic condition.

Related to this is the obsession with the Jews, which is, I fear, Pound's problem and ours. And by ours I mean that it is a murderous problem for the Jews, of whom this writer is one, and a moral problem for those who are not. For both, it is a question of the anti-Semitism not being susceptible to being refined into the paradisal, by Pound, and of us (readers) being unable to digest such obsessive ineradicable hatred into some beautifully overall biography, of which this would be an 'unfortunate' digression.

This perspective may help to unfold the dilemma in which we as readers find ourselves with respect to the opening of the first *Pisan Canto*, where the reader experiences a sense of crystalline beauty, with no sense of grittiness or texture in the verse, or in the ideas it postulates:

> To build the city of Dioce whose terraces are the colour of
> stars . . .
>
> (74, 425)

The experience is like looking at a beautiful or intriguing organism under a microscope to discover that the forms are a lethal bacillus.[1]

Thus the reader is placed in a most extreme situation, where s/he may, perhaps, not honestly dissent from the beauty of the verse, here and whenever the referent is the fascist state, yet feels

---

1.   For instance, in her anthology *Against Forgetting/Twentieth Century Poetry of Witness* (1993), the editor, Carolyn Forché, seems unaware that by including the first 175 lines of the first *Pisan Canto* she is including a Fascist declaration. That is indeed bearing witness.

profoundly unhappy on discovering with what the verse is attempting to affiliate the mind of the reader. One observation is that the sense of struggle has been evacuated; we perceive the crystalline order of enforced oneness, but do not see directly the imposed structure of the fascist state. Nor is there an indication of what has gone into or what continues to be fed into the making and continuance of such a political organism. From those 'terraces . . . the colour of stars' one could not guess, for instance, that in 1926 Mussolini suppressed all opposition, or what those antecedents of the state were which Hemingway describes so graphically in chapter thirty of his *A Farewell to Arms* (1929). Or, in case it may seem that I am dealing in some biased way with the formation of the state and not its practice, one would not gather from these 'terraces' 'the colour of stars' that Mussolini's Italian conquest of Ethiopia (1935–36) involved the state's use of poison gas on a defenceless civilian population. If we accept Flory's assertion that Pound was against war, how square this with his continuing support of a regime that acted thus, and continued its aggression in 1939 by its invasion of Albania? I had not intended a litany of such acts, but only to question Flory's assertion that Pound was against war.

The case for beauty, where struggle has been eliminated, is unanalysable unless either one scrutinizes its political application or asks whether this kind of beauty may in some ways be defective. It is hard to do the latter, first, because the accomplishment of the verse is of a high order, but second, because its achievement wires into something to which many are susceptible – the condition of paradise and its concomitant beauty. One might even ask if Pound's hatred of Jews, and apparent distaste for Judaism, isn't to do with some cultural challenge it presents to his love of the lucid and pure paradise. Though in fact there is room for coexistence. Indeed the two cultures are necessary for their ongoing cross-questioning of each other's premisses and creations.

To recapitulate the crux. The version of paradisal culture which, unlike Dante, has digested away the elements of which it is composed, or were antecedent to it, or in which any sense of struggle and conflict has been anaesthetised, constitutes one aspect of the poetry of *The Cantos*, for which Pound strove. Another component in this crux is the historical and political, where Pound endeavours to present the model and instance of what he considers right government and social conduct (Confucius, Mencius, and more doubtfully, the Renaissance Italian figure of Sigismundo Malatesta). The material of this latter (Cantos 8–11) is not so much offered, or even presented, but chopped into approximate lineage. The often quoted 'Siggy, darlint, wd. you not stop making war on insensible objects, such as trees and domestic vines, that have no means to hit back . . .' (10/42) is not simply a relief, because of its humour, but inadvertently, because that humour seems to expose the bombast of his (self) hero who, one imagines, is indiscriminately blazing away at everything, including the defenceless flora. Is this a case of the unconscious in Pound getting a temporary and welcome upper-hand?

It has taken some twenty-six years for the contrasts between Eliot's *WL* virtually finished 1921 and *The Pisan Cantos*, finished in 1946 (published 1948) to emerge fully. This comparison could be offered in a four-part figure whereby Pound, in the earlier part of his writing life, seems surer of his critical judgements than of his poetry, whereas Eliot emerges (with Pound's help) surer in the drive of his verse than Pound, yet at the same time less assertive in his criticism than Pound.

Eliot's poetry moves with greater confidence, and, eventually, with greater and more willed authority, than Pound's with his finely filamented lyrical modesty. It is a surprising outcome, for the combative, no less racist, Pound, to be producing a more supple poetry. And though it might be argued that Pound's suffering in his cage in Pisa, in the DTC, induced the character of PC's, it should be added that he could not have made this poetry (which is no act to divert himself from his suffering) unless the components were alive in him.

For though the work is constantly interrupted by spasms of racism, fiduciary obsession, not to mention outbursts of coded support for fascism, it also offers a lyrical delicacy which constitutes the best writing in the (Pisan) Cantos.

Of course, the negative argument is that what holds *The Cantos* together is Pound's obsession with fiduciary matters, in particular, with usury. And further, that the anecdotes and the re-creation of various witty exchanges and judgments acquire, in their profile and compaction, the quality of a trope. Yet when we read and enjoy substantial passages in the PCs, what holds each of these together arrives through the rhythm, whether in metrical or free verse. Pound makes quite frequent use of a four-pulse line, tending to make the syntax coincide with the end of the line, yet not complete itself in a sentence – for many lines (and then not registered by a full-stop).

It is this line-by-line completion within the syntactical flow that gives
a sense of upright steadiness and reassures the reader; and enables
in him/her the confidence to continue. And thus, this assurance
that he (Pound) will continue his adherence to the fascist state even
though it now exists in the mind only:

> I surrénder neither the émpire nor the témples
>
>   plúral
> nor the constitution nor yét the cíty of Dióce
>   (74, 434)

Both lines could be read either as four- or five-pulse (and the first
of them as six-beat) but the completeness of syntax line by line
within the continuing sentence is plain. And again, a few lines later:

> till the shrine be again white with marble
> till the stone eyes look again seaward
>   The wind is part of the process
>   The rain is part of the process
>   (74, 435)

where here the first of these lines is ambiguously four-pulse, though
it could be read as three-pulse; but where the next three lines are
unambiguously three-pulse.

So a consideration of rhythm, whether four-pulse with caesura,
three-pulse, or five-beat, sometimes in pentameter (iambic), and
sometimes in lines in stepped formation, – any consideration of
rhythm involves more than a counting of stresses. It necessitates
a feeling, and a being able to recognize the movement of the lines
in relation to the flow of the syntax, and the line-unit, and thus
the lineated portion of the syntax within the sentence-flow. This
needs a little effort, though once one has done that, it becomes a
natural part of one's reading and response.

That the description, so far as it goes, offers a means to reading,
doesn't modify my sense that such is the easier aspect to describe.
For what underpins the rhythms and often informs them is a two-
fold quality. First, though it sounds strangely old-fashioned to as-
cribe it to a modernist, there is the lyricism and the response to
nature. Second, and this indirectly relates to the first, is a sophisticated and thus sometimes witty stoicism, not properly present
before these Cantos, though perhaps implied in the Mauberleys.

What underlies, and perhaps underpins, the lyricism and his gratitude to nature, is – I was about to repeat, somewhat unthinkingly, what has been said before concerning the man of *The Pisan Cantos* – humility. But can this properly be said of a man who wrote:

> As a lone ant from a broken ant-hill
> from the wreckage of Europe, ego scriptor . . .
> (76, 458)

Yet if these generalizations are of value as serving to undertone an overall sense of this part of the whole of *The Cantos*, then maybe the word is 'acceptance', without rancour, and with defiance. Though sometimes with a waspishness reserved for the side he remained opposed to:

> Pétain defénded Verdún while Blúm
> was defénding a bidet
> (80, 494)

And to continue this tack, for the moment, there does not appear, whatever suffering is present in his work, to be any awareness of the sufferings of others, in the camps, to which he indirectly contributed. These inmates, at least, were provided with neither table, typewriter nor paper, nor is it conceivable that they would have been. Yet Pound had access to these, his suffering notwithstanding:

> Nor can who has passed a month in the death cells
> believe in capital punishment
> (83, 530)

Some critics argue as though Pound's suffering cancelled his offences, but neither back nor forward within the equation is justified. Suffering remains what it is, as offence does. One difference however is that while Pound paid for his treason, though not, I think, for his inhumanity and his racism, if punishment be a form of payment, Eliot did not. Like Pound, there is no tincture in Eliot's war or post-war verse that indicates either his remorse at his racism or, more importantly, his awareness of what was sustained in the camps of Europe. The only possible reference with respect to remorse occurs in 'Little Gidding':

And last, the rending pain of re-enactment
    Of all that you have done, and been; the shame
    Of motives late revealed, and the awareness
Of things ill done and done to others' harm
    Which once you took for exercise of virtue . . .

(CP, 218)

FEELING AND RHYTHM

I have suggested that when Pound's feelings put his verse-making under pressure, like Whitman, the verse tends towards, and in Pound's case may become, metrical. Under pressure, the verse resumes rhythmic congruity and patterning. It is also noticeable, in the Usura Canto (45), that the free verse there uses the Biblical device of repetition and parallelism, sometimes in the form of anaphora; so that through this rhetorical pattern the free verse achieves its own equivalent of metricality.

If for some, these devices give the PCs unity and sequential wholeness, in my repeated readings, which produce increased appreciation, such is nevertheless not the case. They do not constitute a whole, in sum, or Canto by Canto, though by virtue of their acceptance, and their tranches of modesty, and even in places, their tenderness, they are recognizably different from many of the other Cantos. The focus is more personal, even when, in the earlier Canto 47, he presents a beautifully open sexual apprehension. Here, too, the mythic universalizing intention seems to be uppermost:

The líght has éntered the cáve. Ío! Ío!
The líght has góne dówn into the cáve,
Spléndour on spléndour!
By próng have I éntered these h̄īlls:
That the gráss grów from my bódy,
That I héar the roots spéaking togéther . . .

(47, 238)

Still, one notices here the *knowledge* of sex impels the movement into swaying patterned procedures where continuity is countered by each line-unit containing a completed portion of syntax (see Lawrence, chapter 4, below).

I have touched on the modes of lyricism and sophisticated

stoicism in the PCs, which may be seen in contrast to the almost unrelieved persiflage that might finally weary some readers of the *Propertius*. Still, nothing had really prepared the reader for this change. It is hard to measure value for value; between the witty banter of the Propertius episodes, and the inward wit, in the eighteenth-century sense of *wit*, where by a stroke of the imagination the preoccupation of the characters in the Propertius becomes that of the poems themselves; between these two, and the wit of the anecdotes and memories, in particular that one concerning Yeats and Ford Madox Ford (in 82, 525). Which contains a judgement *respecting* truth. This relates to the contrast between the concision of imagery and the uncompromising value put upon high art in the Mauberleys, and the concern with life (including his own) in the more embodied responses of lyricism, stoicism and acceptance, which underpin the PCs.

These are gains; but if we take Propertius and Mauberley as representing two different kinds of accessibility, both related to the world of *res*, of the world 'out there', the PCs, even in their most cohering continuously sustained passages, are elusive and slippery. This is, as I never weary of saying, due in part to their disjointedness, so that they do not join up either sequentially, or interconnectedly in the strategy of a mosaic. But it is also because the poem under the intense pressure of external events without, and perhaps through disappointment within the poet himself, has shifted not to *verba*, the construct of the poem, but to the re-creation of the world's effect upon the inward man. Thus the gods and goddesses in the PCs have become more registers of his responses than deifications of experience.

So how best to respond to the PCs since without response no deep lasting enjoyment, no remembering and returning to them as works, exists. And without this, praise and valuation are, largely, invention.

I have made a list of those parts of the PCs (I don't expect there will be any surprises) to which readers may respond. I should try to describe the parameters which structure and limit my choice, even where there operates, for this reader, opposition between the lyricism and the fascism it appears to espouse (as in the opening of the first PC). Not surprisingly, these touchstones are to do with responsiveness: 'I have been hard as youth sixty years' (80, 513).

Another way of presenting this responsiveness is to suggest that without love there is little communication. That may seem simplified, but I think it is rational to say that love (including self-love) has an object, and that its most frequent and successful though not invariable operation involves reciprocity. If these truisms seem not worth the saying, I would add that although we might assent to them, we seem less capable of extending their evaluative application in a poem. So without requiring that either the mode of affection or accessibility provides the only basis for evaluation, it seems that most readers arrive with a certain relief at these cohering and sustained passages, which some critics have called 'set pieces'. Of course, as with the touchstone of love, a confrontation of evil, and the mode of hatred, or derision – these will also sustain the reader – though perhaps finally in some diluted sense 'sustain'. Which disdain is in part the area in which the Mauberleys work. Though in the long run hatred and contempt probably isolate those who do the hating, and break down the energy involved in communication. At any rate with these tentative and protracted suggestions in mind, I offer the list concerning *The Pisan Cantos*. Canto 74, with particular reference to the opening (425–6), concluding with

'but a snotty barbarian ignorant of T'ang history need not deceive one', and the praise for the defeated fascist regime and its present place in the mind

(430–1)

Canto 76, 458:   the 'lone ant'

457:   'nothing matters but the quality/of the affection'

and

the portion beginning 'Lay in soft grass'

– these two passages have a kinship in feeling, though their referents are clearly different.

See also 466: 'nothing counts save the quality of the affection'. Canto 79, 487–92:   the sustained Lynx passage beginning with 'Old Ez folded his blankets'.
Canto 80, 513:   Tard, très tard je t'ai connue, la Tristesse
I have been hard as youth sixty years
with a back reference to 512, 'Je suis au bout de mes forces' (I am at the end of my strength).

514/15: 'Oh to be in England now that Winston's out'
– this passage leading to the murder of Le Portel, and so, on to
'Tudor indeed is gone'
Canto 81:   'Libretto' leading to 'What thou lovest well remains',
519–22;
Canto 82, 525:   the anecdote concerning Yeats and Ford beginning
'and for all that';
Canto 83, 528:   the portion 'and you might find a bit of enamel';
530:   the 'death cells' passage, 'Nor can who has passed';
531:   equity and rectitude beginning 'And now the ants
seem to stagger';
533:   'When the mind swings';
536:   'Oh let an old man rest'.

THE RE-ESPOUSAL OF FASCIST LOYALTIES

An immediate difficulty in the first PC (74) is not that we don't, but
that we clearly do, know whose deaths Pound deplores and mourns,
above others, the nature of whose deaths and subsequent treatment
he expresses with tender outrage:

> Thus Ben and la Clara *a Milano*
>   by the heels at Milano
> That maggots shd/eat the dead bullock
> DIGONOS, Διγονος, but the twice crucified
>   where in history will you find it?
>   (74, 425)

There follows 'yet say this to the Possum: a bang, not a whimper'
(425). The clear reference to Eliot ('possum', his nickname) is ambiguous, but implicating. Is it merely a reference to Eliot's *This is
the way the world ends/Not with a bang but a whimper* ('The Hollow
Men')? And if it is no more than that, it is still, at the very least, a
reversal of Eliot's quietest catastrophe. The fascist world in which
Pound was deeply implicated, with 'a bang not a whimper'. That
much is also clear. Yet why is this addressed to/for Eliot? Why laid
at his feet? We must be careful not to construct a fraternity of fascist minds, merely because we have a fairly clear idea of Eliot's
attitudes, some of which were near-fascist, and his anti-Semitism.
After all, all Jews are Jews, but not all Jews are left-wing! And in

any case, since so many Jews had been destroyed by Hitler, Eliot's anti-Semitism was at that stage of the European Jewish remnant partly redundant. Yet it seems possible that Pound was calling on his friend to remember their similar outlooks and filiations, Pound's explicit and declared, Eliot's hidden and now silent, except for his subsequent support for his friend. Yet these lines might have reminded Eliot that he, too, was in some danger. For Pound, there is no ambiguity in his expressed filiation:

To build the city of Dióce whose terraces are the colour of stars.
The suave eyes, quiet, not scórnful,
                    rain álso is of the prócess.
Whát you depárt from is nót the wáy,
and ólive trée blown white in the wind
wáshed in the Kiáng and Hán
whát whiteness will you ádd to this whiteness,
                    what cándour?
'the great périplum brings in the stárs to our shóre.' . . .
the wind álso is of the prócess,
                              sorélla la lúna
Fear gód and the stupídity of the pópulace . . .

                                                        (74, 425)

The ending of this unambiguously implies not merely a contrast between 'god' and the 'populace', the one whom we fear out of piety, and the populace we fear because of its arbitrary and fickle power. Perhaps he would not have feared the populace or have had contempt for them had they continued their support for the fascist regime. Or perhaps, and more likely, they would in any position be contemptible. It is not only that we are to flout democracy by insulting all but our rulers, (the god(s) are inapplicable here), but that Pound allows no room either for debate, or dissent from this proposition. By (his) definition, those who do dissent are 'stupid'. If we in any way oppose it are we, as readers, also stupid? We are far from the humility with which these Cantos are associated. It appears as plain anger with the turn of events (the Allies' victory) that has thwarted his hopes. This anger and despair undertone the lyricism here.

One understands Pound's anger and despair at the collapse of the regime, but how he treated his opposition is of great concern to us, his readers. Moreover his inflexibility, in the verse, has repercussions

in as much as it plays back on the beautiful parts that precede
this final line (above), involuntarily endowing the passage with an
inflexibility from which the lyric apprehensions suffer.

The line 'Fear god . . .' is not hard to deal with. Much more difficult to associate with are the lines 'To build the city of Dioce
whose terraces are the colour of stars' ending in

'the great periplum brings in the stars to our shore'.

It is perhaps despair that grounds this acceptably old-fashioned
and romantic use of stars as pin-points of, if not hope, at least of
aspiration for that which has been destroyed but which, in Pound's
mind, is the theoretical summation of what is best. In imagery and
aspiration, this is not too distant from

> Scatter, as from an unextinguished hearth
> Ashes and sparks, my words among mankind!
> (Shelley, 'Ode to the West Wind', 66–7)

If we stand back, for a moment, from the link that, as I read it,
Pound wants to make between this 'city' and fascism – and perhaps
not a link but an embodiment of it – we may be able, and willing,
to read this as a presentation of what is ideal; the city of God, the
city of all that is ideal, in ethical terms, of good government and
wise conduct.

In her attempt to consider the links with the fascist state that
Pound clearly makes, Flory will assure us that

> 'the partisans who came to arrest him found him busy with the
> *Book of Mencius*. When he left with them, he took his edition of
> Confucius's *Four Books*. . . . He has no doubts about the perennial
> wisdom of Confucius's writings as he asserts obliquely. . . . in
> "washed in the Kiang and Han/what whiteness will you add to
> this whiteness, what candour?" This is part of a quotation from
> Mencius which Pound gives in full in his Confucius. . . .'
> (Flory, 185 ff)

All this and much more smells of the lamp, but not in any good
odour, for it seems to this reader that in hastening to reassure us
that this is Mencius and Confucius, which it may well be, she is
anxious to disburden Pound of any filiation of fascism – as if, if

one has the Confucius, one couldn't have the fascism. Is that so? I do not think 'Old Ez' (a benign vignette of himself) would have thanked her for making a dissociation of things, or so it seems to me, that he himself has been at pains to affiliate. For by drawing on and implanting the ideal drawn from the two Chinese moral philosophers, Pound is actively seeking to make their substance subserve his vision of the fascist state: 'the city of Dioce whose terraces are the colour of stars'.

Similarly, for 'a man on whom the sun has gone down' (74, 430), in

> What you depart from is not the way

harbours, of course, this doubleness, as though Pound himself were seeking to establish the moral authority of the fascist state, not only in its intrinsic worth, but by its association with the moral analects whose value opponents of the fascist regime would accept. Nevertheless the right way most have deserted, involves a misplacing of our understanding of that right way, which is the regime of fascism. And in 'what whiteness will you add to this whiteness', we have a beautiful apprehension of purity, though also of such whiteness being eroded by dust 'olive tree blown white in the wind'. Thus Pound carefully inserts, in this somewhat non-linear passage, whiteness standing for both purity, which cannot be improved on ('will you add to') as well as the whiteness being scoured white 'by the dust' (experience and suffering), purity intrinsically, purity suffering, suffered and dying.

At this point commentators assert there to be clear discrepancy between what Pound believed, or wanted to believe, and the nature of the regime. In a sense that is clearly true, yet we do not need *commentators* to tell us, even if we assume that Pound chose to ignore such differences. A conscious discrepancy between what vision of fascism he offers and the regime in action is brutally visible. It is less than candid on the part of such commentary to use this difference between his vision and the regime's actions, for yet again we are on the way to attempting to exculpate, or excuse, or claim Pound's innocent ignorance of the real fascism. What he supported and appeared to condone, and what he did not. Thus to use the discrepancies between Pound's writing and the reality of the regime (not to mention its alliance with Nazi Germany) seems to me to constitute an attempt to bend the nature of reality, by which, it is implied, Pound was perhaps unaware of such reality, or chose (perhaps) to ignore it for the sake of the 'better' part of fascism. It might be better to accept that what Pound wrote (and did – his broadcasts) did not come from delusion or some attempt to persuade himself, against his better feelings. None of that is visible. On the contrary, it may be appropriate for us to accept that, mistaken or not, or in some small measure because he needed to earn money for his family, these professions of support for and idealization of, fascism are a conscious part of Pound's thinking and beliefs. What Pound wrote was in knowledge. What his defenders seek is to suggest that he wrote (and acted) in naivety and innocence. Pound does not need others to make excuses for him, and it is morally better for us readers, in the widest sense of the word, if we dispose of such attempts to mitigate what he wrote in defence of fascism. It embodies difficulty enough.

If we do this we may at least be able to focus on the problems. If we cannot resolve some of them, that too unearths a truth.

For this reader, the difficulty is indeed situated in the discrepancy between the regime and the way in which Pound's vision of it is presented. This might seem as if I am acceding to the Flory position of Pound's willing himself to believe in the good efficacy of the fascist regime, in which he was however much deceived; but I am not. There is no strain in Pound's presentation of his vision throughout Canto 74, and elsewhere; 'the terraces . . . the colour of stars', 'the great periplum [that] brings in the stars to our shore' (periplum/peri*plus* is 'voyage round the coast-line, usually of the Mediterranean'); and all such beauty here, including 'The suave eyes, quiet, not scornful' denied 'by the stupidity of the populace'. Surette considers these eyes to be Aphrodite's (*A Light from Eleusis*, 201), but again, the same argument applies. These may belong to Aphrodite, but it is not inconceivable that they are also Mussolini's (authority, not gender, is the point here.) Or is it possible that Surette's reading is an overmythic one, and that these are the eyes of the Italian dictator alone? The proximity of the dictator's fate with the 'suave eyes' appears to permit a reading in which the eyes are those of Mussolini.

And on the other hand, I read no sense of a man (Pound) not knowing what he says, and what he does not. It is the highly articulate poetry of a man whose views express a beauty and a politics with which we may not (or may) agree. The problem is a fairly clear but not simple one.

When the poetry is ugly, or inflexible, we may discount it as poetry. When it is beautiful, we cannot dismiss it on the basis that it embodies the vision of a regime whose acts we deplore. We must accept that such poetry is an expression of Pound's beliefs and responses, and that his vision of the regime is intended. In that case, either we are mistaken about the regime, if we believed it to have been evil (some do not), or we accept that it is possible to write beautiful poetry which embodies the evil inhering in some political dogma.

Rather than merely dismiss the vision, which might itself be a 'stupid' act, or claim that Pound was deluded or wilful, which may not be much of an improvement, we may have to consider the possibility that there may be something flawed, or defective, in such beautiful poetry, or indeed all poetry, if it is suffused, allows itself to be suffused, with an evil vision, or suffuses that evil with beauty.

It is true that the embodiments lack detail

> rain also is of the process

yet in context this generality is also, perhaps, a metaphor for the 'eternal vision' expressed in those eyes (Mussolini's/Aphrodite's). Indeed the passage is notable for its thoroughness in embodying that 'periplum' to which all of the Mediterranean contributes – 'brings in the stars to our shore'.

It could be, and frequently has been, argued that it is not the business of poetry to consecrate regimes, and that therefore we should not force it to do so here. But the awkward thing is that that precisely is what Pound appears to want his poetry to do here and his readers to understand it to be doing. If we say that it is 'only the poetry that matters', as Eliot did, we risk a schizophrenic view of a poetry that has been made to have no application to the world in which we live – thus 'verba', to the exclusion of 'res' (82, 525).

It is a situation where the poetry has been corralled into some 'as if' condition, more a condition of perpetual metaphor than *verba* even, entirely metaphysical in its apprehension of and relation to the world in which we live and die. Even if we leave aside the political dimension, which neither Eliot (*pace* Empson) nor Pound was willing to do, such would be a grave reduction of poetry's business. Which is not to say that poetry must always be political, but that some part of social transactions, its cruelty as its benignity, must always have silently crept into the substance of the poetry.

The view that the world and poetry are unconnected predicates a poetry constantly pushing itself free of the world – that is, its source of inspiration. Clearly that will not suffice, for though most art has a proportion of metaphysicality, an 'as if' part, this exists by virtue of that other – the existent world.

But it may be that just as we can never see ourselves in the same way after the two world wars of this century, so we cannot see poetry in the same way again, as the beautiful, immune, undefective creation we had thought it was, or hoped it might have been. By the time we reach the assertion concerning 'a snotty barbarian ignorant of T'ang history' (of which this reader is one) we are, regrettably, back in that obsession where a particular culture ('history') Pound believes in must guarantee the 'gemlike flame' of purity and moral value. Unlike Pound's defenders, I do believe that he, and Eliot, were politically dangerous, as was the man Eliot revered, the Frenchman of *Action Française*, Maurras.

We must find in Pound a vision additional to the fascist one yet without its erasing our recognition of what Pound is asserting in that respect. This is hard to do. Thus if we say that Pound deplores 'the total interest sweated out of the Indian farmers' (74, 426) we must still balance this against the 'stupidity of the populace' of which the farmer is a member (or are we dealing with agrarian sentimentality?). Similarly, we are required to consider what may be a contradiction, or tautology, in that first line of the first PC.

'The enormous tragedy of the dream in the peasant's bent shoulders.' Is it, perhaps, the cosmic tragedy of all peasants, their labour constituting their tragedy in those 'bent shoulders'? This might be the case, although we might not usually suppose this kind of sympathy to be active in Pound (except maybe in a sentimental mode). If the tragedy inheres not only in the invariable labour that bends these shoulders but in the dream in 'bent shoulders' that derives from the weight of some event, it may be that the death of Mussolini and his Mistress, together with the termination of Italian fascism, is what Pound envisages as the tragedy expressed in those 'bent shoulders'. There is a sort of double system in the verse, whereby the tragedy is established in the peasant in a beautifully contoured and flowing line and then, in its second system, related to the tragedy, as Pound sees it, of the end of Italian fascism. If this interpretation is near the truth, then, coming at the head of these

PCs, we are hardly being invited to forget Pound's mourning the termination of Italian fascism, or to disremember his allegiance to the system. As to the 'twice crucified' and 'where in history will you find it', this ignores contemporary history, but especially the camps, of which Pound[1] was, being party to Italian *fascism*, a co-worker.

This passage with its mode of suffusing connection moves, in its implications, in possible relation to the single line surrounded by non-sequiturs

> nothing counts save the quality of the affection
>
> (77, 466)

(though the line may connect with the lines a little further on, 'the feeling that Mr Eliot may have/missed something', meaning 'affection').

Whatever its connections, it is indeed a tenderly confessing line, in the utmost contrast to 'the stupidity of the populace' and the 'ignorant' 'snotty barbarian'. It may be that it is designed to stand out by its being isolated. If so, it stands forth, in isolation, in its simplicity, and by virtue of the colloquial 'counts' (= matters). It also stands out through the rhythm, which refuses to sound hackneyed by sliding into an identifiable rhythmic or metrical form. It thus deflects sentimentality.

A FEW INSTANCES OF DISLOCATION, AND ONE OF UNITY

Because there are so many instances of dislocation it is hard to cite something representative of this. And it is also in any case possible that without knowledge of, say, myth equal to Pound's ('leave it alone if you don't understand it,' he has said), or an understanding of how he has adapted the myth's received version (besides, according to Surette, his having defective knowledge), one may miss the supposed connections in this ubiquitous element in his verse.

Yet disconnections exist.

Mt Taishan is a sacred Chinese mountain, a consciousness of

---

1. But see Victor Brambert's review of *Benevolence and Betrayal*, *T.L.S.* (5 June 1992), p. 12.

which Pound imposed on the mountain he could see from the
DTC at Pisa. Thus

> surrounded by herds and by cohorts looked on Mt Taishan
> (74, 432)

'Herds' may be flocks grazing the mountainside of the actual perceived mountain, or imagined herds grazing the actual but not to
him visible Mt Taishan. Or it may be the 'herds' of other people
he feels 'penned' in by in the DTC. 'Cohorts' presumably means
'guards' (or perhaps the other prisoners). There is a space, followed
by

> but in Tangier I saw from dead straw ignition
> From a snake bite
> (74, 432)

and then an account of how from the holes in the tongue resulting
from a snake-bite 'fire came'. How perceive the connection between
these two which latter, moreover, has the conjunction 'but', which
implies connection rather than mere sequentiality; 'but'. 'But' what?
In case it may seem I select in a hostile spirit, I offer next a passage
in which Pound touchingly acknowledges the generosity of Mr
Edwards who has stolen packing cases to make Pound a table,
presumably so that among other things he may write; but in any
event, from a human decency that provides comfort in that desolation where a prisoner may be sentenced to death: Thus Mr Edwards

> 'dóan you tell nó one
> I máde you that táble'
> (74, 434)

What Mr Edwards has done is an act of charity presumably against
'regulations', doubly so since it both eased the condition of the
prisoner and was constructed from stolen material; hence Mr
Edwards' 'charity'. And also, presumably, 'methenamine' is a charity because it 'eases the urine', the medicine being presumably dis-
pensed by the institution, and therefore legal; madly so, since they
might both instigate comfort for the prisoner and then execute him
soon after. And this contrasts with Mr Edwards' illegal charity,
though both are beneficient if, that is, I have correctly guessed

here the function of 'methenamine'. If this is correct, however, the mention of the medicine in the narrative provides one more detail in his autobiography, having both isolated and contributory value. The uncharitable part is that the narrative quite heartlessly loses Mr Edwards' act, it supplying instead a means for reflecting on the idea that the greatest charity ('the greatest of these is charity') subsists amongst those who 'have not observed regulations'. Mr Edwards has subserved Pound's didactic narrative. The dislocation serves to lose Mr Edwards so that Pound may make his joke about charity and ultimately sting the institution that has penned him. All this may be so, though the jump is great; yet if correctly construed, offensive, even if we get an insight into Pound in his more sensitive moments. The irony is that Pound's camp, and other camps that preceded this one, elsewhere in Europe, had few Mr Edwards.

A different and sustained passage in which myth, and love, and the visible animal and vegetable world cohere is the Lynx 'section' (79, 487–92). Flory's account of it is excellent.

'O puma, sacred to Hermes' (492) is less than helpful in as much as it is the Lynxes that are otherwise to 'Keep watch over my wine pot' (488). The Lynxes do not fully take over continuously until 'O Lynx keep watch on my fire'.

Flory (205) quotes Kenner as saying that Pound's wife, Dorothy, told Kenner that Pound wrote the 'Lynx chorus' for her. It is a moving claim.

Surette (40–1) tells us that Pound confused the very different Mysteries of Eleusis with those of Dionysus, the god of wine, whose rites involve the votaries being in a condition of madness or 'enthusiasm'. Though among the animals sacred to Dionysus were the dolphin, serpent, tiger, *lynx* and panther.

The Mysteries of Eleusis, or the Eleusinia, were, on the other hand, a celebration of Demeter (Ceres) and her daughter Persephone (Proserpine). These are figures of fertility, in agriculture. Demeter's name probably meant, or signified, earth, and she was protectress of the fruits of the earth. Her daughter, Persephone, abducted by Pluto (Dis), god of the underworld and death, is detained there from late autumn to spring by Pluto on the basis that she had eaten six seeds of a pomegranate he had offered her. (She had eaten a portion of the fruit in the underworld, his domain.) Lawrence uses the myth correctly, for his own purposes, in his great poem 'Bavarian Gentians' (see chapter 4, below). Surette claims (40–1) that Pound quite without any authority but his own related the

Mysteries of Eleusis with the Troubadour poets of the middle ages, and further, though with some slight basis ('minority view'), that Pound linked the Troubadours with the Albigenses. The Albigenses, near Albi and Toulouse in southern France, embraced the Manichean heresy and were destroyed by Pope Innocent II through the agency of the Englishman Simon de Montfort, the father of the English parliament. Democracy even in embryo has its darker side.

Though not in complete agreement, commentators seem, more or less, to accept that the Lynx passage embodies a mixture of Eleusinian deities, Aphrodite (Cytherea) and a minor goddess, Pomona. Thus Dionysus' Lynxes (Surette, 217.) At this point one is tempted to throw up one's hands and declare the match a draw – between Dionysus and Demeter. On what basis may we conclude Pound to be proceeding?

The fruits involved are the grape, pomegranate, and, by implication, the apple ('cider', Pound, 491). The Lynxes seem to be invoked as protection. The conclusion ends in wariness, even dread. Surette tells us that the three female figures are not especially reassuring (they may correspond to his wife Dorothy, and Olga Rudge, and Bride Scratton). These new figures are Persephone, a rather sombre goddess described as the Juno of the underworld; Artemis (Diana) the virgin huntress and associated with death; and Maia a 'couch-mate' of Zeus (and mother of Hermes). Near the close of the Canto (79, 492) we have 'aram/nemus/vult' (= the grove needs an altar); and these may be altars 'exacted as restitution for the suffering which their love for Pound had brought to all three (women)' (Flory, 206). This is hidden matter, and the rhythmical recurrence in, for instance

> O lýnx, gúard mý víneyard ⁄
> As the grápe swells únder vine leaf . . .
> [Hélios] is cóme to óur móuntain
> (79, 492)

does not convey more than a kind of choric and dance activity, and does not overtly lead us into such an interpretation. However, dread and propitiation may perhaps be obtained by riddling the myths, as Surette and Flory have done, and to both of whom I am indebted.

Yet this hiddenness of meaning is distressing because despite my belief that when rhythmic and sustained continuous passages occur, there meaning is delivered, the Lynx episode, except via the myths, and then only in some hidden way, may mime into some religious celebration but gets us no nearer to what is happening and into what 'larger' scheme of these PCs one should fit it. In a general way, we learn that love is invoked, dreaded, and propitiated.

To return to the question of politics and Pound's adherence to the defeated fascist regime. This gets embodied in mythic form, immediately after his referring to himself as 'a man on whom the sun has gone down':

nór shall diamond díe in the ávalanche
    be tórn from its sétting
first must destróy himsélf ere óthers destróy him.
4 times was the city rebuilded, Hooo Fasa
    Gassir, Hooo Fasa   dell' Italia tradita
now in the mind indestructible, Gassir, Hoooo Fasa . . .
and four gates mid-wall Hooo Fasa
and a terrace the colour of stars

                    (74, 430)

The fascist state is represented by the destroyed African kingdom of Wagadu in its still awaited fourth incarnation. Add this to 'Hooo Fasa' ('Hail to the tribe of Fasa'), with an extra 'o' to Fasa in line 6 (above) that seems to represent a redoubling of hails and cheers on behalf of it, and it tells us that Pound's undiminished loyalty remains – undiminished, though henceforth in the mind, there, at least, indestructible, line 4 (above). (I am indebted to Stead for this last, 304–6.) I think we must accept that Pound remained a fascist, perhaps until his death. When he returned to Italy in 1958 he gave the fascist salute (Ackroyd, 100). Why should we attribute this only to Pound's flair for self-promotion? Why should we doubt it because *some* find it morally repulsive? That is not a sound basis for separating Pound from his stated loyalties and beliefs.

And the loyalty to the fascist state, offered in the Cantos, fits with the autobiographical tenor, and tendency, in this and parts of the other PCs.

Sometimes this autobiographical flow relates details of day-to-day existence in the DTC eased by acts of kindness, principally, it seems, made by Black soldiers who worked there, such as the Mr Edwards who made the table for him. Thus the declaration of adherence to the defunct fascist state, done quietly, or in myth, bears all the marks, not of bravado but conviction. We have no reason to doubt what he tells us, in a condition, moreover, when there is none to mislead him (*pace* Flory).

To return to the quotidian details, and the moving relief he describes, some of which is found in his observing the life of small creatures going about *their* business:

the lizard: 'A lizard upheld me' (74, 428)

the ant: (76, 458) though here as a figure representing himself 'ego scriptor' (I exclude the famous passage 'the ant's a centaur', 521) but I include 'And now the ants seem to stagger' (83, 531) and (83, 533) 'When the mind swings by a grass-blade'

the wasp: 'Brother Wasp is building a very neat house' (83, 532, and several other places)

'Ladro the night cat' (74, 438) and 'Prowling night-puss' (80, 498) birds, on the wires, and ubiquitously. But see 82, 525;

though see, also, the Whitman

reference 82, 526:   'O troubled reflection

'O Throat, O throbbing heart. . . .'

Whitman wrote in 'Out of the Cradle Endlessly Rocking':

> O troubled reflection in the sea!
> O throat! O throbbing heart!
> And I singing uselessly, uselessly all the night.
>   (*The Complete Poems*, 279)

Though Pound's recurring to Whitman here seems not to do with Whitman's theme of the beloved partner destroyed by death. Thus the uses Pound makes of these creatures is various, but in the main it is to do with a grateful sense of community with the small creatures, and for the solace and delight they give him in their unwitting fellowship.

In general, this seems to contrast with his regard for his fellow-humans, when (unwittingly perhaps, because, for instance, they are Black) he regards them as not his equals. Thus, as I have suggested, the gratitude towards Mr Edwards for the table turns into an intellectual and more self-interested point concerning larceny on a small and grand scale; which, one supposes, is an offshoot of his preoccupation with usury and the habitual dishonesty of most governments, and their disregarded mandate only to govern justly and honestly. From Pound's perspective and disposition it is permitted to forget an individual, who has done him great kindness, disinterestedly, and at some personal risk, in the interests of such larger and more 'important' issues. Thus fascism. In this respect it is not reassuring to find him comparing himself with or even replacing Christ in

> with Barabbas and 2 thieves beside me . . .
> (74, 436)

Is this a joke?

It is in such side-shots rather than with the great passages that we get the off-duty thus unguarded sense of what part of Pound's disposition and attitude to humanity is. Yes,

> As a lóne ánt from a bróken ánt-hill
> from the wréckage of Európe, égo scriptor . . .
> (76, 458)

is a perspective of a small creature, he being one, but it is Pound alone who comes forth from the ruck as the heroic 'lone ant'. The border-line between even the most tentative humility (ascribable to size and scale here) and pride in 'lone ant' is tenuous.

Yet to put it the other way about, it is in this community of small creatures, of which he is and is not a part, and his gratitude for their unwitting fellowship, that the most moving, authentic signal of humility occurs, where Pound seems *not* to see himself as subserving some larger purpose.

'Nothing counts save the quality of the affection' (77, 466) and the earlier formulation, in 'nothing matters but the quality/of the affection' (76, 457); and the moving admission of his feelings, in another language

> Tard, très tard je t'ai connue, la Tristesse,
> I have been hard as youth sixty years
> (80, 513)

all testify to the greenness of feeling in him, and its willingness as well as ability to express itself.

Nor before going to these larger portions should we miss those moments where the birds perched on the camp wires make musical notes as if on a stave for music (Stead writes well on this: 313–14). The imaginative wit here shares some kinship with Pound's respect for truth over witticism, as in

> , and for áll that old Fórd's conversátion was bétter,
> consisting in *rés* non *vérba,*
>   despite William's anécdotes, in that Fordíe [William=Yeats]
> never dénted an idéa for a phráse's sake
>
> and had more humanitas ⊨ jen
>
> (82, 525)

We find an even more modest instance of the touchstone concerning truth and value

>   and you might find a bit of enamel
>   a bit of true blue enamel
>   on a metal pyx or whatever
>   omnia, quae sunt, lumina sunt, or whatever
>   (83, 528)

It is found – the modesty – in the second 'or whatever', which colloquially modifies the Latin, and, with the Latin, forms part of the hexameter. The colloquial phrase prevents the whole line from becoming 'heavy' – solemn. The meaning of course is not portentous, though its expression within the metricality might otherwise have run the risk of seeming so.

TUDOR, AND OTHER MATTERS

Believing that free verse had got out of hand, Pound and Eliot resumed the practice of quatrains modelled on Gautier, where two out of four lines are rhymed between alternate unrhymed ones. This may create a sense of suspension, or dissonance, though in that usefulness it is by far the lesser instrument than Owen's slant or half-rhyme; see, for instance, both his 'Insensibility' and 'Strange Meeting' (pub. 1920). In a broadcast in the 1960s, the late John Lehmann described these '1920' poems of Eliot's as 'brilliant', an opinion I don't share. Pound, however, caught the partly lyric, partly narrative, sometimes ode-like versatility of the quatrain in his Mauberleys; and in the second Mauberley, section IV, this rhyming scheme, effects apt suspension and disjunction:

> 'I was
> And I no more exist;
> Here drifted
> An hedonist.'
>
> (*CSP*, 221)

Even the slightly torqued syntax of line 2, which would more usually be rendered 'I exist no more' (but which in its ordinary form would make no sense) is right for this somewhat precious aesthete-hedonist. At the same time it conveys Pound's judgement of the man's dislocation from society (Flory thinks these Mauberley poems are principally a mode of 'self-criticism', 102–6, and especially 104).

I do not wish to side-track the reader into a reconsideration of Mauberley, except to suggest that what Pound did with 'part-rhyme' in that poem he did again with 'Tudor indeed is gone', (80, 516), this time using Fitzgerald's 'Omar Khayyam'. There, the third unrhymed line beautifully conveys the 'but', suspended, sense within the otherwise sweet, heavily-rhymed ambience. Compare

> Iram indeed is gone with all his Rose,
> And Jamshyd's Sev'n-ringed Cup where no one knows;
> But still a Ruby kindles in the Vine,
> And many a Garden by the Water blows.
>
> And David's lips are lockt; but in divine
> High-piping Pehlevi, with 'Wine! Wine! Wine!
> Red Wine!' – the Nightingale cries to the Rose
> That sallow cheek of hers to incarnadine.
>
> (p. 112)

with

> Túdor indéed is góne and évery róse,
> Blóod-réd, blanch-white that ín the súnset glóws
> Cries: 'Blóod, Blood, Blood!' against the góthic stóne
> Of Éngland, as the Hóward or Boléyn knows.
>
> (80, 516)

Pound takes and adapts not only the original 'Iram indeed is gone' but also the 'Wine! Wine! Wine!' The Persian is a hardly less desperate plea – though it is in subsequent contrast to Pound's 'Blood, Blood, Blood' – with its cry for the momentary arresting of the transient with hedonist pleasure.

In another sense, Pound's quatrains differ from those of 'Omar Khayyam', for where the latter is arresting the present in momentary pleasure, Pound, in a kind of lament, is recreating the past so as to give it life in poetry. And more complexly still, Pound is noting what has gone from both the England he knew, and the England that many years preceded him. And all this is done in his favourite device of – I had almost said pastiche – but that is not right. It is a mode of translation whereby the nuances of Browning's 'Home-Thoughts, from Abroad' (also Italy) are transposed to Pound's 'home-thoughts' in Italy, under differing circumstances. ('Oh to be in England now that Winston's out', 80, 514).

Pound here makes an unmagnanimous thrust at one of his two enemies, Churchill (the other being the American, Roosevelt). The target formulated in the line 'Oh to be in England now that Winston's out' is partly malicious, for Churchill, who was surely one of the architects of the Allies' victory (and himself half-American) was therefore partly responsible for the downfall of fascist Italy and, in a sense, of Pound himself – also 'out'. For as Churchill was thrown out of office by the landslide Labour election victory of 1945, so Pound is himself 'down-fallen' by the Allied victory. As ever, the tone is critical if not knowingly so. The Socialists ('labour') will, in their 'vacillations', and presumably their 'mistaken' policies of government and money-system, make a mess of things ('let the bacon come home' = 'the fat is in the fire'?). At any rate, nothing good is foreseen there, notwithstanding that the opposite thrust of the fascist and Nazi regimes has come to nothing. Pound has lost the war, and is now fighting the peace. He is allowing his malice, and lack of magnanimity, to overcome his awareness of how things are, and indeed may turn out.

Having delivered his sting he then proceeds, by loose association only, to the stabbing of Lady Anne's Le Portel (80, 515.) Here is a perfect instance of Pound's directing and synchronizing past with present. It is achieved through his remembering an incident from his own past, 'That would have been Salisbury plain', and his other anamnesis, realized in 'and I have not thought of/the Lady Anne for this twelve years'

Nor of Le Portel
How tiny the panelled room where they stabbed him
In her lap, almost . . .

(80, 515)

There is nothing that might prevent his 'thinking' of both incidents,
but what is so imaginative in his 'thought of' is how it interleaves
his actual lived past with a prior past he could not have experienced, except, that is, through reading and imagination.

The Tudor claustrophobia of 'tiny . . . panelled room' and equally
claustrophobic betrayal of 'In her lap, almost' leads directly into the
main passage. I have quoted the first stanza (above); here are the
remaining two:

Nór séeks the çármine pétal to inférr;
Nór is the whíte búd Tíme's inquísitór
Próbing to knów if its néw-gnarled róot
Twists from York's héad or bélly of Láncastér;

Or if a rátional sóul should stír, perchánce,
Withiŋ the stém or súmmer shóot to advánce
Contritiọn's útmost thrów, séeking in thée
But oblívion, nót thy forgiveness, FRANCE.

(80, 516)

The 'indeed' of the first line of stanza one expresses a pained irony;
for Tudor culture (culture being one of Pound's 'heroes'), the issue
of which was the fuller-blown Elizabethan life in its mysterious
elaborate richness, has, essentially, disappeared as a living practice,
with the supervention of the eighteenth century and its very different rationalistic plainness. (One may check this by comparing Skelton
and Wyatt with Pope and Swift; then by comparing Pope with the
short-line 'Songs' of Blake *and* these lines of Pound's.) But as Tudor
and its flowering have vanished, so has what fed into and produced it; that is the Yorkist–Lancastrian struggle, ceased with the
eventual combination of their Houses. Love and War indeed, in
these dynasties of York, Lancaster, Tudor – with John of Gaunt
involved in the spinning of this coalescing.

Pound here offers a luminous view of history where culture and
dynastic power blossom through the using (shedding) of human
blood; as a flower sheds its petals. The word 'blows' concerning a
flower means 'decays', and is never far from the prevailing *rhyme*

of verse one. The rose-symbol of love and virtue (sacred and secular) is white, and red, thus the symbol of the Houses of Lancaster (red) and York (white), who stained the rose of their virtue and love by their struggle for power. The 'Omar Khayyam', 'anticipating' the poets of the First World War, has

> I sómetimes thínk that néver blóws so réd
> The Róse as whére some búried Caésar bléd . . .
>   (p. 114)

which is virtually the fulcrum of Owen's 'Greater Love'. It was left to Rosenberg, in 'Break of Day in the Trenches', to merge, as almost happens here, the perception that the blood of a Caesar *is* the red of the flower (poppy).

At any rate, I read this red as in part 'shed blood' which might then account for why every rose is 'Blood-red'; for the flower would have not only the dynastic blood but the stain in it of the blood shed. Though, certainly, it is also the blood of love, dynastic power consolidated by marriage. But yes, blood-stained (and blanched-white) because of the blood shed to get and retain power. 'Blood, Blood, Blood!' (line 3) – we have been led from blood-rose to rose-blood – implicates love with death, for it *was* love, we may assume, that linked Anne Boleyn to Henry VIII in marriage (Tudor) and which ended her life in execution (legal murder) by which Henry shed (unpetalled) one life for another. But not before Anne gave birth to the future Queen Elizabeth, in the year of her marriage, 1533.

It is a great deal of history in four lines, eight if you include the second verse, but it is there to find; history, not in a partisan or even politically partial sense, but delicately luminous, in which the essentials of love and slaughter (criminality) are fused in images of colour inhering in the flower-petals, with which the rose burgeons life. It is English life, to which Pound is attracted so long as it retains its culture, chiefly that of an inaccessible past; and this love makes luminous the passage.

In the second verse, York and Lancaster have access, not now to direct power, but through their dynastic underpinning of the Tudor fortunes. The root is 'gnarled' because time's root of life has become experienced in that struggle for power; and 'new-gnarled' because it is the Tudor House that has twisted, in struggle, into predominance. The 'carmine petal' (shed blood?) does not question the moral rightness of its success but only, if at all, its 'legitimacy', not infrequently in these matters 'established' by force rather than law and 'rightful' inheritance. York's 'head' or 'belly' of Lancaster could be read as intellect (head) and body (Lancaster), as if Pound might be attempting to characterize each House by giving each a typifying attribute. It feels more like Pound's characterizing the essential human attribute and then arbitrarily grafting head to Lancaster and belly to York (I may be wrong, lacking perhaps some crucial strand of information).

The third stanza may have its meaning rooted in history, in which mode we might think it reasonable to continue reading, as we read the first two stanzas. Thus, historically, not only did England struggle to retain parts of continental France, and harass France continually over a hundred-year period; additionally, the Tudor family had French blood, for Owen Tudor married Henry V's widow, Catherine of France. But that history and its dynastic blood has also flowed into 'oblivion'. And in as much as time has ended that dynastic power, it has also washed into part-oblivion what England had inflicted on France's people, to take the burning of Joan of Arc as only one shameful example of England's conduct. ('Oblivion' is not a concept that this writer fully accepts.) Thus 'not thy forgiveness, FRANCE' 'But oblivion', like Hopkins' 'disremembering'. Finally, though out of order, the 'white bud' of life does not question itself; life must be as it can.

All this distillation may have been prompted by Pound's awareness of his own particular place in contemporary history which, it might be said, not with any satisfaction, 'caught up with him', and questioned him, as he may have questioned himself. *Sub specie Aeternitas* it may be; but where Time is God's history, history itself is human, subject to human interrogation and 'inquisition', a reminder of how the timeless nature of God is implicated in the temporal life of the human, through religion.

The passage is beautiful, and this is not accidental but, rather, the result of creating something which yields beauty as a contingent attribute. Unlike a great deal of the Cantos where, when the matters are adjacent, there seem to be some by-chance or even opportunist connections, this passage is sustained and continuous. It has the light luminous wash of lyric, but the tread of the ode as it seeks to quintessentialize from history the sense of mutability caught, paradoxically, in something perdurable. So this passage in its historical essence is balanced against the preceding one, 'now that Winston's

out'. The specificity of the 'Winston' one and the essentiality of this
other give together a sense of width, not only of human activity,
but of course of Pound's vision. Juxtaposition, and collage, but also
placement, which finally leads him back to the possibility of his
own part in history and his possible removal from it, delivered
in the quizzical and wry

> puss lizard will lunch on some other T-bone
> (80, 516)

for the puss (lizard) is as much a register of some other life (hers)
as other life may be implicated with his.

Canto 81 contains the *libretto* which, in its turn, leads into the
rather fuller-scale music of what, with the possible exception of the
Usury Canto 45, is perhaps the most quoted of Pound's Cantos,
beginning with 'What thou lovest well remains'. This sub-section in
its turn unfolds 'The ant's a centaur in his dragon world'. I am, of
course, implying that love and acceptance are here linked, and that
one appears to be the consequence of the other. This may be Pound's
self-healing moment.

Libretto is 'words for music' (Yeats' *Words for Music Perhaps?*).
We may interpret 'music' variously, on a continuum ranging from
music in a literal sense to what it continues to signify – harmony,
peace, accord. And no amount of deploring that cliché can, or should,
keep these latter suggestions out from the range of possible, indeed
probable, meanings. But of course it means music itself:

> *Láwes and Jénkyns gúard thy rést*
> *Dólmetsch éver bé thy gúest . . .*
> (81, 519)

'Lawes and Jenkyns' were seventeenth-century English composers,
Lawes having written music for Milton's *Comus* and Jenkyns an
Elegy on the death of Lawes. The trope of Dolmetsch, the promoter
and performer of English early seventeenth- and eighteenth-century
music, being the guest of such music, because he is its performer
and interpreter, is a beautiful one. So clear and obvious, unsaid
before, so far as I'm aware. And we shouldn't miss the puns in

> Hás he témpered the víol's wóod
> To enfórce   bóth the gráve   and the acúte?
> (81, 520)

– with the pauses in the second line to indicate pauses in rhythm, perhaps to be found in the rhythm of some music Pound had in mind. 'Grave' and 'acute' mean 'serious', but the former has also the serious meaning of a 'grave'. The double meaning of one brings both closer together, harmonizing them by making each part of a serious mindful music. And to say it once more, the lovely spaces between 'enforce' and 'both', and again between 'grave' and 'acute', not only mime the movement of music, with its pauses in flow and rhythm, but also serve to remind us of the condition of poetry. For the unhabitual spaces make the line hesitate between what it would be without the lacunas, a predominantly *trochaic* 'plus' dance-lilting tetrameter; but also, if we give the pauses value, and redistribute the stresses as a consequence, a predominantly trochaic 'plus' pentameter. It is indeed original, reminding us what may be done by pushing the traditional form to its limits, while still retaining the holding structure.

Such assemblage of rhythm confirms the idea of Pound's poetry being essentially linear, which differentiates it from Eliot's, much of which is dense and complex. The difference is perhaps between the purity of seventeenth-century (English) music and the rich harmonics of, say, Brahms's orchestra. No hidden value judgement lurks in this comparison; there is more than enough room for both, and we wouldn't even notice if there weren't. Word play of the 'grave' and 'acute' – sound counterpointed with death and pain – is essentially linear. The two strands of meaning-reference, to the music, and to death and pain, remain separate, and are expressed as two separate strands of meanings. As we perceive the counterpointing of the words and their meanings, so we may pick up on a further aspect of music's rhythmic possibilities, in the opening stanza of the *libretto*:

> Yet
> Ere the séason díed a-cóld
> Bórne upón a zéphyr's shóulder
> I róse thróugh the aúreate ský
> (81, 519)

By placing 'Yet' on the first line, though it is essentially a metrical part of the second, which parts when read together form part of a four-beat line, Pound creates the impression of music slowly starting-up. Yet of course, that is not the habitual way with music, though Pound creates an illusion that suggests such an idea; for music starts up with the tempo it continues to establish. What Pound has introduced, intentionally or not, is the sense of a vehicle beginning its journey from a stationary position accelerating into an average momentum which process must allow for some initial slowness – music's trajectory analogized here to a vehicle's starting to move. We can 'get' this by noticing that the third line (metrically in effect the second) is also four-beat. Yet Pound unsettles the reader's expectations for he no sooner establishes a metrical norm than in the final line he creates an ambiguity as to whether the line is four- or three-beat. And by introducing the additional syllable of 'the' he makes the line an ambiguous mixture of iambic (u-) and pyrrhic (u-u). The refrain 'Lawes and Jenkyns' changes again to trochaic four-beat. It is a restless passage, yet it mimes the nature of music's capacity for quick changes of tempo, keeping the music-quality through the purity of its verse lyricism. This is also here part of the theme: purity. Yet unlike his theory concerning totalitarian art, and his practice of crystalline creation, it bears some marks of cross-currenting, even as it shows signs of the transcendental – another version of 'crystalline art'. Finally, it is a singing rather than speaking voice.

Once one has introduced an 'uncertainty' principle into a consideration of Pound's verse, it is difficult to be sure if, for instance, the next transition is fortuitous or an intrinsic part of the whole. With the introduction of the love motif – from Chaucer's 'Merciles Beaute' – a love not, I think, as dire as Surette believes – we move from the sense of *harmony* induced by music to one of vision. At any rate, whether the love is dire or not, it has been standard practice to declare that the beauty of the woman one loves, especially if she is unwilling, slays one. It is vision in both senses, for the eyes that fill the space in his tent, Aphrodite's perhaps, since we are speaking of love, this time bring humility. It is gradually and beautifully introduced. And in saying that the passage coheres I am suggesting that it has the coherence of narrative, yet contrives to present its matter as something being or having been experienced. Situational, perhaps. Yet although the experience is presented in such a way as to provide sequential accessibility, the experience isn't traduced into spurious orderliness.

'What thou lovest well remains'

One might argue that he presents, not experience, but a medieval picture close to allegory, where the poet Waller is made to sing and Dowland to play, and both to express love. So the ravishing, achieved by music and by love, is synchronized through the older poetry of Chaucer, where the idea of 'dying' by love was not then so strange. The totality yields what Pound was in need of – lastingness and durability. Thus: if you love properly it will last. Yet for us what is at stake here is whether Pound is skilfully manoeuvring a set piece or whether the outward manifest skills of art correspondingly conduce to an authentic intimacy. Here I believe it is the latter.

There is what looks like conscious ambiguity in the word 'remains', for it means 'last' (permanence), but also its contradiction, meaning death, as in 'the remains of the dearly beloved'. Which is acceptable rather than manoeuvred. One habitually feels that love is in competition with death, and that for as long as there is death, there exists also a sense that love is strong enough to face it and continue.

Thus the famous passage, which many have considered to constitute Pound's offering of humility (beginning 'Has he tempered the viol's wood' and ending with 'this is not vanity' (81, 520–1).

My experience in re-reading this passage is not consistent; one reading makes its didacticism concerning vanity seem prescient. A further reading suggests it to be moralizing and limited. This predicament is absurd, yet there may be reasons for it in addition to those of personal limitation.

Diligent, passive or indolent, readers may experience relief at arriving at such passages which offer a clear (moral) exposition of the familiar lesson of pride's infirmity and the need for humility. Thus accessible meaning and familiar territory combine, indeed conspire, to induce a favourable response in the reader. Yes, I follow that; yes, I concur (with what I have previously learned). All this would tend to elicit positive response and evaluation. 'This is good poetry', we say and 'uplifting'. Thus it does indeed elicit a positive response from numbers of readers, which, by the way, I am far from denigrating.

One critic has suggested that the Usura Canto (45) is 'a set piece' and the same might be said of this passage. Certainly it postulates nothing which has not been said many times, and it is by no means sure that its presumptive confidence allows it to breathe with the kind of sensitivity that we find in Pound's praise for the Italian fascist state, and his lament at its collapse. This places the reader in yet another of those positions where s/he is required to resolve those conflicting responses of approval and denial. Or rather, one is tempted here, in the 'what thou lovest' passage, to surrender overall judgement to moral concurrence in a way that one cannot with the opening of Canto 74 concerning the military fascist state.

It is as if Pound were not only sure of himself at this point, but confident of his readers' responses as well. As if he were to say to himself: I know many will not approve my support of the fascist state, but they will surely underwrite my exposition of the traditional virtue of humility. That degree of certainty may not elicit the best writing. And unfortunately, if this kind of confidence does in any degree serve to muffle sensitive response, here, the metricality, which so often assists and abets the presumptions of a mistaken authoritativeness in a writer, will do as much in this passage. These are the grounds for my unease, but if I may say that lack of confidence in a writer may help to produce some of his/her best work, somesuch ought also to be valid for the good reader. But in any event, tentativeness together with a degree of positive energy is an acceptable combination. But here, paradoxically, in a passage supposedly the exposé of pride, we have a degree of unaware certainty incommensurate with the moral tenor of the theme. And in a period when blind certainty has been the permissive agent of brutality, this is not reassuring.

Yet what does work against the 'certainty' impulse here is the complexity evident in Pound's handling of scale. Paradoxically, it is the structure inherent in the scale that provides the (unconscious) degree of uncertainty in a passage that seems otherwise assured of its own righteousness. If any of this is right, it may help to account for the crux made of two opposed sets of responses, which appear to be incompatible if not mutually exclusive.

At any rate this is the point at which this reader's inability to produce an assured evaluation forces him into exposition. Indeed the attempt to produce such an evaluation may in fact be seen to have been a precondition to interpretation.

Scale. If love is valuable for what it loves, and if it also provides the precondition for a necessary humility, then the (apparent) mortality-gap between 'shall not be reft from thee' and 'The ant's a centaur' is only apparent, and serves to open up the realization of how love demands humility, and how humility is necessary for love and thus for an apprehension of what is valuable. It is the point at which realization takes place, and it is the operation of this scale that does not so much explain as discover it to us.

Scale is not only the means to insight, but is the insight itself, for it is by the perception of the relative that one may be in a position to understand one's own and another's position. Thus the larger and the smaller creatures with their (possible) interlocking relationship.

Yet even as one is about to discuss the question of scale, the crux of uncertainty as a positive component in another's work reminds one that nothing definitive other than a pious wish to be 'open' oneself, and make a similar plea to the writer, emerges. Yet of all attributes, complexity, as opposed to linearity, is probably the most likely structure to engage openness and disengage from that sense of (disabling) confidence, which is probably the single most inhibiting factor in contemporary English and Scottish poetry now. The side-swipe is not intended to be offensive or even provocative; it is made to remind ourselves that in the best Eliot, it is the metricality in cooperation with the *complexity* that keeps the expressive poetry 'open', even when the subject-matter and the upper-level attitudes that inform it are not.

So despite Pound's preference for linearity and contour, complexity in this passage comes through his engaging with scale; if we can get past the dismissiveness of 'the rest is dross', we are well placed to consider the whole and cooperate with Pound as readers.

The centaur is, here, a figure with potential either way, though it would probably be rash to suggest that the potential for good is necessarily vested in the human rather than the part that is horse. To which part do we assign the 'half-bestial' nature with which Webster's Third International endows the centaur? Is it perhaps the human half underpinned with the animal that has the capacity for change, rather than the entirely human; though this is not to say that the human part will avail itself of this capacity. In this context of possible change, if no other, vanity is an obstacle:

'Learn of the green world what can be thy place ...' That advice consorts with such as those small creatures Pound continues to observe in the PCs (82, 525 for example), though it remains for the reader to make those connections. The 'lesson' probably best communicates itself in the kind of continuous exposition we have here; and in medieval, almost bestiary fashion, seems to deliver the heuristic opportunity to perceive that the green world of nature reliably provides the moral exempla of modesty:

In scaled invention or true artistry . . .

This is a new Pound or, perhaps, the emergence of a previously hidden one. 'The green casque', the helmet and armour of the ant, or the carapace of any insect, has naturally and without immodest display exceeded human 'elegance'. The word for the outmoded equipment of a warrior works well, for the old word for armour, 'carapace', has been re-applied by botanists to signify the exo-skeleton of an insect. The insect may itself be said to be 'armoured' against pride in that its natural elegance renders vanity superfluous.

The mechanism in this passage, 'Pull down thy vanity,/I say pull down', is that of scale. The meanings are numerous, but the main one seems to suggest that the world is fearsome – 'dragon' – and in such a world the ant necessarily grows comparatively prodigious – 'a centaur'. This is not the creature's vanity, for it probably has none. What actuates it is the desire to survive and in this it acquires the abnormal size and ferocity of the centaur. An alternative reverse reading would run like this. In his own limited world, which is dragon-like in ferocity, not size, the ant nevertheless inflates its behaviour to the size and ferocity of a centaur, thus rendering itself absurd in comparison with its normal size and conduct. Both readings are probably valid, and indeed I suggest that one is the necessary agent of the other. They do not cancel each other, for by having the first, which is a function of modesty, and the second, which is the instance of absurdity (human vanity), we are able to make a contrast and draw such conclusions as are necessary for the lesson, and re-apply it, of course, to human conduct; with the added proviso that human conduct is invariably like the second, which is vain, and that the natural world is more habitually, except perhaps in courtship, more like the first. But then everyone makes allowances for the theatre of courtship, knowing in any case that one's experience of sex is that of being chained to a maniac in the shape of one's desires. The little phrase 'it is not man' is presumably not ironic in this passage of straight morality, but we can easily make it double up to yield irony; for although it is not manly or properly human to be vain, it is, indeed, only too human with respect to our habitual conduct. In all this, the scale provides the natural fulcrum between inflating vanity and natural modesty in this double three-part comparison.

The passage concludes by moving into free verse, and contains a graceful punning (manly) reference to Blunt, a pre-First World War acquaintance, who is the touchstone of true culture (see photograph in Ackroyd, 33). Though having said 'free verse', the rhythms tend towards congruity, even if the tone tells us that the ideal and the lessons of the metrical libretto are now delivered. The idea is sung, but not the task of fulfilling what it has sung. To act is not vain; to fail to act is culpable.

We indeed notice the tendency towards rhythmic congruity, and it will serve to remind us of Whitman's similar tendency in his intenser passages; though with Whitman we find a syntactic – and – as rhythmic a patterning. Nevertheless the whole passage here patterns the syntax and in doing so contributes to the singing quality. Even the stepped lines, made of pentameter, give the pause and lilt of music –

> Púll dōwn thy vánity
> > How méan thy hátes . . .
> Púll dōwn thy vánity,
> > I sáy pull dōwn . . .
> > > (81, 521)

where the singing tone balances out the somewhat assertive hortatory moralizing. The effect would certainly contribute to assertiveness if the lines were run on as pentameter; whereas the stepped lines, of interrupted pentameter, carry a sense of hesitancy within certainty, yet redouble the exhortation.

Finally, with respect to this music, the medieval 'imitation', the slightly antique touches of language and the rhetoric combine to produce not only coherence but music. In its turn this music becomes a metaphor for harmony, a right world if we would only live rightly within it.

A rider, of a kind. One notices that from the beginning of the 'vanity' passage no foreign word occurs. The reverse form of this observation would consist in asking what the effect on his verse is of using foreign words and phrases from *European* languages that Pound might expect some of his readers to have some knowledge of. What effect, for instance, do the words 'Ed ascoltando' (81, 520) have on the tone, rhythm and pace of the passage in which they are embedded? I am suggesting that the rhythm of the verse is in some

subtle sense altered by the presence of foreign phrases, especially
when they are designed to dovetail with English metre:

> ómnia, quáe súnt, lúmina súnt, or whatéver
>   (83, 528)

My feeling is that Pound was aware of this, but in any case it may
be that others have written on this version of the macaronic. If not,
there is a field of inquiry.

4

D.H. Lawrence, Poet

THE TRAJECTORY OF LAWRENCE'S CHANGING
VERSE STRUCTURE

To move from Isaac Rosenberg or Wilfred Owen to Lawrence entails a shift from the iambic (u-) to the anapaestic (uu-). And with respect to a comparison with Rosenberg it seems to involve a change from a harsher, old, unflinching directness to a modern speech-ridden, flowing, multisyllabled, colloquial language, where speech is at the centre of the pulsar. In *this* sense Lawrence, even in his iambic and other *metrical* verse, is contemporary in a way that Rosenberg is not. It is the change from the frontal directness of one to a more delicate yet pulsing sinuousness of the other, and per-haps this indicates why Whitman remains at the centre of contem-porary verse-writing. 'Whitman was a crude observer,' compared with Lawrence James Reeves claimed (176), adding,

> Since Chaucer established the supremacy of iambic metres over the native alliterative verse, no poet has successfully deviated for long from the iambic norm . . .
> (*D.H. Lawrence's Poetry: Demon Liberated*, 180)

Of course, we will never know, because of the lack of techno-logy, how people *spoke* in conversation, and how they spoke their iambics when they read their poetry aloud, or performed it on stage. I read some years ago that we 'know' that in the past vowels tended to be longer in people's mouths, but I'm not sure that such supposed knowledge of how earlier speech sounded, or how poetry was spoken, is going to help one to accept Reeves' authority on the iamb. In any case it is much more complicated, for within the ideal notion of what an iamb[1] sounds and reads like is the question of

---

1. There is a considerable amount of anapaestic movement 'gashed' with heavy stresses in Hopkins. In Milton quantities of spondees, which constitute duration, sometimes with, sometimes without, stress.

what we can perceive of its natures at different times and in different poets. That is, within the term, we may be speaking of a different rhythm coursing through what looks like one form, which is named, say, iambic pentameter. One might find that one is encountering an anapaestic tendency in what is nominally an iambic structure. For although English metricality counts both syllables and stresses, it also seems to me that one metricality, such as iambic pentameter, may have cross-currenting in it a different rhythmical tendency. The work of Hopkins is an extreme case, but there are others – Milton, for instance.

I have not forgotten that I mentioned Rosenberg with Lawrence, and I would add that the most extraordinary fact of the comparison between the two poets is that the five years' seniority Lawrence had over Rosenberg does not dissolve the crux that writers more or less contemporary should be such different makers. For Rosenberg is in certain respects an older version of English poetry than Lawrence. Lawrence's poetry relaxes more into current spoken English than Rosenberg's. And what a spoken Tongue it is.

There are further things to be said; for whereas Rosenberg's compositional trajectory – in so far as we have it before the war destroyed him at the age of twenty-eight – moved from metrical, to mixed metrical and free verse, and, in his latest dramatic verse, to free verse, Lawrence's was more complicated. Lawrence died in 1930 when he was forty-four. Within that period, and who knows what he would have done given more years, he started as a metrical poet, with energies that would not always comfortably fit into the metrical rhyming mode. And yet he ended by resuming, in a number of poems, a metrical verse. Writing to Edward Marsh, the editor of the five influential anthologies of *Georgian Poetry* (1911–22), he declared on 19 November 1913:

> It all depends on the *pause* – the natural pause, the natural *lingering* of the voice according to the feeling – it is the hidden *emotional* pattern that makes poetry, not the obvious form.
>
> (*Selected Literary Criticism*, 80)

And earlier, he had written to Marsh on 18 August 1913,

> Sometimes Whitman is perfect. Remember skilled verse is dead in fifty years – I am thinking of your admiration of Flecker.
>
> (*Selected Literary Criticism*, 77)

With hindsight, and given his tentative but unexplored and probably now unexplorable relationship with Imagism, one can see Free Verse coming. Eventually, what he wants to say, and how he wants to speak, will not fit into metrical verse. The transition occurs in the volume *Look! We have come through!* (1917), but the essay 'Poetry of the Present' (1919) actually anticipates, indeed monitors, the developments taking place in Lawrence that produced the later *Birds, Beasts and Flowers* (1923). Of (his) free verse, he wrote:

> The strands are all flying, quivering, intermingling into the web. . . . There are no gems of the living plasm. The living plasm vibrates unspeakably, it inhales the future, it exhales the past, it is the quick of both, and yet it is neither. . . . This is the unrestful, ungraspable poetry of the sheer present, poetry whose very permanency lies in its wind-like transit. Whitman's is the best of this kind. . . . The clue to all his utterance lies in the sheer appreciation of the instant moment. . . . The quick of the universe is the *pulsating, carnal self.* . . . Much has been written about free verse. But all that can be said, first and last, is that free verse is, or should be, direct utterance from the instant, whole man. . . . Free verse toes no melodic line. . . . Whitman pruned away his clichés – perhaps his clichés of rhythm as well as of phrase. . . . The quick of all time is the instant. . . .
>
> (182–5)

One sees that the quick, the instant, the plasmic and fluid are what Lawrence was after in his free verse. What he omits is of course as interesting as what he includes in his statement, for in *BBF* the free verse is contained and structured by variations of Hebrew parallelism – what Hopkins called a 'figure of grammar'. And one can see that parallelism, with its start–stop mechanism, usually organizing a syntactical unit to coincide with a line, is, compositionally, the opposite of what he claimed he was doing (above). Parallelism is the structure that contains the quick and fluid. Parallelism replaces metre.

Lawrence goes on changing, and develops. The best of *Last Poems*, published posthumously in 1932 (edited by Richard Aldington), has, most notably in 'The Ship of Death', a tendency to reintroduce (and reinvent) iambic pentameter. But in such a way that he could not have used it had he not been practising free verse before (see below).

ANSWERING SOME CRITICISM: A POET WITH FORM

Those hostile to Lawrence's free verse argue that the alleged clum-
siness in his metrical rhymed poems indicates his inability to use,
or construct, any form. Yet this ignores the many metrical achievements such as 'Discords in Childhood', 'Cherry Robbers', 'Gipsy',
'Baby Running Barefoot', 'Last Words to Miriam', 'In Church',
'Piano', 'Hymn to Priapus', 'River Roses', 'Meeting Among the
Mountains', 'Giorno dei Morti', 'Desire is Dead', 'Nottingham's
New University', and of course, 'The Ship of Death'. There are many
others, but this should have been enough to discredit his supposed
inability to create metre. Somesuch criticism looks to be behind
Philip Hobsbaum's assertion that Lawrence's change from Hardy
to Whitman as a model was disastrous. Lawrence failed to realize
that

> behind the apparent discursiveness of Whitman, lies a patterned
> association of ideas linking up the various strophes. Lawrence
> took a decisive step when he left behind the verse which was that
> of Hardy . . . for the dispersed cadences of Whitman . . .
>
> (*A Reader's Guide to D.H. Lawrence*, 21)

Lawrence apparently failed to perceive and thus re-create in his
own free verse the interlinked responses and ideas one finds in
passages of Whitman's. The implication of this is that when Lawrence used the metrical norm provided for him by, among others,
Hardy – however clumsily he worked it – his incipient disorder
and formlessness were contained. The metrical norm even induced
some order in his verse. Conversely, his failure to appreciate the
filamenting in Whitman's free verse encouraged formlessness once
he disposed of a metrical norm (note the implication that free verse
tends towards formlessness, by its nature). R.P. Blackmur makes
such an attack in his essay 'D.H. Lawrence and Expressive Form',
in *Form and Value* (1957, cf. *Language as Gesture*, 1952):

> When you depend entirely upon the demon of inspiration, the
> inner voice, the inner light, you deprive yourself of any external
> criterion to show whether the demon is working or not. . . . That
> is the fallacy of the faith in expressive form . . .
>
> (256)

One notes also that the remarks concerning Lawrence's alleged 'hysteria' (263–4) seem predicated in the main upon what Lawrence wrote in his 'Preface' (1928) and derive less from an open reading of the verse.

Nevertheless defenders of Lawrence appear loath to quote Blackmur, thereby strengthening his and other's animus. Lawrence, on the other hand, made use of the organizing structure of parallelism in his free verse, as late, for instance, as the poem 'Phoenix' from *Last Poems* (see below).

WHY IGNORE LAWRENCE'S POETRY?

In her extremely helpful and readable *Acts of Attention: The Poems of D.H. Lawrence* (1990, revised edition) Sandra Gilbert argues – many things concerning Lawrence's poetry. Thus, he wrote poems in the mode of modernism; that he was (marginally) affected by Imagism (see chapter 2, above); and that he contended with three impulses in his poetry: the Demon, as Lawrence called it in his Foreword to *Collected Poems* (1928), the conservative (and somewhat literary) young man and the fiction writer himself. She also deals extensively with the alleged Sartrean duality in Lawrence of *en soi* and *pour soi*, which is of limited use in considering Lawrence's 'creature' poems. But her overall tendency is to explain the poetry in terms of its ideas. This strategy may be intended to counteract Blackmur's charge of formlessness and hysteria, but in any case the poetry is examined for its ideas without the criticism having recourse to the poetry itself, which is surely not the most effective way to deal with Blackmur's strictures. So the poetry is turned inside-out, considered as a vehicle for, or an expression of, ideas, not for what it is as poetry. Clearly, a wholly *technical* consideration ('skill') will tend to induce boredom, yet it seems perverse to consider a poet's verse largely to the exclusion of how those ideas, feelings and attitudes are embodied with it. Conversely, I argue that without the poetry, the ideas would have a different life and meaning. Gilbert herself argues somesuch point (see pp. 247–8) concerning the poem 'Wages'. If we look at meanings, we are also bound to consider not only how the gradual relinquishment of metrical for (an in part) free verse affected his work in *BBF*, but also what effect his partial return to metrical form had on some of the verse in *Last Poems*.

THE 'RHYMING POEMS': 'PIANO' AND 'DISCORD'

One of Lawrence's favourite words in 'Rhyming Poems' is 'boom[ing]'. It occurs in his 'Discord in Childhood' – 'a male thong booming and bruising' (36), and in 'Piano' – 'in the boom of the tingling strings' (148). These are two strong pre-free verse poems, the latter arguably one of his best shorter poems. One reason for rating these poems together with 'Cherry Robbers' (which follows 'Discord in Childhood', in *The Complete Poems* (1972, 1980)) amongst his best rhyming poems is that, following my suggestion as to what Lawrence implied in his designation 'Rhyming', one finds ease and congruence between form and substance. This needs immediate qualification. The first point is that what 'Discord' and 'Piano' share distinguishes both from 'Cherry Robbers'. For despite one's sense that the theme of cruelty and mockery which, unlike Gilbert (p. 51) I see embodied in the figure of the girl's:

> 'I will see/If she has any tears'

meaning, I suggest, 'not many', the theme seems to exist as much for the form as vice versa. Like Housman, though I prefer it to Housman, it seems to perform using precise metricality and bolstering almost aggressive rhyme – 'Laughing at me/I will see'. All the rhymes are sonically full, and regularly and symmetrically placed (unlike the reversed pattern between the two stanzas of 'Discord').

A different kind of tension inheres in 'Discord', which makes 'Cherry Robbers' appear, in a negative sense, a more literary achievement, whereas in 'Discord' and 'Piano' the language is more inventive because more evaluative. It is as active as Dylan Thomas's cross-referencing language in his early poems. So not only the uses of 'booming'/'booms' but, in 'Piano', the caressing menace of 'insidious mastery of song' and delusive power in 'great black piano appassionato'. The rhyme is as regular and 'full' in this poem as 'Cherry Robbers', but what has entered both poems is what Gilbert terms 'the novelist', and what I call the experiential. For it is my suggestion that since Lawrence began and ended as a poet and had long periods when he was writing more poetry than fiction, it is not the novelist working these poems but the experiential capacity, which itself accounts for the novelist. Thus what underpins 'Discord' and 'Piano' is not a fiction writer's techniques but the experiential capacity, which subtends both the poetry and the fiction. 'Discord' and 'Piano' are not immediately perceivable as metaphysical poems because the experiential element, by definition, is not metaphysical. But if this experiential capacity can be considered to contain essentializing truths, it is because of the power Lawrence, for instance, generates in his creation of the actual. The actual generates the essential. Yet this nearly always ensures that Lawrence's poetry is understandable, though this attribute seems, for some, to preclude further exploration. Additionally, it seems to be acceptable to some that the experiential is hardly worth having.

Some such ordering of priorities may account for why Lawrence's poetry presently gets read at schools but not, usually, put on university syllabuses. On a 'higher' level we do not apparently expect or want our poetry to be experiential. We leave that to fiction. And this may lie behind the withholding of complete approval in such a fine poet and good critic as Iain Crichton Smith, where he says in his essay, 'The Feeling Intelligence' (*Towards the Human*, 1986):

> Thus it is that we say that this sort of poetry ('the self-delighting intelligence of the feelings') is not necessarily the greatest poetry but it is a category in which Scottish poetry is weak.
>
> (152)

It's fine, the tendency of this argument seems to be saying, to give the senses their due, but there is something finer. There may be, but by arguing for the conventional estimate of Lawrence's achievement, the experiential as a whole seems once again to be downgraded. It dances about as 'the self-delighting intelligence of the feelings' – as if that intelligence weren't in the highest sense religious, sharing and communal – those core attributes I believe to be, rightly, at the centre of Crichton Smith's evaluating processes. At any rate the finer thing is there in Lawrence's poetry. And whether, in 'Piano', you go with Leavis's seeing the adult as mastering the child's emotions, or with Gilbert's seeing Lawrence as giving the emotions full expression *through* the adult, there appears to be agreement that the child in the man 'weep[s] like a child for the past'. Lawrence's strategy here is indeed complex. Overtly we are not to give way to (childish) emotion – 'In spite of myself, the insidious mastery of song' (148). Yet we are to reverence that which lives in the child's experience of both the sacred and the music, not to mention his surviving (adult) love for his mother. I cannot see that this should invite our deploration, or anything other than a positive response to this creation of interconnected, partly transposed, child-and-adult experience. Indeed, it is with this very intrication of child and adult that the poem's *language* works. The contrast is between the 'boom of the tingling springs', which is both the piano itself and the feelings the total experience continues to rouse, and the *subsequent* musical experience, in some ways judged to be inflated and wanting: 'great black piano appassionato'.

For one sets that passion against 'the small, poised feet of a mother', 'who smiles as she sings'. 'Poised' implies control over strong feelings, and itself does a great deal of work in co-operation with the spondaic noun in 'poised feet'. Moreover both 'vain' and 'clamour' obtain strong emphases, and this serves to raise up the somewhat negative 'clamour' (as in 'clamouring for attention') to be further qualified by the two meanings of 'in vain' and 'vain' (vanity). The rhyming of 'clamour' with 'glamour' might suggest that the 'childish days' are no less suspect than the implied 'glamour' of the present singer, but finally we receive the morally approbated figure of the mother and her 'small, poised feet', since this is what the narrator evidently remembers with positive feeling.

In certain respects the 'male thong booming' of 'Discord', presenting the parental 'dreadful' violence, is more *essentialized* than anything in 'Piano'. The possible exception is indeed that 'appassionato', which is both admired and felt to be slightly faked, exaggerated through the gestures of art rather than informed with love and even religion ('hymns'). Whereas there is nothing exaggerated and everything essentialized in the expression of 'thong' in the male voice and its menace.

Certainly both poems arrange themselves round the experiential factors of sound – 'tree' and 'ship' in the first stanza of 'Discord', and, in 'Piano', the contrast between the 'boom of the tingling strings' and the singer's 'appassionato'. Though to be just, it is her power that evokes in the poet his mother and *her* music.

LAWRENCE AND WHITMAN, A QUESTION OF DELICACY: PROSE AND VERSE

Lawrence not being Whitman, we must tend to be wary of Hobsbaum's stricture concerning Lawrence's apparent failure to apprehend Whitman's interlinked stanzas. In fact Gilbert is acute here, indicating that Lawrence's free verse poems are invariably shorter than Whitman's because Lawrence was less an epic more a lyric poet.

Gilbert also distinguishes between English and American poetry, suggesting that the rhythms of the latter are more delicate, and subtle, than those in English poetry. This is perceptive non-value judgement; and it may be that because American intervened its fresher second-comer English at a time when Western culture had become more sophisticated, we must expect an apparently epic civilization, such as America's (and Russia's), to find its greatest contradiction in having to develop and redesign its strong formative energies of the newcomer in the sophisticated delicate mode of older cultures.

This exigency may be at the back of Whitman's greatness – he is after all America's only great poet. For Whitman does indeed desire to be the epic poet, perhaps of democracy even more than of America, and for this the energy must thread its delicacy in the most delicate way. This may be one reason why Whitman in the main relinquishes metricality *and* uses the parallelism found *unlineated* in the English Bible. (See Benjamin Hrushovski in *The Penguin Book of Hebrew Verse* (parallelism).) One must be epic but in the new mode of democracy – the new faith – and so find a different 'metric' – a rhythmic form appropriate to new requirements. Only it can't be done in metre itself (one imagines oneself in Whitman's position!) because this repeats the civilization of England (Whitman had little respect for his contemporary Tennyson, and Hopkins was certainly critical of Tennyson's poetry and sensed a kinship with Whitman). Besides which, metre isn't delicate enough for the latecomer, as the *prose* practice of the poetic Emerson suggests. In this sense, the more parochial assessments notwithstanding, as Rosenberg said of Emerson, 'This man paved the way for Whitman' (*Works*, 289). Emerson's writing is important, and it would be useful to have an investigation of Emerson's (prose) delicacy of perception, expression and tone. (I am aware of Richard Poirier's *The Renewal of Literature/Emersonian Reflections*, 1987.) And in respect of delicacy, consider G.S. Fraser's metaphysical-and-sensuous 'taste in the head', which he, amusingly, insisted on patenting to himself.

Yet although the rhythm has to be delicate and therefore eschew metricality, it has also to filament an epic realization in something, paradoxically, very solid, very built (see 'Song of the Broad-Axe', for instance). And since, as with Lawrence, the Bible was from childhood at his disposal (his mother was a Quaker), and the water repeatedly lapped on Long Island, as he indicated, parallelism containing delicacy, the scent and its nuance, together with the epic, would be just dandy.

It fitted wonderfully, and felt new even if, in all respect, we recall Smart's prior *Jubilate Agno* with its antiphonal structure. This would appear to place *Lawrence* awkwardly, especially since, in 'Poetry of the Present' he had professed[1] Whitman to be his new forebear. But in a sense this is Lawrence's mistake. Whitman isn't Lawrence, but rather one who freed Lawrence to consolidate himself anew, even if his narrative impulse (not precisely the same thing as a novelist's) sometimes interfered with the poet's more essentializing labour. And if it can be said that Lawrence was more lyrical than Whitman, he was not more delicate: with Whitman the nuance is in the verse itself

> the flag of my disposition
> (SoM, line 101)

And this, one of so many instances of delicacy obtained from conjunction, is more delicate than anything I can remember of Lawrence's. It is metaphysical travelling via Emerson (his 'squares of snow') though not, perhaps, something that Lawrence was interested in creating.[2] Respecting Lawrence's supposed femininity, his is a somewhat masculine psyche. Lawrence's apprehension of women, Sandra Gilbert is at great pains to emphasize, was acute; and his apprehension of the Shekina, the female god principle, without and within us, was similarly so.

DELICACY, ENGLISH AND AMERICAN

At any rate, the question of delicacy *qua* Whitman and Lawrence needs pondering. Has the language of English coarsened over 150 years? Are the Americans more soft-languaged than the English? Is there a delicacy inhering in American English we English have been too superior to notice, but which Lawrence, together with Rosenberg

1.   Though he had been reading Whitman as early as 1908, when he was 23 (cited by Gilbert, 28).
2.   Notwithstanding Daleski's suggestion in *The Forked Flame* (1965).

and Gurney, perceived? And if this is so, is it what prompted Lawrence to discover Whitman as his replacement ancestor? Or, and this is offered more as an additional possibility than an alternative: is written language finer-sifted than spoken? Thus it seems to me that although poetry is closer to speech, it is nevertheless the written component in poetry that refines ('Heard melodies are sweet, but those unheard/Are Sweeter', declares Keats's 'Grecian Urn'). Does the written give a finer, more supple grain, rhythm and texture to poetry than the verse element itself? This possible condition may have to do with the intrusion of prose, its rhythms and its voice, upon poetry; at any rate, one sees how complex the task is of trying to analyse the crux.

Some of these conjectures will be blown away – poetry is supposed 'To purify the dialect of the tribe' (Eliot, 'Little Gidding'). Yet if that is so, it purifies dialect not language. Too much purity is clearly not desirable, producing attenuation, from which American verse may presently be suffering. The opposite is also an affliction: too much of the speaking voice, transposed into written verse, may coarsen, though we are also told that the connection between speech – the living language so-called – is essential for the written language as much as for the health of poetry. Yet perhaps beneath our unquestioned assumptions something quite contrary to them has been working away. For if poetry is closer to speech than prose is, it might follow that from necessity prose works harder at language to produce its *texture*; and that by having to labour more to work within something akin to the nature of speech, it ultimately replicates, or rather, creates, out of its artificiality, a more hard-won and rendered artefact. Conversely, the simple-minded transcription of verse into a predominating prose version of verse doesn't work, and notwithstanding what Pound recommends, his finest verse does not practise this. The best of *Mauberley*, and the *Pisan Cantos*, clearly has this prose grain, but it is *within* the verse itself, whatever prescriptions he had dosed others with. Finally, a truism. We speak poetry but write prose. The interaction between the two is good for all three. So for all that Owen is the more English writer, it is Anglo-Jewish Rosenberg's poetry, perhaps because it incorporates this attribute, that has a finer grain.

The argument, if it is worth considering, needs to be transferred back to Whitman and Lawrence. Admittedly, Whitman's verse seems at least as oratorical (not orotund) as Lawrence's. Yet his long lines may be closer to the spirit of parallelism (and thus to a written code) than Lawrence's, just as Lawrence's repetition may be more speech-oriented; though presumably their impulsions derive from attention paid to the Bible. But Whitman's lines, usually longer than Lawrence's, are as a rule more sustained by a written component than the later poet, being more jointed by punctuation; even the original series of dots in SoM might be regarded, like Emily Dickinson's dashes, as more part of a written than spoken code. The distinction is hard to make.

In Whitman's verse there are hardly any enjambments. One critic has suggested that his end-stopped creation was an attempt on Whitman's part to transcribe verse for recitation, but this suggestion subverts the entire enterprise of Whitman's syntax interrelated as it is with his lineation, and seems unlikely. At any rate, the lack (or presence) of enjambments is not part of what we might regard as spoken language. And the parallelism, so essential a part of Whitman, of which *repetition* is the result rather than the designing part, comes from a Bible to which we may, it is true, listen, but which we read. And even if we do listen, we attend to something written down, and, essentially, written in a translation transcribed into prose; that is, non-lineated transcription. We very few of us speak in translation, though we may read it. The written mode tends towards the character of prose.

My fellow-poet Rodney Pybus has suggested that one important difference between American and English poets is that where American poets reading aloud will diverge considerably from the printed text as far as lineated rhythm is concerned, treating the print more like a musical score, English poets will read much more closely to what is printed. If true, this might seem to suggest that American poetry is closer than English to speech. It might also suggest the reverse. That American poetry is so bound by the printed, written, composed (composure) version of language as to be closer to prose. And that this might account for why there is in the American poets' reading aloud a greater, sought-for, divergence from the printed poem than there is in her/his English counterpart. If this, or any part of it, is allowable, then we are in a position to consider Lawrence's free verse, and its on the whole lesser delicacy than Whitman's because of its being, having, to a greater degree, the nature of the spoken voice. I would in fact argue that Lawrence's shift from metrical to free verse indicates his desire to interpolate more of the speaking voice into his poetry than the metrical verse permitted him. It's worth having a look at the last two poems of

Look! We have come through (1917), 'Frost Flowers' and the more sustained 'Craving for Spring', which were written in England (the last has the ascription 'Zennor', where Lawrence and Frieda lived, until expelled from Cornwall by the military authorities in October 1917). It is also in part true that these two poems, as Lockwood says, 'already have the characteristic features of [BBF]' (p. 100). Yet not quite. If one compares

scýllas and yéllow-háired héllebore, jónquils, dím anémones,
even the súlphur aurículas,
flówers that come fírst from the dárkness, and feel cóld to the
  tóuch,
flówers scéntless or púngent, ammóniacal álmost . . .
('Frost Flowers', 270)

with 'Pomegranate', the first poem from *BBF*,

Pómegranates like bright gréen stóne,
And bárbed, bárbed with a cr̅o̅w̅n̅.
Oh, crówn of spiked̅ green métal
Áctually grówing!
(278)

what one notices despite the word 'ammoniacal', drawn from the modern language of chemistry, is a contemporary feel to the language of the latter poem, due, I would argue, to the governance of speech rather than the preponderating, or still strong, element of that written language in 'Frost flowers'. Thus,

Do you méan to téll me you will sée no físsure?
Do you prefér to look on the pláin síde?
(278)

Lawrence's insouciance requires the spoken voice, rather than the written hand. Hands have no tears, or laughter. The language of the latter poem is noticeably more compact. At any rate the monitor is the speaking voice and I offer speculatively the suggestion that Lawrence, after the war, living in exile with his wife (they were married in 1914), and not for the most part speaking English, except with her, felt the need of spoken English, and produced that in his verse. The contingent is invariably a factor in composition.

To revert to the written aspect of his prosody, I have noticed that when Lawrence's lines are end-stopped, by punctuation or syntactical termination, there is a tendency to greater delicacy. Whitman, as I've said, rarely attempted enjambments and Lawrence was not at his best in using them. In this he might have learned much from Wordsworth:

> Nor will I quit thy shore
> A second time; for still I seem
> To love thee more and more.
> ('I Travelled among Unknown Men')

Clearly it is not simply a question of where to break the line so much as where the energy of the syntax intersects, with maximum effect, with the line. Punctuation in prose must often do what lineation, when used well, does with greater effect in verse. For equally clearly the line is also a form of energy, though having built into it the possible checks of its energies, in the syntax itself as well as in the line ending. If the speaking voice is the main abetter of all this we get a less supple, less flexible, less rich line than if the other elements are each given their rightful, and needful, interplay. Such impoverishment may also have to do with the spoken voice having to strain in order to execute those functions it has subverted. On the other hand, it is the voice that forces inventiveness into the poem, as if to counterbalance the missing contribution of those other factors. This invention may be checked by considering 'Peach', or indeed many of the fruit and tree poems. Gilbert tends to account for *BBF* in terms of Lawrence's alleged hatred of human beings in this stage of his life; and which in its denial of the human being releases the energy into the *en soi* life of the creatures he re-creates in his poems. This seems plausible so long as one disregards the condition of the speaking voice itself which is, after all, speaking not only to 'himself' but with others. About and sometimes for creatures moreover that are, in many respects, versions or aspects of the human creature.

THE HUMAN AND CREATURELY LIFE IN *BIRDS, BEASTS AND FLOWERS* AND OTHER POEMS

The negative aspect of Imagism's objectivity is that in recreating the creature (or object) in its appearance, Imagism misses the life.

Of course, this is a crude formulation, but so much is missing from Imagist poetry as to prompt one into suspecting that one of the unconscious motives, screened, perhaps, from some of its formulators and practitioners, is that in shedding some of the factors that normally cluster a writer's involvement with the creature s/he wishes to re-create, the writer was thereby making it easier for him/herself. Furthermore, one asks, in what sense one can be imagistic and objective in writing, and in what sense it is desirable. Perhaps our passion and care for the creature, in its life, constitutes the proper meaning of 'objectivity', rather than the so much valued detachment and dispassion. Dispassion probably obtains and offers very little, though by concentrating on what one sees and feels one makes the necessary moves towards excluding the otherwise supervening ego. I quote again the portion from 'Pomegranates':

> Pomegranates like bright green stone,
> And barbed, barbed with a crown.
> Oh, crown of spiked green metal
> Actually growing!

The difference between seeing and wonderment is summated in that last line, 'Actually growing!' complete with exclamation mark, which serves to de-reify the creature.

Of course there is, as others have observed, Lawrence's provocative relationship with his readers, not least of all in the sexual implications of both 'Pomegranate' and 'Peach', but none of that could occur unless there were first the response to the 'felt life':

> Why, from silvery peach-bloom,
> From that shallow-silvery wine-glass on a short stem
> This rolling, dropping, heavy globule?
>
> ('Peach', 279)

In a way that is difficult to explain, the rhythmic impetus communicates the poet's appreciation of the creature, which act extends into pleasurable and delectable metaphor.

This physicality that breaks down the taboos concerning the pleasant and its opposite is responsively expressed in the next poem of this serial group (not 'sequence'):

> In the médlar, in the sórb-apple,
> Wíneskins of brówn morbídity,
> Autúmnal excreménta;
> What is it that reminds us of whíte góds?
>
> Góds núde as blánched nut-kérnels . . .
>   ('Medlars and Sorb-apples', 280)

And since I have made such a commotion, by criticizing Sandra Gilbert for speaking of the poems' ideas rather than their poetry, I should remark on the difference in the poetry – the passage from 'Pomegranate' being concentrated and immobile, while this last has a mobile, enjambed, flowing lineation:

> Medlars, sorb-apples,
> More than sweet
> Flux of autumn
> Sucked out of your empty bladders
>   (281)

The first concentrates a perception of the fruit, and this latter expresses the 'wonderful . . . hellish experiences' of the one who has eaten it:

> perfect drunkenness
> Intoxication of final loneliness.
>   (281)

The enjambment separating 'sweet' from 'Flux' serves paradoxically to suspend the flux and sustain its movement, and thus, since it is 'sweet', sweeten it more. The short lines, however, emphasize the more than sweet sweetness of the fruit, and return back upon the receiver their essentialized active nature.

'Grapes' considers the implications of drunkenness, or perhaps the better word (not because it is the more respectable one) might be 'intoxication', involving as it does the more suffusing quality of 'toxic' – rather in the way that Tolstoy in *What is Art?* spoke of the diffusion of art as 'an infection'. It is such inebriation that brings one to 'the brink of re-remembrance' (286).

Of what? Or rather, what does the poem suggest? It is something that 'dry' America (= 'Prohibition' introduced 1919, repealed 1933) seems to not want to remember; and on that account it is strange to this reader how cerebral Gilbert makes this 'blood-consciousness' sound together with our effort to recover it. As if the latecomer Americans have the blood-consciousness problem (though Lawrence seems to deny this) at a greater remove, and, even so, theoretically. But this is to evade a problem. It is difficult to describe what ought to be at the core of being alive, and perhaps our difficulty in part constitutes the syndrome of what Lawrence would say is awry. Certainly the first three poems of *Last Poems* and 'The Man of Tyre' (also of *Last Poems*) make clear the 'god-given' attributes that are desirable.

Lawrence found it hard to express his apprehension of (non) human life because what he wants to avoid is expressing life in the form of an idea. Because ideas at best only approximate to an idea, not a mode of being. In 'Flowers and Men' (*More Pansies*) he defines his sense of this being by negation:

All I want of you, men and women,
all I want of you
is that you shall achieve your own beauty
as the flowers do.

Oh leave off saying I want you to be savages.
Tell me, is the gentian savage, at the top of its coarse stem?
Oh what in you can answer to this blueness?

[I want you to be as savage] as the gentian and the daffodil.
Tell me! tell me! is there in you a beauty to compare
to the honeysuckle at evening now
pouring out his breath.

(683–4)

Not entirely by negation, though there is probably no single poem that might fetch the sense of being alive into the light. Instead we must see round the phenomenon, somewhat in the way Rosenberg did with his[1] several uses of the 'root' image to express different if related aspects of one idea.

In 'Cypresses' (*BBF*) Lawrence depreciates 'Roman virtue' (297) which, he tells us, destroyed the subtle, delicate and thus life-embodying Etruscan culture.

---

1. See Jon Silkin, *Out of Battle*, ch. 10, and D.W. Harding, *Experience into Words*, ch. 5.

> wavering men of old Etruria:
> Naked except for fanciful long shoes,
> Going with insidious, half-smiling quietness
> And some of Africa's imperturbable sang-froid
> About a forgotten business.
>
> (296)

And what others had, the Romans, because they had not, destroyed, perhaps out of fear and envy. European empires have been 'built' this way, not least of all that one forced by Britain. So the Romans conquered 'the slender, tender-footed' Etruscans. Here through the dark glass of a dead race, or one absorbed into another, we get such a glimpse as Lawrence had, a register of life, the sensitivity and responsiveness of which ('delicate magic of life') had not been entirely darkened by the legal, conquering and acquisitive nature that Rome seems to have had.

In the Mediterranean area the cypress is considered to be the tree of death, thus being here in apposition to the Etruscans, who are dead.[1] Yet something of their spirit survives, in the cypress itself as Lawrence apprehends it, in 'the sinuous, flame-tall cypresses', which melt into the 'wavering men of old Etruria', 'their way . . . like cypress-trees in a wind'. But I have omitted the key epithet that characterizes the secretive character of their life, found in the word 'evasive'. And again, their 'subtle' life is partly sensed, and ineptly recreated ('bungled'), in Leonardo's *Mona Lisa*. As if the older Mediterranean, of which Etruria is a glimpsed instance, flickers through with the subsequent demise of the Roman Empire.

TELEOLOGY, OR ALTERNATIVELY, LETTING LIFE EXPRESS ITSELF

Another way of viewing the difference between Whitman and Lawrence is to notice that for all Lawrence's plea for an openness, which he does not regularly or even usually transgress, he is nevertheless considerably more teleological than Whitman. And teleology is after all involved with closure. This can be understood in the two versions of 'The Ship of Death', where, in the first unsectioned and, paradoxically, much more Whitmanesque version, the ship (compare

---

1.   See also Lawrence's letter to Edward Garnett, 5 June 1914 *re* 'the old stable *ego*' and his novels with their 'allotropic states' (*SLC*, 18).

both versions of Lawrence's poem with Whitman's 'Passage to India', especially its two concluding stanzas (437)), as Whitman might well have had it, journeys to 'oblivion', whereas in the latter, more characteristically Lawrentian and I believe better (sectioned) version, the received one, the ship returns. The revision instigates teleology. We perceive the goal and conclusion of return rather than the dissolution into oblivion, and this teleology is comparable with that in the third, usually preferred, version of 'Bavarian Gentians' (there is a later fourth version, 1042).

I have indicated that Lawrence's rhythms are more insistent than Whitman's and I now suggest that the flowering of this insistence has teleology as its root. You need to be sure to instigate a goal or termination in your work. Teleology and purpose almost irresistibly combine to produce some version of insistence, likely among many manifestations, to express such a nexus in rhythm and prosody.

Whether such connection exists as strongly and causally as I believe, both teleology and prosodic insistence are evident in one of Lawrence's finest poems, 'Almond Blossom' (304–7). And this may be the point most apt to disagree with Gilbert's ascription of a largely *en soi* (in itself) character to the poems of *BBF* – *en soi* because, allegedly, Lawrence so hated mankind. There is something anti-biblical in this and, I think, unlikely. For without denying Lawrence's bitterness at the war (*Kangaroo*, chapter 12, 'The Nightmare') and his particular suffering during it, it seems as if the *human* characterization here specified in the flower's 'Gethsemane' (306) (garden of pain) is made to inhere in both the flower and poem. The plant is magnetized *towards* the human, and, for all purposes, it is that partly god-like kind of human who suffers for the world's sake. The messianic character of the tree is human, though (in part) ascribed in the metaphor of the Christ-God. So it seems as if the *en soi* ascription is only technically correct and provides no insight into what the poem is deeply expressing. Which is this truly 'iron age' in which the almond, with its 'deadliest poison', puts forth what looks like iron, appropriate for the age, and its blossom, appropriate for its own responding nature.[1] (See also 'Bare Almond Trees', 300–1.)

---

1. But see W.C. Williams's 'An Elegy for D.H. Lawrence':

> Dead now and it grows clearer
> what bitterness drove him . . .
> (*Collected Poems*, Vol. I, p. 393)

It may be argued that such is anthropomorphism. Intersecting with all this is the redemptive compulsion that this is a tree making poison, 'In supreme bitterness', as it were in response to the age of iron in which it lives. The distortion of its life is a measure of its total context, as its flowering is the measure of its generosity, like Christ's. The 'Gethsemane blood', messianic but self-creating blossom, which is sore-hearted, is also 'life-blissful at the core'; and this connects the poem with 'Flowers and Men' (above). Its blessing is both beautiful and painful, costly and finally, in this Shelleyan winter ('This is the winter of the world'), it is painful for it:

> Ópen,
> Ópen,,
> Fíve times wíde ópen,
> Síx tímes wíde ópen,
> And gíven, and pérfect;
> And réd at the córe with the lást sore-héartedness,
> Sóre-héarted-lóoking.
>
> (307)

The poem is a complex act of worship, being composed of Lawrence's praise for the creature's own complex but essentially positive and responsive nature; but alongside this is the creature's fundamental nature itself, which is open, jubilating and engaged in the act of praise. In the quotation above this is sustained (crucial mode) by end-stopping repeated lines that are nevertheless enjambed in an ongoing syntax – a fine subtle achievement – delicate and triumphant.

Lockwood thinks that 'Sicilian Cyclamens' is (also) an instance of Lawrence at his best in the mode of *BBF* (though the group in fact has many modes). Like 'Baby Tortoise', its joyful inventiveness holds up its single type of life as the reciprocal mirror of many:

> Slōw toads, and cýclamen léaves
> Stíckily glístening with etérnal shádow
> Kéeping to ēarth.
> Cýclamen léaves
> Tóad-filmy, éarth-iridéscent
> Beáutiful
> Fróst-fíligreed
> Spúmed with múd

S̄n̄ail-nácreous
L̄ow̄ d̄ow̄n.

(310)

And of the plant as a whole, though chiefly of the flower,

> Greyhound bitches
> Bending their rosy muzzles pensive down,
> And breathing soft, unwilling to wake to the new day
> Yet sub-delighted.

(311)

It is a form of synecdoche where the cyclamen is an instance of 'pristine' life, 'Pelasgic', that is, of the pre-Greek race; for Lawrence locates most of his yearning in the pristine life of the Mediterranean. And as such 'they' are the instance of man before they became men. This dawning of life, finely creatured in the flower, gets another incarnation in the swiftness of the hare, whose velocity is an index of that spontaneity and freshness of true and unspoilt life:

> The hare suddenly goes uphill
> Laying back her long ears with unwinking bliss . . .

(311)

'Unwinking', untremoring, blissful but without the 'sore heartedness' and burden of the 'Almond Blossom'. Lawrence does not hesitate to make his meaning explicit, thereby giving his creatures the literal depth of his symbolic meaning. As he says,

> Ah Mediterranean morning, when our world began!

(311)

His – I would not say en soi condition, of conscious and not yet wary life, is wonderfully spoken up for. It is life feelingly conscious of its condition, hardly, in that sense, unaware of itself. Lockwood's claim that Lawrence lacked the terminology to express himself in this pre-Sartrean era, besides, perhaps, deriving from Sandra Gilbert, seems to have missed Lawrence's point. Then seemed it very bliss to be alive. 'Bliss' is not an 'unconscious' or even unaware condition.

However, in this poem another voice has more strongly entered, that of he who speaks on behalf of, rather than he who enables enactment; and we will find this voice suffusing more of the poems in *BBF*. It needs tact and restraint to let the creature perform its acts and express its being, as against the lesser achievement of the speaking for it. Greater tact still to speak for, but in the nature of, that creature. Of course, in 'Mountain Lion' the creature is the still-beautiful victim of its Spanish-speaking Mexican slayers; 'Hermoso es!' So there is still existential justification for the narrator doing the creature's work for it. Someone must speak for the dead. Yet something else is present – the authorial voice – which, in its detestation of the slaying, has the greatest difficulty in not monopolizing the sensuous life-centre of the poem; and in the termination of the poem, it shifts the focus off the slain creature and onto the narrator-speaker himself, who, arguably, is not the author but the fictitious (indignant) quasi-witness. And yet it seems as if in order to embody truly the flux of the creature's life, one must love it as one did the almond blossom

> Fragile-tender, fragile-tender life-body
> (306)

Of course, the creature there is being spoken for, yet such is the intensity of the apprehension that it feels as if the creature is not bespoken for, but speaking from and of itself.

If such generosity falters, the tendentious didactic voice may increasingly occupy the life-space. But yes, of course, the 'Creatures' group *is* vital, the poetry virtuous *and* sensitive. Thus

> And I, a many-fingered horror of daylight to him,
> Have made him die . . .
> ('Fish', 339)

It is wonderfully responsive and responsible, but – yet what is the way out of the dilemma – the poet is somewhat conscious of his sensitivity. As well he might be.

In 'Man and Bat' we have the situation of a bat having taken refuge in Lawrence's room, and the man's equal determination to evict him:

> It was the light of day which he could not énter,
> Any more that I could énter the white-hot door of a
> blast furnace.

He could not plúnge into the dáylight that stréamed at
  the window.
It was ásking too múch of his náture. . . .

(344)

Of course, empathy for a bat does not establish, *prima facie*, that
sympathy for human beings! (I am thinking, once more, of Gilbert's
assertion that Lawrence wrote *BBF* because he had, in effect, lost
sympathy with the human creature.) But that last line, 'It was asking too much of his nature', is telling because it implies that sympathetic insight requests and, in this instance, obtains, a recognition
of the creature's nature. Given such a recognition, and Lawrence's
willingness to appreciate and act on it, it seems less likely that
his sympathy with the human predicament had been exhausted.
But, to pick up another thread of the argument, we respond to the
efflux of insight, 'Light of day'/'blast furnace', rather than the creation of language. For the fusion of insight *and* language on a more
developed level we must wait for the poems comprising 'Reptiles',
such as 'Snake' and the six 'Tortoise' poems, all of which combine
the wonder of the language in 'Almond Blossom' with the insight
of these 'Creatures' poems.

BRIEF INTERMEDIATE NOTE ON METRICALITY IN *BBF*

I noted above that although *BBF* is comprised of free-verse[1] poems,
passages of metrical verse are embedded in a number of them. For
instance 'Cypresses', the sixth stanza, beginning

Amóng the sínuous, fláme-táll cýpresses
That swáyed their léngth of dárkness áll aróund . . .

(296)

the stanza is not entirely in iambic pentameter, but sufficiently so
for it to indicate that Lawrence had found a use for it in his free
verse. And in 'Almond Blossom', stanza 6, beginning

But yóu mistáke, it ís nót from the ský;
From óut the íron, and fróm óut the steél . . .

(304)

1. Of *BBF*, 'a book of very free poems', *Letters*, 515.

the use of iambic pentameter is consistent throughout the stanza, except for the last line, with its ripple of feeling,

> Sétting supréme annúnciátion to the wórld.

That lovely ripple in the line (or else it might be read as hexa-meter, but given the context of the whole stanza it is more likely to be a 'ripple' within a pentameter) – that movement corresponds in some way to the quaver in the concluding line of Hardy's 'Channel Firing':

> As fár inlánd as Stoúrton Tówer,
> And Cámelot, and stárlit Stónehénge.
>
> (*Collected Poems*, 288)

And similarly, we find in 'Snake', stanza 9:

> Wás it cówardice, that I dáred nót kill hím?
> Wás it pervérsity, that I lónged to tálk to him?
> Wás it humílity, to féel só hónoured?
> I félt so hónoured . . .
>
> (350)

It might seem as though I am agreeing with James Reeves' 'no poet has successfully deviated for long from the iambic norm' (*D.H. Lawrence's Poetry*, 180), but though not wishing to appear a dissent-ing voice, I would suggest that something different is going on in poems that are, substantially, in free verse. Yet what is it?

Perhaps in a sense, yet a most peculiar one, which the late James Reeves would not, I think, have accepted, Lawrence is using the 'iambic norm' for particular, and in Reeves' terms, ironic purposes. But by 'ironic' I do not mean 'irony'. Rather, Lawrence is using the metrical earlier established norm for the specialized purpose of interpolating a particular voice and especial feeling.

In all three poems, and there are many others in *BBF* in this mode, the free verse, which has many faces and characters, is, among other things, speculative. It is not Coleridge's appalled 'What if', but a voice discovering, in perplexity, the very best in itself. Thus the isolated Romantic poet, precursored, as Richard Holmes has indicated in *Dr Johnson and Richard Savage* (1993), by the figure of Savage, and the earlier Johnson himself.

Leaving aside the biography which might, however, support the idea I am advancing, Lawrence's *uncertainty*, after the First World War, as to the nature of human society and the human animal, including a perplexity concerning his own nature, forced him to explore his uncertainty, but also to express his wondering affirmation for the quick of creaturely life. Free verse was the most acceptable instrument he found for this, Lawrence's strong desire for teleology and closure notwithstanding.

An understanding of this wish for partial resolution, however, may help to explain Lawrence's use of metrical verse in *his* free verse poems, or, at least, account for the effect of certain metrical passages within that corpus. Of course, it could be said that here was a convenient mode for Lawrence to touch home on, when he wanted to; Lawrence the exile in life as much as in his verse. But that, I think, is to ignore the effect of these metrical passages, which is in certain respects remarkably similar in all three cases. It is not, I think, difficult to say what that is; it offers at any rate, what I would term 'limited certainty'.

In all three passages, and they are notable for their verse as much as for their convictions, there is the certainty predicated upon the discovery of positive value. 'Among the sinuous, flame-tall cypresses' – 'there at least'; and 'But you mistake, it is not from the sky', and 'Was it humility, to feel so honoured?' – 'for I did'. Though the nature of *that* feeling has yet to be disclosed (below). I am not saying these are the only feelings effected in these complex metrical passages, but I am arguing that in poems of exploration and uncertainty flashed into expression by the instrument of free verse, these metrical passages flash out as moments of certainty in a world that is felt to be anything but.

That in itself is a great ironic achievement, neither odd-ball, as some critics suggest Lawrence is, nor falsely rhetorical.

CREATURES: A MODE TENDING TOWARDS THE DRAMATIC

In the 'Reptile' poems, a number of impulses are brought together while at the same time their range is increased. 'Impulses' is a vague word, so I had better define it.

It is strange that in the flower poems (above), creatures who cannot speak or respond are themselves so powerfully responded to; that by the same un-visible reciprocity, they are in the poems tacitly given the means to respond. Thus the 'sore-heartedness' of the 'Almond Blossom', flower and poem, ought to correspond (gently) to the male tortoise's coition cry; yet the filaments of response in 'Almond Blossom' are so strong that in their being concentrated on they appear to elicit a response from the flower (plant) that seems less author-instigated, or mediated, than that in any of the reptile poems. In that sense the flower poems are nearer Lawrence's core (and perplexity?), and in that sense are more lyrical, though the lyric character generously endows the flower rather than the poet. Certainly, this lyrical, sensuous character is more intimate and essentialized than that in the reptile poems, poems which are closer to the mode of drama-novel. Is this realism on Lawrence's part, or something even deeper?

The reptile poems instigate something new. I don't know whether the 'Creatures' poems 'Mosquito' and 'Bat' and 'Man and Bat' preceded in composition the 'Reptiles' poems. But suppose that these poems bring in an element of intimate repugnance, and strangeness (as with 'Fish'): and that they also bring, as 'iron' had done in both 'Bare Almond-Trees' and 'Almond Blossom', a vivid use of the ordinary, colloquial word-object into the literary context. We end up with a sense of Lawrence's working language-and-life hard, yet with ease.

Instances of this abound, but to cite a few. The mosquito is a (dull) 'clot of air' (332) and likewise the bat in 'Man and Bat' is 'like a clot' (345). The fish is 'Curvetting bits of tin' (335), and 'the small fish fly like splinters' (338). And of the fish that (sadly) he caught, it was 'gorping'. So much for language, when the colloquial and quotidian are multiplied upon the literary. Nor does Lawrence rest it there, but introduces what might be called the 'feelingly' scientific. Thus in 'Turkey-cock', 'Your wattles are the colour of steel-slag' . . . 'Cooling to a powdery, pale-oxydised sky-blue' (369) and in 'The Blue Jay' he addresses it as 'You copper-sulphate blue bird!' (375) – Lawrence seems to have responded to mineral blue. (See also Roy Fisher's 'Starting to Make a Tree', chapter 7.)

But this is to name only one aspect. In 'Creatures', especially the bat poems, there is what might be described as the rhythmic equivalent to onomatopoeia. Thus with Tennyson's creatures, in the bees' sound of the 'murmuring of innumerable bees', the purpose of 'innumerable' is to have the plurality of sound produce an effect of infinite number, of voices if not of creatures. In Lawrence's bat poems we have the lineation re-creating a sense of bat-flight, especially of the bat's looping panic as it feels trapped in the room exit for whom the sunlight bars. It is notable how generously Lawrence manages this creature once he grasps that to get him to leave of his own accord 'was asking too much of his nature'. As he says,

> the human soul is fated to wide-eyed responsibility
> In life . . .
>
> (347)

And he gets the creature out. In observing this, I might once more qualify Gilbert's too cerebral imposition of *en soi* onto the poems of *BBF*. For what is the terror and interacting horror between bat and man, if not of a realized consciousness, in which both are party to an understood life. The bat is not human, 'admitted', but in this transaction between them they are both interacting creatures, zoologically, and here, I think, the perhaps enforced distinction between *en soi* and *pour soi* dissolves. 'Wide-eyed' responsibility is entailed for the bat, yet so is it between humans. Thus to extend this point, there is interaction, and, in there being so, a separation and relationship between creatures, that did not occur in the same way in the flower poems. The rhythmic equivalent of onomatopoeia:

> Néar the céiling as íf in a wéb,
> Stággering;
> Plúnging, fálling oút of the web,
> Lúnging blíndly,
> Héavier;
> And clútching, clútching for one sécond's pause,
> Álways, as if for one dróp of rést,
> One líttle dróp . . .
>
> (345)

is the instrument whereby Lawrence initiates narrative and drama. The danger will be if both the narration, 'the act and process of telling a story', and the narrative 'what it is you actually recount', (Eagleton, *Literary Theory*, 106) take over at the expense of the poetry's other elements. How successfully can Lawrence 'engorge' a complexity of elements and reconcile coexistence in the one poem? Yet with narrative-narration has come something slightly other, which might be described as 'drama'. For although there evidently is drama in prose narration, there probably is, in Lawrence, as in other poets, a more immediate physical sense of interaction in the poetry than in the prose fiction. This is open to question, but if we allow that prose fiction is usually concerned with how people interact, it might be said that poetry is probably more concerned with how it feels to interact, and may bring in a greater quantity of that with its essentializing and compacting activity. If fiction tells us more about people, poetry may tell us more about what such people (*and* creatures such as the bat) feel in a totalizing life situation. At any rate I don't think it's enough to separate out prose-fiction (the novelist Lawrence) from the poet and his demon. That is to be too much guided by both Lawrence in his Foreword to the 1928 edition of *Collected Poems* and, perhaps, by Sandra Gilbert, tempting though her distinction between these two is.

'REPTILES'

In 'Snake', as in the bat poems, we have 'encounter' or 'drama', though in 'Snake' there is more on-behalf-of narrative-narration than in the poems concerning the bat. Yet having said that, the creaturely realization in stanza 3, with the lovely internal-rhyming delicacy of 'drip' with 'sip' – the latter such an unexpected verb for a snake's act of drinking – is entirely generous, and the narrator invisible:

> He reached dówn from a fissure in the eárth-wáll in the
>   glóom,
> And trailed his yellow-brown sláckness sóft-béllied dówn,
>   over the édge of the stóne tróugh
> And résted his thróat upon the stóne bóttom,
> And whére the wáter had dripped from the táp, in a small
>   cléarness,
> He sipped with his stráight móuth,
> Sóftly dránk through his stráight gúms, into his sláck lōng
>   bōdy,
> Sílently.
>
>   (349)

However in 'Snake' the encounter is not only with the creature:

I picked up a clúmsy lóg
And thréw it at the wáter-tróugh with a cláttter.

Í thínk ít díd nŏt hít hím . . .

(351)

and

And vóices in me sáid, Íf you were a mán
Yoụ would táke a stíck and bréak him now, and
finish him óff . . .

And yet those voices: ('of my education')
If you were not afraid, you would kill him!

(350)

Of all Lawrence's *BBF*, this is probably not only the most moral
of his parables but, as the moral trajectory travels alongside the
narration, the most explicitly didactic in its unfolding. There is nothing to weary the reader in this, partly perhaps because it is directed
at the narrator and only indirectly, on reflection, upon the reader.
That is good strategy without any covert slyness, engaging the reader
because one believes that such was truly Lawrence's experience
and response. In the poem is triple involvement, between man and
creature, and with his divided self. Yeats's dictum that we make
poetry out of the argument with ourselves is in this case well
founded:

The vóice of my educátion said to me
Hé múst bé kílled,
For in Sicily the bláck, bláck snákes are ínnocent,
   the góld are vénomous. . . .

But must I confess how I liked him
How glad I was he had come like a guest in quiet,
   to drink at my water-trough
And depart peaceful, pacified, and thankless,
Into the burning bowels of this earth?

(350)

The business about the creature's looking 'around like a god' seems,
to this reader, secondary. The first argument with himself cannot,
in any case, involve 'a god' but the two sides of the human psyche

as each interacts with the creature. On the one side of it rejoices the kinship with creaturely life – or much of it. On the other sits, chuckling and fuming with self-important knowledge, the 'voice(s) of my education'. Not that fear isn't potent, but on the evidence of the *poem*, there is only a modicum of it. There is so much more of the recollection of these societal voices, and the macho image of self: 'If you were a man'. It is true that after he has thrown the log in the creature's direction (probably to frighten him rather than to hit him) the snake 'convulsed in undignified haste'. Yet the offence is not against a 'god' or 'king in exile, uncrowned', but against creaturely life, its pact involving its members in an Isaiah-like peaceable kingdom of which the man and the snake are individually a part. The offence committed is against that pact, and involves the rupturing of it. In any case, even mere politeness might demand that he continue to allow the snake to drink, since he was there first.

So is 'pettiness' what Lawrence must 'expiate'? If it is pettiness, then expiation seems on the face of it too strong a word. But the pettiness is in himself, the offence against the creature and the pact of the peaceable kingdom. Probably, Lawrence collapses these complex issues into the word 'pettiness' so as to create as little moralizing uproar as possible, and in that case the reduced word works, drawing the reader to reflect on the smallness of the word and the incident's implicit dimensions. The drama between man and snake, and in himself, has been cut down to size and is, in that, curiously modern. A minimum of fuss maximizes the corollary of how great is the breach in the societal life and conduct of creatures.

THE PEACEABLE KINGDOM

One of my students, Goto Takahiro, remarked that the snake was a messenger between the domains of the human and the non-human. This finely achieved perception puts into another dimension that sense of the prelapsarian Peaceable Kingdom, and intimates by how much Lawrence wishes to restore within our contemporary existence that old (Mediterranean) kingdom. That is to say, with respect to that kingdom, the snake and human are on equal terms. Surely that is *one* reason why, initially, the narrator does not disturb the creature in its beauty ('soft-bellied') but lets the firstcomer drink. And in doing so discovers that he 'liked him'. The argument 'Lawrence' has with both the snake and himself is encapsulated in

And trúly I was afráid, I was móst afráid,
But éven so, hónoured still móre
That hé should séek my hóspitálitý
From oͧt the d̲ark d̲oͦr of the sécret earth.

(350)

In the next stanza we begin to get a shift in the creature's status: it is 'like a god', and what begins as metaphor resumes in the last but one stanza as 'like a king', repeated, and 'uncrowned', but no less kingly for that, and then, outright in the last stanza, 'one of the lords/Of life'. It would be easy to accuse Lawrence of allowing that aristocratic component illicit entry into the poem; except that it seems to work its way in with such finality, that we must take the insistence as meant meaning.

If we do this, we need to take on two different violations of transgressions for which the narrator must 'expiate'. One consists of the transgressing of the pact of creatures of equal standing, creatures who belong to the prelapsarian kingdom; so that when the narrator hurls the 'clumsy log' in the creature's direction (rather than to hit him) he not only violates the creature's dignity, but the prelapsarian condition, or, if it is preferred, the postlapsarian agreement. Yet the other violation is of 'one of the lords of life'; and although to press upon the poem a 'class' reading is, perhaps, crass, my principal difficulty is that these two tend to be mutually exclusive transgressions. For the violation of the universal kingdom depends on its members having equal status, capable of making *equal* if different contributions. To violate the uncrowned king is altogether a different 'country', and itself disarrays the notion of the kingdom of equality, where, by the way, the king of such a country is moral respect and peace. Coexistence. It is a problem I have struggled with for some time without finding satisfactory resolution.

MORALIST

Having offered criticism of a poem of Lawrence's, I should say that it is presented in the belief that Lawrence is one of the major poets of the twentieth century in English. It seems necessary to offer this slightly prancing assertion not only because of Lawrence's ambiguous status as a poet in the domain of higher education, but because of this reader's unease with one of the editor's placing of Lawrence, the poet, in his introduction to the standard *The Complete Poems*. Vivian de Sola Pinto wrote (p. 5):

> It may be argued that the only possible form for great poetry in this age of science and realism is the novel or prose story, and there can be no question that Lawrence's poetic genius finds its fullest expression in prose works like *The Rainbow, Women in Love, St Mawr* and *The Man Who Died*. Nevertheless, his work in verse is a very important part of his literary achievement. He said something in his verse that he could never have said in prose, and his best poems are among the most valuable and significant in the English language written in the twentieth century. Indeed they may be described as examples of the only kind of great poetry that can be written in the world in which we live.

Of course, if there can be no question 'that Lawrence's poetic genius finds its fullest expression in prose works, such as *The Rainbow* and *Women in Love*', there can be no arguing it. But despite this, and notwithstanding Leavis's idea of *The Rainbow* being a 'dramatic poem', it seems worth suggesting that when we read the poetry, it is not prose fiction that we read. Lawrence seems to have thought so too. But there is also to consider the somewhat damaging piece of praise in 'Nevertheless, his work in verse is a very important part of his literary achievement', which puts the verse into a poor second position. It is a competitive perspective, which not only places the verse in that position, but predisposes the reader, who is more or less willing to meet Lawrence's poetry on open terms, to see it through a somewhat concessive filter before s/he even starts to read it. It is not that one would wish De Sola Pinto to be generous, but simply to let the reader alone.

Lawrence is many things, but it could be said without deterring a reader that he is, among other things, a moralist. So that when Pinto says that 'He said something in his verse that he could never have said in prose' (p. 5), one could reply that whatever Pinto meant, it is not that the poetry expresses itself differently but that its basis of declaration is different from that of the prose. This is a difficult argument to make good, but it is based on the idea that the morality in the poetry is different because more inclusive. Can something be more inclusive?

In his 'Why the Novel Matters', Lawrence wrote that 'The novel is the book of life' and

> To be alive, to be man alive, to be whole man alive: that is the point. And at its best, the novel, and the novel supremely, can help you . . .
>
> *(Selected Literary Criticism*, 107)

And in 'Morality and the Novel' (1925) he declared:

> The business of art is to reveal the relation between man and his circumambient universe, at the living moment. . . .
>
> *(Selected Literary Criticism*, 108)

There are two positions here – I'm not trying to catch Lawrence out – one of which is to do with the novel ('whole man alive') and the other to do with 'art' ('the relation between man and his circumambient universe'). Just so. Although in fact the poetry of *BBF* does neither of these exactly, for it includes people both explicitly and implicitly. And then there is the relationship between the 'circumambient universe', which is not so much between that and *people* as between *all* creatures and 'itself', where people are one part and thus, by definition, are not the consideration of the whole thing. Yet if the moral judgements are delivered by 'man', such as the one writing the poems, in the *poems* the creatures also (sometimes) perform judgements. Thus even a dead one, such as the mountain lion, who obtains from her slayers in their own tongue the admission 'hermoso es!' 'it is beautiful'. Thereby suggesting (the dead creature might be 'saying') 'you were wrong to kill me' and 'why did you?' The snake and man morality is partly of the novel, in as much as an element of its focus is on the conflict within the narrator/persona. But the struggle *within him* in relation to the snake is not part of the novel; as I have been trying to suggest, in its relation to the peaceable kingdom, it is a perspective of cosmogony. Universal relationships are not, as a rule, the material of the novel; not, at least, as Lawrence seems to see it (above). But they are the subject of poetry.

So to risk repeating this, 'expiation' is to do with an offence committed not against another human, but in respect of the universal compact. As Sandra Gilbert has so well observed, while irony is (locally) present in Lawrence's verse he eschews the ironic mode, which, Davie believed, provided in the 1920s the more relevant modes. 'Eliot's ironical modes were more fruitful . . . [than] the models which Hardy provided'. Thus he considered those to have been the most valuable for twentieth-century poetry (see *Thomas Hardy and British Poetry*, 1972, 138). The important question, though, is not whether Lawrence does not employ local circumscribed irony – which he does – but if his poetry, its vision, is cast in ironic questions and perspectives – which it is not.

All this is said by way of trying to describe in what way the (universalized) morality of the poetry ('wide-eyed') differs from the morality inhering between humans in the reach of the novel (fiction).

As we may easily see in 'Mountain Lion', this is not a question of excluding morality between humans, which is most acute in the collusive meeting between the pairs of human beings, but of developing and extending that morality to include the slain mountain lion, and what is implied in *her* death. Thus the human animal is not excluded from this totalizing morality, which the novel appears not to operate.

So in 'Elephants in the Circus', the third poem in *Pansies* (1929):

> Élephants in the círcus
> have aéons, of wéariness róund their éyes.
> Yet they sit úp
> and shów vást béllies to the chíldren.
>
> (425)

The tasks that the elephants are forced to, to earn money for the circus-owners, is implicated in the 'aeons of weariness round their eyes'; and their vulnerability is underscored by the for them unnatural posture, in which they display their 'vast bellies'. But it is to children they are shown, so that these latter are collusively included in this corrupting enslavement of the animals, for money. This role of the children here resembles that of the children in war's 'desperate glory', in Owen's 'Dulce Et Decorum Est'. It also needs remarking that the sensuous, allusive, apprehending morality of Lawrence's poem is finely countered by the two-line structured parallelism – 'Elephants . . . have/Yet they . . . and show'. It is not that the poem exclusively relies on either morality or parallelism, but that it brings both into conjunction, and so consolidates its achievement. And in noticing that structure of parallelism, one might suggest that what metrical verse does with it, in the propositional-type verse of the early Augustans, free verse does more insistently, using it, however, as its principal *structural* component. This is an interesting development in free verse, for whether it is a result of not using metre, or else a replacement of it, the parallelism becomes in this type of poem (see also 'Phoenix', below) *the* structural component. It may be that Lawrence's 'natural *lingering* of the voice . . . the hidden *emotional* pattern that makes poetry' (*SLC*, 80) has transmuted into a form. And perhaps, in this, we may have discovered a tendency in Lawrence for feeling to shift into, or find, a form under its own pressure.

No less than in 'Snake', the burden of 'Elephants in the Circus' represents the broken compact of the Peaceable Kingdom. But in the remainder of the 'Reptile' poems there is a shift from the relationship between human and non-human creatures to that between creatures, whose lives, sexuality and 'family' life parallel human lives, to their mutual illumination. So this group of six tortoise poems enacts the life of other sentient lives. The dim life in the garden between the human couple and the serpent (shadowing 'Snake') becomes, in laconic reversal, the substituted comparative lives of tortoise, child and parental lovers, whose activities bear bleakly but with humour upon our human lives.

It is as if the story of the Garden had been abruptly ceased to resume another postlapsarian one, where we both laugh at, and commiserate with, the human and creaturely plight.

There is another change between 'Snake' and the tortoise poems. Most of the former poem, with the exception of the four opening stanzas, is mediated through the authorial voice. In the tortoise poems, the role and spread of the authorial voice has been reduced to make way for the tortoise activities. And what life!

If Keith Douglas's wit is the blade of his courage (as I suggested elsewhere), so Lawrence's humour comprises some part of the energy of the 'quick' as he apprehends that in the creatures' plight.

'Baby Tortoise' initiates the following-on from 'Snake' of the tortoise poems, and this jetting connection of humour and cool endearment in these poems has to exert all its capacities, if it is to effect the passage from tragic recognition that in low-key concludes 'Snake' to the heartfelt family antics of the parental tortoises; the male 'crucified' by, and into, sex, more than his stoical, seemingly oblivious larger mate.

Some of this wit in enactment consists, in 'Baby Tortoise', in seeing how many other creatures may be perceived in momentary and fragmentary resemblance with the central figure, yet without this disturbing the creature's essential being. The comparisons are hardly ever merely physical, though they are physical, but employ the physical to instigate spiritual insights with regard to both the creature as tenor and the others as vehicle:

> A tíny, frágile, half-ánimate béan. . . .

It has a

> tiny beak-mouth . . .
> upper hawk-beak

and is said to row like a

> small bird . . .
> Rather like a baby working its limbs, . . .
> Challenger,
> Little Ulysses, . . .
>   little Titan, . . .
> Stoic, Ulyssean atom; . . .
> Voiceless little bird, . . .
> Like a gentleman in a long-skirted coat. . . .
> Invincible fore-runner . . .
>
>   (352–4)

It is a great deal for the creature to support with 'All life carried on your shoulder' like Atlas; but he manages. Yet the extraordinary fact is that the more personages, creatures and roles are pressed upon the baby tortoise, the more strongly formed the creature becomes, its appearances, out of all these fluxes of others, printed in overlapping identities into one: his own. Perhaps this composite unity is intended to establish cosmological rather than only human (merely human?) analogies.

Thus the next poem, 'Tortoise Shell', views the dorsal part of the creature, and examines the religio-sacred value of the cross lapped into the shell, 'the first eternal mathematical tablet' (355). In so doing, the structure is careful to demythologize itself of Christian possession and proprietorship, even to eschew any crypto-religious dominance by Christianity. If the creature has 'his five-fold complex-nature' (356)

The Lord wrote it all down on the little slate
Of the baby tortoise . . .

(356)

when turned helplessly on his back he is nevertheless as vulnerable as a 'sprottling insect' (sprottling = sprawling, kicking about
helplessly).

So that when we return to the laconic endearment of the parental and family behaviour, anterior to it all is not a Christian but
a sacred sense of the creation, which the Lord made, and 'wrote'
on the back of the tortoise, who constantly adverts to it in his
'perambulating' motion (a nice sly use of the word in 'Tortoise
Family Connections', 357).

Yet if this is in place, there is perhaps an element of unconscious
unkindness buried in it with respect to his wife Frieda, where Lawrence, in 'Connection', proceeds to enact the unfamilial behaviour of the creatures. Frieda, of course, had left her husband Ernest
Weekley, and their children, to live with and eventually marry Lawrence. It cost her, particularly in relation to her children. Something of the pain the separation from her children entailed *may* be
seen in as much as after Lawrence's death Frieda copyrighted the
Lawrence estate into the possession of Angelo Ravalgi (whom she
subsequently married) together with the Weekley family. Not the
Lawrence family.

At any rate we may read Lawrence's grim yet almost gleeful and
very comic registration of unfamilial feeling in 'Tortoise Family
Connections':

It is, no use my saying to him in an emotional voice:
'This is your Mother, she laid you when you were an egg.'

He [baby tortoise] does not even trouble to answer:
  'Woman, what have I to do with thee?'
He wearily looks the other way,
And she even more wearily looks another way still,
Each with the utmost apathy, . . .

(357)

In this, of course, is the marginally scandalous use of and reference
to the exchange between Christ and his mother, when he declares

'Woman, what have I to do with thee? Mine hour is not yet come'
(*John*, 2.4).

We may notice something of Lawrence's evolving different styles,
signalled perhaps by his use of markedly different line-lengths and
syntactical structures. Less radically, Whitman effects this in *Out of
the Cradle* where, in operatic structure, the recitative/narrative is
printed in Roman, and the high-point emotional aria utterance (of
the widower male bird) in *italics*. Here, with Lawrence, the longer
and shorter lines enact differing functions, though no invariable
rule or pattern as to what each structure does shows up. In general,
as with the above, the longer lines, often occurring in a sustained
flight, as in stanza 3 of 'Snake', enact rhythmical description, or
narrative, and the shorter trenchant lines are used for dramatic or
emotional emphasis. Thus the three lines that express the apathy
between son and mother

> Incognisant,
> Unaware,
> Nothing . . .
> (357)

may, in this respect, be compared with the short lines in 'Almond
Blossom', especially those in the concluding three stanzas, the repetition of which, prosodically and syntactically, is used to float the
emotion.

So, the source of Lawrence's vitality in *BBF* is in both the essential 'quick', delivered in a mixture of repetition (stability), and in
the invention (as in 'Baby Tortoise', above); and these are delivered
in varieties of style, more various than Eliot's, for instance. Consider the subtleties of character brought to bear in

> As for papa,
> He snáps when I óffer him his óffspring,
> Júst as he snáps when I póke a bit of stick at him,
> Because he is iráscible this mórning, an iráscible tórtoise
> Being tóuched with lóve, and dévoid of fátherliness.
> (357)

In part, the subtlety derives from 'papa' being both a tortoise
and a partly replicated human. If we say that his irascibility in
love is purely tortoise in character, we shall have to cope with the

fact that this is not always only true of tortoises. If we say that all
human beings are thus in love, we will likewise have to cope with
a one-sided ascription. The subtlety consists in the reader's being
oscillated between both man and tortoise, man as father/lover, and
tortoise as father, but definitely lover. The two-sided comparison is
asymmetrical and the humour derives in part from this.

As for the baby tortoise,

> Does he lóok for a compánion?
>
> Nó, nó, dón't think it . . .
>
> (357)

This last line is, of course, a 'counter' of the speech of the time, but
by enrolling it in the enactment and the discourse Lawrence gets
it to fulfil its social function in a form of doubleness. The baby
tortoise 'doesn't know he is alone', and at the same time we are
offered a knowing overall view by which we may observe him
with humour and sympathy. And, after all, are we so different? The
anthropomorphic comparison, this time brought to bear on papa's
offspring ('like father, like son') is deliberate, and similarly oscillating, intensely witty and affectionate, as we may see with the 'three
little brothers' being 'like little perambulating pebbles'. The wit is
both affectionate, and distancing, to the extent that, as Brecht would
have us do in Classic Theatre, we are to use our intelligence to see
what results from a comparison between us and 'them'. The poem
clinches the comparison with that lovely enjambment, and indeed
deeply affectionate enactment of love (which Graves borrowed)

> To róam, and féel the slów heart beat
> Tortoise-wise . . .
>
> (358)

On one side of the enjambment is the human, and on the other –
both him and us. The fine, inconsequential (yet completed) ending

> And biting the frail grass arrogantly,
> Decidedly arrogantly.
>
> (358)

has the effect of centering the father for the next episode in the
family activity, which, in 'Lui et Elle', is sex:

She is large and matronly
And rather dirty,
A little sardonic-looking, as if domesticity had driven her to it.
Though what she does, except lay four eggs at random in
      the garden once a year
And put up with her husband,
I don't know.

(358)

Increasingly so, there is a fleck, a flaw, a sting in Lawrence's apprehension of his paradise, for if she 'only' lays 'four eggs at random . . . once a year' (358), she also – but in the same breath – does 'put up with her husband'. Which as we shall see, is a great deal; though it is also a great amount for himself, 'crucified into sex' (361). For the *tortoise* situation, comparable to the habitual, by no means invariable and contrary human one, is that she is larger and seemingly indifferent as to whether she will have and endure sex with him; whereas he, smaller, 'dapper' (that comic, damning word in the context), intensely desires it, indeed is compelled in 'his isolation' to make 'his effort toward completion again' (361). It is in this being strung between several polarities, and their ensuing tensions, that Lawrence achieves his effects of comic pathos (she 'pitying her', 'I pity Monsieur'); in the shuttling journeys of sexual attempts, and comic successes, that end in sudden and awefull consummation.

I said earlier 'varieties of style'; and might also have said varieties of mode, underlying which is another set of polarities, in a sense an answer to Plato's ideal against which we are that primal model's imperfect versions. By bringing in the template of myth, for instance, in the 'earthy house-inhabiting Osiris' (361), but collating it with the contingent, mortal, quotidian elements of our lives – or the tortoise's – Lawrence conflates, or rather, compacts, Plato's ideal and version into one entity in which the unchanging sacred and the contingent human comprise one module. Thus we find 'Osiris' and soon 'that mud-hovel of his slowly rambling spouse' (361). How much wider this set of references is than the novel's. And again, both male and female are characterized in 'domed boats bumping' in the comic pathos of sexual necessity. We are hardly different.

'Tortoise Gallantry' in its very title brings irony, for he is reductively *like* a 'Stiff, gallant, irascible, crook-legged reptile,/Little gentleman'. The syntax and enjambment do not advise us which way to attach 'Little gentleman', so we are left to revise his being, from reptile to 'gentleman'. His conduct, as ours often is, is anything but the poised urbane behaviour implied in 'gallant' ('a gallant' – and Lawrence may well have read what Whitman had to say in the 1856 letter to Emerson, 'This empty dish, gallantry' (771)). He is certainly not in control, of any situation. This has the effect, as Lawrence suggested in 'Lui et Elle', of soliciting our sympathy. He is

> Driven away from himself into her tracks . . .
>
> (363)

and in this line we perceive how he must follow her if he is to complete himself, whereas she is, relatively, indifferent, if 'allowing'. He is also removed from his own 'tracks', that is, from his own self, which condition is Plato's understanding of love and ecstasy (SOD = 'the state of being beside oneself with passion'). It is love that possesses him; he does not possess himself, or her.

'Tortoise Shout' concludes both the tortoise group and the larger one of 'Reptiles'. And we may suspect we have followed the creatures to their 'end', their sexual completion. Yet we may not have been able to anticipate that the 'shout', the sound, the cry, implicates other animals, in a peaceable kingdom which, however, includes pain; where we find – 'the scream of a frog', 'a nightingale's piercing cries and gurgles', 'the scream of a rabbit', 'amorous cats', 'a terrified, injured horse' and 'the sound of a woman in labour', among others. It is a wonderful list, as wonderful a compilation as Whitman might have made, and if not quite as inwoven as that of Whitman in SoM, concerning the male body's attributes in relation to nature (see Chant 24), it rivals it; not so much in delicacy, though that is there in, for instance, the 'nightingale's cries *and* gurgles' (my emphasis), but in the drive of its realism and intensity –

> The first elements of foreign speech
> On wild dark lips . . .
>
> (366)

The reader is brought back, not only to that crucifixion entailed by desire, but also, and ideally, to that exemplary wholeness entailed in the act:

Torn, to become whole again, after long seeking for what is lost
The same cry from the tortoise as from Christ, the Osiris-cry of
    abandonment,
That which is whole, torn asunder,
That which is in part, finding its whole again throughout the
    universe.

(367)

The rhapsodic long-lined appeal of the conclusion seems earned.
Or rather, the rhapsodic tone, lineation and rhythms have been; but
what has intruded into the account appears to be the author. Perhaps this should be commuted negatively to somesuch figure as
'teacher' or 'didact'. One may not object to that, but what is harder
to take is the interruption of the narrative of creaturely enactment
by a preacherly authorial voice in a last-say role. It is grandiose and
biblical as in, for instance, 'torn asunder'. It is not so much that one
objects to the voice either, but that one feels Lawrence is obeying its
language and its mode rather than using it in the interests of the
poem. The language of another age, the original Arabic or Greek
translated into seventeenth-century idiom, is exerting pressure
on the language Lawrence would normally use, of his time. I am
not disputing the importance of Lawrence's communication in this
last stanza, but suggesting that other elements have ruptured the
kind of mode Lawrence has established for most of the poem. To
check this, one may compare the ending of this poem with that
of 'Almond Blossom'.

I suggested above that I would come back to the considerations
of prosody and lineation. So I offer two observations. One is the
flexibility with which Lawrence employs his *short* lines. In 'Mountain Lion', the flux of forms is between relaxed long-lined description, with which the poem opens, and the short lines. These latter
are dramatic, as we see in the opening of the encounter with the
two Mexicans who have killed the creature – 'He trapped her this
morning, he says, smiling foolishly' (401):

> Mén!
> Twó mén!
> Mén! The only animal in the world to féar!
>
> Théy hésitate.
> Wé hésitate.

Théy have a gún.
We have nó gún.

Thén we áll advánce, to méet. . . .

(401)

This is sufficiently and evidently dramatic to need no further comment, except to point to the executive (non-grammar-bearing) comma in the last line above, between 'advance' and 'meet', which serves to enact hesitation. It is followed by the confluence of four humans hastened on by guilt and collusion.

Or consider the short lines, which essentialize the poem's mourning the slain creature, in

It is a mountain lion,
A long, long slim cat, yellow like a lioness.
Dead . . .

(401)

'Dead' is not a single word Lawrence couldn't have placed in the rhythmical context of another line. It is part of his strategy of correlating descriptive lines with those of ideas or actions. Then again, it articulates the tight-lipped anger at the slaying of living beauty:

He trapped her this morning, he says, smiling foolishly.

'Trapped' is right. It is the language of evasion seeking collusion, as indeed are the refractions in 'smiling foolishly'. And of course, the phrase refers the reader back to the other couple in this encounter, who also 'smile, foolishly' in collusion – 'as if we didn't know' – 'We have no gun'. Everyone is in the know and each partly understands the motivation of the other, and the gun-power of one. 'Foolishly' here is resonant with ironies, both between the pairs of 'accomplices' and between the narration and the reader. This ironic discourse is sealed with the sad recognition

He is quite gentle and dark-faced . . .

(401)

which appears to suggest that gentleness can also do violence. He seems gentle, he probably is, *and* he has killed her. And we behave like fools in that we greet them as if we did not know, and they smile

foolishly both knowing what they have done and that we realize –
but they have a gun.

Second, the verse in long lines. If we take the pentameter as the
upper register of median length, the longer line presents another
outreach of Lawrence's versatility, in the stanza beginning 'Lift up
her face'. This frequent long line expresses experience within the
capacity of everyone, and it culminates in the pang-like 'brilliant
frost of her face' (402). It is followed by the short-lined telling apprehension of her beauty, cast in the very language of her slayers:

Hermoso es! [It is beautiful]

And in using the word beauty we might become aware of another
use of it, in the connoisseur-like language of 'What a beauty'. 'Yes,
shot her this morning, sir', which commutes the creature to an object
for the collectors. 'He is quite gentle.'

Certainly, the Spanish interjection clicks on a further change, as
we move from the internalized comment of the stanza concerning
her beauty to a sense of mourning in

So, she will never leap up that way again . . .
(402)

with the comma (again) after 'So', instigating a voice of both mourning *and* restrained anger. Without which it would, perhaps, lead the
reader into maundering regret for the loss of the creature. For the
anger represents, at least, the sense that what has happened ought
not to have, and that, if language can achieve anything, we will
perhaps impede such actions in future. Poetry changes nothing,
perhaps; but one might note the control of strong emotion in the
apparently marginal punctuation, as it shifts the balance of voice
off the author and onto the authority of the narrator. Yet the last
stanza may be construed as the didactic and angry voice of the
author, which, off-balance, threatens to subvert this fine poem:

And I think in this émpty wórld there was róom for me and
a móuntain líon.
And I think in the world beyond, how easily we might spare
a million or two of humans
And never miss them . . .
(402)

The arrogance of this is – chilling. If we say that this fails to register the future rise of fascism, we can at least affirm that the First
World War, which Lawrence so deplored, accounted for some 21
million killed – 'And never miss them'. In recurring to the missing
white frost-face of that slim yellow mountain lion we pick up on
the aristocratic strand that I suggested doubled the considerations
in 'Snake'. In 'Mountain Lion' this occurs in 'Her round, fine-
fashioned head ... And stripes in the brilliant frost of her face'.
'Fine-fashioned head' implies 'this aristocrat of animals'. Of course,
Lawrence is entitled to his aristocratism, but it shakes the basis of
the poem's appeal to the reader as much as it did in 'Snake'. It
constitutes, all round, a lapse rather than another oversight.

CONGRUITY IN FREE VERSE

Attentive readers will have seen that in the free verse of BBF there
are (as I have suggested above) clusters of metrical lines, a number
of them approximating to iambic pentameter. More subtly, there
exist passages which have the pace of metricality, if not a sometimes more rapid one, but which are not metrical. Yet these passages are comprised of lines which complete themselves in a mode
that compares with the completeness of metred ones. An instance
of this occurs in 'Baby Tortoise':

> To take your first solitary bite
> And move on your slow, solitary hunt.
> Your bright, dark little eye,
> Your eye of a dark disturbed night,
> Under its slow lid, tiny baby tortoise,
> So indomitable. . . .
>
> (352)

Some sense of the creature's progress here is, with one exception, to do with the lack of syntactical repetition, which, when it
occurs, tends to create a sense of marking time. Syntactical repetition
is of course a mode used in Hebrew parallelism (see the analysis
of Lawrence's 'Phoenix' below). The structure of such parallelism
invariably entails repetition, with either literal or in effect syntactically end-stopped lines. But when end-stopped lines are *not* formed
in syntactic repetition they convey a sense of *congruity*, even though

in metrical, and perhaps in rhythmic, terms there is none. And if this end-stopped character is dove-tailed into continuous syntax (as above) this strengthens the *effect* of congruity. If to this we add an evenness of discourse and/or tonality, the sense of congruity is further strengthened. It is prose-like, plain – an elevated plainness – such as we find in Wordsworth, and is itself, as Fred Beake suggests, a remarkable achievement. This is the rejoinder of free verse to metricality's congruence, enabling, perhaps, a greater flexibility and even, possibly, a greater liveliness. It is not everything, but it is a great deal.

METRICALITY AS A DEVICE, AND AUDEN'S PERCEPTION OF LAWRENCE'S 'LIGHT VERSE'

Auden's provocative essay 'D.H. Lawrence', in *The Dyer's Hand* (1962),[1] takes a minor strand in Lawrence and makes it his apprehension of one of Lawrence's principal virtues. It says more about Auden's lesser substance and achievement as a poet, and critic, than anything, but it serves to concentrate our attention on yet another aspect of Lawrence as a poet and, in particular, on his 'Nottingham's New University'. Wrongly, I believe, Auden groups this with Lawrence's so-called doggerel. Sandra Gilbert cites Lawrence as recording Frieda's response to his shorter, laconic poems in 'loose little poem form; Frieda says with joy: real doggerel' (*Letters*, 1106; Gilbert, 243). It seems possible that this is the source of Auden's use of 'doggerel', but we should not grudge his possible retrieval of the comment. The argument isn't worth having, though we ought to inspect this and other poems from *Pansies* (1929, both editions), not only because of the intrinsic value of many of them but also, as others have noted, because they lead into *Last Poems* (published posthumously, 1932). Critics have also noted the overlap, and concluded, incorrectly I believe, that there is a lesser disjunction between the *Pansy*-type poem and *Last Poems* than is sometimes supposed (cf. Aldington). Yet some such connection exists, as Sandra Gilbert observes in what she feels is Lawrence's sense of impatience in these shorter poems, impatience which feeds into the (concealed) economy of *Last Poems*. For paradoxically, in *Last Poems*, there is both an abridgement of trajectory in comparison with many of the

1.   Yet see in the same essay: 'Most of Lawrence's finest poems are to be found in the volume, *Birds Beasts, and Flowers*' (*D.H. Lawrence's Poetry*, 236).

poems in *BBF*, and at the same time a greater relaxation, not always however resulting in less tension.

In the meantime, consider 'Desire is Dead' and 'Nottingham's New University', both from *Pansies*; and, for metrical succinctness, 'Hymn to Priapus', collected in *Look! We have come through* (1917). In weaving together the unlikely pain of guilt at being 'unfaithful' to his mother, yet enjoying a sense of release in that very act, Lawrence concludes in the 'Hymn',

> Gríef, gríef, I suppóse and suffícient
> Gríef makes us frée
> To be faíthless and faíthful togéther
> As we háve to bé.
>
> (199)

Here the metricality is not yet the device it becomes – a sort of weapon – as in the 'University' poem. But it has some such thought-driven laconic sharpness, harder to achieve were metricality with rhyme not available. In the 'Priapus' poem, the metre lightly tries on necessity as the justification for his actions. It is halfway to being the same kind of rapid deposition of *ideas* that in the 'University' poem becomes both the substance of the poem as well as its mode:

> From thís I léarn, though I knéw it befóre
> that cúlture hás her róots
> in the deép dúng of cásh, and lóre
> is a lást offshóot of Bóots.
>
> (489)

A lesser poem, perhaps, but is it a lesser achievement? '– By Boots I am M.A.' being a recognition of the financial and enabling source of some of the university's (tied?) assets. It is comic because it is trenchant. There is narration, of course, and what also holds the poem together is the stanzaic deftness coupled with insight – 'culture has her roots/in the deep dung of cash'. Dung! Perhaps there is as much work in that as in the whole last stanza of 'Hymn to Priapus', and, in particular, the slightly self-conscious nonchalance and defiance in the paradox 'Grief makes us free'. Surely not. But if there is a sense of operating a rueful paradox in the earlier poem, what drives the later poem is animus, put through the machinery of conscious metricality.

'Desire is Dead' is five lines, and I quote them:

Rhymes
A   Desíre, máy be déad
B   and stíll a mán can bé
C   a méeting pláce for sún and ráin,
C   wónder outwaíting páin
B   as ín a wíntry trée.

(504)

Where many of *Pansies* are composed in the symmetry of ideas
rendered line by line in free verse, this uses that method with
metricality. By doing so, Lawrence adds a sense of firmness to the
onflowing desolate, but not defeated, feeling-syntax. Its one sentence rhymes, poignantly, the sense that desire may be dead but not
the life of the person, 'wonder outwaiting pain'.

As with the stanza from 'Baby Tortoise' (above) with regard to
the effects of congruence and onwardness in *free* verse, so here, but
conversely, for this is *metrical* verse. Yet it shares with the 'Baby
Tortoise' stanza – the rhyme here studding in the pauses which the
single sentence syntax opposingly matches – a sense of, each time,
pausing and holding back the completed syntax, as each line builds
the idea into its assembling whole. This is a fine achievement, and
foreshadows the metrical achievement in the opening stanzas of
'The Ship of Death' (below). That is, this latter poem's metricality
could not have been achieved but for the long practice of free verse.
As with Eliot, though hardly ever with Pound, some features of
metricality and free verse blend, in both these poems.

LAST POEMS

The short poem 'Phoenix' should also be quoted in full:

Ideas
A   Are you wílling to be spónged óut, erásed, cáncelled,
A¹   máde nóthing?
A   Are you wílling to be máde nóthing?
A¹   dípped ínto oblívion?

If nót, you will néver really chánge.

B   ⎡The phoénix renéws her yóuth
     ⎣only whén she is búrnt, búrnt alíve, burnt dówn

B¹   to hót and flócculent ásh.
C   Then the small stírring of a néw smáll búb in the nést
     with stránds of d̲o̲w̲n̲ like flóating ásh
C¹   shóws that shé is renéwing her yóuth like the éagle,
C²   immórtal bird.

(728)

Parallelism and free verse

By now the reader will recognize my identification of parallelism
with free verse as a kind of shibboleth. Certainly, in speaking of
Pound's free verse in comparison with his metrical (in chapter 3) I
suggested that stylization in the form of anaphora, in the 'Usura
Canto' 45, was one way in which Pound replaced the structuring
recurrence of metricality. I have always suggested (above) that in
place of metricality Lawrence substitutes end-stopped lines, cent-
ring the strategy upon each line containing an idea. It is also of
course a way of separating lines from each other. What bonds them
together, in 'Phoenix', is an intricate structure of parallelism the
working of which I indicate with letters.

It is a compact piece of intrication, with the interconnected lines
of stanza 1 worked in contrast to those in stanza 3, through and 'on'
the fulcrum of the single-line stanza 2.

So much for structure, and so much, incidentally, for Blackmur's
charge of formlessness and hysteria. (The attacks on Lawrence by
Eliot (*After Strange Gods*) and Blackmur (*Form and Value*) suggest a
shared animus.) It might be reasonable to ask, in this situation of
damaging accusation, whence comes the hysteria, which indeed
has many forms. Since both are dead, one from disease and he the
infinitely greater loss, the other, a great loss, also, alas, dead by his
own hand, it is better to ask what such a structure as Lawrence
used, achieves. We may remember that Lawrence had little respect
for the ostentation of form, and for its implementation, through
what he called 'skill' (above).

The structure in 'Phoenix' enables an overall relatedness in the
three incremental repetitions in stanza 1, line 1, and in stanza 3, line
2. Ultimately, however, their intricated strength lies not simply in
their organization and structured argument, but in their being predicated in situations which Lawrence could count on his readers sharing, or at least, appreciating. In stanza 3 it grows out of, admitted,
the *imagined* condition of the phoenix, who suffers re-birth through

being 'burnt alive' (3/2). The 'situation' is familiarized enough for us to imagine somesuch process; but the one in 1/1 is referential, founded on the child's use of the school slate (which saved the lives of many trees) or else of the teacher's blackboard – probably the former (and one I can remember from the infant school I attended in south-east London). Lawrence makes the outward structure alive, not so much through the rhetoric, which is subservient to his meaning, but by the poignant interlocking of a child's experience of learning, with the adult's learning his/her final 'lesson' concerning death. 'Are you willing?', Lawrence asks; a question he answers directly in 'Bavarian Gentians' with the 'let me guide myself' (below). Unlike the child, whose possible unwillingness will probably lead to ignorance, which is bad enough, the adult's willingness will lead to some final understanding and proper closing of one's life. For it is one thing to die, another to take one's death into one's own hands. Which is a profounder experience and process than education, as we have seen in 'Snake', crucial though the latter is. Nor should Lawrence's capacity to render vital, creaturely, experiential responses be used – as if it were intellectually reprehensible – to obscure his own intellectual achievement.

I may have suggested that this poem is made of symmetry, and to an extent this is true. But I have kept behind the question of rhythm. In brief, the insistent rhythm, compounded of questioning directed towards his own self, is structured into repetition, composed of parallelism.

Last Poems, like *Pansies* and *More Pansies*, often uses in its poems a modified narrative, which filaments connections between each poem, though the connections between them are principally those of idea and subject. It is not only that each poem embodies an idea or nexus of meanings; it is that the poem following isn't isolated by the previous poem's termination. For the previous poem provides the origins of the succeeding one.

This is felicitous, but has dangers. One evident one, which Lawrence does not always avoid, is that the individual poem may lose its autonomy and drive towards fulfilment; and thus let slip its identity as a poem. This can be seen in some of *Last Poems*. But conversely, when the poems achieve autonomy, their connections with each other strengthen the individual poems. This may be seen with 'The Ship of Death' and some of those poems that constellate it: 'Difficult Death', 'All Souls Day', and up to and including 'Sleep' (724). The recurring vocabulary emphasizes this sense of connection. Just as 'Shadows' (726–7) looks 'back' to SoD, so it looks forward to 'Phoenix' which, as the 'collection' is printed, is the concluding poem.

Last Poems is extensive, yet even so I will include from More Pansies some reference to 'Flowers and Men' (see above) and 'Prayer'. 'Flowers and Men', with its 'gentian' and the breath that pours from it, anticipates 'Bavarian Gentians'; but it also harks back to BBF. It considers the connections between creaturely life, and exhorts the human creature not to be 'savage' and abandon his/her fullness, or to give up on achieving 'your own beauty' (683).

So even if, thematically, this beautiful poem appears to offer a bridge between BBF and Last Poems by virtue of its concerns and values, many of Last Poems use less and less argument and oppugnancy – or less and less engage a hidden or implied opponent. Whatever disappointments Lawrence has felt with his fellow-human have been abridged to make way for prototypical models of humanity – the Greek gods and, for that matter, the Greek humans. It was after all to the Mediterranean that Lawrence returned, to die. Thus in 'The Greeks are coming' (687)

it is ships of Cnossos coming, out of the morning end of the sea, it is Aegean ships, and men with archaic pointed beards . . .

As with 'Sicilian Cyclamens' it was

Ah Mediterranean morning, when our world began!
Far-off Mediterranean mornings,
Pelasgic faces uncovered,
And unbudding cyclamens . . .

(311)

so here it is, succinctly, yet in relaxed mode, 'out of the morning end of the sea'. And in the following, 'The Argonauts' (687), it begins with 'They are not dead, they are not dead!' 'I must watch them still', whereas the 'ocean liner' 'leaving a long thread of dark smoke', in the previous poem, deposits something like 'a bad smell'.

Observing connections is not sufficient. We need to interpret the poems partly through their interconnections. So 'Prayer' (More Pansies, 684) connects with 'The Argonauts' – 'with bright, crescent feet'; but more evidently it connects with 'Invocation to the Moon' (Last Poems, 695).

I base this, partly, on the evident verbal interlinkage, but partly on the interlinking imagery. The poem puzzles Lockwood, and I won't pretend to a correct reading. And of course, it is dangerous to extrapolate from one to another poem on the basis of shared imagery. Yet if we look at the premiss of 'Prayer' (684) without, for the moment, pressing impatiently for meaning, this seems to be provided in

> Give me the moon at my feet. . . .
> For the sun is hostile, now
> his face is like the red lion.

In 'The Argonauts' it is

> the moon, who remembers, and only cares
> that we should be lovely in the flesh, with bright,
> crescent feet . . .
>
> (687)

In 'Invocation to the Moon', the goddess, or preceptress, becomes more present and more omnipresent:

> Be good to me, lady, great lady of the nearest
> heavenly mansion, and last! . . .
> Now I must enter your mansion, and beg your gift
> Moon, O Moon, great lady of the heavenly few . . .
>
> (695)

and then

> Fár and forgótten is the Vílla of Vénus the glówing
> and behínd me nów in the gúlfs of spáce lies
> the gólden hóuse of the sún . . .

and

> and one warm kind kiss of the lion with golden paws –
>
> (695)

The polarization is akin to 'prayer' – between moon and sun – except that here the sun is not hostile, and it is 'behind me now'. If

we read the sun as a figure of life and potency, is it too direct to
suggest that the reader is to take the moon as presiding over death?

> because naked you are more wonderful than anything
> we can stroke . . .
>
> (695)

What gives one pause is 'great lady of the heavenly few', for the
dead are legion, and will presumably outnumber the living at the
world's end. But if 'the heavenly few' are merely the immediate
clustering bodies of earth, sun, moon and a few others in the vicinity, we do not have to cope with what might otherwise look like
another bout of incipient aristocratism. If we continue our reading
of death as this poem's prognostication, there does not appear to be
great difficulty – for us, readers:

> Lady, lady of the last house . . .
> be good to me now . . .
>
> (696)

And remembering how Lawrence makes his poems' concerns
interlink, and once again that even though metaphorical this does
not deny the word (sign) its referential capacity, we may read the
next poem, 'Butterfly', as both a creature flying out to sea, to its
death, and the winging soul likewise:

> Farewéll, farewéll, lóst soul!
> you have mélted in the crýstalline distance,
> it is enóugh! I sáw you vánish into áir.
>
> (696)

'I saw you vanish' seems to insist that indeed Lawrence witnessed
this, and thought *that*. For it seems most interesting to this reader
that anyone should wish to deny the direct, fairly evident meaning resting in the surface of this poem. It is true, of course, that if
one denies this directness of meaning, one removes the linguistic
inquiry upon which, in a sense, but only in a partial sense, literary
inquiry is predicated. Yet it also seems possible that those who *insist*
on a verbal obfuscation of a comparatively clear self-intuitive text
do so in order to escape from taking on the heavier task of investigating the life-questions Lawrence poses here. One has the image of

a postmodern critic who has spent his/her life flickering the surface of a text, only, in the next life to be presented, suddenly, with
death and the suspension of his earthly muttering. Deal with that,
Death says.

For one may remember that in preparing for death, as Lawrence
is, in these poems, and in the next, 'Bavarian Gentians', he has earlier on been estimating what, in dying, he is leaving behind. And
what its value.

In considering this image of death and moon we need also to
weigh the life-aspect of the sun in the Mediterranean, which, we
peoples of the North take for granted, is life's prime manifestation.
In this respect the note on Apollo in the Smith's *Smaller Classical
Dictionary* is well worth citing:

> In Homer, Apollo and Helios, or the sun, are perfectly distinct,
> and his [Apollo's] identification with the Sun, though almost uni-
> versal amongst later writers was the result of later speculations
> and of foreign, chiefly Egyptian, influence. – Apollo had more
> influence upon the Greeks than any other god.
>
> (43)

This is instructive, for it casts its 'light' on Lawrence's Mediterranean apprehension of, not only the gods, but the interlinkage with
them of those who worshipped, or, at the very least, respected them;
even if 'respect' shades off into fear. Thus in 'Middle of the World'

> I sée descénding fróm the ships at dáwn
> slim náked mén from Cnóssos, smiling the archaíc smíle. . . .
> And the Minoan Gods, and the Gods of Tiryns
> are heard softly laughing and chatting as ever;
> and Dionysos, young [,] and a stranger,
> leans listening on the gate, in all respect.
>
> (688)

See also Whitman's 'Gods' (296–7). The copula 'And' in 'And the
Minoan Gods' does a lot of work. On one level it joins what 'I see'
– 'slim naked men' *and* 'Minoan Gods'; yet on another stratum it
subtly blurs the nature of the one with the other – those who are
gods with those who are god-like. The next poem, 'For the heroes
are dipped in scarlet', makes this association a little stronger:

They are dancing! they return, as they went, dancing!
For the thing that is done without the glowing as of god,
   vermillion,
were best not done at all . . .

(689)

No, they are not gods. And yes, the glow 'vermillion' is ambiguously sited, syntactically, so as to belong to both.

So much for men-gods. The same kind of verification of woman
with the goddess Aphrodite is made in 'The Man of Tyre', one of
the best of *Last Poems*, and in its doing this, shows how economical
and relaxed Lawrence has become:

both, breasts dim and mysterious, with the glamorous
   kindness of twilight between them
and the dim blotch of black maidenhair like an indicator,
giving a message to the man – . . .
Lo! God is one god! But here in the twilight
godly and lovely comes Aphrodite out of the sea
towards me!

(693)

Although 'Desire may be dead' for Lawrence, he yet acknowledges
that deepest of *recognitions* of beauty, in sexuality, interfusing it in
turn with the majestic beauty of Aphrodite, 'the goddess of love
and beauty'. In making these understandings of a life perhaps
denied to him, but not to others, it seems slightly ungenerous to
insist that Lawrence hated humanity plurally or person by person.

The long lines of the poem are sustained rhythmically, and sustain the mimetic movement of a person wading through and out
of water; and in doing this, the adjectives, beating out and spreading their sustained meaning, are enabled to convey a sense of the
extending present, such as we discover, and Lawrence had need of,
in 'Bavarian Gentians'.

One finds this gathering and issuing of life in 'Whales Weep
Not!' – Is it injunction, or description? In his 'Herman Melville's
"Moby Dick"' there is somewhat less sympathy for the whaler than
the whaled:

The gaunt Ahab, Quaker, mysterious person, only shows himself
after some days at sea. . . . Oh, he's a portentous person. He stumps

about on an ivory stump, made from sea-ivory. Moby Dick, the
great white whale tore off Ahab's leg at the knee, when Ahab
was attacking him.
   Quite right, too. Should have torn off both his legs, and a bit
more besides.
   But Ahab doesn't think so. Ahab is now a monomaniac. Moby
Dick is his monomania . . .

                                                          (*SLC*, 380)

It is against this perception, and perhaps one other

   What then is Moby Dick? He is the deepest blood-being of the
   white race; he is our deepest blood-nature . . .

                                                          (*SLC*, 391)

that the apprehension of the whale is set. As it is in apposition to
this criticism that we may understand

and out of the inward roaring of the inner red ocean of whale-blood
the long tip reaches strong, intense, like the malestrom-tip and
      comes to rest
in the clasp and the soft, wild clutch of a she-whale's fathomless
      body . . .

                                                               (694)

How artfully placed is 'fathomless'. And

And bull-whales gather their women and whale-calves in a ring
      when danger threatens, on the surface of the ceaseless flood
and range themselves like great fierce Seraphim facing the
      threat . . .

                                                               (695)

The sustained nature of the adjectival syntax (as in 'Almond
Blossom', above) is congruent with the sustained sexuality, and the
sustaining nature, of the bull whales seeking to protect their tribe's
life from the predatory white Americans. Too strong? One refers
the reader back to Lawrence's Ahab. And wasn't the blubber of the
whale used to provide *light* for such as Emerson? Poor Emerson!
Nevertheless, it is against this vision of sexuality and maternity (only
partly Blake-like) that Lawrence enters his preparation for death.
   So Lawrence must take on death, and somehow make life out

of it, for after it what is there? And in that case, death is not *pace* Wittgenstein an event outside life but, within the ambit of the poem if nowhere else, an event within the midst of life, and so, to be attributed to it.

This is perhaps the difficulty that Lockwood confronts when he says that he cannot properly understand 'Invocation to the Moon'. Whereas by referring that poem back to 'Prayer' he might have felt easier in himself concerning the meaning. Binary principles are 'out', so I will suggest only that there appears to be a binary principle of existence which includes both life and death, in which the moon is death's.

Having done some such with the 'Invocation', Lawrence is free in 'Bavarian Gentians' to concentrate on the gentians and have them bear something of the same doubleness in his 'house'. And what doubleness! As Hermes in 'Maximus' (692) and 'Dionysos' in 'Middle of the World' enter the domestic domain, so here, in Lawrence's house, Pluto's bloom of dark light issues forth from the gentians – the light of the underworld. Of which Pluto is the ruler, with Persephone being his companion for half the year – of Autumn's 'frosted September' and winter.

That 'darkness invisible' (697) of stanza 3 is probably redeployed from Milton's *Paradise Lost*, where in Hell

> A Dúngeon hórrible, on áll sídes róund
> As óne great Fúrnace flám'd, yét from those flámes
> No Líght, but ráther dárkness vísible.
>
> (1, 61–3)

The essential point of these gentians is that they give off the light of death's place 'where darkness is *awake* upon the dark' (my emphasis) and, with 'their' light, conduct him to his death –

> léad me thén, léad the wáy . . .

The mixed accentual and durational character of these rhythms driven with loose reins pays off, for the two lead on to an expression of that determination in action which arises from assent, rather than from consent to an injunction.

Thus across the space between stanzas the repetition of syntax in 'lead/lead' to the gathering determination of 'Reach/give' indeed conduces to the final determining responsibility of let me gúide m̄ysélf

Here the emphasis on 'guide' and on the second syllable of 'myself'
tells the story of Lawrence's 'wide-eyed responsibility' for his own
death. It is one of the high points in the poem, and, in a poem of
expansive rhythms, it expresses, in its marked inflected and durational rhythms, initiating active and firm conduct.

The relative nature of time, which also joins with the binary relationship between life and death, is expressed in that implicating
comment, 'just now' –

> even where Persephone goes, just now, from the frosted
> September

that is, from the life of the earth to its winter and death. For
Persephone is the figure whereby the fertility of spring and summer dies back into late autumn and winter. And though it implies
fertility and renewal, we are at the same time reminded that for
Lawrence, as for all of us, it is a renewal different from nature's:

> Seasons return, but not to me returns
> Day, or the sweet approach of Ev'n or Morn,
> Or sight of vernal bloom, or Summers Rose,
> Or flocks, or herds, or human face divine; . . .
>
> (PL, III, 41–4)

If we catch the echo of all of that in Lawrence, it is because whatever 'awake upon the dark' means for him, it is not the return
of 'Day or human face divine' that is invoked. The thickening
dark tells us so, for it is the dark light that is now stronger than
Demeter's pale lamps, 'which give off light' as she, Persephone's
mother, goes daylight-looking for her daughter. Thus this wedding
of Persephone's life with Pluto's death-life, 'the lost bride and her
groom'. The key-note is not so much 'bride' as 'lost bride'; for however much there is a life of a kind in death 'awake upon the dark',
'where blue is darkened on blueness', it is always darkness, and the
life in this underworld must always be 'lost'. If the ship in 'The
Ship of Death' returns (below), here, the bride is lost, as in such a
wedding must we be.

Although many poems intervene between this and 'The Ship of
Death' (716–20: SoD) the latter is, I believe, the right poem to link

with 'Bavarian Gentians'. The usual hermeneutic procedure is to offer an interpretation of a poem's meaning and as casual rider add, 'and see, it works like this'. Or offer a gloss on the language-strategy but omit any reference to the meaning of the poem, as though Lawrence had no end in view. This seems unlikely. Two versions of SoD exist, one in unsectioned Whitmanesque verse, and the later (what seems to be the later) received version. This received version is 'The Ship of Death', and the one I call Whitmanesque is titled 'Ship of Death'. There is also a short poem called 'The Ship of Death', which in some measure corresponds to the received version, but only in some senses, and then only with respect to sections II and V. But there is one clue to the received version which appears in that short poem of the same name:

> The little ship with its soul to the wonder-goal . . .
> (965)

It is that 'wonder-goal' which links us with the received version because it implies for the soul, destination and teleology. This perspective may be focused up, for in the Whitmanesque 'Ship of Death' we discover that the ship simply disappears into 'oblivion':

> Oh lovely last, last lapse of death, into pure oblivion
> at the end of the longest journey . . .
> (964)

Whereas in the received version, this lapse into oblivion is reversed, and the poem receives teleology:

> And the little ship wings home, faltering and lapsing
> on the pink flood,
> and the frail soul steps out, into her house again. . . .
> (720)

The poem ends with

> For the voyage of oblivion awaits you.
> (720)

But my sense of it is that such oblivion has been pre-empted by the return, in some form, of the little ship with 'the frail soul'.

So Lawrence would seem to have some end in view, and this may be argued on the basis of his changing the *tendency*/direction of the poem from oblivion to conclusion (return). If we can accept the idea that there is such a change, and that the received, sectioned version has teleology, we can extend an interpretation by looking at the syntactical and prosodic strategy of certain parts of the poem.

But before attempting this it's worth noticing, over the period of Lawrence's verse writing, interrupted however by premature death, the spiral tendency of his methods of verse composition. I say spiral rather than circular because although Lawrence started with metred rhyming verse, and later moved in some of the best poems (like 'Song of a man who has come through') in *LWHCT* (1917), to free verse and wrote most of *BBF* in that mode, there is in *Last Poems* a tendency to write poems the lines of which begin to have rhythmic congruence, and in some of which there is metricality. The tendency is just that, to return to a verse of regular recurrence. But even when Lawrence writes metrical verse as in, say, the first five sections of SoD, and most notably in the poem's magnificent first five lines, it is metred verse blended with some of the improvisatory impulsions of free verse. Thus while the first five lines are wonderfully achieved metrical lines, at least the equal of those opening *The Waste Land*, the syntax does not behave like the partner of metricality, composed in rational completed formal syntax, but in some senses works athwart the metre; which serves to make the structure both more substantial and, in total, strange (*ostranenie*). I quote all of section I and the first four lines of section II:

> I   Now it is autumn and the falling fruit
>   and the long journey towards oblivion.
>
>   The apples falling like great drops of dew
>   to bruise themselves an exit from themselves.
>
>   And it is time to go, to bid farewell
>   to one's own self, and find an exit
>   from the fallen self.
>
> II Have you built your ship of death, O have you?
>   O build your ship of death, for you will need it.

The grím fróst is at hánd, when the ápples will fáll
thick, almost thúndrous, ón the hárdened eárth . . .

(716–17)

The syntax that opens the poem is strange, 'Now it is autumn'
seems to indicate that the sentence means to be transitive, as if
to base its structure on 'It is'; but while it is grammatically acceptable to have 'autumn' as the complement of 'It is', the remainder of
the 'sentence' will not properly fit this grammatical strategy. It is
easier to read the whole sentence as if it were structured with the
intention of reaching some syntactical conclusion which, however,
it never obtains. It offers merely the condition of autumn. At this
stage, incompleteness is at the very heart of the poem's meaning.
If the syntax in the first stanza is ambiguously incomplete, the
second stanza clearly is grammatically incomplete, and its being so
reinforces the sense of the first stanza's being so as well. The third
stanza, with its continuing 'And', behaves as though the previous
stanzas had formal, logical, completed syntaxes.

Indeed in creating the sense, in syntactical terms, of the left
hand being oblivious to the right hand's 'strange' behaviour, Lawrence contrives to create for the design of the whole of the first
part that which the Russian Formalists identified in modern verse
as *ostranenie* – the capacity to defamiliarize and make strange. Only,
with Lawrence, this is no mere device, or even a reflection of the cultural ethos, but to do with the very core of the poem's meaning. The
rapid foreshortening of the established pentameter, which ends the
first part, further disconcerts the reader's responses by foiling his/
her rhythmic expectations. The whole mode of *ostranenie* is intensi-
fied by wracking the syntax within the traditional form of iambic
pentameter that would normally demand and get traditional syntax. It is the behaviour of the metre that finally strikes one as odd
since it seems apparently unaware of the conduct of its carrying
syntax.

This mode of elliptic syntax is in its improvisatory character
more characteristic of free verse, more habitual to it, than metrical
verse. That is why so much metrical poetry must, since the advent
of successful free verse and its modes of improvisation, struggle
to sound natural and take full account of what its readers and poets
have been devouring meanwhile. Otherwise it will seem to have
been swept into some backwater. And this is to the benefit of
neither free verse nor metricality.

The habitual mode of metrical poetry inclines towards the synoptic and authoritative. In his free verse Lawrence has shown us – we think of the snake *sipping* with 'straight mouth' and 'straight gums' – not merely how focused he could make his creatures appear, but also how close he could bring them to our view and feel.

In 'The Ship of Death' the 'apples' seem large, the scale achieved, paradoxically, by their being compared to the frangible and evanescent drops of dew with which transitory human life used to be compared. If the dew-like apples can bruise themselves an exit, their size and velocity must be considerable. (This logicing constitutes an attempt to unfold the effect of these pictures.) A similar result of *ostranenie*, through enlargement, is achieved in the second part, with the second stanza, where the apples will fall 'almost thundrous'. A different, equally strange effect is achieved in the third part with the child-like *formal* answer to the question composed of allusive vocabulary taken from *Hamlet*:

> And cán a mán his ówn quiétus máke
> with a báre bódkin?
>
> With dággers, bódkins, búllets, mán can máke
> a brúise or bréak of éxit fór his life . . .
>   (717)

It is in the nature of this poem to tease disconcerting strategies through its formal metricality. With such strategies the so-called certainties of life are questioned, and made perhaps more precious as they and life depart. And the familiar effects of metricality are defamiliarized by the infiltrating strategies acquired in the practice of free verse.

But of course it is, in considerable amounts, metrical verse that Lawrence uses in this poem, and it is the combination of metricality with free verse modes that makes the poem so quick and fresh in its transit to death, and its return from oblivion. A further mixing of modes is effected through Lawrence's implanting of 'quietus', the effect of which is to play up the basement-like language of ordinary speech with the gravitas of Shakespeare's Renaissance diction.

And so, as I have suggested, the ship makes some kind of return. The sense of that awe-full mixture of conditions Lawrence was in the midst of is what the poem attempts to steady, in a certain variety of forms, before delivering its wholeness to the reader. It is this holding together of mixtures, of modes that would not normally easefully consort, and which most poets would not try to bring into coexistence let alone into cooperative union, that makes the poem the triumph (and loved poem) that it succeeds in being. In the end Lawrence brings together his background with his life as a writer, that brought him into the midst of English middle-class and literary life; and he also brings his background into play with the life that has disengaged from both, though in business terms, he continued to deal with that middle-class life. In the end, that is to say, the wholeness mattered, mattered supremely, to Lawrence; and this holistic character is, among many things, what he achieves in a poem that is singularly open and unironic. Though it betrays to the careful reader an awareness of how that ironic mode presented itself to him as a possibility he did not choose to take. In that sense, 'The Ship of Death' contrasts with *The Waste Land*, and shares something with the conclusion to *Four Quartets*.

That awareness of an ironic alternative is, I think, opened up in

Have you búilt your shíp of déath, Ó háve you?
O búild your chíp of déath, for yóu will néed it . . .

(717)

'You' might of course be self-address, but it is not Lawrence's frequent mode, and the tone here filters outwards rather than inwards. Behind, but not obscured by, the assuring and assured 'for you will need it', lurks, I feel, the sense of mockery that redesigns 'Et tu Brute?' – you, too, will die; which is there, but not pressed on the reader. Had it been pressed, the irony would, willy-nilly, have been pulled along with it, might even have initiated such a mocking bruising sense. The reader is not, however, wounded with this understanding, but merely, with considerable calmness, told that in experiencing what he (Lawrence) does, he passes on a sense of it, without malice or envy, to those who are not presently beside death.

5

Dylan Thomas

Reading Ralph Maud's *Poet In The Making (1968)* and his *Dylan Thomas/The Notebook Poems (1989)* has confirmed my sense of Thomas's major achievement. I use the term major advisedly, having in mind the attacks, or the more subtly depreciating commentary, upon his worth as a poet (and a man) by poets still living whose work (in this reader's opinion) have little chance of being within sight of Thomas's achievement.

Others have made *ad hominem* attacks, of which some have been variously dealt with by Empson in at least one of a number of fine essays on Thomas included by John Haffenden in *Argufying (1987)*. The personal attacks are the more galling because by these means such persons appear to be seeking to discredit the poetry. This does not seem proper, and if we were each arraigned for what the world knows of us, quite apart from what we know and admit of ourselves, to ourselves, which person's worth would remain? At any rate, given Empson's defence of Thomas (see in particular the reference to his caring attitude and intention towards his parents), it seems unnecessary to go over what a disinterested reader may examine for him/her self.

What may still be useful is to give a careful reading to a few selected poems in the hope that collectively this will achieve an overall view of his achievement, as a poet, as well as develop further the course of this book.

It seems sensible, for instance, to remark that, Maud's 'free verse' of the notebook poems notwithstanding, almost all of Thomas's poems are firmly, and clearly, metrical and frequently use full or slant rhyme (though 'Fern Hill' contains no rhyme I can detect). This still needs saying, as much as to claim that the syntax in the 'early' (first printed) poems (many of the poems in succeeding books are also in the true sense 'early' and derive from the note-books) that their syntax is straightforward and direct. This is important since their complex meanings are kept in place by means of the clear metre and direct syntax, and which ask the reader to ponder these contrasting modes of means and meaning. Moreover, once we have established the formal attributes of metre and syntax, we can more readily identify the location and nature of the difficulties. I hope it goes without saying that many of the 'earlier' poems are difficult.

I used to console myself by saying that Thomas's achievement lay not in his contribution to thinking, and perception, but his language. That where one read Lawrence's poetry for his apprehension of creaturely life, his sophisticated atavism, and his rational thinking (as well as for his language), with Thomas, the poetry relied on its linguistic achievement. Plausible; but the linguistic complexity consists, I now think, of a complexity of attitudes rubbed through each other in such a way as to produce a necessarily complex linguistic result. Yet what are these attitudes? One may easily say they are comprised of sex and religion, yet it is the poems' achievement to be both embedded in these as well as in a perspective that overviews them. At any rate, I thought it might be helpful to interpolate the notebook work into my reading of some of the received versions of the poems since the published poems emerge from a general background parts of which are comparatively plain and simple. What one gets is a sense of developing density and complexity, rather than a complexity that otherwise might appear from the published work *sui generis*, precocious, or even wilful. These strictures are usually made by those who look for (or write) a version of prose-like propositional verse such as is the subject and method of Pope's *Essay on Criticism*. The objection is not to Pope but to the insistence of such canonical devices so applied that – don't we agree – this is the only way to write poetry. This insistence will frame even such poems as 'The force that through' endowing it with an appearance of docility and mediocrity. Whereas Thomas's achievement (Empson is right) lies in a richness that, in its balance and sanity, sets up a distinct mode of poetry, and adds (confusingly for us all, perhaps) a plurality of awareness, to our ultimate but not perhaps immediate enrichment. The poetry not only pluralizes the vista but extends the limits of our vision.

These claims are perhaps of the kind that prompted Empson (once again) to compare Thomas, for his richness, with Shakespeare; the comparison between linearity and complexity spurs one to examine the claim concerning Thomas's complexity.

In doing so one notices that whereas some of Shakespeare's

complexity is pun-based, the characteristic complexities of later writers, those of Blake, Shelley, Rosenberg and Thomas of course, often involve a different kind, not so much of puns but of other genres. For the play of meaning through puns is usually predicated on singular self-involved linearities intersecting momentarily, only to plunge on their separate ways without further consideration or consequence. The mode has vitality but obvious limitations. And that Shakespeare may have thought it was an insufficient mode is implied in the kind of complexity in *Anthony and Cleopatra*:

> The crown o' th' earth doth melt. My lord!
> O withered is the garland of the war,
> The soldiers' pole is fall'n: young boys and girls
> Are level now with men; the odds is gone . . .
> (*Anthony and Cleopatra*, IV, xv)

Complexity of this kind occurs in Blake's 'green' (and cf. Pope's 'And the fresh vomit run forever green') where in Blake's 'Nurse's Song' (*Experience*) we get the nurse overhearing the children 'heard on the green' and her admitting

> The days of my youth rise fresh in my mind,
> My face turns green and pale.

The idiom 'green with envy', which is the green identified with the nurse's face, is forced to resonate with 'fresh' and with the innocent green of childhood and its potential for growth. 'Green' is also the green of the village, belonging to the community, and this contrasts with the singular self-interested envy of the nurse's 'green'. Blake's revitalizing of the positive 'green', with all its associations of 'pasture' and natural richness, helps us the more to appreciate the 'green' in Thomas's 'The force that'. There is some element of punning in Blake's green, but his two greens interact to produce much more than the pun's momentary illumination and amusement. The richness engendered involves ideas, morality, considerations on the theme of envy and its effects; and of course, the way complexity works linguistically, lit up by language, should not be lost on us.

The richness of what might be called interpretation of entities (I am not convinced Hopkins exerted no influence on Thomas despite his disavowals) has further ramifications.

WELSH

Lip-service has been paid to Thomas's being Welsh somewhat in the way that it is offered of David Jones ('it was always a pain to him that he did not have the language' – then why didn't he learn it?).

The nature of such English-based assertions lacks diligence and may inspire in the reader a similarly inadequate response. Oh yes, Thomas was Welsh, Hywl and that eloquence & fun. This confident self-approbating stance (that puts out of mind the richness of Shakespeare and the very different kind in Lawrence) is indigenous to a cultural superiority perhaps in part arising from conquest. It will take a tenacious reader not to be put off by such pleasantries.

Thomas seems to have had no Welsh. But he had something of the Welsh culture, as his hilarious slyness of attack in *Under Milk Wood* (p. 43) shows (of Ocky the Milkman and his customer who says of the milk he purveys, 'fresh as the dew. Half dew it is'). Only great familiarity (and affection) can inflict such arrows. In Thomas, the wit, in the eighteenth-century sense, as well as in the modern sense of 'witty', in Thomas is at once local, local and Welsh. So one expects to find, and does find, more intimate and re-creative instances of Welsh culture in Thomas's poetry. And for Thomas's attachment to Wales (and not only his home town, Swansea) see Constantine FitzGibbon's *Life, passim*.

ENGLYNS AND CYNGHANEDD

The *Princeton Encyclopaedia of Poetry* cites the forms of (internal) rhyming thus: 'C. A scheme of sound correspondences peculiar to Welch poetry, involving accentuation, alliteration and internal rhyme. Described by Gerard Manley Hopkins as "chimes", he admitted that they were a main influence on his own formal experiments.'

Without being brought up speaking Welsh, one can only guess at the nature of the tightness of these forms and in what way it embodies the nature of the Welsh language. Yet it seems likely that such rhyming may be the means of underpinning shifts of potentially congruent and/or confrontational meanings and feelings. I am in no position to confirm my speculation, but the proper question here is whether any of these modes entered (and were transformed) in Thomas's English, enabling him both to keep the Welsh

form and use it with a comparative freedom that the Welsh-tongued
poets might not have felt able to employ, especially since in recent
times such poets may feel beleaguered by being part of a minority
language.

At any rate I look to see if there is some congruence between the
Welsh rhyming (and thought) and Thomas's redesigning of this
into perhaps more subtle linguistic and thought congruences and
relationships. For if it is any good that is what a rhyme will do,
rather than achieve some momentary touching up of sounds.

I see the boys of summer [in their ruin]

I sée the bóys of súmmer in théir rúin
Láy the góld títhings bárren,
Sétting no stóre by hárvest, fréeze the sóils;
Thére in their héat the wínter flóods
Of frózen lóves they fétch their gírls,
And drówn the cárgoed ápples in théir tides.

                              (*CP*, 1)

In this (the poem's first stanza) there are two principal meanings and one apparently secondary one. The first two, of sex and
fecundity, are interconnected with 'harvest', the fecundating result
of nature, and humanity's gathering of it. Thus 'tithings' and 'gold';
though 'gold' carries the double meaning of fiduciary matters as
well as ripeness (cf. Jonson's *Volpone*). There is also the additional
pun on 'store'. This theme of fecundity in turn interconnects with
that of Jason and the golden fleece, and the feckless get-your-girl
(and abandon her) conduct of which Jason is the instance and representative. 'Apples' and the Jason-word 'cargoed', interrelate the
idea of fertility in humanity with that in nature. But, and here the
secondary theme threatens to overcome these positive themes, we
read of the 'boys of summer in their ruin' and of how their conduct
makes 'barren' the 'gold tithings', with the possible pun on 'lay'.
And this extends into 'loves' being 'frozen'. If we take the moral
view that Jason is an instance of that opportunist immorality always potential in sexual conduct in either gender, but traditionally
and invariably presented as a male attribute, we may pick out
another strand of meaning-chime: 'ruin', 'barren' (tithings plays a
double role in this whole scheme) with 'freeze' and 'frozen loves'.
And of course, the scheme involves the conduct lamented in 'Setting no store by harvest', which is why 'the boys of summer' are in

'their ruin'. It is conduct improvident (in contrast to 'tithings'), both morally and in the general scheme of things, to behave thus feck-lessly. But the richness of the immediate harvest, and its continu-ally beckoning potential, is never obscured, and does not obscure, the richness of the ultimate harvest – that of a patient garnering, some sense of which is implicit in the communality of 'tithings' – which is how 'we ought to behave'.

'Tides' is complex because it supports the background idea of ships and voyage, 'Jason' and 'drown'[ing]. But it also instig-ates the idea of fortune – 'There is a tide in the affairs of men' – so that in one sense this wanton feckless behaviour is of consequence. But this momentary trespass of Buddhistic indifference on a pro-vidential Christianity is not really permitted to gain ascendancy, because we need to ascertain what meaning 'tides' is metaphor of. The answer to that little mystery seems to be the impetus of sexu-ality and its somewhat ruthless operation, in some. So that what may appear at first to be a soft-pedalled secondary theme becomes ultimately of such importance as to threaten the very fertility to which it is germane and cognate.

All this is repeated in the poem's other stanzas (Empson and others have said that Thomas's poems do not develop beyond their initial premises). Yet, though I am not sure this stricture is correct, in this poem we are flounced upon two ultimate contractions of contradictory meanings:

> We are the sons of flint and pitch.
> O see the poles are kissing as they cross.
> (III; last two lines)

One notes the jaunty ballad-marching rhythms of the penultimate line which immediately give way to the movement of exclamation and strong feeling embodied in the iambic pentameter of the last.

I am too much of a holist not to want to reconcile the mean-ings I have been teasing out. If 'we' are all obstinate, unregenerate 'sons of flint and pitch' (all sons touched with darkness and the adhesions of sin) these impulsions of good and less good harvest-ing (as ye sow, so shall ye reap) are reconcilable and, in patches, redeemable. The poles (polarities) are 'kissing', inherent in that act of good and less good possibilities, and as 'they cross' (quarrel, con-tradict, thwart) they also form the figure of the cross, sign of ultimate redemption. 'Without contraries is no progression,' Blake observed.

Analysis cannot do justice to the interconnections taking place as the poem moves forward. 'But seasons must be challenged or they totter', gains complexity in its marginally self-parodying next line where (tedious) predictability is expressed in 'a chiming quarter'. This is what the clock does whose punctuality is like death's – an irony that is true, not paradoxical. Certainly to sustain such argument over 54 'kissing' lines induces respect for Thomas in this reader.

> 'The force that through the green fuse drives the flower'
> (CP, 9)

Here is stanza 3 of a 22-line poem. The whole is comprised in five stanzas in each of which, except the last, are two lots of two-line iambic pentameter surrounding single four-syllabled lines that tend to act like a 'bob', some of which are in decelerating spondees:

> The hand that whirls the water in the pool
> Stirs the quicksand; that ropes the blowing wind
> Hauls my shroud sail.
> And I am dumb to tell the hanging man
> How of my clay is made the hangman's lime.

The poem is composed on the principle of ' "There's this" but "there's also the other" ', in which contraries are balanced in such a way as to further the paradox that the very muteness this is supposed to produce also finds expression and eloquence. And, as Ralph Maud so finely observes, the stanza also entails 'compassion'.

The rhythmic structures also play a role in this 'this but that' strategy. The 'bob' effects a halting of the movement (and ideas) initiated by the two opening pentameters, so that the two which follow the retracting movement of the 'bob' must once more start up the business of the stanza, and of the poem overall. The last two lines of the poem have, ambiguously, the character both of the epigrammatic clinch of the Shakespeare sonnet, and the ride of the Petrarchan sonnet in which the argument is variously, but with respect for the structure of the whole, distributed to a conclusion. That these lines have some of the Shakespearean sonnet character is due to their embodying the villanelle-like character in the refrain that threads the poem, 'And I am dumb to tell'. This has the effect of circulating the meaning through the poem, like blood. But in as much as the poem ends with an entirely different, non-recurring line (though concluding a crucial part of the poem's multi-fold theme), this tends to draw the poem from this crux of obstinately retained release-recurrence structure.

Dear me! one would think it unnecessary to stress the complex capacity of the poem, but it's worth remarking how the strategy of the concluding two lines – recurrence and non-recurrence – embodies the poem's theme: that life creates, besides much else, its own death. So, providing one knows the rules, one knows that one is 'dumb to tell' these very axioms one is, in the poem, in the process of constating.

Again, we have paradox in the form of an irony that is *true*. That is, the irony consists in the truth being of larger consequence than the irony it displays in 'green age'. And how finely complex that is. For 'green' 'age' is not only youth containing its prospective age, but age containing its retrospective youth. Additionally, we have the grief that is 'green', fresh and perhaps grieving, which comprises one of the poem's interlinked themes. Compassion. For in spite of the human muteness the poem works with a totality greater than its eloquence; to grieve and in part to sympathize. And this is the point at which to remark that the social component of the poem has, largely, gone unremarked.

This indication acquires particular relevance in stanza 3 (above). For whereas in stanza 1 we read a comprehensive imaginatively rendered condition of age, which is that which destroys, in stanza 3 the manufacture of death is not by age but by natural disaster or human agency.

The hand (force of nature) that whirls the pool is, like the infirm quicksand, one malevolent aspect of nature. The hand (human intention) that ropes the blowing wind constitutes the art and practice of mariners. This is the positive harnessing of nature (the force of the wind) but the hand, age's or God's, causes my death and wraps my cadaver in the shroud which is also a sail (sea as life's journey-area).

So that Thomas easefully manages to make the positive sail (journey, exploration) into the instrument that wraps the corpse, prior to its being committed to the life that wore itself into its death. This confirms the theme of the poem which is that life ('greenly'!) gives itself to death through its act of living (cf. Keats' 'Ode on a Grecian Urn').

But Thomas hasn't finished with 'rope', for this is also, here, the implement used to hang a man, who is then further destroyed by his being deposited in the quicklime. This was the English way, in the last century and the first years of the twentieth, of disposing of the bodies of executed murderers. So the lime drinks the blood and eats the flesh. This in turn refers to the condition of Christ's body (executed) and so, in turn, refers to the Eucharist in which those who participate eat his flesh (wafer) and drink his blood (wine). Consubstantiation; though a Christian lady in Japan took me to task in 1993 for my application of the word thus. Perhaps the poem is at this point saying that we are all part of this barbarity and share the guilt:

How of my clay is made the hangman's lime.

'My clay' is my body, also subject to death and decay; but in this instance the poem cites, 'we' have killed the man who has transgressed. The physicality of the words blocks an attempt to euphemize our collective contribution to a singular infliction and punishment. So rope ropes together the meanings that have ramified from the first stanza, which projected death as an inevitable disaster of our bodies, to death as allegedly 'condign', a punishment inflicted by humans on humans, which is unnatural and denaturing to both. There are other doublenesses in this extraordinary poem, such as that which leeches (1/4) since, as the metaphor has it, *time* feeds on the living 'fountain head' – but it also springs forth life.

I have so far omitted to examine the richness of 'fuse', but before doing this, I should indicate the oppositions of meaning contained by the sonic similarity in 'Drives' and 'dries' (2/2). And in passing should note that 'mouthing' implicates both the action of sucking at the nipple (as a fountain might be said to do at its source of water) but also of that which 'mouths forth', giving water. This of course anticipates the explicit 'fountain head' in 4/1.

As for 'fuse', Empson and others have dealt with this, so that further commentary feels like trespass. Even so, the word draws one into indicating its meanings – such as the process of melting, agglomerating, as well as the time-bomb motif echoed in 'blasts' (1/2) – and also into suggesting how the time-bomb idea holds together the poem, since we all await the inevitable. Against 'fuse' therefore, we have the act of resistance which is the protest of language, the active creative business that continues despite the inevitable event. Such doubleness comprises the phrase 'crooked' for the flower (not 'dishonesty' but disease/age/deformation); since the *greenness* implicit in fuse (melt, fluidity, sap and thus life and growth) is the only answer, besides language, to death, albeit an autonomic one. But it is in language, a not involuntary act, that we declare our humanness, as other creatures do in their lives; hence the compassion and poignancy of 'dumb', for we are inclined to be rendered dumb by the strength of the coming-on of death. Yet what renders us dumb also causes us to resist that muteness.

'AND DEATH SHALL HAVE NO DOMINION' AND 'AFTER THE FUNERAL'

The dilemma (it exists) can be simply put: that the poem sacrifices the wonderfully pervading complexity of the best poems to the dramatic presentation of (heroic-style) resistance to inevitable death. And also, that it succeeds despite this because of certain lines that spring from this very limitation.

> Where blew a flower may a flower no more
> Lift its head to the blows of the rain;
> Though they be mad and dead as nails,
> Heads of the characters hammer through daisies;
> Break in the sun till the sun breaks down . . .
>   (*CP*, p. 68)

Also add in, 'Or waves break loud on the seashores . . .' This line seems to break down into an easy rhetoric of simple effect culminated in 'loud', where 'break' almost expresses what 'loud' has no need to render. And by doing so, sadly obscures the doubleness of 'break' which refers to both 'waves' and, by implication, 'people'.

The lines that conclude this stanza and the poem are altogether different, and it is the warrant of their forthrightness that they match this directness with complexity and delicacy. 'Blew' in 'blew a flower' is, of course, a flower tossed in the wind, but it also means dying or dead where 'no more' enjambs – not on to something different but onto more of the same. Thus 'blows of the rain' names the agent of destruction. Rain blows in the wind but the initial meaning of 'hammer' is destruction, confirmed by 'nails' in the next line and the intentness of 'hammer' in the one after. But by way of adumbrating the poem's theme that death shall have no entire success, it is not so much that the heads of the daisies are hammered down by the rain as that the 'Heads of the characters' hammer through into existence. The mild 'characters' are simultaneously cognate with daisies and all such living vulnerability – thus 'character' meaning eccentric as well as a character in a play. Also, to have character (= strength). Here 'hammer' builds on this reversal of break, hammer, destroy. 'Break in the sun' suggests break down, but it is the very persistence of such 'character' to go on until the sun breaks down (= as a result of such persistence the sun, as a tyrant, breaks). It is this subtle hovering between being broken and breaking another down with one's persistence that expresses the non-aggressive character of survival. This hovering is expressed through rhythms with a strong basic but varied metrical structure (see scansion above).

The notebook February 1933 poem (129) is not as good and does not have the concluding stanza of the received version.

AFTER THE FUNERAL (IN MEMORY OF ANN JONES)

In the February 1933 notebook (129) what corresponds with this poem is simpler than the received version, lacks its rhetoric, and has a quality the rhyme emphasises which might be described as spry:

> Join in the hymns, and mark with dry bright looks
> The other heads, bent, spying, on black books.
>
> (130)

The hostile reception given to these mourners in this Pope-like neat couplet (notwithstanding the awkward 'bent' and 'spying') finds some amplification in the received version; but the large change between versions entails a lessening of the animus towards the mourners as it reapplies the energy to a celebration of his aunt, the dead Ann Jones.

As with 'And death shall have no dominion' the poetry ultimately triumphs out of the rhetoric that at first appears to vitiate it. This is assertive judgement of a poem universally praised. Still, my unease focuses on the englyn-like internal rhyme which in some forms, normally spaced out over two lines, is here (and in other places) closed-up into mere alliteration and assonance, emerging in rhetoric:

After the fúnerál, múle práises, bráys . . .

I couldn't deny the effectiveness, but what saves it from hammer blow results is the thinking's dispersing subtlety, the associations of which are rich. 'Mule' associates obstinacy, and implicated in it is stupidity, an almost dunce-like over shaped praise for the dead woman who was perhaps not treated over-well by the community when alive, and who was possibly amongst the less prosperous of them:

I knów her scrúbbed and sóur húmble hánds

seems to touch that. At any rate these implications appear to deny that authentic grief and homage, and thus generous feeling, are being offered to the dead woman (which from Thomas's letter concerning his aunt's death he himself did not have much of at the time). Yet authenticity of feeling is what the poem sets out to establish as the desirable attribute, and by which it seeks to establish its own warrant. The ostentation of inauthentic mourning is compounded in the mule's 'brays' that traditionally connotes stupidity and boastfulness (though this is unjust to the creature). The difficulty with such criticism is that it may in its self-righteousness begin to resemble the negative image it seeks to impeach. Difficulties of the same order apply, for this reader, to 'judgement clout' (9). Thereafter, with such moral throat-clearing done, there is a change (this is not a poem without development and outcome).

In a róom with a stúffed fóx and a stale férn . . .

The rhetoric is quieter and it allows the imagery to share in the poem's totality. Moreover, thinking is leached into the poem through this imagery. The objects (above) adorn the dead woman's parlour ('best room') but are conventional reflex manifests of gentility, part of a room used for Sunday visitors. There is an element of pathos underlying the 'stuffed' and 'stale' and thus a complexity is initiated in which if the bogus attributes of these prized rural objects are set up against 'humped Ann', the pathos reinforces the sense of compassion we feel with Thomas for her 'scrubbed and sour humble hands'.

This quieter passage broaches one of the great richnesses where the poet risks his presence in the poem (as Geoffrey Hill does in 'September Song') by drawing attention to the poem's (and his) rhetoric in a 'monstrous image'; seen to be too large, and acknowledged as tasteless. This risk succeeds, and its success is strengthened by the prepositions which work so directly and finely: 'for her' means both on her behalf, and 'as she would regard it' were she alive. A similar strength inheres in 'out of praise'. Praise causes its own magnification of her and at the same time so magnifies the person as to remove her from the praise it seeks to entail. This is Thomas at his best, and in a mode much different from the richness of 'I see the boys' (above). 'And need no druid of her broken body' similarly works both ways, in and out of her life. She is in no need of a druid (bard = inflated poet) now she is dead, and indeed never needed one. That was not her way, her life. Yet with characteristic indirection Thomas is able to justify his rhetoric, for the Welsh poet is a bard, one who praises, and his position in the English-language acknowledgement of this Celtic tradition with its attached obligations makes for interacting complexity between the two traditions.

We are bards, in English, in Welsh mourning, for one whose 'flesh was meek as milk'. This affirmative nexus further throws into question the value of the gentility of the 'fox' and 'fern'; it also strengthens the authenticity of her humble character (her condition is part of her character) which might seem to be one of those virtues an expression of which death often seems to encourage.

Though these are moments in the midst of louder language. By the time we read 'I know her scrubbed and sour humble hands' the rhetoric has strengthened the poem, because the language is grounded in that area of poetry (indeed all 'creative' writing) where language is faced both towards the language to which it is committed and the exterior reality to which it refers and which it re-creates. This double facing is probably recognized by Thomas most sensitively because most easefully deployed in the phrase 'I know', which works both to relate a fiction and to assert the conviction of a truth the poet recognizes as being veracious. Further, this knowing turns into condemnation in that the 'sour humble hands/Lie with religion in their cramp'. The hands are cramped, but so is the effect of religion cramping. This is the collusion between the Church and vested interest which serves through the deployment of alleged virtue, in its puritan guise, to depress the individual in the interests of service. In this nexus 'scrubbed' tells us a great deal. 'Scrubbed' refers to the cleanliness of the flesh, but it also articulates an abrasive over-concern with cleanliness in a number of directions, which again includes the pumice-stone effect of religion, via the adage 'cleanliness is next to godliness'. Through societal insistence this cleanliness often slides into being godliness. And somehow, in a way that is not easily explained, 'scrubbed' also implicates the effect on those 'humble hands' of their having done a lot of scrubbing, humble and hard work to which that poor body has probably all her adult life been dedicated. I say this much because I believe that these meanings are delicately filamented in the workday imagery with which the reader is presented. That the person suffers a related distress is shown in

Her fist of a face died clenched on a round pain . . .

The aggression of 'fist' is inverted into the equivalent negative infliction of suffering, expressed in the dual-purpose 'clenched', before being finally rendered in 'pain'. Further, 'clenched' was probably her habitual condition, that age increased, and which, finally, and monumentally, moved into the sculpture of death, where an idealized Ann is turned from a living sculpture of pain into death's. 'Sculptured' serves several masters. But mostly it ambivalently gestures towards art. Sculpture is an art-form, and a positive realization. But this is living sculpture, the condition of which (pain) we don't have the right to 'appreciate' in the way we might feel we do have the right (even perhaps the obligation) to approach as art. Pain is the act of sculpting, and Ann in her condition is the result. She is stone because hardened in death, but what looks like a monument to her virtues and her suffering turns out to be a protest against her likely suffering: and the enjambment 'monumental/ Argument' makes sure that we appreciate the difference between an actual monument and the hapless way in which this woman cannot remain her own monument (!) *and* continue to testify to her suffering. Thus 'hewn voice' means 'sculptured' (art) but it also means cut off ('hewn') by her death. In the end we are left with the ambiguous art of her life, and the erasure of the woman in her death, even though the effect is one of a fertilizing, catalystic actuating of the poet into a state of compassion. Then the emblems of gentility, the fox and the fern, are made to 'twitch' into love and seed. And by the time we reach the last few lines, the exaggeration of 'forever' has become endearing since we realize that he, too, knows he is unlikely to last 'forever'. The rhetoric has become reflexive.

THE HUNCHBACK IN THE PARK
A REFUSAL TO MOURN
IN MY CRAFT OR SULLEN ART

If contemporary poetry's accessibility remains a contentious issue, I'm not sure if earlier poetry didn't also cause problems. Consider Byron's famous crux.

> For the sword outwears its sheath,
>   And the soul wears out the breast,
>   And the heart must pause to breathe,
>   And love itself have rest,

What, one might ask (with Empson), is the meaning of line 2?

But perhaps our difficulty is that the imaginative energy of our culture has for some time been concentrated in the novel, its readers' interest and energy being oriented towards character and (until recently) narrative. In this respect A.C. Bradley's concern with character is nineteenth-century criticism of fiction redeployed on Shakespeare. And if poets haven't stopped producing cruxes, readers have currently withheld their best energies from poetry, for fiction.

Yet this said, twentieth-century poetry can be difficult, especially for those who expect to track it the way they do prose. The current premiss (even for a number of poets writing in the 1990s) seems to be that readers should use on a poem only as much energy as they do on prose of comparable length. 'Bites'. Readers' transactions of this kind are ungenerous and little is likely to come of them. For although it is true that modernism asks much of a reader, the perspective in which Byron's central character in *Don Juan* operates is as complex as that of *The Waste Land* and *The Ship of Death*.

It has been said that after 'Altarwise by owl-light' Thomas recognized the cul-de-sac created by his linguistic acts. But the publication of 'The Notebooks' by Ralph Maud raises questions of both 'subsequent' and 'later' as well as effecting correlations between these terms and those of 'difficult' and 'accessible'. Thus the simpler and more difficult poems do exist side by side in some of the notebooks and it might therefore seem that we should not speak of *later* work moving in the direction of simplicity.

Such an argument cuts both ways. If the two kinds of poems really do coexist in some notebooks (we needn't insist on defining exactly 'two kinds'), then it could be said that about the time that Thomas was first *publishing*, selecting complex poems for his first book, *18 Poems* (1934), he was almost certainly choosing the poems he at that time thought were his best (see letter to Pamela Hansford Johnson of 2 May 1934, quoted by Maud in *Notebooks*, 40).

On the other hand, the more accessible 'The Hunchback in the Park' also coexisted in embryo in the 1930–32 *Notebook* (109 see FitzGibbon, pp. 280–1). Thomas's sale of the four notebooks, through the bookseller Bertram Rota, to the Lockwood Memorial Library of the University of Buffalo in 1941, probably implies that not only had he sufficiently quarried this early material, but that he was also ready to move on. Putting the elements together it might seem as though the following process ensued. That Thomas first of all elected to publish from the Notebooks the more complex poems, and even developed them as he thought necessary, in that direction, of which, though belonging only in part to the Notebooks, 'Altarwise' might nevertheless seem the culmination. But that having done so he then chose to write, as well as choose from the Notebooks, the more accessible work (typically 'The Hunchback', though see below), culminating in *Deaths and Entrances* (1946); and that the sale of the Notebooks terminates somesuch fluctuating process. Of course later he wrote additional, simpler poems, which seem not to have come from the Notebooks: 'A Refusal to Mourn' and 'In my Craft' are instances. The existence of these poems outside the Notebooks – I mean their having been written independently of the Notebooks – would appear to support my conjecture that Thomas at first published the complex poems but later chose to work more direct and accessible material from the Notebooks. Although ultimately without back up from these (re-) sources.

The hunchback in the park (CP, 111–12)

And yet *this* direct accessible poem has its source in the 1930–32 *Notebook* (109).

Considerations of the poem's accessibility necessarily interlock with those to do with meaning, though the Notebook version is ambiguous evidence in these questions. But in noticing the almost declarative tone in such accessibility in the received version we might (I do) regret the loss of the lovely sonic play in

> [He] Sees the molten figure on the water,
> Misty, now mistier,
> And hears its woman's voice;
> Mister, it calls, hey mister,
> And the hunchback smiles.
>
> (*Notebook* 110)

This would appear to correspond to these lines in the penultimate stanza of the received version:

> Máde all dáy until béll time
> A wóman figure withóut fáult
> Stráight as a yóung élm
> Stráight and táll from his cróoked bónes
> That shé might stánd in the night
>
> (112)

This latter is wonderful writing, yet 'writing' (I say this with much hesitation) is what it has become, sacrificing the intimate interjection of 'Misty, now mistier' and the extreme delicacy of its punning with 'Mister'. For isn't this the point of both poems, that the crooked man daydreams his exact wishful restorative opposite; and so this interlinking pun does it in a way that the later substituted, more declarative, simplicity doesn't. On the other hand (and we might consider that this poem was probably revised in July 1941; Maud: *Notebook*, 249), the poem was rewritten in the midst of war, and who knows what horror of information was then becoming available to Thomas. So that what this experienced dimension of the war finely adds is that of the confrontational element between the children's mockery and the hunchback's loneliness and vulnerability. Thus 'A cripple children call out' in the first Notebook version develops into all the persecution of which children are capable – into the hunchback's torment with the drinking cup that 'the children filled with gravel'. And the acid commentary, almost an aside

But nobody chained him up

(though effectively they did). This establishes the motif of baiting and even of persecution, 'Dodging the park keeper / With his stick that picked up leaves'. For though syntactically it is the boys who dodge the keeper, the absence of punctuation encourages the reader to include the hunchback in the act of 'dodging'. Ultimately the hunchback-outcast is more vulnerable to authority than the truant boys. And we may also relate the stick of the keeper to the dead leaves it (he) picks up – the hunchback is a dead leaf (dead soul, yet not actually so). This condition of the hunchback is continued throughout the poem until the narrative culminates in the wild innocent boys following (not pursuing, and it's a subtle difference) – following the hunchback to his home – a kennel – fit for a chained dog (another hidden instance of Thomas's use of the folk material of adage). The resolution trembles between Edenic vision and a realistically offered simplicity, not perhaps quite credible, or reconcilable, except in the guise of Prophecy. Would such boys have made a pact with him (almost become him ('followed'))? Or perhaps the times have changed since Thomas's day. Or perhaps a kinder difference exists between Welsh and English mores.

The questions subsume my unease that the resolution of the poem into accessibility has also released, perhaps, a slight tinge of unrealistic sentiment (sentimentality is too strong an ascription). Such a touch is present in the last line of the first, *Notebook* version (above):

And the hunchback smiles.

Yet there is a difference. In this first version the smiling depends only upon himself. The ending of the ultimate version, however, shows Thomas's fine capacity to open the poem out beyond interlocutions with himself (*pace* his hostile critics) to the mister's relationship with society – boys, dog, nurses, swans, and park keeper (authority). One notices that the syntax and meaning need little punctuation, and that only the minimum of fullstops is provided – with the exception of punctuational stanza spaces.

So what gains, what losses, in a comparison between this accessibility and the reader's harder initial work required for the more complex poems? To ask this is to confront the attribute of complexity which presently (under threat?) is still judged to be one of the crucial prerequisites of good poetry, as Empson explained in his 'Preface' to *Seven Types of Ambiguity* (Preface to second edition, XV). To answer this one returns to the question of puns, raised earlier. Not excepting 'crooked' (stanza six) 'lock' in the first stanza is the most noticeable. The hunchback is

> Fróm the ópening of the gárden lóck
> That léts the trées and wáter énter

until Sunday evening.

'Lock' and its nexus of ideas is probably a later addition to the poem, and if this is so, it shows how Thomas has admitted complexity without complicating the linguistic element or the narrative's flow.

'Lock' includes 'unlocking' for none could enter the park unless the park keeper opened it in the morning. More significantly it also refers to the hunchback's unlocking (releasing and regenerating) of his lovely restorative perfect opposite of himself (yet part of himself also):

> A woman figure without fault
> Straight as a young elm . . .

And this unlocking or flowing out of the perfect image relates to one other meaning of lock, which is, of course, the mechanism that restrains, controls the level of, and admits, a body of water, into a lower stretch of itself. This meaning appears to be operative because 'the trees and water [that] enter' cause a reflection until nighttime, when reflections cease. Thus what is brought, pastorally, with water in the morning light corresponds with what is released from the hunchback in the creative restoration of himself by day, and which flows back to him at night when the 'woman figure' stands guard.

This ebb and flow has profound implications. The reading is tenable, and consonant with the essential, merciful, compassionate humanity with which the hunchback at large in society's public domain, the park, is treated. And this is said notwithstanding the boys and their function in the poem.

But compare this poem, originating in the Notebook of 1930–32, with 'I see the boys of summer' (above) from the August 1933

Notebook, and one sees that the earlier simplicity of the *first* version of 'the hunchback' is apparently *followed* by the complexity of 'I see the boys of summer'. And that the complexity of 'lock' added later still and which is germane to the whole poem is of a kind less 'intrusive' than that in 'I see the boys'. Of course 'intrusive' is debatable, but the drift of this argument may make it possible to indicate that Thomas seems to have returned to the narrative simplicity of the truly earlier poem ('Hunchback'), as against the complexity of 'I see the boys', a complexity one must encounter if one is to enter the poem at all. Whereas the complexity of 'lock', and its implications for a deeper reading, do not impede a partially adequate reading of an accessible poem. Put simply, the richness of 'I see the boys' is not linguistically present in 'The hunchback' where the overall concept is readily available. Perhaps the key difference in this is that the more complex poems seem to employ a longer measure than some of the more accessible.

Certainly that is a difference worth much pondering.

A Refusal to Mourn (CP, 101)

Including the fine 'Lie still, sleep becalmed', 'A Refusal to Mourn' is one of five poems in *Deaths and Entrances* (1946), all of which deal with the negative proceeds of war, death. And of these five, four deal directly, except for one, with death by fire in air raids. During the Second World War, incendiary bombs were amongst the commonest infliction on the civilian. In the sense in which we often term Rosenberg and Owen, Thomas is not a 'war poet', but Thomas's work bears and attests to the stress of war, through civilian experience.

Empson probably felt no need to remark this since he wrote within the common ethos of the war: we may need reminding. We may need reminding not only that Britain stood near to extinction, but that there were forces in the country ready to welcome fascism. With hindsight, 'Twenty-four years' may be said to bear an understanding of this. And 'In My Craft of Sullen Art', written in 1945 (Maud, 1st, 42) may, on reconsideration, be said to contain a sense of surviving the threats of war, and, at the same time, a registering, because of such pressures, of what is most precious. In that sense the theme of love and art, 'permanencies' under threat, acquires significance and poignancy. I will return to this poem, where metricality plays such a critical role in its delicacy.

'A Refusal to Mourn' is comprised of four six-line stanzas, three of which are (approximately) congruent with each other. The final (fourth) stanza breaks the pattern to some effect at line 4, this being the turning point and marker line for all four stanzas. Each stanza rhymes ABCABC with further half-rhyme such as 'mother/water', 'truth/breath'. Punctuation is simple and sparse, applied strictly in the first place for sense; consider the commas in the last stanza. Formally, the poem comprises three sentences, the first and longest of which ends with the first line of stanza 3. These simple facts are evident enough, but if we read a joint in the syntax after the end of the third line of stanza two,

> And the synagogue of the ear of corn

the concluding phrase may be read as either statement or question, perhaps as both. Thus 'Never . . . Shall I let pray the shadow of a sound'; or, 'Never . . . And I must enter/Shall I let pray . . . (?)'
This ambiguity that I read in the syntactical intention forms a part of the poem's culminating meaning. Thus, I mourn secretly, though I should not do that, even inside myself, and will never do it publicly. To mourn is to re-emphasize the barbarity of this destruction, and thus negotiate the blasphemy of it:

> After the first déath, there is nó óther.

All killing is wrong (though it may be expedient) and the first death, singular and awful, liberates the occasion of all others. One is too much. The first is so enormous in its own 'right' that it obscures those which follow, so to mourn is to add to that obfuscating process. Thus this last line is a grave full of meanings. I must not, it seems to say, follow the killers, for to mourn is, by inference, to participate in the act of killing. So I refuse, and in this human act define what it is to be human.
On first inspection the negative anthropomorphizing (water is 'unmourning') appears to be dignified and lend dignity to the human act, but on closer inspection 'Unmourning' both supports Thomas's refusal to mourn and contrasts with the refusal. Water cannot choose to do anything (apparently), whereas we humans can (apparently) choose.
The poem's directness and simplicity of expression interact with the form, involving the metricality and lineation. Yet the simplicity builds up its particular assemblage, in some ways a Hopkins-like

compound adjective, in this instance describing darkness (1/3): 'mankind making/Bird beast and flower/Fathering and all humbling' – 'darkness'. It is worth comparing the nucleated complexity of Rosenberg's meaning in 'God-ancestralled essences' ('Dead Man's Dump', stanza 4) with Thomas's more flowing, accumulated expression.

In turn, this accumulation raises questions concerning the formalizing effects of metricality and rhyme in Thomas, in this poem, as against the more compact realization in Rosenberg's free verse in 'Dead Man's Dump'. The comparison yields surprising results since it might be thought that metrical verse (it is often claimed) is invariably more compact and architecturally more structured than free verse. Whereas in this comparison, the assertion is not justified. And to the extent to which it is not so here, the case points up what Thomas does with the interrelationship between the substance and his expression of it. Thus, the formal means of metre and rhyme do not so much interrelate with the substance as occur as a form fixed onto the syntax's different, flowing action. In such a view, the rhyme emphasizes this effect, pushing in its chime rather than co-operating with structure, meaning and syntax.

So, fine as I feel this poem is, after many readings, I also feel reservations such as I've suggested. Closer examination still yields the conclusion that this reservation does not apply to the final stanza, the naturalness of which is due to the interlocking of syntax with lineation, metre with rhyme and all four with each other. But is this poem an instance where free verse might have been more apt?

In my Craft or Sullen Art (*CP*, 128)

This is certainly not the case with the following well-loved poem, the thinking and structure of which is enshrined in its metre and intricate, almost identical pattern of rhyming over the two stanzas. Equally, it could be argued that the traditional metered directness embodies traditional, perennial human virtues. At any rate the poem achieves a candid humility and 'lovingness' – the quality requires a word that hovers between neologism and something informal. Loving-kindness is almost appropriate, except that the term objectifies the feeling the verse radiates. A further reason for de-formalizing the attribute is on account of the poem's unassertiveness. This (or my description of it) may make the poem sound like a failure, yet what holds the poem in place is the coming together of these retiring attributes in a buoyancy imparted by the metricality. Compared with 'A Refusal to Mourn' this poem operates a more sifted intrication of metre with syntax and meaning. And the poem's intrication is assisted by the subtle off-balancing of metricality. Wordsworth does this with a much wider range of metrical forms in his 'Immortality Ode'. But what can be said here is that the smaller overall compass of metricalities is accompanied by subtle off-settings from the preceding or succeeding line's metres. That is, the lines read with greater metrical possibilities when read in total concert.

Thus, while the first two lines are accentual-syllabic (counting both stresses and syllables), the succeeding three tend towards the accentual (counting stresses). It is when we get to

Or the strút and tráde of chárms

(and perhaps the line before) that we find that read to oneself (as opposed to out loud) one can scan the line in another metre:

Or the strút and tráde of chárms

And this double rhythmic possibility arises in the context of line by line rhythmic variation. Here, the subtle possibilities of pace affect the tone and thus the meaning.

For in one, Thomas appears to be mimicing the 'strut' of such charms, and in the other seems to be closer to acceding to the seduction of such a condition. The ambiguity between these two is at the heart of the poem.

In the first stanza the lovers hold the living griefs in their arms. Thomas, poet and persona in the poem, denies that he works ambitiously or for reward, either fiscal or acclamatory ('trade of charms'): and the strategy of the verse, described above, makes this assertion feel authentic which, in the end, is the reader's only way of judging such things.

In the second stanza (and the binary but intermingling character of the whole poem contributes to this effect of simplicity and authenticity) we readers feel that the dead are hallowed

With their níghtingáles and psálms.

With? One notices again how this line hesitates between the accentual-syllabic and the accentual. It is nevertheless the lovers and their quintessential lives for whom he writes, as a form of tribute. 'But for the lovers', in the next line, Thomas uses the accentual as the most emphatic (but not assertive) way of expressing a positive idea embodied in a positive feeling. As the syntax slowly attenuates in an extra clause (line 19 to last but one line of the poem), so the metricality relaxes into closure and the accentual-syllabic mode:

> Who páy no praíse or wáges
> Nor héed my cráft or árt.

It is perfect verse, that does not stand on its achievement.

Fern Hill (*CP*, 159–61)

The boldest possible question might go thus: can this poem stand against Empson's preference for the earlier poems? And as corollary to this, is the cross-referencing complexity of poems such as 'I see the boys of summer' (see above) finally more satisfying than the lyrical directness of the later poems? Further related to these questions is the presence of mannerism and facility in the later poems, a shorthand coinage in such phrases as 'sky blue trades' and 'lamb white days'.

Although, as the fiction writer Lorna Tracy remarked, these are of a lesser order than the 'heron/Priested shore' of 'Poem in October'. This is true, notwithstanding the 'sea wet church' that occurs later in the same poem; the formula doesn't inevitably entail facility. Yet given the level and the frequency of device that occurs in middle and later Thomas, this may prompt some readers to concur with Empson: 'I would have had to say I liked the early obscure ones best . . .', (p. 392).

Yet as I have already suggested, there is not a simple clear division into earlier complex – later simpler – poems, though there may be a discernible tendency in this direction; Thomas's revision of the more accessible easier poems from the notebooks accompanies the later composition of such direct poems as 'In my Craft' and 'Poem in October' and, of course, 'Fern Hill' itself. So what we come out with is a sense that the more direct poems are (a) not all from the later period although (b) the later tendency is towards directness and accessibility and (c) the most difficult of all to state unequivocally, that at their best the middle and later poems of accessibility each have a new sustained lyric benignity, and an intrinsic mode of development and progression. This new progression may help to counter the charge that Thomas's poems do not develop beyond their own original premiss. For if the best early poems are unbeatable in their own terms, yet their kind of complexity justifies the observation that each poem 'only' explores its own premiss.

Perhaps the equation goes something like this: that the complexity involves a ramifying upon itself; the direct poems entail, or at least permit, progression within themselves. The caveat is that directness is more susceptible to a possible sentimentality, of which 'sky blue trades' is an instance. Yet if we were to look at makers only in terms of their defects, if such they be, we would be poorer on account of our stinginess. This, at any rate, is an attempt at the profit and loss graph of the later poems. I should now look in detail at 'Fern Hill'.

Fusion of flowing rhythms with lineation

Both 'Fern Hill' and a 'A Refusal to Mourn' work flowing rhythms. The structure of both poems entails an interrelation of opposites. Thus flowing rhythms and paratactic syntax within a grid, or template, of carefully wrought, repeated stanzaic patterning. Like a stream running through a complex water garden, that repeats its walls, barriers, sluices and locks creating a mesh of attributes without the energy violating or being violated by the structure.

> And green and golden I was huntsman and herdsman, the
> calves
> Sáng to my hórn, the fóxes on the hills bārked cléar and cóld,
>   And the sábbath rang slówly
>   In the pébbles of the hóly stréams . . .
>
>   (CP, 159)

Some critics have drawn attention to the alleged looseness of Thomas's syntax (see above) without noticing that here (as elsewhere) the lineation achieves the positive effect of emphasizing the flow, but not loosening it. Movement here becomes a version of narrative through the formalizing intersection of a dactyllic/anapaestic triple-syllable flow with the lineation.

The narrative

Poems like Day Lewis's 'The Nabara' or 'Flight from Australia', whatever symbolic representation they acquire, derive their impetus from their narrative energy, and only in a secondary sense from language and its interrelationship with rhythm. They are stories in verse, and the verse serves to sharpen the narrative drive rather than vice versa. Whereas Thomas's narrative is embedded in language, rhythm and symbolically realized phenomena such as 'the holy streams'. The poem assembles itself through an intrinsic commitment to its materials, and the disposition of these to one another. In this respect narrative is no different, and when such prototypical elements meet, adjustment to each other is entailed. If one gets the dominance, the other's potency accrues to the stronger, such an accrual however being best satisfied when one member does not exhaust the other. Single parties are not recommended. On the other hand, if the wrong member, by which I mean a member from a competing intrinsically non-poetic form, gains dominance, as in narrative poetry, the danger is dilution of the basic mode. A play with too much poetry suffers loss of drama. A poem with too much narrative weakens its own mode. Yet a mode that continually engages its purity ultimately weakens its strain.

Thomas's mix in his middle and later poems is interesting. The success, as I believe it is, lies not merely in a felicitous blending of elements but a use of elements that cannot be further reduced. *Basic common denominators*, or elements of the periodic table.

The recipe will invariably work. We find ourselves in reluctant sympathy with a criminal who is old rather than one who is in his prime. Babies and young children who are victims of a massacre excite our extreme indignation. This suggests that against the force extended by the re-creation of specific events there runs another force which derives from processes or conditions to which we are *all* subject.

In his later poems Thomas has moved his preferred codes, from sex and religion among others, to youth and age, and if my foregoing diagram holds good, then it would seem that youth and age form a more basic code even than religion, sexuality and politics. Deliberately, or not, adopted, Thomas's basic universal code and its by-products ensure a basic acceptance of his writing if the literary components are working; and the reason why one can speak in these compartmentalizing terms is because the codes are basic.

By the same token the means are less adventurous than in his early poems, and they bid for a popular appeal that has, largely, succeeded.

The other co-functioner of age is nature, and here again, 'Fern Hill' works in that mode. (A work remains to be written on the function of nature in poetry in time of war or its immediate aftermath. 'War, patriotism and nature'.)

Thomas's religious component has been commuted to nature and its 'holy streams', 'holy' not only because the hallowed vision of childhood interacts with the adult lenses but also because we, as readers, associate nature with God's beneficence. So Thomas claims from his readers, a response, a reflex, at any rate an impulse difficult for the reader to withhold or question. So inception in such a medium brings on the reader's responses in reflexes that reciprocate the poem's intentions. In this sense we may feel that poems such as 'Fern Hill' and 'Poem in October' are conservative in a way that Eliot's *The Waste Land* and Rosenberg's plays are not.

So 'Fern Hill' can spring its lenses from the experience of childhood, via the adult who looks back on that childhood as he examines his adult responses to it. As I suggest, the material is traditional, but so is the introvert search and evaluation.

The poem's narrative concludes in a realization of the ageing process as it interacts with a recall of childhood. The gambolling rhythmic onwardness of the poem celebrates that very childhood the poet holds in mature 'greenness' – childhood, 'childhood's' maturity, and its naivety:

> Time held me gréen and dýing
> Though I sáng in my cháins like the séa.

The poem terminates with the very best of Thomas's complex density. 'Green and dying' is childhood and ageing, and in this poem the complex presentation is triple; childhood as it was, childhood experience as it is viewed through adult eyes, and an evaluation of adulthood itself. For to be 'green' with childhood may in certain respects be good but it is also inadult, escapist and green (= naive) to wish to remain so. The tension then is between blessing one's childhood yet in such a way as not to remain enchained by it. Yet not to surrender its experiences either. For though we value being adult we must also remember it is, seen from the ultimate viewpoint, a form or process of dying (towards death). The 'chains' of the next line, then, are these bonds and restrictions, but such restrictions are also the means of producing energy. The sea's tides are in 'chains' to the gravitational pull of the moon, and the waters to earth's gravity. But within such constraints the sea has enormous energy. Indeed its energy, like ours, could be said to derive from its 'chains'. The sea may be said to sing, but 'sing' here seems to imply, self-consciously, poetry, the act of making, as it does in Whitman's 'Out of the cradle'; and in fact Whitman's and Thomas's poems each use a similar group of constituents.

Wordsworth's 'Tintern Abbey' and Lawrence's 'Piano' also come to mind, but Thomas's uniqueness asserts itself in its characteristic density, and the density enacts the irresolvable crux. It is worth remarking the form of the final two lines, which approach that of a couplet form because of the thought process that moulds the pair 'Time held me/Though'. A nice way of concluding a poem without imposing unsuitable total closure.

A CONCLUSION

'Fern Hill' travels a comparatively simple and linear linguistic route; likewise 'Over Sir John's hill'. Whereas, as I suggest, the early poems' language meshes into itself with cross-referential density, while in the later poems there is gathering directness. The 'Poem on his birthday' (*CP*, 170–3) advances a mode that premature death prevented Thomas from developing even more strongly:

> The rippled seals streak down
> To kill and their own tide daubing blood
> Slides good in the sleek mouth.
> (4/7–9)

There is a movement from 'I see the boys of summer' to these lines, where the language directly engages with the crux of 'killing to eat' – as it does with greater emphasis on the cruelty in 'Over Sir John's hill' (*CP*, 167–9). In the 'birthday' poem the seals appear to be involved in reciprocal slaughter – 'their own tide daubing blood'. In this poem Thomas is, once again, ballad-maker. In 'Over Sir John's hill' he is 'young Aesop' and he is 'fabling' what he sees. The appeal is to traditional situations, the expression rhythmically lyrical,

> for the sake of the souls of the slain birds sailing.
>
>   ('Over Sir John's hill')

I have since read Seamus Heaney's lecture 'Dylan the Durable? On Dylan Thomas' (1991), in *The Redress of Poetry* (1995). I don't accept the equivalence Heaney apparently wishes to impose on Thomas – 'he was a Welsh version of what Patrick Kavanagh called in the Irish context a "bucklepper"' (p. 125), and can only add that my position on Thomas is not changed by what he has to say. I find positive and exegetic criticism often more challenging and more persuasive.

Heaney takes a serious look at Thomas, and forms a judiciously and moderately severe view of the man and his work. Yet had he admitted a wider range of poems, together with detailed textual examination of one or two, he might well have come to conclusions of a less contrasting kind on the work. It is more various in character and achievement than Heaney suggests.

Heaney also speaks of 'Thomas's anti-intellectualism' (p. 140). It is a familiar charge, yet it is precisely the appearance of the Mind, in many of the poems, that confronts Heaney's use of this ascription. So I not only instance the poem 'There was a Saviour', but suggest that interested readers consult the extended consideration Winifred Nowottny gives it in *The Language Poets Use* (1968, pp. 187–203).

The lecture 'A Torchlight Procession of One: On Hugh MacDiarmid' (*Redress*, pp. 103–23) is dated one year later than that on Dylan Thomas (1991). Perhaps because certain aspects of MacDiarmid's poetry touch Heaney's sympathies, the judgements are not merely fairer to the subject (although they are), but are intrinsically sounder. The exploration of MacDiarmid's work is absorbing, and so for that matter is his handling of Marlowe's 'Hero and Leander'.

6

Basil Bunting and his *Briggflatts*

There is a crux Ted Hughes considers in his essay 'Myths, Metres, Rhythms', from his collection *Winter Pollen* (1994), which arises from the domination of accentual-syllabic metre (such as iambic pentameter), where you count up the lines' stresses (five) and the syllables (ten). And this same principle of counting stresses and syllables applies to other metres within the accentual-syllabic system. This structure, however, differs from the accentual one where you count the stresses but (within reason) do not total the syllables in the line; nor within reason need you have a fixed number of weaker syllables to balance the stressed ones. You may, for instance, have a line of four stresses, two either side of a caesura (as in Anglo Saxon verse), and this line be integrated with head-rhyme or alliteration. (And of course, accentual verse and 'sprung rhythm' are cognate.) Hughes's point is that the accentual structure was depressed by the rise and subsequent dominance of the accentual-syllabic line.

So accentual verse went under, but not out; and apart from a period between Chaucer and Tudor poetry, it desponded, perhaps through the unthinking confidence of accentual-syllabic verse. Some of this argument may be read in Hopkins' letters in those parts where he is critical of Tennyson's poetry (as was Whitman). But for those who want to read, feel and hear accentual poetry and cannot manage Anglo-Saxon or Middle English (as I cannot), they should read as much as they can of Langland's *Piers Plowman* and of Hopkins. Read Coleridge's 'Christabel' and his preface to it. Read also the plays of Eliot; and, additionally, catch the form, especially in the durational syllables, as one of the prosodic strategies in his *Four Quartets*. All this may disclose a form asking to be used, one capable of expressing rhythms with a radiating vitality, often a rugged one, different from the smooth confidence of a verse-line that counts stresses *and* syllables.

The question is not only in what state accentual verses survives but what its partial defeat and damage has cost the accentual-syllabic forms. In a situation where one entity triumphs, both suffer, the conquered in the obvious way, the conqueror paying long-term dues for unchallenged supremacy. A not effectually challenged supremacy benefits none; the struggle not only weakens but requires an assertiveness that damages the sensitive operation of the dominant mode. Again, a form conquered is not necessarily one destroyed, and it may be that the accentual form continues to sap the energies of those poets using accentual-syllabic forms because of their inability to listen attentively to the rhythms of other modes. It may be that one, or all these in combination, has (have) weakened the accentual-syllabic form: for a form is a living thing, and when its practitioners cannot impart their full vigour, subtlety and critical sensitivity, when it subsists in smoothness without tension, lacking, for instance, the indirections of stress and duration working in the very best of Wordsworth's verse, we have only an empty form.

There are further consequences. If the prosody of one form together with its culture is subdued, it may nevertheless intermittently emerge, either in a version of its own form, or its existence may enable something else. It may access other forms in lieu of itself, especially if the dominant form is weakened; and such may indeed help to account for the emergence of free verse, or unmetrical poetry such as Smart's *Jubilate Agno*, or Blake's Prophetic Books. And of course Whitman, and all those others who practised unmetrical poetry in the same American period.

Thus Imagism appears to be a verse mode actuated by ideas concerning 'the hard clear image' (see chapters 2 and 3); equally, it may be the product of an energy disengaged from the accentual-syllabic mode finding its rhythmic impulse in free verse.

This then is the suggestion; that free verse grew, not only as a variant of accentual verse, but also within the context of those depleted energies of both accentual-syllabic and accentual verse. It is also likely that verse making use of duration emerges as a consequence of such debilitation. And while what Peter Makin, in his excellent book on Bunting, says is true – that duration (quantity) in English verse tends to convert into stress – yet there are ways of enabling stable durational (long) syllables. Put a long syllable after (or near) a stressed one and you may succeed in preserving the length of that syllable:

In héavy barley season.

and

In súch soft air
(I, 40)

PROSODY AND THE INDIVIDUAL VOICE

If 'Villon', 'The Spoils' and even 'Chomei at Toyama' struggle to establish a prosody, they do not properly get beyond this; it is poetry subservient to its writing, not a poetry implicating idea/experience.

Briggflatts is a truly created and creative poem because – I almost said (with Bunting) – of its music. (Though Bunting's claim that in poetry it is its music that matters seems contradicted by his having actual music – Scarlatti – played between the sections of *Briggflatts*.) Yet *Briggflatts'* music, its interaction of prosody, lineation and syntax, works because the poem takes up a complex of shaped experiences demanding form and expressiveness. The poem's meaning is part of its prosodic character, which, together with sound, constitute the poetry's 'music'. *Briggflatts* is, principally, free verse, not verse with its metre taken from it; although like Eliot's, it is rarely very distant from the ambit of metricality. If it expresses stress and duration, and uses rhythmic congruence, it switches readily when a different rhythm is required. Compare:

Péns are tóo light.
Táke a chisel to write.
Every birth a crime,
every séntence life.
(I, 41–2)

and

Máy on the búll's hide
añd throūgh thě dale
fúrrows fill with máy,
páving the slówworm's wáy.
(I, 39)

with the sensitive, evasive side-stepping from rhythmic congruence in

> White márble stáined like a úrinal
> cléft in Ápuan Álps . . .
>
> (II, 45)

One reads the verse imbued in its meaning, and so we accede,
not to the proposition of music's primary importance, but to a sense
whereby music is the means by which meaning is made. Without
meaning, there is no music of poetry, only sound, which is something different. It is one thing to listen to poetry in a language one
does not understand, another to evacuate meaning in a language
one comprehends so as to concentrate on its sound.

Bunting's verse is declarative, presuming an occasion that requires a heightening of spoken-language, street-speech, arbour-
whisperings, broadcasting – all that simulates a reality 'out there'.
In that sense *Briggflatts* is more honest than much contemporary
verse, which snuggles up to the supposed reality of a low-tension
conversation (language), while offering scenes of simulated but often
unfelt violence (external reality). It presumes an intimacy with reality
because it purports to be an indistinguishable part of it (realism/
illusion). And this may be one reason why the lineation of much
contemporary verse seems arbitrary (free verse) or mechanical
(metrical). It seems so because, with the former, the line-lengths do
not work in relation to syntax. For to do this would be to acknowledge that the poem's language is not a simple replication of event
or speech, and that the poem needs to recognize those prosodic
structures it apparently seeks to bypass. This can be tested by incur-
ring the slow cursor of Bunting's sullen disenchanted yet intense
voice, the *cantare*, in its constantly oppositional, objection-finding,
factious, even carping intensity. The voice, as it works with rhythm,
lineation, syntax, is almost refractory. But it forces the grumble to
habituate to a more comprehensive feeling, and, in this sense,
musicalizes it without denying its character.

This needs saying because much of Bunting's verse other than
Briggflatts seems to play out the discovery of being able to lodge
the fractious in verse. At its less achieved, this is mannerism, the
polemics of the elegant. *Briggflatts* incorporates this, and the music

deepens into a commitment to, a feeling for and an evaluation of, experience. There is rarely a 'see-here' to distract the reader from the narration.

So with the exception of 'Chomei' which Robert Woof nevertheless, in *Stand* (8/2, 1966, p. 29), found somewhat 'ruffling' in its tactics of contemptuousness; with parts of 'The Spoils', and the whole of 'To Mina Loy' and some shorter poems, the achievement seems to consist of *Briggflatts*, with the other works disenabling an expression of experience as they struggle with prosody.

Whereas *Briggflatts* blends language with experience under great pressure. Additionally, it is the fury of creation itself that matters with *Briggflatts*; not only the experience embodied in language, but the necessity to create, in itself a theme implicit in the whole work, analogously explicit in those portions which refer to music. We remember that although it is with language that Bunting was pleased to work, for him music is the creation of which words are the attributes. The Russian-Jewish poet Mandelstam also spoke of his poetry in the musical analogy of 'composing' (see *Hope against Hope*, Nadezdha Mandelstam). So perhaps we may appraise the poem's meanings in certain respects like a piece of music, where the assemblage of themes in the poem resembles the way themes in music are put together, to reflect and to interact with each other. A fugue is a simultaneity of meanings, like a metaphor compressed and then immediately yielding some third meaning.

Briggflatts does not compress in this way. Thoroughly modernist, it collates themes without conjunctive discursive explanation, even with respect to 'and', 'but', 'yet' and other mediators. This tactic has the effect of leaving open many options of meaning, but also of rendering experiential material less in the form of abstract argument but in that experience the words render.

So, grasping the method in its musical analogy of blocks of adjacent meaning may help us to understand the meaning(s), as much as it also frustrates the expectation of *explanation*. In as much as music does not explain itself, we are also in *Briggflatts* oriented along other circuits of experiential understanding, in which pleasure is included as a mode of comprehension. So if, as I suggested with Eliot's *The Waste Land*, we think of *Briggflatts* in terms of blocks of meaning, and for a moment disregard the diagram of peaked climaxes that Bunting drew for his friends during the interview (see *Agenda*, 16, No. 1 Spring 1978)

we get this (Roman numbers refer to sections of *Briggflatts*).

I: Children's experience of love; and a mason (the girl's father?) chiselling a grave's name and insignia. This key episode acquires a synecdochic, representative character partly through the poem's rarely providing names, and none of them identifying characters as would a narrative poem. First appearance of Bloodaxe.

II: An apparent if unspecified connection between the autobiographer's leaving behind the person with whom he was initiated into love (in rural north England) and a falling into poverty in London. Note the reference to Tottenham Court Road which bounds the east side of north Soho (post-First World War?) then more the locus of artists and writers that south Soho became after the Second World War. With strophe 4, the Viking boat (of Bloodaxe?) appears. A considerable amount of *Briggflatts* seethes with the sea.

Self-critical doubt raised concerning the integrity of the implied autobiographer through the formulation 'unconvinced deserter' (45). The status of this 'desertion' is multivalent, but one particularly notices the double negative. A deserter is one who is, presumably, 'unconvinced' of the value of that which he 'deserts'; whereas this 'deserter' is 'unconvinced' about his want of conviction. However the leitmotif of the narration recurs which is finally re-envisioned in V (58) with

> to humiliate love, remember
> nothing . . .
>
> (II, 45)

The 'White marble' (II, 45) that begins strophe twelve leads into a second glimpse of masons cutting rock into the stone for graves (this time in Italy). This passage briefly resonates with what accompanied the initial sight of stone-cutting (I), the experience of love.

The two-beat, four-line section in four stanzas serves to sound the hand-craftsman's cutting of stone in the next portion. The construction of graves constitutes a way of dealing with death that may be peculiar to human beings.

This leads into

another Bloodaxe portion

which changes, in the course of a stanza, to nature despoiled in its own operations and predatory acts (parable for human actions?). Thus, 'cannibal slug' (47). Without a break, it leads into the (triumphant?) sexual act of Pasiphae's guiding the bull's organ into her

> nor loaded spirit sink
> till it had gloried in unlike creation . . .
>
> (II, 48)

One notices how the rhythm stresses 'unlike' with 'creation', in such a way as seemingly not to condemn the act, and, in this, contrasting with Hell and the shit-eaters of the section III (49–50).

III: Hell, its vendors and eaters of shit. From which context it appears that the Greek Alexander (Firdosi's Persian version) ascends. With courage, but with foolish pride, he climbs the mountain his followers refuse to attempt, and at its summit he sees the angel Israfel (III, 51) waiting to blow his trumpet. The blast of this will be the signal to end the world (and creation?). Passing into sleep, Alexander wakes, having fallen literally and symbolically from the mountain-height to the ground and the slowworm's advices – 'jeering', claims Makin. If we see this as autobiography enacted, it is one of the poem's high points, essentially a moment of experience, not contemplation. The lesson of humility, not humiliation, appears to be reinforced, in this fable-like portion, with the slowworm's providential care for itself

> Good luck to reaper and miller!
>
> (III, 51)

which self-care seems to act on the Alexander-man; it brings about the business of one's raising oneself, and leading home in a condition of humility and understanding.

IV: The two long concluding lines of the previous section (III) anticipate the shift and signature of this one.

That is, long lines spell out the defeat of the Celts by the Saxons, in the former's vain attempt to defend their territory against the Saxon's extension of power. The outnumbered three hundred warriors and their not numbered retainers are feasted for a year, in preparation, though perhaps with little expectation of their winning the battle. They are defeated at Catterick.[1]

If we are to interpret Bunting's almost synonymous celebration of their physical prowess with their defeat

> young men, tall yesterday, with cabled thighs
> (IV, 53)

the inference seems to be that, in Bunting's view, they expected their destruction. This is perhaps echoed in the almost predatory nature of the autobiographer's and the poet Aneurin's celebration of the dead

> I hear Aneurin number the dead and rejoice,
> being adult male of a merciless species . . .
> (IV, 53)

where the celebration of the activity of the warriors erases the question of mortality and its relevance. Instead this is reserved for the women who 'wake discontent'. Makin cites *Y Gododdin*, ed. A.O.H. Harman (Llandysul, 1988, 178n, 41).

I refer to the Aneurin translated by Tony Conran:

> Diademed in the forefront, wherever he went; . . .
> Breathless before a girl, he paid for his mead . . .
>
> Men went to Catraeth, keen was their company.
> They were fed on fresh mead, and it proved poison-
> (*Welsh Verse*, 114)

The desolation after the battle (see also Geoffrey Hill's 'Funeral Music' no. 7, chapter 7 below), supplies nature's predators, and the whole scene offers a paradigm for an aspect of nature. The cruelty ('cruel owls') of the two Welsh poets, Aneurin and Taliesin,

---

1.   'By about 603 the fort at Catterick was in English hands', Makin, 178, 178n; Jackson, *Gododdin*.

is contrastingly *echoed* in the presence of the two Northumbrian saints, Aidan and Cuthbert. Makin is especially interesting, and illuminating, on this latter (see Appendix 3, 'St Cuthbert in the hands of Bede', 331–3). The lines concerning the saints are mysterious, but they appear to identify a strand in common, not so much with the two Welsh poets, as with the warriors these poets celebrate. For the cruelty of the Welsh poets identified in Bunting's phrase 'cruel owls' may involve a recognition that they, too, feed on the slain warriors for the substance of their verse:

> Aidan and Cuthbert put on daylight,
> wires of sharp western metal entangled in its soft
> web . . .
>
> (IV, 53)

Whereas it is the saints' *fortitude* that is fused into this metaphor, and this of course is what they share with the slain Celtic warriors. This conjecture seems to be confirmed in the next encomium where the saints 'put on daylight' 'not for bodily welfare . . . but splendour'. Certainly, this is what the slain warriors share with them, though their actions conflict in the extreme.

(Does this reflect Bunting's own pacifist actions in the First World War, as contrasted with his course of action in the Second War?)

Whatever the answer to such a reading, both warrior and saint appear to contrast with the predatory and weak Bloodaxe. And as if to foil any conclusion, summary or otherwise, Bunting ends this historical 'episode' with the pained sceptical assertion

> Follow the clue patiently and you will understand nothing . . .
>
> (IV, 53)

There follows a passage fertile with praise of music, in particular, Domenico Scarlatti (54), and this is juxtaposed, once again, with narration recollecting the early love and the tender provision of what *she* offers in her loving acts. As it turns out, the recollection is poignant because the love is never resumed (see V, 58). We repeat that prior sequence in section I, of an almost retributive poverty rewarding his 'desertion' of love. There is no attempt to solicit the reader's sympathy or soften the image of the figure and his experience:

> where rats go go I,
> accustomed to penury,
> filth, disgust and fury ...
> (IV, 55)

although the self-critical appraisal elicits this reader's sympathy.

V: The implication of rewarding nature with the attributes of music (in strophe one) is that both share in an active and creative design, whereby design and process appear as reciprocal reflections of each other's continuity – life. Whether that, in turn, implies a belief in Bunting of a deity, as Donald Davie believes – 'what the poem itself has set in motion' ('God and Basil Bunting', *Poetry Review*, 83, no. 1, p. 83) – is not proven.

The virtue of *Briggflatts* is in its active capacity to identify wholes (design) and at the same time to create a sense of the astringent local instance. In this last Bunting homes to Northumberland, itself intensely and consciously local, the life of which is at once characteristic, yet also a version of vitality found elsewhere, in other life with its own bent and characteristic:

> féll-born mén of precise ínstep
> léading demúre dógs
> from Twéed and Till and Téviotdale, ...
> Their téeth are white as bírch,
> slów, under black frínge
> of silent, áccurate lips ...
> (V, 57)

'White as birch' echoes spring, and the dogs with 'accurate lips' echo the 'men of precise instep'. But this 'spring' and the whole precise life are caught in the north's sharp light of winter, and seen in the context of wintering age. And still returns the love of youth, spring, and the ethos of section I:

> Fifty yéars a létter únanswered;
> a visit postpóned for fifty yéars.
>
> Shé has been with me fifty yéars.
> (V, 58)

'With me' is and is not so, and in the combination of that lies the poignancy of the narrative set in this context of winter and ageing;

for 'postponed' seems to suggest both the possibility but the unlikelihood of the love being resumed. And with that the coda is, after death, mere confirmation of unrealized possibility suspended for ever in that place.

RHYTHMS AND STRUCTURE: IMPLEMENTING A MEANING

The values that Bunting seems instinct with are not difficult to name: an independence of mind, without which the feeling and thus the capacity for goodness falter. In section V (58) the much-quoted phrase 'free of our humbug' and the words 'firm' and 'steadies', to cite simple well-founded instances, provide the verbal clues. The rhythms reconfirm these values.

In chapter 2 I suggested, *pace* Charles O. Hartman, that Whitman wrote free verse, which, however, in some passages of excitement and intensity approached and sometimes realized metrical verse. Consider, for instance, the openings of both 'When lilacs last' and 'Song of the Broad-Axe'. Something of this seems observable in Bunting, though it is less easy to be certain what one observes; for the short lines, of which much of *Briggflatts* is composed, can suggest a metricality, or hover round it, by virtue of the few syllables that stock each line. Yet what one often experiences is feints and evasions of such regularity, in a recurrence of stress or duration. When *patterns* of stress take place, they are often pronounced and evident:

> Táke a chísel to wríte.
> Évery bírth a críme,
> évery séntence lífe . . .

In this instance the '*i*' sound as in '*Psyche*' enclosed in those single-syllable line-ending words reinforces the rhythmic congruence.

The five lines that follow have a similar intent of metricality (and feeling) but, following the full-stop after 'pen', yield to lines that have neither metrical congruence within themselves nor with each other. They are in fact asymmetrical:

> Love múrdered neither bléeds nor stífles
> but jógs the draftsman's élbow . . .
>
> (I, 42)

The craftsman could be the poet; and the breaking-step from the rhythmic congruence seems to reflect an almost humdrum disintegration that ensues from the abandoned (betrayed?) love. As the rhythmic count dwindles, reflecting perhaps a corresponding reduction in love, so the draftsman, via the concluding rhyme he bangs home, designs the lettering of the gravestone. This is, presumably, the acts of the mason, steely blue-eyed and copper-moustached, who shares something of the character of the fell-men with 'precise instep' walking their dogs in Northumberland (V, 57). This wiriness associates in IV with Aidan and Cuthbert who, in 'their' puissant Lindisfarne 'illuminated' mode:

> put on daylight,
> wires of sharp western metal entangled in its soft
> web . . .
>
> (IV, 53)

Symbolically the sharp determination of thread (intention?) is necessary to make the overall 'soft/web'. The image registers both a cultural perception and the perception of a style of a certain people whose individuation is reciprocally formed with the culture. And despite the reversal of stress in the first two words 'wires of', so that the rhythmic emphasis falls on the sharp 'wires', a positive cultural register is offered. This is partly achieved through the primarily dactyllic five-stress line that expressed the energized aspiration of this way of life.

Individuation returns one to the questions raised in the poem's ascription 'Autobiography', for the poem is allotropic. The poet passes through many guises, child-lover, indigent young man, Bloodaxe, the Aidan–Cuthbert axis, Alexander, and finally the older man remembering in winter the 'return' to love postponed for fifty years. Even when critical of Bloodaxe and Alexander, who are each aspects of the central figure, he is all of these, and in this sense the poem is centrifugal. Autobiography as a figure from life.

So these are not opposed but reciprocal processes in which autobiography is a means of enabling a narrative and an illumination of values. So the others' values say something concerning the man and call upon the continuing northern culture of which he is an instance. (See Bunting's beheading discourse.)

The slow, sparsely syllabled lines that compromise much of

Briggflatts strike home the values of fortitude, obduracy – and fortitude in the humbling process of epiphany and learning (the slowworm episode that ends III, 51–2). Of course, this gets careful rhythmic enunciation, yet where Bunting claims that music is what most matters, I suggest that rhythm in *Briggflatts* is the executive of meaning. (See 'A Note on Briggflatts' and 'The Poet's Point of View' (Three Essays, 34).)

THE POET – OUTSIDER AS VISIONARY

In the last chapter I sidle up to the familiar concept that some of our best poets criticize their society by standing themselves outside the citadel. Examples of poets in, half-in, alienated or absorbed (by success, its lure, or bromides) into society are many, and make this an important question for readers of twentieth-century poetry. Other poets might be chosen to demonstrate their outsider potency, but all the poets I have examined in this book (and the others I have had to omit) are examples of those who have had to negotiate this question; and although reciprocity of readers is vital to poets, there exist, as the Prophets appear to have understood, alternative strategies in negotiating this reciprocity. It is clear from Hopkins' criticism of Tennyson that there is implied a negotiation with an imaginary readership that, linguistically and prosodically speaking, placed him (Hopkins) outside the pale, though the *material* of his poetry placed him within in a way that pertained neither for Blake nor for much of earlier Wordsworth.

Wordsworth's early Jacobin positioning alone marginalized his possibilities for inclusion, and the essentializing of his *feelings* (which Coleridge identified in part as his 'freshness') also defamiliarized his work for readers. He made his readers, and he makes us. Whitman's visionary democratization of his territory suggests a socialization that consolidates his poetry with a supposed existing peaceable society. But this surely is the wish, not the reality. The Quaker kingdom never has been in even one small aspect an effective part of America's contract; and 'When lilacs last' mourns not only the death of a president but, arguably, the extinction of the basis for that vision. Not that we should be pessimistic. Nevertheless the tenacity of the wish in Whitman's 'Reconciliation' goes in fear of that loss.

Free verse was practised by others at the time, but Whitman's later attempts to soften the originality of the first *Song of Myself* (1855) reveals his awareness of his *exteriority* as man, as poet, and social being. And one of his earliest influences was upon a literary movement that did not use the English language – that is, German Expressionism. Furthermore, Ivor Gurney and Lawrence were English not American responders. So for that matter was the Anglo-Jewish poet Isaac Rosenberg. (See his 'Emerson', *The Collected Works*, 288–9.)

Leaving aside the question of Wilfred Owen's homosexuality, his traditional but modernized responses enabled him to engage in an argument with his society during the First World War, the conduct of which was predicated on action from which he dissented. Rosenberg's more radical dissent (see my *Out of Battle*) wanted inclusion within English verse, but his responses are those of an even more developed visionary than Owen was, and his prosody remains more exploratory. Moreover his desire to reinvigorate society is predicated on a radical criticism of it (cf. his playlet *Moses*, 1916).

As I have suggested (see chapter 2) Eliot's case is more ambiguous, where, in the final section of *The Waste Land* (1922), he consolidates his position with that of religious orthodoxy. Whereas I argue that Pound achieved some of his best poetry facing the possibility of execution (though Pound's story is indeed a tangled one). Yet his vision of a redemptive society was remote from the Italian fascisti who made use of him and whose position he continued to endorse (see above, chapter 3).

And Lawrence? Lawrence and his wife Frieda became exiles after the First War (see above, chapter 4) yet the poetry does not appear to register this. The kingdom of God remains within. As with Owen, Lawrence's criticism of society is predicated on a contract with a traditional use of the *language*, though prosodically his verse is more exploratory than Owen's.

Prosodically, Dylan Thomas's solutions are traditional metrical ones (see above, chapter 5), although the language is, especially in the earlier poems, compressed and cross-referenced in a mode most poetry in English could or, at least, did not then negotiate. And Bunting? Prosodically he is a modernist, yet which 'modern' work does *Briggflatts* resemble? More realistic than Pound, his resulting dissent is thus that much more radical. Local, historical, he is in these aspects traditional, even if the kingdom of the north does not (now) exist. Even if certain attributes of it continue. In this respect,

his concern with an ideal society constitutes a traditional underpinning of his vision of human conduct.

BUNTING: TRADITIONAL AND MODERNIST

Here, Davie's concern with Bunting's putative Christian underpinning emerges, although even in the instance I am about to offer,
it is ambiguous. Citing J.W. Burrow, Makin indicates that 'God's
goodness had once guaranteed the goodness of the creation; now it
was the goodness of creation that guaranteed the very existence of
God' (Makin, quoting Burrows, 274). So the slowworm's testimony

> Ripe wheat is my lodging. I polish
> my side on pillars of its transept,
> gleam in its occasional light . . .
> (III, 51)

is not mere trope in which the wheat becomes God's cathedral
('transept/gleam') but a stage in an argument in the evolution (!)
of Christian belief, where science is conscripted to help prove the
existence of God. The method of looking is essentially scientific; the
detail is crucial for, as with Hopkins, it is part of the inscape. *Pace*
Johnson, the poet is, here, required to number the stripes on the
tulip even if the grounds for doing so are not purely aesthetic.
As with Hopkins they were not purely religious, either.

The position of *Briggflatts*, in religious terms, is both traditional
and historical. Equally surprising, although the poem uses the modernist strategy of juxtaposition placing side by side blocks of narration or episode without explanatory connective tissue, the syntax
(like the religious imagery) is an unexpected mix of the formal,
traditional and elliptic where, with the latter, the syntax is shorn of
pronouns. Compare

> One
> plucked fruit warm from the arse
> of his companion, who
> making to beat him, he screamed:
> Hastor! Hastor!
> (III, 49)

with the lines below. For in this quotation above the co-ordinate noun clause, 'who/making to beat him', has the traditional qualities of leisurely prose discourse, in both structure and tone hovering between eighteenth- and nineteenth-century architectonics; and it wouldn't dream of operating the compaction of ellipsis. And this in turn has an effect on the rhythm and the prosody. So compare this above with the lines concluding the first stanza of section I, which are not mere abbreviation:

> Máy on the búll's híde
> añd thröūgh thĕ dalē
> fúrrows fill with máy,
> páving the slöwwörm's wáy....
>   (I, 39)

This jams together two syntaxes each comprised in two lots of two successive lines. The month of May is upon the bull's hide and in the dale; furrows similarly fill with the effect of the month. But a moment's thought will also reveal the possibility that the first 'May' might not only be the month but the shrub; the syntaxes not only interlock but conjunct two ideas (or two perceptions of spring) in their interlocking act, and prepare the way for the slowworm. The word that connects the two pairs of two lines is not conjunctive; it is the simple sensuous idea of May (and perhaps the shrub) – the season of the North and all it bestows. Such syntactic and 'idea' strategy is modernist, and in reading Bunting we need to accommodate the traditional with the modernist. And this is an instance of this book's preoccupation – the need to reconcile the traditional (metrical) with the modern (free verse). And in inspecting this interesting phenomenon of mixed broadcasting

> Páinful lárk lábouring to ríse!

one notices the lack of the verb 'is', thus forming an untraditional syntax expressing traditional matter. The creature's continuing effect leads into the mainspring, behind which is the imagination that launches the whole, rhythm being the executive of all this. Let's see.
 In the line above, the alliterating 'ls' enact some part of a bird being unnaturally ponderous, and this alliteration (in a traditional manner) works either side of the caesura, marked by the comma. Certainly, Makin is right when he tells us that in the stressed

language of English, 'all' quantity (durational or long syllables) tend
to convert to stressed ones. The observation is judicious, yet my
reading would suggest that a coinciding of stress with duration
occurs on the first of both syllables either side of that separating
comma in this four-pulse line, but that the last syllables either side
of the comma achieve that most difficult thing in English (English-
English) duration. It might take a phonetician to explain it to us in
the utmost schwa, and then again, it might not. It's in the total run
of the line that we mark the difference between stress and duration.
And if this listening is true, then we unlock the sense of pain in
energy struggling against inertia, which is indeed the burden of all
life. As if to confirm this, the line-idea is followed by the hammer-
chisel onomatopoeia of

In the gráve's slót
he lies. We rót.
(I, 39)

which the perfect rhyme strikes home.

It seems important to leave the magnetic first section, even if
the poem's premisses and themes lie there. Perhaps part of its at-
traction is the way in which the disparate themes are cohered, not
simply through the narration concerning the children-lovers, and
the daughter's father-mason. The cohering is as much to do with
how the poem (and this section in particular) trades in its imagist/
objectivist (object-re-creating) inheritance fusing narration with image. In this way the section mediates between the image as the representative instance of a symbolic activity – 'masoning' – and the
specificity of the lovers as well as the mason himself. But neither
mode can free itself of the other, and it is through the rhythm that
this tension in the section exerts its extraordinary power.

The second section advances by developing the narration, but,
perhaps because of what such narration demands, does not have as
much tension and coherence as the first.

The sea-experience develops in this section, and with it (44) the
sense of Bloodaxe as a ruthless, predatory voyager (not the character of a strong person). This second term contrasts with the love
manifested in sections I and IV and with the presence of Aidan
and Cuthbert (also in IV). It is hard to assess Bloodaxe's judged
relationship with the predatory, parasitic life of the city in the
autobiographer's

toadies, confidence men, kept boys . . .

(II, 43)

It is a somewhat self-righteous list, and assuming the writer's probity, which we must, it is nevertheless difficult to imagine a human being who is immune to touches of different imperfections when he impugns others. Aesthetically, it is also hard to align this version of predatoriness with that of Bloodaxe; perhaps what they all have in common is not so much their predatoriness as their weakness. This is not registered in either case, and I think it possible that one of the weaknesses in the modernist position, which itself, in English, at least, derives principally from Imagism, is its insistence on a perfection that probably originates from Pater's 'To burn always with this hard, gemlike flame' (see above, chapter 2). Thus under the guise of aesthetic formulation, the difficulties of life, and the condition of imperfection, which is the human condition, is not allowed for.

In section II (I am slowly building a case for this section's coherence!) this quality of squalor identified in the opening strophe of the section is (45) extended to the landscape, which, in being compared to a urinal, is discredited by the metaphor. This seems hard luck on the landscape, but as with so much in rhetoric its execution is effective. And presumably the 'marble stained like a urinal' is, via the modernist strategy of assemblage, some residual matter extending, or perhaps reflecting, the moral squalor of the human parasites. It certainly seems to contrast with the mason's stone and his activity in section I, in the question of cleanliness, though, as it turns out, the stone will serve the identical use here as it did for the mason in the first section. And this strategy fairly reveals the strengths here as well as the difficulties of modernism.

Thus on the one hand the accommodation, via the aesthetic and what it has to teach, of specificity; the way, for instance, the stone is extracted, as it were, from rock, and worked in graves that constitute the Italian churchyards – and even, perhaps, in part into urinals ('marble middens'?). On the other hand, the specificity gains its strength, it seems, from a refusal on the poet's part, *qua* modernism, to explain either the meanings of the partly symbolic (?) specificity as well as the connections between the parts, the blocks of narration, or episodes; so that the reader is left to supply and conjecture a meaning. This enables a richness of meaning, by association, to enter the reader's transaction with the text; but it also

makes it difficult to get at the totality and make those very connections that might enable the richness.

At any rate at the end of this strophe we are left once again
with the axis of remorse, regret-guilt, responses that pervade the
poem and which are to do with 'discarded love'. I may not be
the only reader to welcome the leitmotif strategy as one means
of understanding the whole poem – if that were possible for any
one reader. For (barring the 'coda') the poem concludes with the
love 'postponed' for fifty years (V). And if we read the poem as
'autobiography' we may carry with us the sense not of a narrator
who doesn't know that outcome of the story (that is, one who
purports to be unfolding the narration as it happens) but, on the
contrary, one uniquely in the know with regard to the (his) life.
As Montaigne noted, in defending himself against the objection to
autobiographical material in his essays.

Further on occurs the murder of Bloodaxe. Here again modernist specificity serves the poem well, where this is expressed in
unsquared-off, glancing rhythms, that express both the slyness with
which the murder is achieved as well as the horror at the deed:

> Loaded with mall of linked lies,
> what weapon can the king lift to fight
> when chance-met enemies employ sly
> sword and shoulder-piercing pike . . .
> (II, 46)

The 'lies', as Makin indicates, probably indicates the character
of Bloodaxe – not so much the lying to others but to himself – the
concealment from himself of his weakness, which, in totality, serves
to augment his cruel and predatory character (not modifed much
by the mores of Viking society). This in turn serves to bring about
his murder ('sly') – as if like brought about like. The whole tale
seems to be one of uncondoned natural justice, as the glancing
rhythms, augmented by the hyphenated compound adjectives
(above), show. The rhythmic effect of these lines is uncertainty,
which, in those days and for 'rulers' of Bloodaxe's ilk, might seem
to be the one certainty in their lives. The carrion-feeding vultures
(47) the 'codling/moth' (whose larvae feed on apples), the 'ragged
lettuces', spider and 'cannibal slug' all attest to the predatory aspect
of nature which, by juxtaposed association, underscore the *human*
predation to which this section attests.

There are always two ways of reading a passage in poetry (and prose), one of which is what the words say, and the other what the rhythms with the words express. Syntax is another interlinked mode of expression, and even if we allow for expediency as a component of expression – the contingent means available after patient working and reworking – the rhythms are, even so, the tacit mode of expression underpinning what the writer may have felt, whatever the upper semantic layer.

Thus the reading of the Pasiphae ending to section II (48) is better enabled if we set aside our (possible) human repugnance and try to attend to the evaluative feeling rhythmically expressed: Thus after Pasiphae had guided the bull's organ ('seed') into her

> nor did flésh flinch
> disténded by the brúte
> nor lóaded spirit sink
> till it had glóried in únlike creátion.
>
> (II, 48)

It may seem a perverse reading to suggest that a negative appraisal of Pasiphae's 'gloried' is inappropriate, but rhythmically, with the reinforcing rhyme, a positive is the final effect I believe to be created here. The rhythms are firm, the 'nor'/'nor' of the syntax is congruently placed, and the syntax itself, distributed clause by clause in each line, creates the effect of certainty, which the four-beat rhythm upholds. The final accentual movement of the last line quoted attributes both spasm and willing certainty to the whole act.

If, following modernist practice, we now set this reading against Bloodaxe, his murder and the generally predatory and dishevelled character of his nature preceding this passage, an altogether positive reading of this Pasiphae episode, as against murder and general predation, seems to result.

SECTION III

In a diagram of the climaxes in *Briggflatts* (first printed in *Agenda*, Basil Bunting special issue 16, No. 1, Spring 1978) we find a series of mountain peaks:

This occurs in an interview on 4 November 1970, between Bunting, Peter Quartermain and Warren Tallman. The picture looks neat, yet is it accurate enough? Bunting represents the third section as peaking above the others, and says:

> the middle one . . . it's a different thing . . . a nightmare or a dream or whatever you fancy . . .
>
> (*Agenda*, 15)

Yet Bunting may be imposing an orderly and narrative-like structure of an older and more traditional kind (I dare to suggest) perhaps inappropriate to the *Briggflatts* of other readers.

Perhaps all I am cavilling at is that it is not a climax, but a sustained plateau, a raised continuity that hasn't the climactic quality of a peak. But then why should the poet be kept to his diagram?

Yet the plateau-like achievement of this section is the effect – sustained rather than climaxed.

It is surely Hell – the shit eaters and vendors – with the almost-coy Hastor who

> raised dung thickened lashes to stare
>
> (III, 49)

and will buy no other shit-loaves but (as I understand it) his own. This is powerful enough, if marginally regressive, and possibly vengeful (Hastor = Astor, the newspaper owner?). But the passage (49–50) survives the feel of a grudge. Hell is powerfully touched in, with a quirkiness that effectively settles the vision in the mind. There, for instance, are those incapacitated with the laughing-sickness 'till fun suffocates them'. It is that 'fun' which at first dissonates, with laughter, and then, in its sheer oddity, achieves its vision of perversity.

It seems that the ascent from this is in some respects from out of Hell. The extended climb, up the mountain, is made by Alexander alone (his followers will not follow him), and in a sense it is a spiritual ascent. But if it is triumph, it is lonely, and achieved in pride; which might suggest that Hell has been carried up within the Alexander figure.

Bunting (*Agenda*, 9) claims that the 'central' portion of the poem 'as I knew from the beginning' was Alexander's 'interview'; and the Persian version of the legend, 'one of the very early ones', occurs in Firdosi's *Shah Nameh*. Achieving the 'peak unscaleable' Alexander is humbled ('interview' is a strange word) by his sight of the angel Israfel, who appears not even to notice the human who has reached the summit. As for Alexander, he perceives the angel with swelled cheeks, ready with his trumpet to sound the note that will bring the world's end. Yet the wonderfully delayed rhyme of 'delay/clay' suspends that judgement and its ensuing act. The old-fashioned touch of allegory balances the same kind of specificity and symbolic instance that the poem achieves in section one:

> Yet delay!
> When will the signal come
> to summon man to his clay?
> (III, 51)

I had at first felt that a separation between narration and specificity had occurred, but I withdraw that, and think the fusion extends, with fineness, into the whole episode with the slowworm. It is a quirky sensuous picture of slowworm (the lizard family):

> a cold squirm snaking his flank
> and breath leaked to his ear . . .
> (III, 51)

This is the slowworm, making tactile and audile intrusion on the man who has fallen asleep after the experience on the mountain. A lovely and unviolent way of bestowing a humbling lesson upon the man. It is the word 'squirm' that makes the experience intimate, and gives it wit with the word 'leaked.' Thus the communication between the two creatures is achieved and in so doing solves the problem of conveying the speech (communicating breath) of a creature without such capacity. 'Snaking' is also inventive. It restores to literalness the metaphoric sense of snaking, and at the same time communicates the reptilian nature of the slowworm, while darting its wit at the reader.

The metricality also carries the vividness of this life. For if

> a cold squirm snaking his flank

is a four-pulse line, while the next

> and breath leaked to his ear

could be read as a three-stroke line (or even a two-stroke one if 'breath' is hurried onto 'leaked'), they are each counting both the syllables and those syllables bearing stress-duration. The same is true of the next two lines, 'Ripe wheat/its transept'; and the continued effect of the metricality, quirkiness and personal feeling, which latter is what makes *Briggflatts* triumph, brings together narration and visualization.

After which Bunting is in intimate control. The slowworm is seen and endowed with (anthropomorphic) character so that, however, when he blinks, it is not, as with a human creature, a sign of nervousness but to do with his own piercing capacity. The creature's confidence increases:

> Good lúck to réaper and míller!
> (III, 51)

The slowworm is the equal of reaper and miller – he who cuts and he that grinds. With a finely unexplained transition (another feature of modernist writing) the voice becomes the narrator's. This encounter with the slowworm, who leaks humility into the Alexander/poet figure, is a high point in the poem. The encroachment of rhyme, together with lines that are so short that we cannot with certainty know whether to read the verse as free or metrical, hovers the traditional conclusion of section III between tradition and modernity. Additionally, the ambiguity and uncertainty of how to read these lines, metrically, slants us across the two systems of metrical and free verse, and thus analogizes the state of mind in Alexander, as both conqueror and humbled man. To complete this sketch of the concluding lines' prosody, the transition of humility is finalized in a pair of separated longer lines, flowing and subdued, conveying a sense of Miltonic quietness both without and within, as if nature concurred with the slowworm's lesson.

SECTION IV

Fŏllŏ̆w t̆he clŭe pátĭĕntlў̆ ănd yŏu w̆ill und̆ĕrst̆ănd nŏthing . . .

(IV, 53)

This sardonic incomplete conclusion contains a particular history, which is that after the battle of Catterick (above) the Anglian kingdoms of Deira (Yorkshire, approximately) and Bernicia (Northumberland and Durham) both rose. But they rose cultured in part by a mixture of Celtic Christianity, which blend is 'responsible' for the culture that produced the tough delicacy ('western metal entangled in its soft/web') of the Lindisfarne Gospels. (What part did Cuthbert play in the production of them?) Davie seems unable to accommodate Makin's view of Cuthbert's importance (*Poetry Review*, 84). For Davie, the important question, perhaps the most important, appears, from this article, to be the question of Bunting's Christianity, and his belief, or not, in God.

There are entangled here a number of difficult questions. One is whether belief in God and Christian belief are synonymous. For *some* Christians they may be, and may have to be. But from where I stand, as a Jew, I would question this. I suppose it depends how wide an embrace the oecumenical one is. The next question is to what *extent* Bunting did or did not believe in God, and to what extent, if it can be ascertained, this affected his poem, and thus our reading of it. Next comes a more difficult question, which is to do with the poem's aesthetics. I ask to what extent we must decide on Bunting's religious beliefs before deciding on the nature of his aesthetics? For both Makin and Davie this would appear to be the issue, though perhaps Makin was not well advised to attack Bede for his alleged distortion of Cuthbert. For in doing so he allowed the argument as to the nature of Bunting's religious beliefs to assume a prominence that is perhaps unnecessary for an assessment of the relationship between the northern culture of Northumbria and *Briggflatts*. The crucial citing (on which Makin bases his aesthetic argument) would appear to be a portion from 'The Codex' (tape), part of a lecture on poetry that Bunting gave at the University of Newcastle (while he was Literary Fellow). Thus, first to simplify detail till only the barest essentials of it are left; second to weave an enormous number of such details into an intricate pattern which yet keeps perfect balance and proportion; and thirdly to set your central theme with infinite care in just the right place ...

concerning which Makin had written that such was what he (Bunting) wanted for a newly re-constituted Northumbrian art (Makin, 222).

That this is what Bunting wants for his own poetry is clear enough. And in *Briggflatts* he appears to situate his work in that tension between 'barest essentials' and 'enormous number of details'. This might be a way of putting the formulation (above) where I suggested that specificity, which is the strength of much modernist practice, combines with the instantial representative impulsion to produce a unitary product. And that this carries with it some such religious sense as many poets might admit to, Bunting, I believe, being one.

However the related problem is that the Lindisfarne Gospels themselves seem to be predicated on a belief in God, and an ascetic approach to life. This would appear to accord with Bunting's requirement of 'barest essentials', and it is this humility predicated in 'barest essentials' that seems to be at the heart of all that Makin admires about Cuthbert, and which gives the saint's humility that strength which political power does not wield.

And that seems to bring one to the threshold of *Briggflatts*. For as Makin appears to suggest, when Bunting was employed (during the war) in positions in which he of necessity had and used power this did not coincide with a poetic fertility. The case is of course unprovable, but it can be indicated that when Bunting was in 'Hell' during his sixties he produced *Briggflatts* out of the depths. I do not subscribe to the naive notion that destitution and/or suffering are predicates for good writing, but I do believe that power is probably alien to it. And furthermore, I believe that the enforced ascetic nature of his life (those 'barest essentials') perhaps coincided with his adult experience over a considerable period, or periods, and probably consorted with that northern respect for essentials and distrust of luxury, of which he, Bunting, is a sufficient example.

So that the clue which followed patiently will provide no understanding becomes, in this whole context, the understanding itself. It is where one starts from, as it is where Bunting himself seems (see interview with Jonathan Williams), blindly enough, with *Briggflatts*, to have begun.

It is in part negative of course, though with a balancing understanding to be drawn, if one will. Thus the lice that have contempt for the clothing (IV, 54) that houses them are themselves instantly vulnerable to the flame that destroys their bodies. That seems intended as a measure of understanding, for us.

Yet for all the hard lessons that the poem embodies, this section with long discreetly flowing lines, though not relaxing its vigilance on the hard clear image, still manages to express a life of tenderness and experience that lies outside the immediate grasp of such hard strategy. The love reappears:

> Light as spider floss her hair on my cheek which a puff
>   scatters . . .
>
> (IV, 54)

Once again, it is not only in the sense, or for that matter in the clear pictures the long line expresses, but in its multisyllabled flow that the important part carries. For its flow conveys even more feeling than such nevertheless evocative words as 'floss' and the intended intimacy of her hair on his cheek. And the echo of mortality, which attends the hair's scattering at the lightest breath. The tenderness of this is seen in the way in which 'scatters', which is available here for many different uses, such as 'scatter my/thine enemies', is here, with its feminine ending, the line's final echo. In its trisyllabic tendency, and with the final unaccented syllable, the line's rhythm effects its sense of something infinitely vulnerable.

We get a full sense of this by contrasting these lines, indeed almost all the section, with the lines in the last passage, which revert to the hard spare beat of short measures:

> Where rats go go I,
> accustomed to penury,
> filth, disgust and fury . . .
>   (IV, 55)

The verse mediates between the rat's strategy and the human's rat-like one. And in as much as both are striving to persist, each is turned against the human – the rat against all humans, the autobiographer against those stronger and more ruthless than he. The rat's evasive valiance is admired, though both the creature and the human in their struggle are 'unreconciled' with each other, and with the wider condition they share. It is thus in the nature of this bony-footed verse that the subsequent free-verse lines plot out the strategy of resistance to vicissitude, but are cohered in a tempering harmony with the assistance of assonance and alliteration.

SECTION V

With the start of the year's ageing we recall how, traditionally, we harmonize a year's cycle with the uncycling life of creatures, which harmonization implicitly acknowledges the ironic disparity between the two processes.

In this last section (excepting the brief 'Coda', which is past seasonal fluctuation) we are in the winter's part of nature's cycle; and remembering that *Briggflatts* is among many things 'autobiography', we are thus with the narrator in his age (the narration makes evident the gender of the narrator).

The first strophe links the dripping icicle (life?) with music. And then, through music's climax, to that of the 'year's end' – this last seeming to form an inexact analogy. The year's end neither 'glows' any more than it ends in crescendo, if we except the festival implicit in the human but not the natural cycle. Nor can I make the correlative required transition from melted icicle, and I am similarly frustrated by the problem that it is precisely at the year's end that icicles can't be expected to melt even if in age life does. If this is pedantry, I'm reminded (not consoled) by the fact that Bunting's verse, imagistic, objectivist, is usually exact in these respects. One thinks of oxter, of the 'thole pin' shredding 'where the oar leans', the grommets, halliards and all the other cited parts of the Viking ship (II, 44) and one remembers also the exactness of the urinous marble of the Alps (II, 45). Perhaps an anxiety to pull together the trajectory of the whole poem's parts produces an uncharacteristic and wilful poetic act.

But how beautiful the next stanza, mediating beween delicacy and toughness in 'whey-blue haze' (V, 56). Of course there are many kinds of beauty; it is an easy word with which to adorn a passage, or image, but in the Northern characterization

> fell-born men of precise instep
> leading demure dogs
> from Tweed and Till and Teviotdale ...
> (V, 57)

it is the unusual ascription 'precise' struck against 'demure' that produces the beauty. It is a loving partnership that gets bonded in contrasting characterization. What gives these characterizations a force that reaches the fuller nature of synecdoche is the mode that, through its strong individuation, acquires representative power, not only on behalf of men and their working companionable creatures, but of the types and features, the nuclei even, of a culture. Beauty, then, is not decoration but a decoction, an essentializing representation under heat (pressure) that establishes an illusion of permanence – in as much as we use the word 'world' as referring to something that lasts. In this essentializing sense beauty appears to be thrown against Bunting's notion of music, and to emerge as an essential of meaning-in-presentation.

Yet we shan't escape from Bunting's 'music' so easily since we find we do have a characteristic mode of Bunting at his habitual best, which is the short line. How short? Usually two to four emphases, durations themselves marked out by few surrounding syllables, these in their sparseness not always weak. Further the lines (above) give, as with Lawrence, an uncanny sense of being parallel, even though the movement of each is not congruent. I believe that this sense results from an arrangement of the syntax whereby propositions separated by lineation are disposed in such a way as to correspond or impinge on each other semantically.

And for music, we reckon with Bunting's short lines, moving slowly, since it seems that the tread is comprised in length as well as stress, Makin's excellent observations on stress and duration in English verse notwithstanding.

And what, one may ask, is the meaning of Bunting's long durational syllables? It is, perhaps, to do with lament:

> Fífty yéars a létter unánswered;
> a visit postpóned for fífty yéars.
>
> Shé has been with me fífty yéars ...
> (V, 58)

'Years' is durational, I believe, rather than stressed, and the chiasmic arrangement of the word in the first two lines emphasizes the word (the meaning and import of the whole narrative) to have it confirmed in parallel sequence in these last two lines. Accentually the lines are congruent, though not identical.

As for 'lament' three things translate into it. First, quite apart from its being such, it repeats the revelation of what we already know from section one: 'a visit postponed', and that first partnership never subsequently joined up to sever such postponement. It continues in place of connection or resumption. Postponement continues, which is cause for irony and lament, though the irony is quickly deflated in his having had a sufficient life. The second thread of this lament is that not being with him, she has so been in him. And third, the chiasmus of 'fifty years' above is trodden out slowly. It is the way with pain, which is not severed, and which in its duration is infinite – in the way the long syllables briefly express it. Finally it (lament) is an 'image' of what is mortal, and of how mortality is briefly existent in time.

7

Some Poets Now

Acceptable speech? That which predominates?

Before the First World War it seemed as if the middle classes (and perhaps the petit bourgeoisie) felt their strength and aspired to establish their speech as the dominant mode.

This is visible in R.H. Mottram's *The Spanish Farm Trilogy, 1914–1918* where, without any intended irony on Mottram's part, the two English officers, after some formal protest on the part of a socialist-minded other-ranker, are simply bursting with good-natured merriment at the earnestness of the other-ranker. The *author's* apparent blankness suggests his unquestioned assumptions that the middle-class officers possess the stable common sense and wisdom from which all understanding beyond reasonable doubt issues. It is not a tricky moment for Mottram, but a triumphant one.

Since then the centre of gravity has shifted, and not only the position where the proper centre of power should reside is in doubt, but whether there is or should be one, and whether indeed the assumption of unquestioned supremacy itself is tenable.

If the question of whether speech initiates or is a reflection of a shift in power is worth raising, the issue cannot be concluded. What one might say is that the speech that presently prevails has become abbreviated, perhaps more evidently heartless and less leisured. The language has in certain respects become pluralistic (not the same thing as a shared democracy) – has also become a deafer language, with smaller groups each competing for recognition – perfectly justifiably – within the total English anglophone. At the same time each seems unable or unwilling to hear another locus than its own. Sensuous language, and its inseparable correlate, rhythm, have suffered in this shift, not because the newer speeches cannot find the means to express sensuousness but because each may not want or have the patience to do so. Or perhaps because each needs more time to gather and route its energies and enter them on their expressive trajectory.

The rhythms pulsing and lashing away in our lives – how can one begin to discuss this intelligibly? The question begins to bifurcate into what we speak as a response to stimulus, or pressure, and what one expresses within the code(s) of poetry written and printed. But one thing seems likely: that there is a continuous fusing and separating between actual speech and speech redesigned in written poetry. My examples here will at least indicate the crux I am raising even if they will not bear the weight of it as reliable instances. At any rate my first instance of speech is that of the young lad who, in the early nineteenth century in Britain, faced with execution, for some trivial offence, says to his hangman

'Pray sir, do not hurt me.'

This purports to come from actual speech. The next comes from speech mediated in dramatic iambic pentameter:

> Thou'lt come no more,
> Never, never, never, never, never . . .
> (*King Lear* V, iii)

I have puzzled to find out why the former should move this reader, at least, more than the latter. Of course I can only speak for myself – but both seem instances expressing tenderness. The first, though seemingly on behalf of his own person, suggests a capacity for tenderness, the second, spoken by Lear about his daughter, solicits our tenderness for him in his loss.

The first solicits tenderness from his executioner from whom we know none will be given. The second expresses Lear's anguish and takes hold of our tenderness. The first, as far as we know, is direct solicitation, and appears to indicate respect for him who will destroy him. The speaker offers to share a code of speech even if the executioner rejects it – if for no other cause than his livelihood.

There is a further way of examining this. The first instance is unbearably intimate; and who is to say it is less accomplished speech than Shakespeare's? What seems to be happening in this first is that we have speech passing over from impulse into consummation, saying everything that should be said about a victim and his/her predator (hangmen were and are predators hired to do the job for a paymaster). It establishes, in language, the shared relations between humans. On the other hand, Shakespeare's is consummate

– what? To call it rhetoric is to miss the principal burden of the question, which is that the danger of converting speech into literary forms and codes can damage the energy and sensitivity of that speech. Which danger discloses one reason why this reader believes Wordsworth to be a greater *poet* than Shakespeare, for his forms mediate living *speech* with greater care – awareness – than Shakespeare's appears to. Or one might say that the language that was available to Wordsworth (rather than Shakespeare) was a richer locus of common speech, more centrally poised and available then than it had previously been.

Wordsworth's assault on the diction of later eighteenth-century verse, of which Gray's sonnet is the typifying instance, constitutes, whatever Coleridge's mocking arguments against his intimate friend, an argument for bringing speech into a position more centrally available to writers. For making speech the basis for poetry, rather than poetry enclosing its own language in a position where no permeable membrane works between its language and that constantly spoken and changing. Wordsworth felt the growing point of British speech (he seems to have been acutely aware of Burns, for instance) and he modestly situates his poetry there. In Lear's moving lines, Shakespeare seemingly redesigns speech into a literary mode possessing great energy, but, beside the speech of the young victim, it discloses to this reader a deficiency I attempt to identify.

POETRY AND MUSIC

In *c.* 1948 the American critic Edmund Wilson declared that the iambic pentameter did (does) not express 'the tempo and language of our lives' ('Is Verse a Dying Technique?', *The Triple Thinkers*, 1962 (1952), p. 35). A closer inspection of Eliot's *The Waste Land* and Lawrence's 'The Ship of Death', both within twenty-five years of Wilson's assertion, and, moreover, Robert Lowell's 'The Quaker Graveyard in Nantucket' (*Poems 1938–1949*), does not corroborate this. Moreover his disinclination to investigate the achievements of free verse makes this reader suspicious with respect to his melting down the distinction between prose and verse. His post-symbolist discovery of musical essences common to both modes appears to be actuating this assertion; and yet when all his objections are explained we still need to consider his deploring the want of *music* in some periods of verse:

The Greeks (he says) are *singing* about the landscape, the Romans
are fixing it for the eye of the mind. . . . in the Elizabethan age, the
English were extremely musical. . . . What has really happened
with Pope is that the musical background is no longer there and
that the ocular sense has grown sharp again. After this, the real
music of verse is largely confined to lyrics . . .

(36)

This appears to suggest that one kind of poetry sees with the voice
that speaks and another (perhaps with a greater ambit) apprehends
life with the singing voice. But his principal objection appears to be
that metrical poetry has not the capacity to express contemporary
life sensitively, and that in any case the essential singing voice shared
between prose and poetry is not an attribute contemporary poetry
is properly using. That all this is said in prose, and that it ignores
certain central achievements in nineteenth- and twentieth-century
verse, should not go unnoticed. But neither should we lose sight of
music, which on the one hand might be used as a term to describe
the interlocking of syntax with lineation and rhythm, but one also
used to denote sound, which of course cannot be separated from
either prosody or meaning. More than that, 'music' might imply
the comprehensive integration of a poem, something that we may
experience with *The Waste Land* and *Briggflatts*.

Such integration brings one again to those boundaries of speech
actual, and speech modified by the code of written language (speech
intended to be written down), and thus to the fluid-electric area
between and/or overlapping both. The (continued) vitality of *The
Waste Land* as well as much of Lawrence, and of *Briggflatts*, suggests
that this is an alive, sensitive area, and that probably the ambiguous relations between poetry and speech are at least as fertile as
those between prose, with its more written-down character, and
the wavering indirections and onwardness of speech.

ROY FISHER: LANGUAGE, OR WHAT IT REFERS TO?[1]

'I must say Roy Fisher's work does add up impressively.'
(Tomlinson's letter to this writer, 18 April 1972)

1.   All dates of *composition* supplied by Roy Fisher in a letter to this
     writer, of 20 January 1988.

Fisher's poetry encourages one in the belief that language is his primary concern, yet what is odd here is that his poetry is full of subjects and themes ('The theme is indeed important!'; Wordsworth). In fact, there is an integrated tension between how he writes and what he shows concern for. And in this integrated yet unstable relationship his poetry will invert either way, into one or the other emphases. Given that his strengths are with language it seems even so that when he de-characterizes his capacity in this direction he produces some of his best work: 'Starting To Make a Tree' (*City*), 'After Working', and in particular its cognate 'For Realism', 'The thing about Joe Sullivan', the complex ending of *A Furnace*; and what anticipates that long poem 'A Furnace', the evasive, slippery, characteristically deliquescent 'Wonders of Obligation'.

Proper for such fluidity, almost a synonym in Fisher's case for modesty, and for deference to the reader, we find that with the exception of full-stops Fisher often omits punctuation, preferring, apparently, to achieve its function through line-endings. Of course his syntax is meticulous and, in this, and its formality, it contrasts with his conversational manner and tone (not colloquial). Thus the voice together with the syntax oppose the fluidity of his free-verse moving through line beyond line of enjambment, whether actual or simply that of punctuational absence.

This system of oppositions integrated with fluidity, careful lineation and formal completed syntax is played in a relaxed conversational manner (see 'Seven Attempted Moves'). And being relaxed it accommodates several modes, including wit, of which Fisher has plenty (see 'Paraphrases'). It is a strangely complex mind yet not one wasting itself in a narcissistic elaboration of this but instead offering its responses with much directness.

The early *City* (1957–61) embeds the autonomous poem 'Starting to Make a Tree' (25), a prose poem in what feel like stanzas rather than paragraphs. It has three salient characteristics. First, the quiet aplomb of the language coupled with its metaphysical daring. Thus, nature enables trees, but so denatured is the condition of our city (ies) – we would now say 'polluted' – that we must 'make' a tree from our urban and industrial detritus. And so (stanza 1) the 'faggot of steel stakes', where 'faggot' must remind that such are the cuttings originating from a real tree, yet where our (natural) desire to have a tree is so strong that we are obliged to construct one from what our society has produced (and discarded) – steel 'stakes'. What nature does, we *make*.

Second, the waste of the city and its despoliation of what is nature's and thus (seemingly) untainted. Fisher produces a fine simultaneity of opposites in 'burnt, chemical blue of the soil'. For by underscoring the 'blue' as 'chemical blue' he implicates both the natural atmosphere and the chemical toxins we have made, and, putting the two together, he identifies pollution. A similar strategy entailed in the same stanza is seen in 'washed with a pale brownish smoke'. It is, of course, 'washed' that does double duty (cleaned and sullied), although, in fact, it effects the third thing, of implicating the painters 'wash' of colour. Fisher has advanced imagism into a lyrical and ironic condition.

Pain and indignation are harboured in the chaste language, voice, syntax and movement that re-create the barbarity of industrial waste and its inflictions on the humans, especially those living near the factory (most likely those who work in it, although that has changed recently). Yet consider the following that comes from the later 'Wonders of Obligation' (1979, 155)

> I saw
> the mass graves dug . . .
> ready for most of the people
> the air-raids were going to kill: . . .
> provided
> for the poor of Birmingham

And this sober dismay at the treatment individuals receive at the unkind hands of authority ('provided') is found in the earlier 'For Realism' (1965). And if in the 'tree' poem there is yet another constituent, found in the subterranean sly sexuality of 'groin', 'bole' and 'thrust' in stanza 8, this subsequently becomes converted to overt human affection in 'For Realism' – as if this were the benchmark of human conduct. In 'For Realism' (54–5) affection becomes evident, expressed in the poem's uppermost layer, and thus, not surprisingly, the verse bristles with punctuational traffic directions too numerous and various to indicate in a single quotation. Yet for all its affectionate detail, the poem finally accommodates a deploration of insensitive bureaucracy the implied minatory character of which may be understood by the much more brutal authority to be found in the almost adjacent poem 'Seven Attempted Moves'. At any rate we find the mild yet tart rendering of British bureaucracy ('For Realism') in

> A cónscience
> búilds, láte ...
> (55)

– that is, not only builds late, but constructs high-rise apartment blocks that appear to destroy both privacy and communal life together. The poem concentrates, not on this alleged 'replacement' of housing, but on the life and community some of which has already been 'scraped' away. To some readers this may read like an unofficial endorsement of conservatism; for this reader, it is an appreciative recognition of the vitality and filamented life of a working-class community rammed up hard against the factory ('Lucas's/lamp factory'). Such a works provides, not community, but the means for its own profit on the one hand and work within the active community on the other. It is fortuitously part of it, but just as 'any old group of people would do', so any old business would do as well. Here is the community:

> plénty of life there stíll,
> the fóodshóps open láte, ...
>   the windows háve
> láke strétches of sílver
> gáshed out of téa gréen shádows, ...
>   A réalism
> triés to recórd, befóre they're góne,
> what silver fílth these dráins have rún.
> (54–5)

If the neighbourhood drains run with filth (from the man pissing publicly, for instance) it is the summer evening that colludes with the people (for example, the woman stepping over the stream of urine) to make such filth 'silver'; summer also colludes with the poet who, in his 'realism', records it, and, with the reader, recognizes such veracity. A similar paradoxical strategy transforms the 'light' factory (!) – violent gashes of 'silver' 'gashed out of tea green shadows'. It is a beauty stained in domesticity, which defines its urban nature, as well as the intimate texture of the community. It is against this that we are to set the belated menacing acts of bureaucracy which mistakes the nature of its charity and its caring. A bureaucracy that has not replaced the beauty of a communal summer's night. The poem is an argument wherein it tricks itself into deploring those same allegedly humane bureaucratic acts it might on the face of it have been prepared to endorse.

In trying to do justice to the poem's duality one notices how the punctuation bristles up in the midst of this flowing enjambed syntax, to remind and warn us, it might seem, of what is being destroyed. That is, the syntax and punctuation is full of winding about and qualification (see especially the first three stanzas). The fluid beauty and sharp punctuational-cum-syntactical disjunctions together rehearse positive and negative simultaneities: part of the old community remains but is overseen by the newer heartless buildings (high-rise) that will soon extend and be the pretext for the destruction of the remaining older community and its values. The pissing man has a part to play (contrast this with the bank clerk's urination in the *prior* version of 'The Fire Sermon' in *The Waste Land* – see chapter 2). He too makes up the value and aplomb of the older community, for as he pisses into the corner, so the women step over the stream, and, in doing so, both fastidiously avoid the waste and accept the act going on in public. Thus are taboos absorbed into the community *and* its infringements tolerated.

'Wonders of Obligation' (1979), almost fifteen years subsequent to 'For Realism', is, by contrast, less thematically graspable, less concentrated, more allusive, less apparently an ordered total form – which is not to say that it lacks structure. Consider a point at which protest stiffens into formality:

> I want
> to remark formally, indeed
>
> stiffly, though not complaining,
> that the place where I was raised
> had no longer deference for water . . .
> (161)

For water! But yes. The syntax orthodox, the tone (at this heightened moment) formal: the protest against the fundamental lack of respect for one of earth's fundamental substances – water – thus life – itself. So it is like the poor in this poem, characterized as 'Mother, of Birmingham' (155), and then, like the way they are treated, they who every day observe the mass grave into which the authorities 'openly' expect them to cram so, with comparable lack of care and respect is the water treated. There is abundance of it (water) and them (the poor), so they exact from no one a need for respect. The structure of the poem is one of allusive protest, on behalf of life, against the way it is treated.

So with water, thus with syntactic flow. Therefore we should additionally note that the punctuation is sparse, maintained mostly for the necessities of syntax. And in this we witness the character-istic Fisher, his making a flow sustained and controlled, and thus checked in its fluid virtues, by lineation.

In contrast to the flowing, orthodox and *un*fragmented syntax, the modernist mode of innocently placing together seemingly dis-connected passages that do not follow logical or narrative sequence is the method Fisher uses. As Eliot's *The Waste Land*, for instance, requires the reader to piece together the sequences of sections if not sub-sections into a whole. What the poem means thus involves the whole run of it.

As with a number of Lorna Tracy's fictions in the collection *Amateur Passions* (1981), the instigation of seemingly unconnected facts, or essences, makes its *effect* without, at first, making *sense*. We don't know what her disparate mini-narratives, episodes, im-pressions, mean – and must wait patiently for them to coalesce, as they do in the best of her fictions, into suddenly accelerating revelation.

As with 'City' and 'For Realism' there is in 'Wonders of Obliga-tion' an 'alongsidedness' (adjacent is the lifeless synonym) formed by nature and urban life, and this forms the obliquely emergent collocation of meaning.

If Fisher can say of urban reality, for instance

> I'm obséssed
> with cámbered tármacs, cóncretes,
> the wáshing of ráin . . .
>
>   (162)

he is also 'obsessed' with these plants and moths, the *mormo maura*, 'the huge fusty Old Lady moth' that is winging itself against the window-glass to come in and taste the light, close-to. Or similarly as he seriously, humorously, and thus movingly, brings forward the plant he has potted

> I'm véhemently and stéadily
> párt of its lífe . . .
>
>   (163)

In the seemingly necessary urban life, not by any means seen by Fisher as all negative, the creaturely life exists, subsists, oddly – and survives. Which, against the odds, is, with some luck, and some good fortune, what the poorer, more vulnerable human beings will do (Fisher hopes) as they nurture the communal decencies that have been built up with such difficulty over a long human period.

CHARLES TOMLINSON: SELF MAKING CONTACT

In his essay 'Tomlinson's "Under the Moon's Reign"' (*Double Lyric*, 1980), the late Merle Brown speaks of

The sarcasm of the poem – heightened perhaps by a touch of envy at the popularity of Larkin ...

(160)

and this conjecture may be used to assist in a crux not unlike the one discussed in chapter 2 concerning the earlier and received versions of the seduction scene in Eliot's *The Waste Land*, that shared by clerk, typist and Tiresias. I suggested there that in a number of respects I thought the earlier version to be considerably better than the received because, prior to the intervention of Pound's editing, Eliot had instigated a robust and unpleasant disgust which the received version in fact made more unpleasant by abating that disgust, the scene becoming more prurient, respectable, though less effective. Somesuch question also afflicts Tomlinson's work, to do with the arrogance and self-enclosing solipsistic character, which arrogance however, when pushed hard by the poet, makes contact with those things he claims to disdain.

For the danger is not so much with the arrogance, which is more a symptom, but the solipsism that cuts him off from the world in which he as poet lives with apparent reluctance, disdain, even anger and hatred. But, as I suggest, with some poems the stronger the negative response(s) the more emphatic the connection with the world of which he cannot but be a part.

The poems I have chosen in order to explore these and other conjectural understandings are: 'A Meditation on John Constable', 'On the Hall at Stowey', 'The Ruin', 'Under the Moon's Reign' (four poems), 'For Miriam' and 'The Flood'. The claim that the poems with the strongest, perhaps negative, feelings are amongst his best

is a difficult one to sustain especially since some of the work
involves characteristics I do not like. But in any event I believe
aggression is present in some of Tomlinson's earliest writing. In 'A
Meditation on John Constable', the terms of the mind's operation and the subject on which it works seem to offer a mild and
inoffensive project. The poem is about Art, in England. Could anything be less likely to provoke? Yet the poem offers an unexpected
arrogance and dogmatic superiority, the aesthetics supposedly
impersonal.

> The érrors of a mínd, so tempered,
> It can forgó all páthos; for what he saw
> Discóvered what he was, and the hánd – unswayed
> By the dictátion of a síngle sense . . .
>
> (34)

This expresses not merely a dislike of involvement with 'pathos'
(which we might bracket with vicissitude and suffering) but a
distaste for an expression of vulnerability as much in oneself as
others. It also appears to implicate the capacity and right to be an
arbiter –

> the hand [Constable's] – unswayed
> By the dictation of a single sense –

This appears to deplore the sensuous condition and to predicate the
desirability of our senses being ruled by 'knowledge' and intellectual understanding – but of course such a mind must believe that
it possesses and supports these right attributes. It has most likely
formed these conclusions by observing, and probably disdaining,
those whose conduct lives more in the senses and feelings. Perhaps
the operative word here is 'dictation' because, if the senses are to
be subordinate, it follows that something else must and should
dictate. It is a mind triumphant and assured of its rightness

> The ártist lies
> For the impróvement of trúth. Beliéve him.
>
> (35)

The coolness of the language-paradox works not only to repel the
reader but in so doing to establish the superiority of the writer's

judgement at the expense of the reader's response. This is backed up by the supposedly moral argument 'For the improvement of truth', in which I detect no irony except for the conscious assertion of the paradox. Rather, the irony would be supplied by the reader who might seek to question the poet's confidence.

Isometrics

The American critic Calvin Bedient identified what he described as Tomlinson's isometric movement (equal syllable measure). Of course, not all syllables can be of 'equal' stress or duration, but the point about this movement is that it tends to remove stress and admit duration, enabling a *gravitas* that is cognate not only with calmness but with authority. Tomlinson's vocabulary too has a certain authoritativeness – 'expunged' and 'conflagration', for instance – predicating intellectual certainties validated in a Latinate diction rather than enacted in the more immediate Anglo-Saxon words of physicality that express the more uncertain condition of bodily experience and response. As for the rhythm

        a single sense
Bodied the accurate and total knowledge . . .
As the adequate gauge, both of the passion . . .
                    (34 and 35)

so that one begins to see that this isometric 'passion' is part of long annunciating syntaxes – the poet is indeed in control. In the above scansion one can pick out the stress, but the long spanning quantitative, durational features which assemble the line reinforce a voice that expresses a certain disdain for the reader, educated, or less so. If the reader then says that s/he likes this manifestation it puts one in the position of endorsing such disdain; but liking is not the only response to strong verse (in the non-Bloomean sense). Such a response might involve an almost appalled fascination with this superiority. It is art but an art consciously elevating itself into a position as arbiter. And the pairs of lines, alternately ranged left and indented, provide a visual *formality* which might reinforce all this were it not that there is no metricality to flesh out this appearance of, say, hexameters and pentameters alternating. It is a prosodic trompe l'oeil Tomlinson has used throughout his work.

'On the Hall at Stowey' and 'The Ruin'

Both poems are concerned with the neglect, or abandonment, and the consequent decay or vandalizing of fine large houses – those which were part of an estate. (In a letter to this writer, Tomlinson has indicated his working-class/petit-bourgeois origins.) I would agree that the destruction of such buildings through the (concealed) volition of councils (after tacitly allowing them to decay, with the intention of ensuring subsequent demolition) or through the knowing or unwitting collusion with vandals ('urchins') is deplorable. Yet additional questions are raised by the rebuke delivered in both poems. 'We' it seems are to blame for failing to sustain such houses, through our apparent indifference to or contempt for what they allegedly represent, a fine culture and taste. Albeit they were brought into being by the labour provided from the social group to which Tomlinson's and this writer's forbears might have belonged. Lawrence was correct when he wrote (see chapter 4) 'that culture has her roots/in the deep dung of cash'; but it might be truer to say that such houses, never primarily art objects, are cash, the conversion of some people's discomfited labour into the comfort, shelter, welfare, and perpetuated privilege of individuals from a different group. So that the style of aristocratism and authority wielded by these and other poems from such a sensitised and independent writer surprises one. Further, the style is disturbing in as much as the complex syntax seems, to this reader, to belong more with that of a socialized authority and affected superiority than to arise from the exigencies of a comprehensive apprehension. Indeed the style here is in some ways *simple* talk, rather than that represented by Rosenberg in the *cri de coeur* to his patron, Marsh; 'surely as simple as ordinary talk' he wrote concerning his poem 'Break of Day in the Trenches' (Letter to Marsh, 4 August 1916, *The Collected Works*, 239). And again, to Gordon Bottomley (also in 1916): 'Simple *poetry* – that is where an interesting complexity of thought is kept in tone and right value to the dominating idea so that it is understandable and still ungraspable' (238). I quote Rosenberg on this question of 'simple' partly because I believe that Tomlinson shares with this writer an admiration for Rosenberg (see his 'Isaac Rosenberg of Bristol', 1982).

Even so these are two poems that display superiority as they confront the destruction of fine houses the style and culture of which are, it seems, a cut above our own. It is a fine point as to whether the poet Tomlinson's berating of our age does not, in his own eyes, raise the poet above the general contemporary ruck. Yet at its best, the style, in its anger, burgeons into savage force in the 'comedy' which results from a tree, growing in the doorway of 'The Ruin', battling it out with the door itself:

> For a week, the swift traffic of demolition
> That mottled with oil their stagnant rain,
> Advanced through the deepening ruts,
> Converged on the house, disjointed, reassembled
> And carted, flung (what had sprawled unhinged)
> The door into the wreckage and burnt both.
>
> (47)

Punishment?

The irony of some third party official council-vandal burning both contestants as they each struggle to survive is too obvious to dwell on, and is very fine (and horrifying). The style that conveys it goes beyond the irony that it purveys, the anger surprising both the reader and, perhaps, the poet into an accumulating complexity that results in a directness released in iambic pentameter. Again, we might notice that the balancing syntax, an instance of which may be seen in the first line above, is, in such equilibrium, in reciprocal relationship with a durational as much as a stressed verse. The durational element adds a pendulum of gravity; though what we see, in both these poems, is a muffled 'conflagration' of anger motivated more by the experience of a talent pulled in two unexpected directions. It is not a great capacity richly divided, as in the case of Lawrence. One might compare these two poems with Fisher's 'For Realism' and his 'Wonders of Obligation' (above).

'Under the Moon's Reign' (four poems)

Tomlinson published his collection *The Way In* in 1974, and pp. 15–20 make it unequivocally apparent – seeing is believing – that in the title *Under the Moon's Reign* are subsumed four poems, 'Under the Moon's Reign', 'Foxes', 'The Dream' and 'After a Death'. In 1980 the late Merle Brown's critical book *Double Lyric* appeared in Britain and America, and contained the chapter 'Intuition vs.

Perception: On Charles Tomlinson's "Under the Moon's Reign"'. In 1987 Tomlinson (re) published a 'revised expanded edition' of his *Collected Poems* in which all such 'frontiers' and therefore connections binding together these four poems, are removed from the reader's eye, thus, in this reader's opinion, revising what appears to have been the *poet's* original intention. One might never guess that Tomlinson had originally linked and given an overall title to these four poems. In 1980 Merle Brown's chapter made it clear that up to that date this *group* was Tomlinson's real achievement whether or not 'the poem may signify little or nothing in relation to his (Tomlinson's) career' (Brown, p. 175). It is possible that Tomlinson did not read that appraisal of his work – possible, yet perhaps unlikely. At any rate, the attempt to deny the reader any visible evidence of the original linkages, which I would presumptuously like to restore, reads like a wilful dismissal of Brown's sensitive criticism. Whether or not Tomlinson responded in this way, the result does nothing but harm to what remains to date (1995) one of his prime achievements.

My way into these poems has, in part, involved an apprehension of syntax. In these urban, un-urbane poems, comprising one poem, the poised cultivated aristocratization and superiority of syntax, the flow of which is constantly interrupted by judicious qualification, is superseded. Instead, the syntax becomes paratactic (not periodic) even phrase by phrase consecutive, without, in 'Foxes' Moon', the polite deferentially controlling use of modifying conjunctions such as 'and'. It is as if initiation, urgency, and even desperation, had overcome the defensive superiority – as if, after all, what use could there be in that? He is surely right? More urgent things attend him and will not wait if he fails to attend to their needs. Thus in place of Larkin's dismissal of England in its 'industrial froth' – it is the word 'froth' that discloses the overtones of superiority (*The Whitsun Weddings*, 21) – is fear ('The dusk was gaining'); and 'sarcasm' (Brown's ascription) in 'England's interrupted pastoral', and even lament in the unadorned plainness, self-aware perplexity and understanding of

> The dream of a city under the city's dream,
>   Proportioned to the man whom sleep replenishes
> To stand reading with opened eyes . . .

(253)

Instead, in 'The Dream', is an understanding of the moon's 'impartiality' ('After a Death'), and thus the satellite planet being unavailable either for consolation or pessimistic notions concerning destruction. To get from the massive impoliteness of the arbiter, in the 'Constable' poem, or those poems on defunct and decaying country houses, to this, is exemplary and heartening, as every achievement of courage is; for this is no less than courage and, disappointingly, the removal of evident interlinkage between these four poems is a partial dismantling of the patience of which the group is composed. Certainly, the foxes who use the nocturnal hours we don't, and who slip away from the edges of the town, in the hours we do, face the moon that, properly speaking, disengages itself of our manipulations if we, rightly, face, not only death but all that continues its operations without any capacity to concern itself with ours. Tomlinson's courage consists in recognizing this, and also in recognizing the foxes' unprideful response to their enabling/disenabling context. In this we may remember the persona's response to the rat, with its grinning fanged intelligence, in Rosenberg's 'Break of Day in the Trenches'.

If the poem 'Under the Moon's Reign' initiates the entrance to night and the rule of the place where the moon negatives the light of the sun as well, in the last nine lines, as waking the sentient human life – a light that takes no sides – it also instigates a shivering entrance into a world ('Götterdämmerung' = complete downfall of a regime) where we are stripped of our control of the actual world, and come 'under the moon's reign'. In contradictory but logical fashion, we must leave our comforting living world of light and its habitualities, where we appear to exert control, and, setting aside our ego, be shorn of its support so as to experience reality.

In the second poem, 'Foxes' Moon', we read of the foxes' night, of the 'interrupted pastoral', of not only what we have done to England, but also of what night does to us (and Tomlinson), through its removal of the day's 'pastoral' ease. Consider the Keats echo in the final poem, 'After a Death'. If we rightly see the foxes' moon, we may measure the extent of this stripping away of support for ourselves and approach a more truthful condition. 'The Dream' (third poem), with its paradigm of orthodox psychoanalytic understanding, offers a complex structure where one's

Shaped by a need that was greed no longer
(253)

– lovely clumsy assonance – and one enters the dream of a city, even more searching because it lies 'under' the city's dream of itself. For in the *city's* dream is the protecting illusion, whereas in this dream of the city's dream is no illusion, and no protection. Instead, we 'stand reading with opened eyes', indeed awake to the strange and familiar urban-scape of reality. And we are replenished.

In 'After a Death' (fourth poem) Tomlinson, with extreme admirable risk, measures out and mourns the death of the unnamed with something like a line from a popular song. In the opening line we find, stripped of those delaying 'and's,

A líttle ásh, a páinted róse, a náme . . .

(253)

He dares to confront the intractability of death with the banality of the song-style which, recontextualized, names what remains to the living. The understanding that nothing remains defines life, which cannot make a contract with the blue sky, heaven and/or its emptiness. In this understanding, where we revert to the moon's influence, it is a kindness the moon distributes, since its light, in its uninvolved shining upon us, comforts us in its lack of offered comfort. It gives us the confirmation of reality and loss in as much as it registers no awareness of our being alive. And what it does not do enables us to come to our senses, and settle with reality, as truthful creatures. That insight comes from strength, and the poetic language, conscious, but unhaughty, creates a true poem.

'For Miriam' and 'The Flood'

A change, but probably no development comparable to that involving the distance travelled from the 'Constable' poem to the group 'Under the Moon's Reign'. But the 'Miriam' and 'Flood' poems have retained the directness of the latter group, although not the complexity, or urgency, that blended complexity with it. And whereas in 'Under the Moon's Reign' the verse *moved* easily to and fro between metrical and free verse (see Appendix, Dennis Silk, below), and achieved an easeful ambivalence between them, in these latter poems some unease enters in the transaction between these modes. 'For Miriam' is predominantly metrical. 'The Flood', the mode of which is old-fashioned narrative (tale-telling), offers itself in a mixed metrical and free verse. Yet the prosody in these poems is ambivalent, and different from that negotiated in 'Under the Moon's Reign'. In 'The Flood' a hesitation exists as how to read the lines, rhythmically – whether or not to read them as metrical or free verse, and such a difficulty here seems – I say this tentatively – to make for an uneasy reading of the poem, a difficulty which has little to do with its meaning. It seems best to conclude that in the poem 'For Miriam' the connection between writer (or persona) and the dead Miriam is a curious mixture of sympathy and the want of it. And perhaps this ambivalence towards the dead woman is reflected in the verse-movement.

Whereas in 'The Flood', the rhythmic uncertainty may result, not from the thematic uncertainty – the couple form an island of life beleaguered by river-flood – but from the taking of an older mode, of narration, with literary equipment now dishabituated to it.

PETER REDGROVE: LOCALIZING MYTH

The norm of Lawrence immediately shows Redgrove's strengths and weaknesses, as it also indicates Rodney Pybus's very different powers. I am thinking here of the latter's 'Little Girl Asleep' (see below). Pybus's poem is alive in each aspect – so far as I can tell – as both poetry and human response. Perhaps the achievement of the very best poetry in our time is to bring such human response into the vicinity of a literary one, enriching and substantiating both. I cannot always feel that this is the case with Redgrove, the rich invention notwithstanding. Here's the view.

Redgrove's two principal executives seem to be mischief and straight unironic wonder – another (partial) instance of good poetry working in an unironic mode – to dispute Davie's claim (see 'A Doggy Demos: Hardy and Lawrence', in *Thomas Hardy and British Poetry*, 1973, p. 138). With Redgrove, mischief shows us evil expressed through straightfaced politeness, or in humour and wit. Similarly he conveys horror (evil), using wit as the expressive agent, and, surprisingly, achieves the same success acting for the good creation (water). But he achieves his best poetry as he plays good and evil together; one sees the complexity of one mode (religion) washed over by the stinging aggression and cruelty – of the wasps (insects recur in Redgrove's verse) – in, for instance, 'The Weddings at Nether Powers':

> A wásp crawls óver the crucifix, sting óut
> Séarching for a vúlnerable part; the sávage vícar
> Strikes, the usúrper búrsts in mélted bútter . . .
>
> (138)

Complexity similarly formed by different and interlocking essences occurs in 'At the Cosh-Shop' (218). The cosh is swathed in silk (the shopman patiently tells him) to draw no blood, and thus conceal the evidence of the act. That is one doubleness, with 'soft silk' serving to contrastingly offset the penile cosh itself. Penile is correct. No sooner do we get silk than we get Redgrove's typically swift unannounced shift to sex which, in such transition, disposes of the need for any rational explanatory connecting matter. We are left with the unmediated connection between violence and sexuality, with the wit seemingly disarming or clothing both the cosh-shop and the sex, for the gentle reader. Those who take the trope as pleasant must cope with the violence, and those who insist on the violence must also cope with the sexuality, the wit, and the notion that violence is 'only' a metaphor for sexuality. This is a typical and successful example of Redgrove's capacity for conveying an overall meaning through a slippery ungraspable mode.

The menace implicit in 'At the Cosh-Shop' is realized in 'Renfield Before His Master'. Although Redgrove is using the same kind of hinge between external reality and metaphor as in the 'Cosh-shop', here, in the 'Renfield' poem, the emphasis appears to be upon external reality. Yet the hinge seems to work here to augment metaphysical speculative impulse; as though there were in Redgrove a mechanism of compensation or equilibrium whereby if external reality (in any given poem) exerted too great a pressure upon him then a corresponding metaphysical, ontological and spiritual impulse would be actuated. In this poem the realities are Renfield, Vlad Dracula and the factory owner Van Helsing. There are the girls mentioned, victims of Dracula, procured by Renfield in return for – what? That is a hard question to answer. More flies, it might be said; but also the power of his own (Renfield's) fear since he is both a catcher of flies for his own spider, yet himself a fly-victim, like those flies he 'loved to eat'.

'Bé that spider whom you féar, Í, Vlád Drácula,

Will só transfórm you, as you wísh,' and showed him hōw
Life flōws in líquid dróps, through fángs,
Créature to créature, in cháins of dróps like wébs...

(160)

Here are both reality and a biological version of ontology, this latter being located in 'Life flows in liquid drops, through fangs'. The reality is Renfield, and Dracula, the spider and the flies. But the spider and flies are not only their creaturely selves (God help us) but an idea of life as we understand it, composed of predator and victim, and, behind that, the apparently (but only apparently) unrevisable idea that to survive life feeds on life, not perhaps as a matter of cruelty but simply for survival. We do not know if 'through fangs' is Dracula's or Redgrove's position, or both, for Redgrove places the idea outside Dracula's speech-marks; at the same time he seems to suggest that this is what Dracula 'showed him' (Renfield). And so, does he show him what *is* and purely what is, according to Redgrove, seen through Dracula; or is it a true aspect of this earth, though only one aspect? Such ambiguity is at the heart of Redgrove. Perhaps it is at the core of us all, but Redgrove seems to be, as it were, indigenous to the area. And although it is dangerous to extrapolate from other poems, the way in which

Life flows in liquid drops, through fangs,

works is akin to other Redgrove poems in which vitality is lodged in the predatory or stinging character of life. Consider the wasp characterized as 'the savage vicar' in 'The Weddings at Nether Powers' (Nether = lower or infernal?).

To extend this question a little further is justifiable, I think, because of the syntax in the line above. For, initially, we get a seemingly benign 'Life flows in liquid drops'; but we must look from whence it comes – out of Dracula's mind. Moreover then follows Dracula's qualification, provided by the separating but mediating comma, 'through fangs'. For Dracula, the 'drops' are blood from his victim – food, but we might readily read the drops as something like sap, or even the blood healthily flowing, without peril, through one's body. Yet the question won't go away because although we know 'through fangs' to be Dracula's perception predicated on his

nature, it can, without too much difficulty, be made to yield a statement about the nature of life. Not the only one, but one sufficient
to make us redesign our perception of life as benign. We can easily
lose sight of or conceal from ourselves the source of our food and
the substance on which our desires are nurtured.

One further comment to do with Redgrove's rhythms. An aspect
of his myth-use involves one's sense that it has not so much taken
the place of religion, but is it. I have already referred to Redgrove's
characterizing the wasp as 'the savage vicar' in 'The Weddings at
Nether Powers'. He also identifies 'the daffodils like Stars of David'.
The displacement of religion into metaphors for nature is an aspect
of this myth-use, but the point I would make is that just as religion may have its *assertive* and proselytizing aspect, so there is
in Redgrove a tendency for this nexus of myth and ontology to get
expressed statementally, and the mode of assertion is sometimes
bought at the expense of a care for rhythm.

It is easier to praise than criticize, but I offer two examples:

'Bé that spíder whom you féar, Í, Vlád Drácula,

Will só, transfórm you, as you wísh,' and showed him hōw
Life flōws in líquid dróps, through fángs . . .

(160)

We have already read these lines; but I now suggest that a reading
of their rhythms may suggest some blankness in the movement.
My feeling is that the first line starts to be rhythmically uncertain
when its swinging trochaic–dactyllic movement reaches 'fear',
whereupon it moves into a spondaic structure. For despite its assertive 'I, Vlad Dracula' the movement is left hanging uncertainly,
probably because of its position in the uncompleted syntax. The
next line, 'Will so transform you . . .', seems to be without rhythm
and the movement, as it were, to fall off the end with 'how'. The
line following has difficulty in starting up the syntax, partly because
'how' tends to be a long durational monosyllable, in the same way
that 'Life' tends to, which word begins the next line. The enjambment is not so much a flow from one line over its end to the next,
but a break followed by a syntactic resumption of the following
line. Although I would add that the next line beginning with 'Life',
and the line that follows it, work rhythmically very well. I think the

problem I have indicated is not confined to a single instance. In the same poem, we find

To thin taut threads under the same sun on which the spider

Dances to eat her is another of them . . .

(159)

where the first line is virtually without rhythm, and the second in something of the same condition. All the executive energy, one might say, has gone into the invention.

This has its consequential dangers not only on account of the intrinsic value of rhythm, but also because rhythm acts cooperatively to secure the balance and centrality of the metaphoric invention, the danger with such invention being that the vehicle (metaphoric element) subverts the tenor (the reality element). Of course, Redgrove may be reading us that very lesson, asking us to re-envision our reality, suggesting that the metaphoric reality may be a better way of understanding what we habitually take to be reality. Epiphany it would seem is greater than that which is epiphanized. Clearly the question of trust enters this – the reader's – and this reader sometimes feels that at the heart of this fulcrum balanced between judgement and invention the mechanism is tipped towards invention at the expense of reality. In which case rhythm in cooperation with syntax would have a crucial part to play, not only in managing the invention but also in inspiring the reader with an instinctual rightness of its operation. The Finnish poet Risto Ahti said, 'Can anyone call reality in question just by claiming it's invented by others?' (*Narcissus in Winter*, translated by Herbert Lomas, 1994, p. 50).

'Living in Falmouth', from the volume *The Weddings at Nether Powers* (1979), is Redgrove's most sustained poem to date, and the 220 lines justify its length. Given the dark aspect of this volume's title poem and the later 'Renfield before His Master' (*The Apple-Broadcast*, 1981), this is in the finest sense a lighter, more benign poem with a greater sense of both foison and (local) external reality. Which is not to preclude the ambiguous last twelfth section. And having complained about the rhythm of some of the shorter poems, this occasionally Whitman-toned, sectioned poem pays greater attention to its movement. Sometimes, as in the first section, the solution to the tasks of rhythm and lineation are found in established modern free-verse practice:

322   *The Life of Metrical and Free Verse*

> there is a móth
> On the rústy táble that spréads out wíngs
> Líke líchened tómbstones . . .
>
> (127)

Similar solutions are employed in section XI. Whereas in the last section, where I perceive some of the address and tone we read in Whitman, he uses that poet's strategy of end-stopping each line and jointing the line within, by punctuation. Thus in the last section (XII):

> The chúrch is very réal, absolutely tóo réal,
> It is réaler than mé, réaler than where I líve;
> If this chúrch is a hóuse then I am a whíte shádow . . .
>
> (134)

Seemingly smaller solutions on a local level lead to larger over-all organizations, as Whitman's 'Song of the Broad-Axe' shows. And as Blake indicates, vision is made up of minute particulars. This I think is one mode Whitman uses in 'Song of Myself', and the 'filamented' (Hobsbaum's excellent word) connections between stanzas, and the leitmotifs across the Chants or sections, bring the long poem together in a non-narrative way – except, of course, that the poem opens with grass and babes, more or less, and ends with grass, death, bootsoles and dust. In that sense, there is narrative, though it exists in the episodic nature of mortality more than the sequence inhering in narrative.

Evidently Redgrove's two-tier system of reality and metaphor works to some extent in the Falmouth poem which is centred on the coastal town and its environs. Yet topography is not ontology, and there would seem to be less inter-filamenting of metaphoric and metaphysical impulses in Redgrove's poem, despite its being so much shorter than Whitman's. It begins with life

> And two-legged dreams make one flesh . . .
>
> (127)

and ends in a movement towards death:

> And my párents who cást mé are móving into the shádow:
>   I follow slówly.
>
> (135)

One set of linkages, which proceeds by the excellent indirection of filamenting the seemingly least important elements, occurs in sections VI and VII, which provide one of the poem's nodes. VI brings in the uprooted oak on the tide which had been 'clawed' from its ground by rains and river. Characteristically, the water is made to have a function, and this in turn leads (marginally) to oysters, and these in their turn, provide the luxury that draws the tycoons seeking to mine Cornwall's mineral wealth:

We wátch the great cárs glíde bȳ to the bóardrooms,
We own ónly tópsoil, the mínerals are resérved,
The gróund is sold únder our féet.
The Oýsters cáll them here, the Blóoms kēep them.
They will ówn éverything. Let the lánd
Pácked with únderpalaçes of góld dripping with óil
Be oýster-tales¹ ónly, tóld to a mining pénis
On a hōtel-bēd in Lóndon; lét it be rúmours ónly, lest áll
Our fiřst-bořn be made miners by the gréat ábsent lándlords:
Not made déep stařved miners by the enórmous ábsent
    lándlords.

(131)

Local industry (mining), trade, money and graft (work/dishonesty). The sexual inducements offered to young tycoons, or perhaps taken by them, correspond to the mining (taking) of minerals from the body of Cornwall ('a mining penis'). We probably shouldn't ignore the phrase which in repetition terminates the last section, 'absent landlords', and which implicates those scandals and abuses involving, for example, England and Ireland. It is an old quarrel providing the substance of Swift's two pamphlets, 'A Modest Proposal' and 'A Short View of the State of Ireland'. Swift was in no doubt of the abuse involving the siphoning off of the resources of the poorer by the richer, more powerful, country; and it seems likely that Redgrove perceives a cognate situation between Cornwall and England, where the former, a Celtic territory with the extant ruins of its own language, has never seen itself as an integral part of England. The for Redgrove unusually sharp and overt political indictment makes it clear that he objects to the exploitation of

---

1. Cf. '[Life] is a tale | Told by an idiot, full of sound and fury | Signifying nothing' (*Macbeth*, V. v).

the Cornish resources; and, for that matter, of one class of people
– 'The old intelligent villagers' with their own culture and skills –
by entrepreneurial tycoons:

> We own only topsoil, the minerals are reserved . . .

In this forthright mode the sexuality, and its correspondence with
the mineral resources of Cornwall, takes on a peculiar poignancy.
Redgrove continues to explore the implications of this local political exploitation with

> lest all
> Our first-born be made miners by the great absent landlords:
> Not made deep starved miners by the enormous absent
>   landlords . . .

The pathos of 'first-born' with its biblical echoes of both Egypt and
Herod (and thus Christ) is clear enough – though with Herod it
was all the children of Bethlehem 'from two years old and under'
(Matthew, 2. 16). The point here is that the first-born will become
sacrificed to the 'absent landlords' by working for them. But the
under-meaning is brought out in the succeeding line where if they
are not made miners were the tycoons not to become their landlords,
they would starve. But mining is a starving business, and if they
become miners they will starve in any case. And in any event what
a fate, to become a miner. Redgrove deservedly takes it all ways,
and the ambiguity is rich and rewarding, to the reader. The long
end-stopped lines wind their way to their intricate and judicious
conclusions, yet the judging never obscures the condition of the
miners. It is wonderfully done.

Also surprising is Redgrove's attitude towards the church, 'abso-
lutely too real', although the surprise probably reflects on this reader
rather than Redgrove. Nonetheless it surprises one that the attitude
towards the church and its symbols is expressed as explicitly:

> And there is that vast cross-death that is worshipped inside,
> Tainting the air with sweats and hymns . . .

> (135)

I detect no irony or countervailing undercurrent and, taken in
conjunction with the previous section and its mild rampage against

the dead and Death, we may cautiously conclude that a religion centred on a symbol of death and suffering (and cruelty) is not to Redgrove's taste. However there exists a difference in the 'death' in the various sections, for whereas in XI death in a sense invigorates and 'the Goddess kisses every child at once' – in the last section, it is death old as that first death in which the dead move into oblivion and the son slowly follows his parents.

RODNEY PYBUS: HIS 'LITTLE GIRL ASLEEP'

In a letter to this writer of 20 January 1995, Rodney Pybus wrote of this poem:

I know I wanted as much *variety* of rhythm and movement here, to suggest the positive, to resist the notion that it's all v. pessimistic. I don't use rhyme, but I do use sound echo, and in places repetition. But who doesn't! . . . For a long time – certainly as far back as this – I've been v. conscious of the mixture – the mixing, quite deliberately at some stages of composition – of Graeco-Latin/Romance based words and Anglo-Saxon/Scandinavian-based words in my writing. It is after all what makes English so rich in sense and sound and vocabulary, and I try to use this advantage the language naturally offers in my writing – the more 'elegant' or 'reflective' polysyllables of the classical mixed with the slower, harder (often), more active, energetic N. European words . . .

Pybus was responding to my request to talk about the means of the poem, and thus what the above eschews is any mention that the poem is about the premature death, before her natural term, of their daughter, who would have been their third child. It seems fair to put it this way since the poem is also candid

The still born silence

(63)

and

Yēs, but íf I were yóunger I'd ásk again
and again where the sóuls are stóred

of thóse who súffer déath
befóre they're bórn . . .

(65)

It is a poem of grief, mourning the death of a daughter anticipated
and hoped-for, but (or is it 'and'?) the reason it is *not* 'pessimistic'
(Pybus, above) is that in a striven-for but measured way the poem
establishes a caring for life, rooting itself in death. Once that is
established, if that is what the poem does, it is this that permits
the work to celebrate the life and mourn its passing.

This is extraordinarily fine, all the more so because it occurs
without its displaying what it does; and although the poem, as the
account taken from Pybus suggests, is a poem of literature, it is not
a literary poem. Its existence is literary, but its roots are in experience and not literature. All this needs to be said because it explains
why the poem is so steady and so balanced. The poem has come
from lethal experience, yet one that the poet has made into a cause
for nourishing life. Once that has been indicated, the literary is free
to flourish without its being offensive and self-referential. It is the
natural consequence of a rootedness in life, and thus adorns life.

'Adorn' is not meant to imply decoration so much as a bringing
out of what is already existent. If a piece of jet or amber adorns the
neck of a woman, it does so because of the woman it confirms and
does not of itself establish her being. And this, I think, is the proper
moment to speak of the mother of the daughter and the poet's wife,
for the opportunity discloses another salient reason why the poem
is not 'pessimistic'. It is a love poem, a poem giving love not only
on account of the mother's loss of her child, but because her loss
brings forth his love which is in any case there.

Something of the mother is refracted through the child who smiles
but does not enter the world: 'It was not to be, none of it' (68).
And in speaking to his wife, 'O my love', he grieves both for the
unborn, dead child and his wife's pain:

the tiny cold clump of
death you have carried . . .

(69)

'you' referring to his wife, whom he continues to address. The
unflinching though gentle nature of the poem is everywhere
available. The heavy 'clump' finely enacts the clumsy life that death

produces, in ironic and fearful contrast to the beauty of the child herself. 'Clump' also carries the sense of plants growing together – clump or cluster – so that, here, 'clump' is the dead equivalent of the living 'cluster'.

Shortly, the poet hears the blackbird and identifies himself (poet = singer) also 'not too full of days', with the bird and its song. The phrase (not too full of days) also implicates the child, though mostly it is he himself who remains interchangeable with the blackbird. Yet just as the bird, in the next verse, became a maker 'artificer' (or poet) of silence, so the poet also learns to make silence in the face of death. The phrase 'artificer of silence' is ambiguous, in that the bird is perhaps at this point singing of death which is 'silence'. But it could also mean that in our death we fall silent. Or that in the face of death, the song becomes silent.

That the verse will successfully bear this amount of textual exploration signifies its basis in discursive rationality, in marked difference from Redgrove the metaphoric basis of whose verse predicates a different approach to reality (see above, pp. 321–3). Where Redgrove, I suggested, will hinge in his exposition between external reality and exploratory metaphor, Pybus (and this is true for most of his poetry with the exception, perhaps, of the section concerning butterflies, 'Admirable Wings' from *Flying Blues*, 1994) – Pybus initiates his version of a recognizably shareable reality such as many of us would accept to be the case, and proceeds to illuminate that with metaphor. A fine instance of this (there are many in 'Little Girl Asleep') may be seen in the first section, 'Now she sleeps' –

I wánted to sée the cólour of háir,

the small brándish of néw fíngers . . .

(63)

'Brandish of new fingers' is evidently what it says; but the vocabulary contains a delicate metaphor for leaves, located not only in 'brandish', but confirmed by 'new', implicating 'new leaves', thus setting linear animal life into relationship with the cyclical life of nature, investigating some very fine and loving reciprocities between that and the unborn daughter.

Every mode has its strengths (and weaknesses) and this strength testifies to the desire, and capacity, to anchor one's psyche in a reality that offers safeguards apparently obtainable from clarities and certainties, and this, I think, is the operational basis of some of Pybus's metaphor. 'Admirable Wings' (above) appears to predicate a changed basis.

This seems to be the right moment to indicate that this is a poem in free verse, the voice of which shuttles finely between the spoken and the singing voice. That is probably not careful enough; Pybus's voice is a speaking one that is perfectly capable of shifting itself into song, but is more naturally at home in a speaking voice that will touch its utterance with music:

> Your mother's hand gently
> strokes your face,
> shapes the setting
> wax, as light
> as winds in summer
> on contours of cloud
> wipe moisture into forms. . . .
>
> (5 Effigy, 70)

We might not agree on what constitutes the music here, but the *cantare* seems to this reader to occur in the movement and tone of

> wax, as light
> as winds in summer

whereas the next two lines with the more scientific and philosophic words, 'contours' and 'forms', melt into the speaking voice again. It is delicately done, and the implication appears to be that the basis of Pybus's utterance is speech which occasionally (or more often than that) licenses music. One finds similar musical moments of a very different kind in Hughes's 'Walt' and his uncle's repeated 'Aye!', in *Wolfwatching* (1989) (see below).

In speaking of this as free verse one should notice the little rushes and leashings-back of feeling held within the fluctuating movement, its 'setting/wax'; thus 'strokes your face' is slow accentual verse that in the next line quickens with feeling, ending, characteristically enough, with the participle 'setting', turned adjective, before it becomes the noun of 'wax' in the following line. This concealedly imitates the movement of life hardening into death – and is another instance of metaphor used to illuminate rather than question reality.

Here the poet addresses his dead daughter. He is the agnostic father, as the mother strokes the child's dead face. The tenderness with which she does this implants a subtle sense of the touch between mother and daughter being sacred (hence the candle reference, in 'wax'), and thus contrasts with the 'agnostic father'. In this section titled 'Effigy' (a figure in stone representing the living body now dead) the child is like life, yet dead, a bodily effigy of herself (see Dylan Thomas's 'After the Funeral', above).

There follows the part which conveys the power of the guilt we may feel if we have produced a life that dies:

> Your eyes, staring deadly,
> drill me with their
> black narcotic . . .
>
> (71)

One notes again the foreshortened last line of the stanza which corresponds not so much to a terminating cadence in a literary form but (as much) to an intake of breath compounded of pain, pity and fear.

His fingers are the bracelet[1] decorating the dead bone. As the poet holds the dead child, he feels death also drawing her, from him. The passage concludes

> I watch the years
> go like candle-smoke.
>
> (71)

The metrical character of that last line is the signature of the inevitable. The unlived life of the child coalesces with years she might have had, *and* with the years of life the parents must now live without her. The candle we may remember is the traditional accompaniment to mourning, in a number of religions, and it also

1. See also the blackbird passage on p. 69 (line 3) for the bracelet image, 'bright bracelet of gold'. It draws something out of Donne's 'A bracelet of bright hair about the bone' ('The Relique', line 6), although in conversation Pybus has very properly suggested that the reference was not consciously formed.

plays a frequent part in ritual, sacred or secular. It has also the symbolic power of life burning (with life) and / but as it does so, using up its life.

The Israeli poet writing in Hebrew, the late Amir Gilboa, expresses an aspect of this crux in his poem 'Here I blow out . . .'

> tell me if
> I should blow the candle out
> so that the holy stump should not
> vanish; or should I in
> horror sanctify
> with burning, this blood, these tears?
>
> (*Stand*, 9/4, 3; 1968)

TED HUGHES: A POET WITH TWO PSYCHES

The risk involved in this suggestion is one taken wholly by myself, but the stimuli comes from conversations with the critic Colin Raw and the poet Ruth Fainlight. Much of the impetus derives from astonishment, and it comes to this: that the two groups of 'uncollected poems' in Hughes's *New Selected Poems 1957–1994* (1995) seem to be written by a poet different in crucial respects from the one who has published the books, with the exception, that is, of *Wolfwatching* (1989). It is not a question of long-standing familiarity with such poems as, say, 'The Horses', 'The Thought-Fox', 'An Otter' and 'Full Moon and Little Frieda'. The differences are those which one can discern, and indicate, by comparing the poems from *Crow* (1970), for which I have reservations, and 'Crow Wakes' (from the first group of 'uncollected'). One must guess the dates for these poems but coming as they do between *Lupercal* (1960) and *Wodwo* (1967), it suggests that the dates of composition situate them somewhere between these two – more or less. *Crow* (1970) is some five (?) years off. But between the poems that comprise *Crow* and the earlier (?) or later (?) 'Crow Wakes' – I am not sure it materially affects the issue at this point – lies the ability to simplify by cartoon as against the willingness to give his character a chance, to allow him breath and space, rather than abbreviate the creation into a kind of vote-winning caricature. This is a longer, longer-breathing, slower-paced poem to do with horror of self and terror at the desire of others to 'Get him'. At any rate this and other uncollected poems make the quotation from Walcott used to 'blurb' the reader – 'It is a poetry of exultation' – seem improper.

This is not to depreciate the value of the poems I have named (above) but to suggest that another poet seems to have been working beneath the one seen in the published books, but which emerged, at last, in *Wolfwatching*. This clearly needs substantiating.

'The Thought-Fox', 'An Otter', 'The Horses', 'That Morning'

It came up until it stood beside me. Then it spread its hand – a human hand as I now saw, but burned and bleeding like the rest of him – flat palm down on the blank space of my page. At the same time it said: 'Stop this – you are destroying us.' Then as it lifted its hand away I saw the blood-print . . . glistening blood on the page.'

('The Burnt Fox', 1993, *Winter Pollen* (1994) p. 9)

'It' is the fox – Hughes is recounting a dream – and the prose piece re-creates what might be called the genetic part of the composition of 'The Thought-Fox'. What I should like to indicate in my response to the prose is that in certain respects it outdoes the poem, in its pathos and drama. Its directness *moves* this reader a greater distance than the poem, though of course the poem is intricate and well contained. Perhaps too well contained, which is the comparison I would make between the 'collected' and 'uncollected' poems. Something has mediated between the genesis of the poem and its release in the finished product – something like, 'make sure this is a poem' instead of 'make sure this includes the experience'. We have been told a great deal about the difference between life and art – too much, probably – it is the truistic distinction contained in the advice the instructor hands to the tyro; yet it may be misplaced. It isn't so much that the novitiate has mistaken the experience for the poem or fiction but that the language hasn't been allowed by the writer to find itself. The danger is that the advice may instruct the beginner into trimming the experience to a compliant or ready-made articulation, and surely this is *un*valuable. In this sense, alone, I prefer 'The Horses' to 'The Thought-Fox', though the latter is a fine poem, the figure in it having the attributes of an actual creature

A fóx's nóse touches twig, léaf . . .

(3)

Although in the last stanza it seems to have double identity:

It énters the dárk hōle of the héad.

This might represent the fox's killing another creature; but if we read the poem with its fluid dimensions, 'The page is printed' seems also to suggest the mind, and the effect on it of the fox's presence and activity. This 'printing' is perhaps like the photograph's negative, where the positive is supplied by the fox itself. Or else, the distinct powerful *presence* of the fox impresses itself prototypically upon the blank of the yet-to-be assembled words – this, too, like a version of a photograph. Yet though these are possible versions of the poem, a full reading is obtained by the tension of the actual and mental, between which the poem operates its mysterious activity, using both the real activity of the fox, and the equally real activity in the human mind that the fox has engendered.

This is very fine, as readers know, yet I cannot help but feel how the even finer possibilities as inscribed in the prose have been let go, in the interests of a poem's poem, a metaphysical intrication that has deflected a very strong experience indeed.

'The Horses' is perhaps a lesser poem, poetically, but one might have to restrict 'poetically' in order to validate the judgement.

A world cast in frost . . .
(7)

will show, however, the capacity to mediate between actuality outside the poem and the articulation of that within it, for 'cast' reverberates an apprehension of both reality-meaning in 'gripped by', but also the sense of a world bearing the designs of frost upon it. Equally, 'cast' will, within the poem, mean 'made by'; as a metal sculpture is 'cast'. There are other meanings, too, like thrown, and that too will yield the other idea of a potter throwing his clay onto the wheel to cast and make, where the potter is God. In which case 'Frost' has the idea of a world implicated with death. But whichever way one reads it, an inhering interaction between actuality (nature) and artefact works. A similar interplay moves

Their draped stóne mánes, their tílted hínd-hooves
(8)

in the word 'stone'.

> going among the years, the faces,
> May I still meet my memory in so lonely a place
>
> (8)

has, some may feel, a roseate retrospective glow but it effectively recasts the experience into memory, without undermining its reality, which, one might say, the more adroit 'The Thought-Fox' does, fine though it is. The clambering rhythms in long lines serve to underpin this interaction between reality and our responses to it, as much as registering the creatures and their 'Stirring under a thaw'.

'An Otter' represents what might be called the Lawrence-aspect of Hughes's work. Not so fine-grained and delicate as Lawrence, Hughes makes the creature palpable within the poem's craft of synecdoche – 'long ruddering tail' – which is also touched into metaphor. And he forms unexpected conjunctions, in section II, for instance, in the underwater otter's lung mingling 'tobacco-smoke, hounds and parsley'. It is the last disparate element that ties the creature into non-human life which is so fine, where all three are part of the otter's environment now.

Another ingredient which compounds a different dimension into his work, is that pre-history, legendary or mythic component: 'from sea // To sea crosses in three nights / Like a king in hiding (section I). Although I believe that this element in Hughes sometimes finesses an in fact more troublesome but ultimately more rewarding transaction with reality. Here is no shortcut or avoidance, the legendary being contained, in both senses, by its being cast as simile. The ultimate condition, and status, of the otter, as a pelt comforting a chair, serves to reinforce the animal's nobility; but this in its contrast with the domestic comfort provided by a chair works the judgement indirectly, allowing the nobility (and the simile) to take on regenerative energy. The balance is as delicate and alive as the child's consciousness revealed in 'Full Moon and Little Frieda' (*Wodwo*, 1967).

'That Morning' (from *The River*, 1983) resembles the earlier, seemingly looser, 'The Horses'. Both are concerned with a terrestrial revelation of that moment in creation when the spirit of life becomes incarnate. In 'The Horses', life is the horses; in 'That Morning', the salmon together with the part played by the predatory feeding bears. In 'The Horses' the desire 'going among the years' is to be revitalized by what 'he' had been shown 'Hearing the horizons endure'. Creation endures and / but must be felt to persist; through the experience of epiphany.

In 'That Morning', the salmon raise 'us toward some dazzle of blessing'. They are life renewing life, and that moment (not in Hughes's but perhaps in our reckoning) is stabilized, recognized and made permanent in the salmon's partial *destruction* by the two bears that 'swam like men // Beside us.' The symbolism of the light is almost not symbolism. The light is the 'glory' of the event, and, like the person's experience of the horses in the earlier poem, illuminatory. But in that morning it is also the moment that creation manifests itself in its inherent duality, in life and the destruction of it, to supply the life of others. The difference of vision between 'The Horses' and this poem is not one of angle so much as completeness. Here the bears 'swam like men', and thus show something to the human witness, about the creatures; but they also indicate the predatory constituent implicated in the being human. To survive means the taking of life whether of a salmon or a lettuce. For Hughes it would seem to be epiphany rather than revelation. Creation in its duality, of life and its destruction, is displayed, and accepted as process. Revelation would entail some heartsearching with respect to one's participating in this; doubleness. One is celebratory, the other reflective, as it is in the prose account (above) of the dream-inception of 'The Thought-Fox'.

Again it is the rhythm in conjunction with the lineation that sets up the meaning, striking into the sense-and-apprehension of the reader's mind beyond what one could possibly expect of the words alone (their lexical character).

The 'Uncollected' poems and *Wolfwatching*

My suggestion is that the looser-seeming poems found amongst the 'uncollected', those not structured upon lyric, or on patterned forms, differ from the more tightly made poems that offer themselves in a structure that announces them as poems. In that sense, the 'uncollected' are riskier and so more courageous poems. Judging from the mixed reception given to *Wolfwatching*, the poems mostly of the same kind as the 'uncollected', some reviewers considered them to be of lesser kindred and drew out their instruments. The failure of nerve was theirs. After a period of thirty years, it would seem that Hughes no longer cares to modify his forms to these simpler requirements. The attack may be seen as an index of the distance he has put between this poetry and the critics' ideas of what poetry ought to be, and their fraternal concurrence might compound our doubts as readers concerning their judgement.

It is not dottiness but being dotty at such length now that makes him languish . . .

Peter Levi tells us in *Poetry Review* (84/4, 1994/5, 51) almost certainly referring to Hughes's prose concerning myth-making; but, by extension, entering his objection into the recent poetry.

There are a number of reasons why critics should have responded as they did, and I offer an alternative possible reason to the one above. The cross of rational, straightforward syntax with the tendency to invest our lives with the mythic (which appears to upset some) makes the poetry seem strange. Perhaps. But it is surely the business of the critic to respond to the unfamiliar and strange – there is surely nothing stranger than Smart's *Jubilate Agno* in English poetry. So I argue that the combination of received syntax (which may offend some modernists) with the mythicizing of twentieth-century life (the traumas of the two European wars, for instance) makes these poems seem at once odd and familiar. And if to that one adds the slow lingering, often durational, nature of Hughes's rhythm – movement – one reads with a sense that Hughes is speaking simultaneously to the reader *and* himself. It is an unnerving experience to cope with, in an art-form where the present boundaries and rules are, perhaps because the field is dominated by critics more than readers, more circumscribing than is healthy. Yet the crossing of boundaries is not *per se* wrong. And the merging of the quotidian with the mythic gives a dimension to our vision. The poems, in their Janus-like positioning with respect to poet speaking both to the reader and himself, involve an immediacy and trance-like pressure in the rhythms. So that if this is taken in conjunction with the relinquishing of the heavy nudging jolly horror of *Crow* – which so many have praised – then the registration of tenderness in the lingering rhythms is a true development. And the discarding of the paraphernalia of farm-stuff and hopping animistic machinery is the more welcome because his poetry seemed incapable of including it. I am for a poetry that is inclusive – as Eliot managed, for instance, to hypnotize the people and objects in his urban landscape into inclusivity with the word 'violet' – 'violet hour' in *The Waste Land*. In the 'uncollected' poems, and many of those in *Wolfwatching*, Hughes manages this natural inclusivity through, I think, the lingering rhythm – and it is a various list: modern war, Amero-Indians, coalmines, popstar and family.

Asserting the existence of tenderness depends on the reader's responsive agreement, and this may be problematic since Hughes's most successful realisation of it is not concentrated in a linguistic tuft of feeling but is achieved in continuous aggregation. The tenderness asks the reader to experience it as a continuity that is, by definition, unimagistic – it is not 'an intellectual and emotional complex in an instant of time' (Pound). To name the poems that most finely achieve this: 'Dust As We Are', 'Source', 'Sacrifice', 'For the Duration' and 'Walt'. And somewhat aside of this nexus of war/family is 'Take What You Want But Pay For It' which yields a tenderness comparable with these others.

There is an element of voyeurism involved in picking out moments of tenderness in these 'family' poems – one such is when the child is combing his father's hair and realises he is touching the skull of a survivor whose tongue is reluctant to speak. The understanding is that the vulnerable father is himself[1] an infantryman whose job is to kill:

> Thére he sát, kílled but alíve – so lóng
> As we were véry cáreful. I divíned,
> Wĭth ă cŏmb,
> Únder hiş wávy, golden háir, as I combed it,
> The fragílity of skúll. And I fílled
> With his knówledge . . .
>
> ('Dust As We Are', 322)

The rhythm, interconnecting with the lineation and syntax, provides a transposed and evaluated rendering of the child's experience of the father's. His combing seems to create this experience, as if by feeling the fragility of the father's skull he 'divined' the rest. So, clearly, the multisyllabled 'fragility' does something mimetic by way of the word's intrinsic meaning, but the short line 'With a comb' picks out the oddness of the instrument of divination which, it turns out, is after all an intimate one, in contact with the man's

---

1. See *Winter Pollen*, p. 215. See also last stanza of Owen's 'Spring Offensive'.

basic 'skull'. We may also notice how the rhythms of lines 1, 2, and 5 move into not so much stressed but durational syllables – 'so long', 'divined', 'filled', and the centres of experience are located in these words, which work out the boy's (son's) intuition, and its results – 'filled/With his knowledge.'

Perhaps the most affecting of these poems is 'Walt', the man who is presumably the narrator's uncle ('His fingers are my mother's'), one who has suffered experiences of trench-war comparable with his father's.

Two contrary risks attach the poet who seeks to create tenderness within a set of brutal experiences. One is that of overlaying the tenderness with an assault of physical horror, supposedly appealing to the reader with – show tenderness for such a one who has suffered all this. Sassoon rarely manoeuvres this way. The other risk is to so suffuse the total experience with tenderness as to evacuate horror. Hughes in these poems hints at the horror, or re-creates it indirectly, and concentrates on the tenderness. He risks and he manages this, creating a persevering leech gatherer-like being.

> He'd crept into my care . . .
> Strange Dead Sea creature.
> He crawled in his ruins . . .
>
> (330)

and

> 'Whý?' he'd cri̱ed, 'Whý can't I júst di̱e?'
>
> (330)

and

> And 'Áye!' he bre͞athes. 'Áye!'
>
> (331)

One feels the mimetic tottering slowness of the pace, itself reinforced by lines, often end-stopped, but each of them formed in a terminated syntax. Or else, more crucially, the lines are not end-stopped by punctuation but rather, like Lawrence's, end on a syntactical pause in an ongoing syntax:

> a full-rigged fortune
> Cast his body . . .
>
> (330)

The complete or partly complete syntax contained within the line-as-unit serves to comfort the reader, and augments the effect of trust which is essential in the communication and acceptance of tenderness:

> And 'Aye!' he breathes. 'Aye!'

'Aye', a word of wider implication than 'Yes', implicates Walt's many responses to life, at different moments, all of which are in certain respects filamented to his experience of war. They are experiences that do nothing to conciliate the reader, and indeed seal him/her from such *experience* as, we may guess, fractured the condition of this man.

KEN SMITH: *FOX RUNNING*

Notwithstanding the fine early poems, 'The pity' and 'Family Group' (*Eleven Poems*, Northern House, 1964), *Fox Running* (Rolling Moss Press, 1980) is probably Ken Smith's outstanding single poem.

Compared with Hughes's work, *Fox* is, in a non-pejorative sense, a poem of meta-language, non-standard language, in certain respects not unlike Aleksandr Blok's *The Twelve* to which I have only had access, I must say, through a number of translations. At any rate Smith would almost certainly have had access to at least one translation of the poem.

Blok's poem is street-folk-knowledgeable. Smith's is streetwise, but the language both poems use is that of a basic slang-speech used to communicate an experience of life more than an *idea* of experience. Thus the language in Smith's poem (and possibly Blok's), unlike Hughes's directly innovative language, is made of clichés, jargon, commerce-speak, slang, argot, punning – one almost wilfully contrary to the traditional and obviously 'creative' language of romantic and neo-romantic poetry. It is a heap of conjuncted and manipulated common (and shared) everyday language, even more current than quotidian language, in as much as it is – given the nature of Smith's poem – underpinned by menace. Fox running, on the run, pursued, hunted by urban pressures, by misfortune, poverty, and by himself and his self-judged failures. Compared with Hughes, therefore, and despite what I have said concerning the 'uncollected' poems and *Wolfwatching*, Smith's language in *Fox* is a cunning almost stolen language of urban society, an ambivalent unstable mixture of working-class, urban, literate middle-class-poet language. It eschews the accepted ideas concerning poetic language ('creative') in order to deliver the lethal haunted/hunted speech of a creature (fox, fox-and-man, man) on the peripheries of psychic and in certain respects physical endurance – a speech that is knowing, toxified and vital, further vitalized, in the main by puns, playfulness and rhythm – of course, a creature out to survive the loss of family and, almost, of himself.

Whereas Hughes's language makes wonderful concessions to urban (not middle-class urbane) speech, but is not of it. The contrast is illuminating, and asks the question as to whence comes Hughes's physical, metaphysical, mythopeic language. I have very little knowledge of Hughes's background and only a little more understanding of Ken Smith's. Perhaps it is more important to see where Hughes locates his imaginative resources (see above for 'The Burnt Fox'). If Hughes's work (excluding, say, the 'uncollected' poems and *Wolfwatching*) moves within the ambit of literature, *Fox* is more subtly, and eventually, literature. First it is writing, composed of devices subsumed to a man struggling to write and fashion the interpretative words for existence and survival.

This may be seen in the rhythms each poet uses, Hughes's often contained in long lines – consider the span of some of those in 'The Horses'. They suggest confidence. Though much of this would be *modified* (though not changed) by what I have said concerning *Wolfwatching*.

This next is speculative. Hughes's verse in its mythopeia appears to spring from a moment of challenge to what Leavis, in *New Bearings* (1932), in reference to the poetry of Edmund Blunden, called 'the immemorial rural order that is doomed' (54). So, in an era that does not any longer base itself in rurality (Britain), the drawing on such rurality is an act of deliberate, strong-minded confidence.

Whereas the reverse must seem to be true of Smith, the son of an agricultural worker (for that story see 'Family Group') who had direct access to rural experience. And as for rurality in a different sense (nature seen 'through the spectacle of books') such could not be the case with a poet of John Clare's calibre, one who worked with nature for a livelihood. Further, an instructive comparison may be had through reading Keats's 'Ode to a Nightingale' and Clare's 'The Nightingale's Nest'. And for further reading consult Heaney's early valedictory poem 'Digging' (*Death of a Naturalist*,

1966). Yet, although Smith's first twelve years were rural, the working-class man becomes the middle-class poet, who subsequently puts himself through all those uncertainties of urban London, where the underground (and overground) rail system is the ('Veins', 13) tracks of fox running (on the run), outcast and neighbour to the similarly outsidered criminal.

Smith's revelation begins with the outcast nature of creatures divided upon themselves:

> Óne eye awáke to his húnters
> and the slávering jáws
> of the húnting dógs, his bróthers ónce
> (131)

and one is immediately aware of a rapid, cursive rhythm which, although much of it looks to be free verse, much has a regular accentual syntactically end-stopped lineation, many of the lines in three or four pulses. Recurring form appears to be the poem's defensive means and constitutes a linguistic capacity to act the survivor. So its pulse is basic, adaptable to jokiness, executive, terse, but – of course – running. The survival predicated in the rhythm is determined, not confident.

Narrative

Though there are wonderful felicitous verbs and epithets – 'first light shivers awake' (144) – as I've suggested Smith's language denies the straight language of discourse and straight poetry (it's unnerving) and rides the other unofficial language – the official spoken language but not the official literary medium – of the street that some of the media are presently in hot pursuit of. The losses are obvious, but so are the gains. It is fresh, incisive, uncommitted, for the most part, to print, and, in certain senses, not part of English literary usage. We find touches of it in Chaucer, I think:

> He wolde the see were kept for any thing
> Bitwixe Middleburgh and Orewelle . . .
> (Prologue, lines 276–7, The Marchant)

that little toss of *knowingness* in 'for any thing' kins with the knowing character of the language Smith uses. It reaches the reader's senses because it bypasses the habitual language of the book and, because in a book, bypasses its own use in the street too. Nevertheless the poem must rely on something else to replace the loss of the language of writing, and I think it finds this replacement of limbs in the narrative structure – there is such, though it is subtle and (perhaps) hard to detect.

The narrative is based on transience, as the title says, and the single character itself 'unstable' in a number of senses. He has no home, and has lost his marriage, in those frightening lines:

> at the énd of a lóusy márriage
> to a wóman híssing in her sléep . . .
>   (165)

The unstable nature corresponds to and is also part of the environment of urban (London), itself partly composed of transients, especially those with whom he has to do, even the DSS officials – not much for you here, sir. Those of us who know, know. But then the character of the creature is not stable, fox, fox-man, man – and it is only at the end of the poem that the creature-human finally establishes himself through facing his vulnerability as a man, rather than trying on his persona as fugitive, a fox. Here are some tentative 'headings' of episodes such as the poem melts from and into – as a creature running from and into life will, or might, experience. Fox running through streets and admitting his condition as outcast, indeed hunted by those very dogs who were 'his brothers once', he gradually finds his way into the arteries of the city – 'tube maps', 'bus routes' (132). Then, the recall of his being a boy bouncing a ball (133), which eventually connects (138) with the man remembering (bouncing ball returning to hand) and releases itself into the hallucinatory (?) meeting of fox with his double (141). The environment, as he acclimatizes to being outcast, settles into hostility, and the street language becomes more pronounced. There ensues a section or two (143–7) in which the scenario of London H-bombed (145) is envisaged with all the knowingness of the politico-scientific language, and mixes with fierce lament for the disintegration of creaturely life under that onslaught. It ends significantly enough with

> Góodbye lóve. Wóman I lóved . . .
>   (147)

the diction belonging to Whitman. He re-establishes himself after this central cataclysmic change into a human being:

> I write or I die . . .
> (147)

he tells us. And close to that, a re-creation of how the love he had found made him who he was/is (148): Dog disguised as fox/Fox. The narrative flashbacks into sardonic assessment of that who he was, 'a good dog' (148) conformist, routinely drunk but fastened into the verities of citizenship – and then of his detaching himself from that, perhaps because he doesn't care for it, but almost certainly because the home (marriage?) is broken. 'I broke it', he says (149), which sounds painfully like admission (rather than confession). From that time out, he is out, and starts to run, no longer dog, but fox (150). The poem becomes even more subject to modes of travel and there follows (151) what reads like the delicate achievement of one re-creating his sense of his own hallucinatory existence (152). He reverts to memories of his marriage and jeers at his own vulnerable need for his partner's faithfulness (and her apparent lack of it) ('So she let you down', 152). The poem focuses into suicidal feelings (153) and into the increasing violent urban racist features, seemingly related to the Thatcher-era (or a symptom of the ethos, it might be wiser and better to say). The suicidal razor-image returns (159), and he imagines, as who has not, what his blank might produce following on his death. 164 sees partial rehabilitation, seeking a room, at least, and (165) listing the jobs he has absorbed to keep alive. Desperation is experienced, and ageing (166), until he learns to face himself, and adopts a serious voice to appraise such truths needful for a strategy of survival:

> whó all belóngs to this blóod then?

The poem appears to trajectory through apocalypse into recognition. If I return to rhythm, it is not only because it is the preoccupation of this book but a part of both the poem's narrative and its metaphor. Rhythm is after all incarnated movement, though it is possible to create the illusion of pause.

I started by suggesting that much of Smith's verse is in lines composed of three to four beats, in accentual verse; but it is also often composed in sprung rhythm, where the syllables in between the stresses are not counted and are sometimes elided. Yet there is another feature which is notable – the unstable disequilibrium of being uncertain whether a line has three or four beats, and of deciding that although you may not be able to do this aloud, in one's head one can read it both either way and both ways – as a three- *and* four-beat line. It is the hesitancy in the line, the tentativeness within the firmness of the rhythmic contour, that makes the verse so good. Here is an example:

> Fox
> ranging the city's inner spaces
> being scavenger of skips parks
> and desirable period residences
>
> Fox wanting to be alongwind
> amongst bracken his own shade
> the breeze at his back . . .

(131)

or

> Fox
> ranging the city's inner spaces
> being scavenger of skips parks
> and desirable period residences
>
> Fox wanting to be alongwind
> amongst bracken his own shade
> the breeze at his back . . .

ELIZABETH JENNINGS

At first it may surprise one how frequently Elizabeth Jennings' passion, with its related perplexities, finds expression through enjambment, until, that is, one riddles the evident fact: that most of the verse is rigorously metered. In English, feeling tends towards trisyllabic expression; so that if metre in Jennings' verse is two-syllabled iambic, then it is not surprising that an alternative release, in frequent enjambments, will occur, syntactically, in unexpected places within the syntax, and created by the urgency of the feeling expressed through that syntax. Additionally, it is likely that such metricality will be quavered, or rocked, by feeling, and the syntax urged through many lines of metre pushed past and beyond those expectations in which units of syntax and lineation take place within line-endings. Such enjambed delivery is found early on in Jennings' published verse. In the by-now famous 'Identity' (p. 17), the syntax skids past the line-endings, acknowledging these, but not pausing or coinciding its syntactic units within these demarcations and terminations:

> Image and passion combined into a whole
> Pattern within the loving mind, not her or his
> Concurring there . . .

(17)

One sees the fine extension, of the second line above, beyond the expectations created by the pentameter of the preceding line. It is also noticeable that this instance occurs in the compelling middle stanza of a three-verse poem, when the energy, meaning and feeling have all paced themselves into momentum. The riving of 'whole' from 'Pattern' – an adjective from the noun with which it would habitually stand united – is countenanced by a more extreme instance, in the next lines, of 'his/Concurring'. And this separation through enjambment is repeated in the subsequent lines. It hardly matters if the pace (energy) causes the enjambments, or the enjambments create a sense of movement, the effect being one of velocity and intensity, further at odds, this time, with the chaste simple language that insists, not so much on control, as limpidity, a version of purity. Even the purity of language, however, has its latent metaphorical guise, in its use of words recognizably part of the philosopher/logician's discourse: 'image', 'passion', 'combined', 'whole', 'pattern' and 'concurring'. The language may suggest not merely control but a mind in control of self; the *prose* of *Every Changing Shape*, with its meticulous word order, does indeed convey that. The verse prosody, however, suggests something other. Yet in pointing to the incline the syntax hastens down, I would add that an examination of feeling/meaning could hardly be taken even thus far without some friendly scrutiny of the prosodic activity. If one tries to get at the sense through lexical examination alone, the meaning moves away.

If Jennings' verse were all enjambed, we would lose its particular achievement. In part this consists of her use of end-stopped lines so as to form an endeavour of discussion/argument/tension through the oscillation between end-stopped and enjambed lines. This, like the language of the 'philosopher' (above), could be thought of as a kind of metaphor since effects beyond immediate verbal meaning are obtained through this pendulation.

There are too many fine poems for me to be able to look even briefly at more than a further four, but I cite 'Song of a Birth or a Death', 'A World of Light', 'Lazarus', 'Childhood in Lincolnshire', 'I Count the Moments' and 'Heyday' as but a few of the fine poems, in which various strategies are operated within a quite confined metrical practice.

We may formulate an equation of sorts whereby the more intense the crux, or the pain, the greater the pinch of metricality and the corresponding resistance to that by the syntax-lineation energy form.

This is seen in the cruxes of 'Song for a Birth or a Death' and 'A World of Light', where, in the first, love needs sex and finds pain, or even violence, endemic to it, and, in the other poem, where peace and purity are *suffered* ('suffered light'). Here pain and mystical apprehension appear to be in reciprocal relationship. Consult *Every Changing Shape* (1961) especially chapter 4, 'The Value of Suffering' (Julian of Norwich), and elsewhere.

The metrical concision made from emotional *stress* may be seen in these two poems. Others of hers, with similar stress, exist, but these two present with unflinching directness the condition of mystical apprehension which, as Jennings indicates in her chapter on Teresa of Avila (*ECS*, 5), brings with its union with God a sorrow and pain that form an inseparable part of this ineffable experience. Perhaps only the second of these poems deals directly with this mystical apprehension but, as Jennings and others have indicated, the terms mystics use to re-create and express such mystical union are frequently those shared with an expression of sexual love. Perhaps we may here reverse this understanding and say that sexual love involves not only pain, but, at its most extreme, for Jennings, some sense of its being inseparable from violence, and that sexual love acquires a mystical arrowing:

> Know that all matings mean a kill
> ('Song for a Birth or a Death', 48)

and

> Yés but the páin still cróuches whére
> The yóung fóx and the child are trápped
> And cries of lóve are cries of féar . . .
>
> (48)

A similar doubleness inherent in irresolvable contradiction (not paradox, which is a species of resolution) is evident in 'A World of Light':

> Yés when the dárk withdréw I súffered líght
>
> (53)

where 'suffered' is too strong a responsive word to be the plaything of paradox. Here the apprehension of light is a suffering of it.

> Ónly a child's simplícity cán hándle
> Such móments whén the hóttest fíre feels cóol,
> And évery bréath is líke a súdden hómage
> To péace that pénetrates ánd is nót féared.
>
> (53–4)

It appears that a child's simplicity is that Christian mode wherewith one possesses the means to be penetrated by the divine light *and* bear with such union.

Yet what also needs indicating is the aptness of metricality to convey the stress, in both poems. If metricality already constitutes a stress, a fitting of syllables into a recurring pattern, this metricality, under the additional stress endemic to the referred to experience, slides through line-endings line on line. One further notices that in a 'World of Light' the line scheme does not occur *within* any of the stanzas, but recurs stanza by stanza on the paradigm set by the first stanza. Thus the rhyme of the first line is repeated by all the first lines in each stanza, and so on. This offers the sense not so much of a fixed but unfolding pattern.

Apart from the prose poems often used (*qua* Traherne, *ECS*, 8) to convey religious experience, 'Childhood in Lincolnshire' is one of the few poems that hovers somewhere near the operations of free verse. However, apart from the concluding line, each of the lines is metrical, but each uses a metricality that establishes no congruent recurring pattern. Clearly this effects variety, yet the metricality enables a single-minded swift directness, as in the pentameter

Só the séa tráfficked wīth imáginátion
(139)

With its sophisticated power vested in 'trafficked', together with
the rocking effect of the extra final unstressed syllable, it is a line
that may remind one of Geoffrey Hill. It is fine metricality. Notwithstanding this, when speaking of the remembered, first experience of the smell of honeysuckle, the verse concludes with

Tíed to its ówn evént and pótent for thát, thérefore, álways.
(139)

The epiphany seems to be expressed, perhaps in metricality, but
also perhaps in a cautiously joyful free verse. At any rate it is the
potency of 'first' and 'always' which gives the poem poignant and
stealthy power. It is worth remarking that the recollecting character of the poem seems somewhat at odds with the poet's assertion
with which she concludes the *Preface*: 'Art is not self-expression
while, for me, "confessional poetry" is almost a contradiction in
terms' (13).

'Confessional poetry' has a broad remit, and this reader would
find it difficult to draw a separating line between the opprobrious
'confessional' and the presumably acceptable 'personal', for all personal work confesses intimacies not otherwise available to the reader.
Indeed one of Jennings' strengths may be found in the directness
with which she renders her feelings, even to the re-creating of what
seem to be specific encounters. Thus this difficult distinction between confessional and personal bears on the poem 'Heyday', which
achieves its status as synecdoche by virtue of the intensity with
which the poet's youth is beautifully and delicately realized:

I hád my flówering tóo bút it came láte . . .
(183)

This might be a reference to her experience of the mystical, but
within the context it is more likely to refer to the previous line, in
which such a flowering of passion has transmuted into a generous
reciprocity and compassionate understanding. Thus the moving
realization of

Thát one wạs shý and whén he fírst kíssed me
It was a child's tóuch . . .
(183)

But this in turn expresses the understanding that passion and compassion, though not mutually exclusive, are not synonymous or interchangeable either. We are not too distant from the realization of 'Song for a Birth or a Death'. This vulnerable and, so it seems to the reader, direct admission, solicits no sympathy. It is properly cast in metrical rhyming lines of iambic pentameter, the first and last stanzas rhyming identically ABCBA. Further, the metricality and rhyme act, not as a form of self-protection, but to intercept solicitation on the one hand, and further irrelevant inquiry on the other. Yet the whole poem is both precise and affective. This leads me to make one further suggestion.

Jennings' participation in *The Movement* may serve to indicate her awareness that she, with others, was (is) a poet writing metrical verse in an overall context where free verse predominates, in quantity at least. This is no value judgement, and because it is not, it permits me to indicate the pressures under which her tough though vulnerable metered verse operates. Metrical verse in an era of metricality neither conforms nor truckles to the norm; it is what it is. In an era which is predominantly that of free verse, it requires quantities of coolness and courage to be neither defiant, evasive, nor oblivious. Metricality[1] needs to be natural and strong in its formality, and the best of Jennings is just this.

DEREK MAHON: HIS POEM OF GRIEF

Some of those free verse poems in Pound's *Lustra* (1916) contradict the belief that irony (and its related modes) is only expressible in

1. Not that Jennings can't be militant on behalf of metricality. In her chapter on St John of the Cross (*ECS*, 6) she quotes with evident approval John Frederick Nims on his 'very vivid rendering' of those poems:

    That means that I have chosen the rhythms and forms of the original instead of turning the content into a slack free verse favourable, perhaps, to thought and imagery, but at what fatal cost to their pulsing blood-rhythms!

    (*ECS*, 63)

    Does this impugn free verse that is slack, or free verse because it is by nature slack? The discussion continues.

the scissoring of rhymed metrical verse. And on the other hand, Mahon's verse supports this latter view. Indeed, Mahon rarely keeps irony out of his verse, and rarely excludes that plangency hidden in the metrical set of irony. He is certainly able to use such a form, although he appears to have assumed that the form provides its own eternal vitality. Whereas I suspect that, through such challenge, the variety of modes inherent in free verse may assist the good poet into freshness and vitality. The real metrical poet (of which kind Mahon is one) knows this because s/he will have experienced the temptation to let the metrical form do more of the work than is proper for the poem. Perhaps the next stage, for poet and reader, is to form an overarching view of verse by assembling a composite perspective made of both free and metrical verse.

It seems possible that the preoccupation (of 'A Disused Shed in Co. Wexford'), driven with looser reins, may have helped to shape what is amongst his best and most accessible work. Irony is present but it subserves 'sincerity', the responsive substance of the text. For instance, in the shed imprisoning the fungi is a keyhole;

> This is the óne stár in their firmamént
> Or frámes a stár withín a stár . . .
>
> (62)

One might argue this 'straight'; but, heartlessly (this being the habitual predicament of irony), one might suggest that this condition is no more than the invariable firmament of low things – a keyhole. It would be wrong to do so. Mahon, habitual ironist, courageously turns the irony upon himself, deploying it with an open self-awareness of his compassion, though signalling at the same time that his compassion conducts its operations with all the self-consciousness of which irony is capable. This notwithstanding, the profitable way to read the poem is to bring compassion and commitment to the predicament of these creatures.

In the anglophone culture, Eliot and Pound, both of whose writing is disfigured by racism, and, in particular, by anti-Semitism, failed, after the Second World War, to register in their work the existence of the holocaust and the concentration camps of Europe and the East. The task of enlarging modern poetry to enable a responsive expression to these exclusively human phenomena was undertaken by, amongst others, Geoffrey Hill, with his 'September Song' (below) and this Irish poet, Derek Mahon.

Hill's modernist 'September Song' is based, not on narrative, but rhetorical and moral structure. His compacting and linking of referents in a tender, controlled anguish, expressed in free verse, contrasts in a number of respects with Mahon's poem which is almost if not entirely metrical, mediated between accentual-syllabic pentameter and four-beat accentual, sometimes composed in an ambiguous hovering between both. And where Hill's 14-line poem tenses itself in free verse 7 out of 14 lines of which are enjambed, Mahon's 60 lines work in such a way that even where they are enjambed the line frequently (in both senses) contains the sense-unit. Its ease is in contrast with Hill's tensed syntax and serves to put the reader at ease in order to appeal, on the presumptive common ground of conscience, to the reader's presumed compassion.

Mahon's narration describes the location of the victims' confinement and their almost total deprivation of light, and is explicit about the causes of their suffering, and inequality, in ways that contrast with Hill's reticent, gentle drive towards non-narrative extreme selectivity of crucial detail. Mahon's poem is expansive in its expression of grief. Hill's is everywhere didactic by implication but nowhere identifiable as such except, perhaps, in the parenthetical stanza where, indirectly, he questions his right to compose a poem dealing with the experience of being in a camp, which he himself never had. Mahon's generous sympathy for the victims precludes such a question:

> They [the victims] are bégging us, yóu sée, in their wórdless
>   way,
> To dó sómething, to spéak on théir behálf . . .
>
>   (63)

A strong empathetic love participates in the construction of a justifiable, acceptable artefact, in which the creatures beg us to recognize their existence and its condition, and to bring a change to such condition.

Mahon's poem engages our sympathies. His faith that the component of goodness is an essential part of our human nature licenses his generosity. He assumes that the drift towards cruelty, or inertia, is not irreversible and that sympathy in each of us can effectively be regenerated. This belief is expressed in the poem's first line

Even nów there are pláces where a thóught míght grów ...
(62)

The poem offers us the places of dereliction, evoked in eerie desolation – a mine 'worked out and abandoned', 'wild-flowers in the
lift-shaft', until we home in on the 'disused shed', one minor part
of the demesne of a 'burnt-out hotel'. Thus in comparison to the
hotel is its ancillary building, abandoned, and neglected, in Ireland,
where the fungi suppurate and despair, and whose inlet–outlet is
a single star formed by a keyhole (star = hope; Mahon is not afraid
to employ cliché). Indeed, it is openly done, our sympathy engaged
by the ease of rhythm, the line-contained sense-units, and by the
fact that it is with the supposedly lesser creatures, the fungi, we are
asked to sympathize. Doing that, by extension we sympathize with
those victims – of natural disaster, in Pompeii, and of human predation, in one of the Nazi concentration camps, Treblinka.

With rhythmic ease, all this occurs through tact and openness,
never in naiveté. The victims themselves have a consciousness that
is far from naive, or they would never be able to identify their
existence with

'Lét not our naíve lábours have béen in váin!'
(63)

'In vain' rhymes four lines above with the seemingly unavoidable
homophone 'pain'. Pain must not be allowed to suffer 'in vain', and
of course if it is recognized, and alleviated, it has not been entirely
'in vain'. Thus 'you see'

They are begging us, you see, in their wordless way ...
(63)

means not only see, but understand, register and act. The 'you see',
placed so centrally and easily in this anapaestic dactyllic pentameter,
allows the poem to identify its didacticism and solicit our actions.
A poem that engages both our sympathies and our active, or potentially active, capacities is a large achievement; and its openness
signals that it is not intended for the contemplation of the reader in
isolation only, but is an artefact that in its success requires from us
an active response.

The poem's achievement could be put in a more fashionably critical way. It achieves simultaneous success both in *verba* (the words in the poem itself) and in *res*, those things in the world to which it refers. What makes this double success, where the metre/syntax contributes so much, and neither *res* nor *verba* is compromised, is charity, which almost despairs but refuses that refuge. The distinction between *res* and *verba* appears in Pound's Canto 82 (*Cantos*, 525).

GEOFFREY HILL: HIS 'SEPTEMBER SONG' AND NO. 7 FROM 'FUNERAL MUSIC'

I wrote an essay on the poetry of Geoffrey Hill published by Grevel Lindop and Michael Schmidt in *British Poetry since 1960* (1972). Extended to include later work, it was published by Peter Robinson in *Geoffrey Hill: Essays on His Work* (1985). I don't feel I can add to it and therefore I offer what I wrote about poems, which I believe to be amongst his best, and I follow this with some remarks concerning rhythm, metre and syntax in both poems.

Hill's use of irony in *King Log* is ubiquitous, but it is not, usually, of the non-participatory and mandarin sort. It articulates the collision of events or brings them together out of scruple and concern, and for this a more or less regular and simple use of syntax is needed, and used. 'September Song' begins:

Undesírable you máy have béen, untóuchable
yóu were nót

A concentration camp victim. There is 'play' even in the subtitle 'born 19.6.32 – deported 24.9.42' where the natural event of birth is placed, simply, beside the human and murderous 'deported', as if the latter were of the same order and inevitability for the victim; which in some senses, it was. Even here, the zeugmatic wit is fully employed. The irony of conjuncted meanings between 'undesirable' (touching on both sexual desire and racism), and 'untouchable' (which exploits a similar ambiguity but reverses the emphases) is unusually dense and simple. The confrontation is direct and unavoidable, and this directness is brought to bear on the reader not only by the vocabulary, but by the balancing directness of the syntax. This stanza contains one of Hill's dangerous words – dangerous because of its too-frequent use, and because these words sometimes unleash (though not here) a too evident irony:

> Nót forgótten
> or pássed óver at the próper time.

'Proper' brings together the idea of bureaucratically correct 'as calculated' by the logistics of the 'final solution' and by the particular camp's timetable; it also contrasts the idea of the mathematically 'correct' with the morally intolerable. It touches too, on the distinction between what is morally right, and what is conventionally acceptable, and touches incidentally upon the way in which the conventionally acceptable is often used to cloak the morally unacceptable. It is one of Hill's grim jokes, deployed in such a way that the laughter is precisely proportionate to the needs of ironic exposure. It is when the irony is in excess of the situation that the wit becomes mannered. But here it does not. So the poem continues, remorselessly:

> As éstimated, you díed. Things márched,
> sufficient, to that end

One feels the little quibbling movement in 'As estimated, you died', as, without wishing to verbalize it, Hill points to the disturbing contrast between the well-functioning timetable and what it achieved. 'Things marched' has the tread of pompous authority which is immediately qualified by the painfully accurate recognition that just so much energy was needed, and released, for the extermination. 'Sufficient' implies economy, but it also implies a conscious qualification of the authoritarian tread. The quiet function of unpretentious machinery fulfilled its programme, perhaps more lethally so because 'quiet' and efficient. One also notices here how the lineation gauges, exactly, the flow and retraction of meaning and impulse, and how this exact rhythmical flow is so much a part of the sensuous delivery of response and evaluation. It is speech articulated, but the lineation provides, via the convention of verse line-ending, a formal control of rhythm and of sense emphasis by locking with, or breaking, the syntactical flow. Thus in the third stanza, the syntax is broken by the lineation exactly at those parts at which the confession, as it were, of the poem's (partial) source is most painful:

(Í háve máde
an élegy for mysélf it
is trúe)

The slightly awkward break after 'it' not only forces the reading
speed down to a word-by-word pace, in itself an approximation
to the pain of the confession, but emphasises the whole idea. By
placing emphasis on the unspecifying pronoun 'it', Hill is able to
say two things: that the elegy was made for himself (at least, in
part) since in mourning another one is also commiserating with
one's own condition:

> When we chant
> 'Ora, ora pro nobis' it is not
> Seraphs who descend to pity but ourselves.
>
>   ('Funeral Music, 5')

But 'it' may also refer to the whole process: I have made an elegy
for myself, as we all do, but I have also made an elegy on a 'true'
event. True imaginatively, true in detailed fact; both, for someone
other than myself. Thus he is also to point to the difficulty of the
poet who wishes, for a variety of reasons, to approach the mon-
strousness of such events, but has compunction about doing so.
He tactfully touches, for instance, on the overweening ambition
of the poet who hitches his talent to this powerful subject, thereby
giving his work an impetus to which it may not be fully entitled,
since only the victim herself would be entitled to derive this kind
of 'benefit'. But he also modestly pleads, I think, with 'it/is true'
that whatever the reasons for his writing such an elegy, a proper
regard for the victim, a true and unambitious feeling, was present
and used. I hope enough has been said here to point to Hill's use
of irony at its best, and to indicate that the tact with which he uses
language is not a convention of manners which he is inertly content
to remain immersed in, but an active employment of the convention, as it cooperates with his scrupulousness. The scrupulousness,
like the pity, is in the language. The theme permeates it.

In the final stanza the concentration is upon the living – us, who
cannot now, 'after such knowledge', assume the selves which we
were. No growth is possible, as it is possible in a season of 'mellow
fruitfulness'; which season contrasts in us now with the skeletal
remains of the camp prisoners. For us, Hill appears to suggest, where

before the autumn fruits were (as for Keats in 'To Autumn') plump and acceptable, they now appear to 'fatten' in overproduction – an obscenity. Yet in reverse association, the fattening brings to mind ideas of being fatted for sacrifice. Thus Keats's subsidiary point in the fourth stanza of 'Ode on a Grecian Urn': the 'smoke of harmless fires' will sting the eyes and provoke harmless tears for other than harmless acts. In the concluding line of 'September Song', 'plenty' denotes not only the plenitude of harvest, therefore, but also the abundance of suffering and, for both the victims and for us, degradation. The tone-mixture in this line is complex; we hear lamentation, irony and indignation . . .

'Funeral Music, 7' concentrates the moral vision of all eight poems within the vision of the battlefield; it has some of the didactic power of *Everyman*, and some of its power of lament:

> Methink, alas, that I must be gone
> To make my reckoning and my debts pay,
> For I see my time is nigh spent away.
> Take example, all ye that this do hear or see,
> How they that I loved best do forsake me,
> Except my Good Deeds that bideth truly.

Here is Hill's poem:

> 'Prowess, vanity, mutual regard,
> It seemed I stared at them, they at me.
> That was the gorgon's true and mortal gaze:
> Averted conscience turned against itself.'
> A hawk and a hawk-shadow. 'At noon,
> As the armies met, each mirrored the other;
> Neither was outshone. So they flashed and vanished
> And all that survived them was the stark ground
> Of this pain. I made no sound, but once
> I stiffened as though a remote cry
> Had heralded my name. It was nothing . . .'
> Reddish ice tinged the reeds; dislodged, a few
> Feathers drifted across; carrion birds
> Strutted upon the armour of the dead.

Our being martial has a part of its rationale in vanity. The more we give conscience the slip ('Averted conscience') the more we are vulnerable to those consequences we thus ignore. 'A hawk and a hawk-shadow' is an ironic pointer to the cave equation: we are the imperfect versions of the ideal predator, whose shadow we are. But the hawk's shadow is real enough, a sign of the immanence of our mutual predatoriness which in fact achieved reciprocal destruction. There is honour, even glory: 'Neither was outshone'. Yet in vanity we mirror each other; and in the moment of the mirroring, which is also ('flashed') the moment of ignition, we fight, blind to each other ('dazzled'), destroy each other, and vanish. The virtue of this poem is that the account is not only moving but further fleshed by the strange, alien presence of 'I': 'I made no sound', 'I stiffened', thought I heard 'my name'. A survivor, a witness? Whatever identity 'I' has, it is as a person of actual, true, moral power that the figure lives. And it is this person's being so alive that makes the morality of the first part through to line seven the more convincing, poised delicately as it is between moral vision and event. 'It was nothing', for no one is left, either in conscience or in living fact, who can call his name, and the 'stark ground/Of this pain' offers a basis for 'nothing'. The carrion birds that strut on the armour of the dead reflect the vanity of the warriors. But the birds are themselves seen as being as foolish (and predatory) as the warriors – as incapable of perceiving how they are observed, in a performance of what they would not dare to do were these soldiers alive. The witness is saved from appearing self-righteous by a posture that expresses perception, humility and bewilderment. Understanding is what flows through and bathes the witness, and not judgement. But the overarching drama is didactic, for both the birds and the dead soldiers mirror the essential dialectic of vanity which, as it is martial, produces destruction. Like the warriors, the birds reveal a predatory blindness to their own 'carrion' condition. By making most of the poem the supposed narrative of one who testifies, the poet avoids the danger of appearing single-mindedly didactic. The devastation points to the ideal judgement.

Hill's metric is as delicate and scrupulous as his meanings

This seems to be the moment to re-engage the discussion of free and metrical verse, but it should by now be evident that we cannot consider the working of rhythm apart from the energy of syntax and its intersection with lineation. A reader's sense of rhythm is affected as much by a poem's rhythmical-and-rhetorical structure as by its interaction with meaning and preoccupation. In this sense the long sentences and extended syntax are as much part of an argument in *Paradise Lost* that Milton seems loath to discontinue as they are instrinsic to his 'style'.

Risking what may appear to be an arbitrary play with numbers I notice that, whether or not by coincidence, each of the unrhymed sonnets (of course) and 'September Song' are composed in 14 lines. The difference between sonnet 7 (and the others) and 'September Song' – between metred and free verse – is immediately and visually apparent.

The free verse poem, 'September Song', is expressed through at least seven enjambments tensed by the onward movement, and they enact momentary suspensions of the syntactical flow without ever violating the syntax's formal structure. 'September Song' thus sets up a formal opposition between what it renders (destruction) and how it renders that in its unbroken syntax. The very first sentence sets up the related sweet reasonableness of rational argument, entailed in its zeugma, while conveying its horrific facts. 'You may have been' is the language of one person discussing the question with another (the victim or a listener). The substance of what is said is that 'you' are to die because of what, not who, you are – or what you have done. 'You may have been' is the locution of rational debate, the syntax taking care to maintain its formality and rationality, seemingly in reply to the Third Reich's express activity of murder.

Sonnet 7 (like the others) works its metrical pentameters, and its relation of metre to lineation, in a reciprocally opposite way (the poems are part of *King Log*, 1968). Thus the question of 14 lines acquires consequence not only because a song and a sonnet were related, but also because, with their development, lyric and the idea of the poem have tended to separate into differing modes of expression, with appeals to differing areas of a reader's responsiveness. Nevertheless, both the 'Song' and the Sonnet are composed in 14 lines, and 14 lines is the space allotted for the sonnet to unfold and conclude its argument and persuasive rhetoric. The space neither compacts nor extends the argument. It is simply the allotted space, just as the concrete gas chamber, such as the one I have seen at Maidanek, by Lublin, in Poland, was a space prescribed for gassing.

Unlike a sonnet, 'September Song' does not unfold related arguments comprised in the debate of a single idea, but it does entail a sequence of rational thought, in that sense behaving in a way comparable to a sonnet.

Sonnet 7 thinks in the structure of a sonnet. The first four lines conclude with a full-stop and contain the first stage of the poem's argument. The following four and a half lines amplify this gorgonizing idea with respect to the armies and their reflecting pride and, with the phrase 'of this pain', end the next sub-section midline (9). The remaining five and a half lines introduce the 'I' without warning. But that is logical. Collectively, armies are victims of each other, but are comprised of individual victims, some of which may or may not have an audible voice of suffering and pain. So on the one hand, the poem is comprised of a moral interplay and moral drama of forces in their reciprocal and murderous pride, and on the other, it is the history of thousands of individuals who perished in the battle of Towton and were each other's victims. 'I stiffened'. And in such argument we notice another thing. Where 'September Song' tenses argument and rhetoric through a number of enjambments, this sonnet end-stops the lines; they start, and they conclude, and their terminations conclude a thought that is nevertheless a unit in an overall argument. This measured starting and concluding is not merely part of the *gravitas*, for which Hill has ever since been paying, but the measure of a strong and true movement, a controlled passionate embodied grief expressed in the tread of unrhymed pentameters:

> Reddish ice tinged the reeds; dislodged, a few
> Feathers drifted across; carrion birds
> Strútted upón the ármour óf the déad.

The restoration of regular strict pentameter in the last line emphasizes the unselfconscious vanity of the momentarily victorious carrion birds and now obliterated if reincarnated vanity of the dead soldiers.

THOM GUNN

In his collection of critical essays and portraits, *Shelf Life* (1994), Gunn has juxtaposed by the chance that is never accidental two tender memoir-portraits, of the critic who was his tutor, Yvor Winters, and the novelist Christopher Isherwood, whose exemplary practice probably confirmed Gunn's suspicions of the ego.

These two portraits might be seen to identify two characteristics that comprise Gunn's verse. One is the plain style which Gunn readily acquiesced in under Winter's tutelage (*SL*, 201) and the other, in lieu of the metaphoric abundance in such as Redgrove, the succinct aphoristic lines scissoring through the prolixity of existence (see his 'discrimination and abundance', *SL*, 11). Not that Gunn is devoid of metaphor, but he tends to the simile end of it, augmenting a meaning or radiation already stated rather than creating one (or several) through the metaphor's focusing of the different components upon each other. To this scrupulous discipline Gunn admired in Winters, yet, with that same scrupulousness, applied in his own prose to note its limiting effects on his verse, Gunn brings a proper sense of the damage inflicted on every part of life, not excluding art, by the narcissistic aspects of the ego. Thus Gunn's admiration for Isherwood, whom, in his restraint, and lack of visible ego, Gunn takes as an example.

These must have been important early decisions for Gunn, made early in his life as both person, and later, perhaps, as poet; and the idea of consciously taking on and showing the conflicts involved may be seen early, in his *Collected Poems* (1993), in the by now well-known poem 'The Wound'.

Before considering it I should like to adopt Gunn's practice of identifying those poems one likes in another's work, by doing that with his. A tentative list would run:

'The Wound' (*Fighting Terms*, 1954); 'Misanthropos' (1965) with a glance back to the syllabics of the first three poems in section 2 of *My Sad Captains* (1961): 'Waking in a Newly Built House', 'Flying Above California' and 'Considering the Snail'. In the section *Poems from the 1960s*, three poems that lie together, 'The Conversation of Old Men', 'The Old Woman' and 'Touch'. From *Moly* (1971), 'Words', which appears to link with 'Touch'. From *Jack Straw's Castle* (1976), 'The Geysers' and 'Wrestling', and from the most recent, *The Man with Night Sweats* (1992), 'Lament', 'All Do Not All Things Well' and 'A Blank' (1992). And of course, I note that for 'Misanthropos' (1965), Merle Brown gave a complete essay: 'Inner Community in Thom Gunn's "Misanthropos"' (*Double Lyric*, 1980).

Aggression preoccupies a number of the early poems, and 'The Wound' puts the problem into the soldier figure of Achilles (one of Gunn's recurring soldier / fighter figures). Achilles is both the soldier subject to the orders of his commander, and, at the same time, freelance and maverick. On the other hand, the freedom supposedly inherent in this maverick condition is itself contradicted by the terms in which it is cast, for although he is a soldier, the wound will only heal – or rather, it will paradoxically break open when he envisages that very thing for which he is apparently constituted, fighting. Thus the divided Achilles-figure is the emblem of seemingly irresolvable internal conflict, for although it is entailed by the requirements of his world, it is engendered by his division within and against himself. One finds this in Owen's 'Spring Offensive' and more overtly, of course, in his 'Strange Meeting'. There may be psychological parallels here, for both poets present problems for which no solution is envisaged.

I have trespassed on the poem's form and expression by concentrating on its meaning, but readers will readily identify Gunn's commitment to recurring metricality and rhyme. In his interview with Jim Powell, in *Shelf Life*, he refers to Bunting's 'tightly disciplined' free verse; so from this we readily appreciate that a commitment to form is synonymous with the exercise of control. Which is why, therefore, his syllabics[1] constitute a moving act of self-criticism, at the same time instigating a way of freeing himself from the limitations of such control in metre:

> My way of teaching myself to write free verse was to work with syllabics.
>
> (*SL*, 219)

And if his practice of syllabics was a way of loosening the succinctness he is in danger of clinching his verse in, his generous essay on Allen Ginsberg prescribes in its encomium a remedy for himself:

> Perhaps we have focused too exclusively on succinctness, since the Imagists, and should have realised that there are other possibilities.
>
> (*SL*, 115)

Other possibilities

'Misanthropos' is in a sense a loosened poem – an extended theme-idea sustained by narrative and the painful self-revelation of the protagonist (he is almost entirely the sole creature, until the poem reaches its final stages of disclosure). The poem is also didactic; and although 'I needed no persuading to also like the plain style' (Memoir on Winters, *SL*, 201), and although the poem triumphs over

1. See Appendix.

the idea that morality necessarily consumes the poetry, this accommodation must have been hard for Gunn. The poem extends through a variety of strict forms, metrical and syllabic. There is no free verse (although there is in *Poems from the 1960s*). Running through the poem I find syllabics (1), rhyme and echo-rhyme in iambic pentameter (2), iambic pentameter without rhyme (3), the echo strategy (6), more syllables, but rhymed in couplets (8), the purposefully discordant, partly rhymed (Gautier-like?) 'Epitaph for Anton Schmidt' in tetrameter of mixed iambic and trochaic. And so on.

The effect of this variety is a summation and *sursum corda* of (Gunn's) forms, as if he said, 'see the variety and freshness achievable within recurring form'.

This variety and freshness, in ever-changing form, achieves irony since the variety expresses what is unchanging, until the poem's denouément – the dogged and single persistence of a man who had been a soldier (server), and who is now an apparently sole survivor after an atomic struggle. The ending in which the enfeebled soldier almost – involuntarily – helps another human – one of a group that unexpectedly appears in this still partly desolated wilderness – is extremely moving. And this section occurs after the exemplary Anton Schmidt is shown to have assisted Jews, in escaping from Poland and the Nazis. Schmidt is discovered and executed:

> He néver díd mistáke for bóndage
> The mílitáry jób, the chánces,
> The límits; hé did nót submít
> To the bláckmáil of his círcumstánces . . .
>
> (144)

presented in almost Brechtian ballad-like narration, Schmidt resembles the Achilles-figure of 'The Wound':

> I wás mysélf: súbject to nó man's bréath . . .
>
> (3)

Yet with a difference. Achilles is conducting his own freedom; Schmidt, with all the pressures of being part of the German army, achieves freedom for those officially designated the target of the Third Reich:

Bréathing the cóld áir of his fréedom . . .

(144)

His freedom lies in an obedience to his own moral imperative.

The episode is out of synchronization with the narrative sequence, for it is we, the readers, who learn of the exemplary Schmidt. But it is not out of synchronization with the poem's narrative progression, standing in direct relationship with the almost involuntary humanity of the survivor (above). And it is this design in the narrative that marks the poem out as risking, and achieving, its didactic purpose. The survivor, as recast Adam.

The disciplined forms that comprise 'Misanthropos', like the discipline and freedom of Anton Schmidt, inhere in the discipline of voluntarism. Somesuch voluntarism was implicit in the figure of 'The Wound' who is forever dividing and healing, and here, one returns to the sustained encomium of Ginberg's poetry, so different from Gunn's, where Gunn says,

the leisurely process of accumulation may add up to a kind of force unavailable to the poets of succintness, the force of the large inclusive grasp as opposed to that of the tightly clenched fist . . .

(*SL*, 110)

It seems that Gunn with his multiplicity of forms, that converge on and radiate from a tightly disciplined idea, is also trying for 'accumulation' and that 'large inclusive grasp' without, at this point, being prepared to loosen up the form of each poem within 'Misanthropos'. It might be put the other way; that the successful tension of the whole poem comes from the variety of poem-forms, each adhering to discipline, while at the same time being prepared to interrupt the notion of straight narration, as Melville did in *Moby Dick* with his disquisition on whales. This variety of forms within a single poem (consider Tennyson's *Maud*) unfolding a single narrative has, at its core, a teleology of self-redeemed human beings. It could also be read as Gunn's aspiration towards a 'large inclusive grasp', which needs to find its form in order to allow the hand to make such a grasp. The poem has its grasp, in respect of its preoccupations: the forensic use of irony to rebuke pride, the gluttonies of the ego, and the folly of weaponry. If the message adds up, do the forms accumulate into a whole?

The poem is a watershed in Gunn's achievement but this note

must attempt to include the achievement that took place in the
1960s with Gunn's writing free verse. 'The Conversation of Old
Men', 'The Old Woman' and 'Touch' (166–9). These three free-verse
poems open up themselves not only to modes of feeling, but ways
of having us feel form-and-feeling. It is in the design of the poem
that a change in feeling takes place. One notices that a respect for
the line, and its pulse, is run with more enjambments than end-
stopped lines. The poet uses syntax to intersect with and draw on
the lines. The strategy is more or less the reverse of Creeley's who
ends his lines and enjambments on the syntactically hesitant word,
in order to express hesitation and fear within the onwardness of having to live one's experience (There is a perceptive essay on Creeley
in *Shelf Life*.) Consider the ending of 'Touch', which is perhaps the
strangest of love poems, both in the individual and in the soci-
etally inclusive sense. The 'I' gets into bed and sinks into it beside
his partner:

> What is móre, the place is
> not fóund but séeps
> from our tóuch ín
> contínuous creátion, dárk
> enclósing cocóon róund
> ourselves alóne, dark
> wíde réalm where wé
> walk with éveryone.
>
> (169)

Earned affirmation.

'The large inclusive grasp' remains the text for his poem
'Lament', which poem bonds with an AIDS sufferer through an
admiration for the sufferer's stoicism, and 'lament' for his early
extinction. Gunn visits – is that delicate enough? – rhyming couplets of iambic pentameter, but the through-movement of syntax,
over a number of enjambed lines and correlative runs of feeling,
engages this feeling with the form. And this co-operation suggests
that through the creation in 'Touch' Gunn has learned to cooperate
with free verse, with the result that the metricality, with or without
rhyme, is not permitted to dictate to experience. With 'Lament',
Gunn shows that he has learned to evacuate the ego, as he claimed
Isherwood did in his best work. And Gunn does this by concentrating in a properly tender way on his subject, who embodies those

attributes he admires; and Gunn does this without ever abandon-
ing him to the literary fate of typicality, which would have been a
gross infringement upon the person and the poem itself. Gunn balances the long sentence with a style that is in part conversation
and in part the prose were this 'conversation' written. It is a delicate
achievement, recording the dying and death of another, but it also
includes the intimacy passing between the two men. The verse is
not invisible – one hears it as verse – the metricality and rhyme
help to ensure that part of the contract; but it fuses a number of
modes, and, in that act, is itself changed.

> Meanwhile,
> Your lungs collapsed, and the machine, unstrained,
> Did all your breathing now. Nothing remained
> But death by drowning on an inland sea ...
>
> (467)

It is a part of the basic requirements of simple language to pare the
feeling into the facing of another's suffering. 'Plain style'. It needs
careful examination to perceive how the 'plain style' here works
cooperatively with the narrative's lethal detail, and, as Winter's
would have inquired, to show the part played by metre in forming the whole. So, 1. plain style, 2. narrative, 3. metre, and 4. grief.

> Meanwhile,

(a)   Your lungs collapsed, // and the machine, unstrained,
       Did all your breathing now. Nothing remained ...
                                                        (467)
and, earlier

(b)   I heard you wake up from the same bad dream ...
                                                        (465)

Under the pressure of grief (4) the language in (b), monosyl-
labically, as in Wordsworth's 'Michael', breaks down the metre
so that there are – to my ear – no stress syllables and only two
final durational ones. One must count the syllables to perceive
the prosodic structure. The lightness of the touch deliberately belies
the strength of feeling. And the monosyllabic words assist in this

because monosyllables by definition have no weaker or stronger syllables, but are moulded to stress by the other factors of meaning and syntax-position in the sentence and line. And with respect to (a) the plain style (1) is modified by the sudden casual introduction of the most appalling fact – 'Your lungs collapsed'. One is again reminded of the casual way in which all of Michael's hopes, vested in his son, are dispersed:

> Wrought at the Sheep-fold. Meantime Luke began
> To slacken in his duty; and, at length,
> He in the dissolute city gave himself
> To evil courses: ignominy and shame
> Fell on him, so that he was driven at last
> To seek a hiding-place beyond the seas...
>
> (442–7)

The nature of the breathtaking effect in both poems is achieved by the governance of the bare economy of the narrative. It is, of course, a matter of individual listening, but, to my ear, the durational syllables (–) as opposed to the stressed ones (/) frequently instigate a lightness of touch which co operates with the plain language to underpin his friend's physical collapse and his own grief. It is enough.

Appendix
Poets on Poetry

Free verse; verse free?

Jon Glover

Whenever one thinks about metre, rhyme and free verse[1] one reaches
for the experts or for one's childhood or for examples. Giving an
account of what a poet *has* done is hard enough; there are so many,
often contradictory, ways of *showing up* (must we always 'analyse'?)
what is there in a poem. Saying what has been done *well* is just as
hard and saying what a poet should do *now* is virtually impossible.

It is interesting to reflect on the extent to which we, as critics and
poets, learn to praise 'unity'. Thus we look to the 'overall context'
of the way in which a poem organises lines and rhythms to govern
the reading of particular lines and phrases. Take, for example, the
opening lines of 'Strange Meeting' by Wilfred Owen[2] and 'Death
of a Son' by Jon Silkin.[3] Owen's 'It seemed that out of battle I
escaped . . .' and Silkin's 'Something has ceased to come along with
me' taken in isolation have some similarities. Both place the subject
in a state of uncertainty ('It seemed . . .', 'Something has ceased   ')
Both create the illusion of using simple English in a grammatically
normal, conversational way. In fact both are probably quite unlike
the way one would use these words as part of a 'real' conversation
(Q: 'Where have you been?' A: 'It seemed that out of the battle . . .';
Q: 'What have you lost?' A: 'Something has ceased . . .' Probably
not). The 'oddness' of the verbal structure in each case is possibly
linked to the fact they are both ten-syllable lines with a fairly clear
iambic echo in the background. They sound natural *because* of the
regularity of the echo although the natural word order has implicitly been altered to establish or 'fit' the echo. After several readings one forgets that there could be any other way of structuring
those words. But both first lines are completely altered when the
second line is added; the rhythms of each are transformed, not
least because Owen's first line needs to fit into the grammar of the

1.   Actually the title of a refreshingly approachable book. G.S. Fraser,
     Metre, Rhyme and Free Verse (London: Methuen 1970).
2.   Jon Stalworthy, ed., *The Poems of Wilfred Owen* (London: The Hogarth
     Press, 1985).
3.   Jon Silkin, *Selected Poems* (London: Sinclair-Stevenson, 1994).

whole three-line sentence whereas Silkin's stops, the iambic echo
is 'refused' and he establishes an initial thoughtful hesitancy:

> It seemed that out of battle I escaped
> Down some profound dull tunnel, long since scooped
> Through granites which titanic wars had groined.
>
> Something has ceased to come along with me.
> Something like a person: something very like one.
> And there was no nobility in it
> Or anything like that.

In Owen the alliterative drive quickly emerges and this profoundly
affects the iambic potential which is largely counterbalanced by the
force of something like a Middle English stress count. The lines
on paper are defined clearly by syllable count, stress/alliterative
count and para-rhyme although, probably, if one simply heard the
poem read out loud the 'movement' of the grammatical sense units
between lines and across line endings would make the listener feel
he was hearing complex free verse. After its initial 'refusals' both in
the sense ('Something . . . Something . . . no . . . anything . . .') and the
rhythms, Silkin's poem becomes equally 'rhetorical' in its progress
to a dramatic conclusion. Yet it turns out that the repetitions and
the implicit question and answer structure of the poem as a whole,
which sound highly organized, are not part of a metrical, regularly
repeating stanza pattern but are actually a form of 'spaced out' free
verse. Again, the listener might be deceived, it does not sound like
what one 'sees' on the page.

But the demand for unity – some defining characteristic – as a
way of 'explaining' either the qualities of 'free verse' or 'patterned
verse', of whatever form, may itself be a red herring. I remember
being impressed (and relieved) by the discovery of 'prose poems'
and poems like William Carlos Williams' *Paterson*, which incorpor-
ated whole sections of 'real' prose. I liked the changes of gear from
verse to prose as much as the rhythmic qualities of each. Was
I making the best of a bad job by identifying in other poets the
'discontinuity' of perception implicit in the different organising
'visions' of combined and contrasted verse and prose as a new, over-
riding principle? Would I be 'failing' as a poet if I used this principle of 'discontinuous' versification and 'dislocated' vision myself
rather than writing in conventional stanzas or, at least, aiming for

respectable free verse? Was poetry that used prose the easiest game of tennis without a net: prose as the ultimate form of free verse?

The first poem to be written of the *Our Photographs*[1] sequence, which was to dominate much of my work for twenty years, was a prose poem, 'Away'. Many others have combined the relative freedom of prose with a more 'concentrated' passage of verse. The verse itself has varied from free verse using short or long 'sense units' to break lines to poems which use a fairly strict syllable count. However, I am aware that a syllable count which does not have an ear cocked to rhythmic pattern can become arbitrary or awkward. A recent reviewer, Keith Silver,[2] has said that the combined prose and verse poems mark a failure of 'versatility in each form'. Perhaps. I suppose I feel enormous respect for any contemporary poet who can, with confidence, use regular patterning structures. Equally, I respect those whose free verse takes on an identifiable, characteristic tone. Am I a victim of 'hearing' too much? Or not enough? Should it all sound 'better' than I can make it now? Could someone else turn my prose into decent free verse? Would this be a form of 'translation' or just a demonstration of better 'craftsmanship'? How does any poet, looking at the blank piece of paper in front of him, 'know'?

1. Jon Glover *Our Photographs* (Manchester: Carcanet, 1986).
2. *P.N. Review*, 105 (Manchester: University of Manchester, Sept.–Oct. 1995), p. 71.

Mixed modes

Dennis Silk

I

It struck me there was an important point you turned away from. Will *one* passage of verse combine the apparently antithetical features, or will say a passage in free verse follow a metrical one? And how will it follow? Will it derive from the previous passage by restating or discussing part of the earlier metrical passage in free verse, doing variations on it, then continuing its own course till a metrical passage succeeds it in the same way? Or is there a way of fusing rhythmically the metrical and free verse passages into *one* passage? Something very like this happens in some stanzas of Berryman's *Dream Songs*. He seems to be testing the limits of song.

I believe some kind of marriage of the two will be consummated, maybe by a new new shift in our hearing. (Both 'news' intended.)

In the old account of the digging of the Silwan tunnel, the miners began at opposite ends, then steered toward one another in the dark as each group of miners heard the other at work.

II A TENTATIVE NOTE ON METRE AND FREE VERSE

In the case of Eliot and Pound, perhaps even Auden and MacNeice, casting around for freer rhythms they had a firm base in traditional metres that can't be taken for granted with later poets. The main cause, probably, is the diminished study of Greek and Latin at school, though there are other general changes in the sense of rhythm that block use of the older metres.

To offset this, perhaps poetry workshops should be run by poets with a good sense of both metre and the several kinds of free verse, and with students who study both.

It may be objected that practice of one style precludes another, or at any rate its incorporation into one's own style. I believe there can only be clear gain.

For the first time, the entire history of English poetry is spread out before us. Poets not properly edited till now include the indispensable Wyatt, Skelton, Smart, Swift, Rochester and Clare. The feminists are clarifying also their own canon of lost women poets, for instance Lady Mary Wroth. It would be sad to lose this new perspective out of a narrow adherence to one form or other of free verse. The open field is wide and long enough to include past (how past?) poetry and the Black Mountain school.

I envisage a cutting room where rhythm has been cut into a huge number of shapes. Unborn rhythms circulate also in this room, and wait for new shapes to be cut out of them by patient and courageous poets. Rhythm extends the entire length and breadth of this room, malleable and generous, and looks around nervously for sharp-eared poets.

Another image would be of a new kind of loom, with more than the one warp and weft. These infinite series of threads will work their way into one another, in ways hard to imagine now. The cloth they weave would be the marriage of the centuries.

A few tentative suggestions, for the most part about longish poems . . .

The first lines of a section following a section say in hexameters recapitulates in free verse some of its images and meanings, highlights them, develops them according to its own logic, then channels its rhythms into a third section, perhaps in couplets. It would be like a window opening, or the collision of waves from different seas.

A free verse section, that is, emerges or is extracted from a preceding metrical one, and a metre can be extracted in the same way from the preceding free verse section. There is a real chance to weave together the great experiments of the century with the older metres (new enough in their time).

One or two more suggestions.

A section with a concrete meaning could be abstracted in a following free verse section, bricks falling all around one's head.

A sonnet begins grandly and ends with a stutter. In a sonnet cycle, the stutter would be picked up and transformed.

Language breaks down into discrete units, then into the excretion of language: grunts, groans, sobs, sighs. A serene sovereign of a splendid and assured verse-movement declines into a winded cross-country runner.

A building-up follows.

Syllabics

Thom Gunn

Syllabic verse overlaps disconcertingly with both metrical and free verse, each of which is defined by what the other is not: for like meter, it depends on counting (of syllables instead of accents), but like free verse, it must avoid metrical pattern. Early examples of syllabics may be found in the work of Robert Bridges, Elizabeth Daryush and Marianne Moore. The trouble with these early experiments is that the long line of Bridges and the elaborate stanza patterns of Moore, being discernible to the eye but not to the ear, tend to make the rhythms indistinguishable from those of cadenced prose or free verse. I find it interesting that Moore, in fact, rearranged some of her early free verse poems as syllabics, thus tacitly admitting a close resemblance between the forms. Much of her poetry is as good as any I know, the life of the language and the agility of the phrasing compensating for any incoherence in the form, but what Moore has done in her syllabic poems is to fit her words into what Hugh Kenner calls a 'grid'. Such a process of fitting has little effect on the reader, who is able to check on the accuracy and ingenuity of the poem's scheme only by counting syllables on the fingers. It is as if the act of counting answered a need on the part of the writer alone: perhaps it provides some objective security in that place beyond meter where improvisation has replaced rules.

This last, indeed, was the charm that *I* found in syllabics. I grew up in my time and place writing in rhyme and meter. But in my twenties, wanting to pursue some of the effects I found in the American masters of free verse, I looked for a way to educate my ear in other musics than the iambic. I found it in the syllabic *short* lines developed with such originality by Donald Hall in his early poetry. In a poem about Charlotte Corday he wrote:

> Charlotte, the will begins to
> revise you to leather. How
> volition hurts the skin of girls!

The stanza is made up of two seven-syllable lines followed by one of eight. Any accent-pattern reminiscent of traditional meter is avoided. The verse-movement that results is of a wondering tentativeness, characteristic of much free verse and syllabic composition, as though the mind were groping after ideas and images, acquiring them only in the moment of transcription. I found this tone very attractive.

Using such a form, which would still give me external rule by which to measure my lines, I tried to teach myself new rhythms. My favourite line was of seven syllables, but I also used eight- and nine-syllable lines with a certain success: in lines longer than these I found my rhythms were becoming too prosy. My most efficient use of the form was probably in two poems I wrote in 1959, 'Considering the Snail' and 'My Sad Captains'. My clumsiest was in a poem called 'Loot'. At worst, syllabics will be simply a chunk of writing chopped into even lengths, which might as well have been composed as prose; but at best, there emerges, against all probability, a certain integrity to the line which the ear starts to recognize. After a few tries, you find that you can compose a poem in seven-syllable lines without having to check on your fingers. (Philip Levine, who was investigating these possibilities at around the same time, has made a similar claim.) Syllabic poetry is a minor form, but it is distinct.

Syllabics were a brief episode in my career. I haven't done anything in them since 1965. They were a stage in my education, after which I have tried out various kinds of free verse, but I have found that I can achieve the widest variety of effects in the traditional accentual-syllabic meter I started out with. (I speak for myself alone, not being proscriptive or theoretical by temperament.)

TWO POSTSCRIPTS

(1)   Here is a short list of good poems in syllabics:

>   Robert Bridges, 'Poor Poll'
>   Marianne Moore, 'The Fish'
>   Donald Hall, 'Three Poems from Edvard Munch' (*The Dark
>   Houses*)
>   Philip Levine, 'Animals are Passing from our Lives' (*Not
>   This Pig*)
>   Alan Stephens, 'My Friend the Motorcyclist' (*In Plain Air*)

It is possible that some of John Donne's Holy Sonnets (e.g. 'At the Round Earth's Imagined Corners') are written according to syllabic principles. Perhaps their masterful rhythmic effects are more easily spoken about in these than in other terms.

(2)   In syllabics you must have a consistent theory of elision. (That of Bridges was very complicated.) You have to decide if you are to count such words as 'history' or 'luckier' or 'different' as two or three syllables.

Forms and inspirations[1]

Jon Silkin

May I make one reservation with respect to Vikram Seth's lucid and interesting essay on his poetry (*LRB*, 29 September), with its persuasive apologia for regular form and rhyme? In his useful discussion of the first four lines of Owen's 'Anthem for Doomed Youth' he rightly says that the fourth version he quotes is *'less* dense *less* compressed than the third draft' and concludes: '"Load every rift with ore" has to be balanced with "Allow the poem, to breathe".' The points are well made, and I take them. But I wonder if the virtues he argues for must invariably be enshrined in regular forms and rhythms – which is, I believe, the implication of much of this essay. Metre and rhyme do not necessarily produce clearer thought or feeling than free verse. I am not 'against' the use of regular form; the poems of mine *LRB* has printed are that way. But Mr Seth's comparison of his own free verse with work of his in regular, stanzaic forms does not establish that the verse was better only because it was regular and metrical. He chose one solution and found it worked. To argue from such a success that regular and stanzaic forms are the better or even the most likely approach seems unrealistic. It may be, for instance, that a success in regular form – producing the effect of ease – may have pre-empted an even more substantial success in another form. Also: I wonder if the regular and metrical forms he apparently prefers do not only accommodate but encourage authorial intrusion and direction. I don't know, but I do wonder.

1. Letter to *LRB* (1988).

Free and metrical verse

Rodney Pybus

As writers and readers we are surely fortunate in now being able to choose from a wide variety of poetic resources, some modern or post-modern, some more than 2000 years old. We may allude to forms or use them strictly, incorporate Biblical/Hebrew-derived parallelism or improvise on iambics, to enrich as well as to offer part of the meaning of the poem; we may engender and pattern rhythm in any number of ways, we may rhyme consistently, inconsistently, or not at all. I still maintain, after some thirty years' wrestling, that it is at least as difficult to write convincing free verse as it is to write a sonnet or rhyming couplets or iambic tetrameters. 'It's no use inventing fancy laws for free verse,' said D.H. Lawrence. No indeed. But, as Auden pointed out, you need an ear as good as Lawrence's, or nearly so, to write free verse well.

It may in part be the fact that my education taught me to write quantitative verse (e.g. passable Latin hexameters and Greek elegiacs, whose metres depend on quantity, i.e. the duration of 'long' and 'short' syllables, rather than on stress/accent), long before I could write a half-decent line in English which has kept me away from strict forms – I've let myself be carried on the language's accentual back towards cadence, and away from chalk-dust and anapaests or dactyls. Perhaps by saying 'too heavily' I reveal my own prejudices. I mean that I believe contemporary English, an essentially accentual language, does not lend itself to superimposed classical metrics, with the exception of iambics. I prefer the 'cadences' of free verse, in the modern sense of rhythmical patterns, the 'flow', not just the 'fall' of the final few syllables or lines. I like the challenge of searching for a new form each time, finding a way out of silence. 'In my book of Genesis', says Charles Simic, 'poetry is the orphan of silence.'

My sense of the old conflict between the metronome and the musical phrase (to borrow Ezra Pound's succinct formulation a hundred – it feels like a thousand – years ago) is that it's time for a truce because the war's actually over, and has been for some time. A surprising number of people disagree, however, so here are a few bones from the skeleton of an argument. (Rumour has it that there are even some metrophiles around who haven't yet realised there's anything to squabble about . . .)

1. Formal verse and free verse are by now surely visible as different sides of the same coin. Or, better, different expressions of the same face. Rhyme and metre are now optional constituents of a form rather than prerequisites. Their aesthetic functions are different from those existing before the mid-nineteenth century, when modern free verse began to appear.

2. Problems arise when this free/metred verse relationship is forgotten/ignored/not realized: the result is too often free verse that really is chopped up prose, expressing, usually, poorly focused emotion or personal responses of no value to anyone but the writer. See *passim* almost any English-American little magazine and far too many books of the past thirty years. ('Ernest', said Gertrude Stein, 'remarks are not literature.' Indeed.) Of course, the result may be metrical verse that's still in whalebone corsets.

3. Whether we use strict metres, with room for due substitution, improvisation, etc. in certain feet or not, rhyme or not, we are using a mode of writing which demands consideration of breath(ing), therefore time (timing), organization and structure, and a relationship between words-ideas-emotions and *the line* before the sentence or stanza/paragraph. (Too obvious to need saying? See any little magazine . . . etc.). Particularly in free verse, we need, very badly need, the *ear*, as well as the eye: if cadences are true alternatives to metre, to give variety of rhythm and therefore energy of various kinds, to enact and convey urgencies or otherwise of feeling, of poetic fulfilment, we need to learn or re-learn to hear them properly. And the foregoing is not a reason to become insensitive to the relationship of lineation to phrasing and syntax beyond the line.

4. The individual writer/reader now finds a tradition different from that existing in the early years of the century. So let us accept that a poet may now use, eclectically, any strict forms without necessarily being typecast as fuddy-duddy, reactionary (cultural-political), in favour of social elitism (it is not a sign of incipient fascism to re-explore the possibilities of *terza rima* in English – witness Douglas Dunn and 'Dante's Drum-kit'), anti-democratic or authoritarian – see Tony Harrison *passim*. It is, incidentally, a somewhat peculiar but, some would say, encouraging 'sign of the times' (though not *The Times*) that Harrison has not only successfully used his strict forms in a thoroughly contemporary way in his

television 'essays' (e.g. *The Shadow of Hiroshima*, C4 TV, 1995) but has been sent to 'read the metre' in Bosnia by *The Guardian*. I wonder how long it is since a newspaper printed anything like this: 'Last night he filed the following poem from Donji Vakuf, which had just fallen to the Bosnian Muslim army.'

Let us accept too that free verse is not a sign of slipshod decadence, democratic allegiance, political correctness, American-worship, colloquial vigour (as if by definition), or mimesis of 'the way people acksherly talk, yeah?' ('Ernest, remarks . . .'). Free verse form can be strict – free verse is not 'free' – according to its own rules: e.g. in the title group of Galway Kinnell's *When One Has Lived a Long Time Alone* (Knopf, 1990) where each of the eleven 13-line poems begins and ends with these words as a line. In between the syntax swerves or saunters, pauses or surges, but never halts by a full-stop till the end of each poem with its tender reflections on loss, inner exile, memory. And for cadence married to varied repetitions, patterns and echoes, themselves reminiscent of the seventeenth century and the 1611 Bible – cadence which has as much emotional, intellectual and persuasive power as metre – one need look no further than MacDiarmid's 'On a Raised Beach' from the early 1930s. Seamus Heaney in 'A Torchlight Procession of One: On Hugh MacDiarmid' (*The Redress of Poetry*, Faber, 1995) rightly uses it to draw attention to Larkin's blindness in omitting MacDiarmid from *The Oxford Book of 20th Century English Verse*. And he is right to use the word 'luminous' about lines such as these – they are like light on an inner sea, though, unlike so much contemporary free verse, they do not try (in MacDiarmid's words) to appeal to 'any easier audience':

> Nothing has stirred
> Since I lay down this morning an eternity ago
> But one bird. The widest door is the least liable to intrusion,
> Ubiquitous as the sunlight, unfrequented as the sun.
> The inward gates of a bird are always open.
> It does not know how to shut them.
> That is the secret of its song,
> But whether any man's are ajar is doubtful.
> I look at these stones and I know little about them,
> But I know their gates are open too . . .

On the practice of free verse

Marvin Bell

What is free verse? Many have tried to describe it by measuring a line. A line might be a unit of rhythm, syntax or breath (Allen Ginsberg claimed to have written 'Howl' one breath to a line), or it might be a unit of thought, or time, or even a visual unit. One could assume only that, whatever else, a line was always a unit of attention. In any case, rules were made to be broken. For the free verse writer, the rap goes: 'Learn the rules. Break the rules. Make up new rules. Break the new rules.'

Talk about 'the line' by itself is never sufficient because lines hold hands with syntax. While the effects of free verse may rest with the line, the secret to composing those lines is in the syntax. Syntax provides the occasions for enjambments and end-stops, as well as for caesuras within lines. Syntax distributes the syllables and, in English, the stresses. Thus, the key to free verse may be the sentence. Which in turn suggests that a poem written in one or more paragraphs, whether one calls it 'prose-poetry' or 'poetic prose', should perhaps be considered also a peripheral form of free verse.

Free verse writers tend to argue that free verse is simply a variation of beautiful prosody: thus, Williams' use of the term 'variable foot', Charles Olson's theory of 'projective verse', and various attempts to scan free verse lines that are none the less open to rhythmic interpretation. In the 1960s, Denise Levertov published in *Poetry* (Vol. 106, No. 6, September 1965) an attractive essay about 'organic form': the free verse poem growing naturally – organically – like a flower. But a truly *free* verse must make room also for the wilful, the prosaic, the imitative, the unshapely (the list, for example, and other patterns of organization that have no necessary relationship to rhythm) – all the 'anti-poetic'. For these, too, in the right hands, can be made artful. Gertrude Stein, speaking about Picasso's paintings, noted that the new always seems ugly. The point here is that the rhythms of free verse are one subject, but free verse *in toto* is another, bearing on definitions of poetry having to do with such aspects of writing as imagination and metaphor that may at times overwhelm considerations of rhythm. It is a controversial subject.

That said, I confess that I am partial to that seemingly 'organic' free verse that 'remembers' meter and employs at least a minimal elasticity of line. I am also partial to a line that knows no bounds. Any attempt to describe free verse must first see it as a variation developed in opposition. Mid-century, there occurred in American poetry an explosion of individual poetic voices in free verse. By the early 1960s, many respected poets, formalists by training, had switched to free verse: Robert Lowell, Galway Kinnell, Anne Sexton, Sylvia Plath, W.S. Merwin, James Wright and John Logan among them. Others – Gary Snyder, John Ashbery, Robert Bly, Kenneth Koch and Frank O'Hara, for example – had not published as much formalist verse, but had certainly been schooled to read it. Surely, even Ginsberg had come by way of the Psalms and the poetry of Christopher Smart and Walt Whitman, texts which by anaphora and other rhetorical devices checked the freedom of free verse.

Of course, there were also brilliant formalists who stayed formalists (Richard Wilbur, Anthony Hecht, James Merrill and Howard Nemerov, for example), and some who seemed to stand in between (one thinks of the syllabics of Donald Justice and Thom Gunn, and the accentuals of Elizabeth Bishop and William Stafford).

By the 1980s, however, free verse had replaced formalist verse as the poetic convention of the time. The freedom of free verse by then permitted a line so neutral in character that it could be viewed as 'transparent', a line that permitted an easy passage of content and which earned credibility because of its 'naturalness'. Also, much free verse was by then being written in deference to the look of the poem on the page. Those who desired a more or less consistent line ended up writing tetrameter, pentameter or hexameter, with sprung feet and an occasional variant line: a 'free verse' closer to accentual verse than to free verse.

On the other hand, one saw a gradual fading of potential in much of our free verse as it lost its power of contradistinction and surprise while becoming the uneventful style of our age. It was still in the nature of free verse to defy expectation. But how to defy further when the reader had become used to both free verse and formalist verse? Poetic defiance in the nineties seems to have been reduced to saying, 'All right, so you expect from poetry – "free" or "formal" – depth, resonance, connectedness, richness, seriousness, and complexity? Well, we'll give you surfaces, cacophony, disjunction, pop, camp, and complication: take it or leave it.'

Perhaps because of its appetite for the 'anti-poetic', free verse has always had staunch opponents. In the late 1980s, a band of young 'new formalists' claimed that free verse was a noble experiment whose time was past, but those insisting the loudest had tin ears, making it difficult to take their word for it. Orpheus needs ears, and so does his audience.

I myself feel easy about the rubbery definition of 'free verse'. The best free verse writer is just another kind of formalist, and understands that free verse must reinvent itself with each new example. Free verse can be a style-by-default; I wouldn't forbid it. But free verse that emerges from a pattern is of another intention.

William Stafford has written that 'an artist is someone who lets the material talk back'. The free verse poet must provide this formal urgency from inside, but then the formalist who does not likewise internalize his or her forms is just as likely to write woodenly. Duke Ellington: 'It don't mean a thing if it ain't got that swing.' Doo-wah, doo-wah, doo-wah, doo-wah.

I have written enough free verse to know that the poet who keeps at it ends up out on a limb. But above and below him in the tree are the lyricist, the epic poet, the dramatic poet, the accentualist, the syllabicist, the writers of sonnets and villanelles and sestinas and pantoums, the compositors of concrete and typographic verse, the prose-poets, the blank verse meditators, the authors of songs and odes and epigrams, and all the others. The sound of poetry is the tree-sound made by all these birds at once, and to my mind it would be a loss to cut off a single limb.

Poetry as discovery and potential

Anne Cluysenaar

When I begin to write a poem (as against getting the first inkling of it) I seem to be harking after something to the right, just at the back of my head. To turn as it were directly towards it would threaten to dispel this impression, and with it the possibility of the poem. So I cast about – always with two or more words at a time, because what I am seeking to hear is a stretch of language running like a blade along the grain of what remains hidden. Any relationship to my subject may seem quite tangential. But from the rhythm, intonation, sounds and syntax of this first phrase I know that the rest of the poem will develop, provided I continue to keep 'in touch'.

Such experiences serve to suggest how intimately rhythm can be implicated in the genesis of a poem and how closely rhythm is related to other aspects of language. I seldom sketch rapidly, returning to tighten things up. Instead, before I go on, each phrase must seem right in itself and in relation to what came earlier. Even so, when the first draft is finished, I may notice rhythms that displease me (no doubt because the speed of reading is so very different from the speed of composition) and it is these that most often cause me to revise. There may for example be uncertainties of rhythm, due to alternative possibilities of pace or intonation. Unmetred verse especially requires one to think hard about how formal or informal word-choice or syntax may guide a reader to the right syllabification of words; while metre, after the first line or two (if only for an experienced reader) will tend to override ambiguities.

Once I have an appropriate rhythm, problems have to do not with creating regularity but with avoiding monotony and creating effects pleasing in themselves (whether smooth or syncopated) and above all significant. Few decisions derive from guidelines provided by poetic tradition; these are too coarse to be given the last word during composition. Instead, I learn from enjoying (or not enjoying) the work of others. New skills require conscious attention for a while, then are internalized. And this is fortunate since it is true, as Baudelaire remarked, that the poet is a centipede whose ability to walk largely depends on not thinking about how all the legs work. I remember for instance learning to reverse the iambic foot after a caesura, and then learning by experience that this 'trick of a trade' applies only if the resulting metrical energy is what the particular line needs and fits in with one's own poetic 'lingo': and there is no rule to tell you when *that* is the case! Which might be said to illustrate the difference between skill and art, and the meaning of the old saw 'rules are made to be broken'.

Holding the many-stranded thread of the initial phrase (now a more appropriate metaphor), I feel my way into a labyrinth only partly foreseen. At this point, overall decisions have to be made about rhythm. This is probably the most fundamental technical choice of all: I have had poems refuse to come in four-beat lines but fly onto the page once the line is shortened to three beats – and this without any other change to the language already found. Assuming each line is going to be based on the same rhythmic principles, it may be built on (1) a fixed number of stresses, but free syllabification (since English is stress-timed, each line will take approximately the same time) – *sprung rhythm* might be a type with added rules; (2) free stressing, but a fixed number of syllables (this allows lines to be of unequal length in time – though of course they need not always be, since I am free to chose the same number of stresses); (3) a fixed number both of stresses and syllables, but an irregular relationship between stress and syllable (which returns me to lines of the same length in time but allows for free rhythmic choice); (4) the same as in (3) but with a fixed overall relationship between stress and syllabification (that is, strict metre); (5) a more complex version of (5), in which although the line can be read metronomically (say, as regular iambs) the sense requires that it be read very freely, so that the placing and number of stresses in a line varies considerably (Shakespeare's sonnets avail themselves of this possibility; notionally five-beat lines may be actualized as anything between (in my perception) three and eight beats and the result, for a perceiver still subliminally aware of the potential metre, is 'counterpoint'); (6) no regularities of stress or syllabification: ad hoc choices to suit significance and of course euphony. Since no verse, as Eliot remarked, is 'free' for a poet who 'wants to do a good job', this last option properly includes the creation of rhythmic contrasts and of patterns of syntax, sound, meaning unique to their context (patterns which may also, of course, be present in lines built on other principles, but which are then perhaps less continuously of the essence).

As a linguist I am aware that, in language-acts I perceive as poetry, phonological, syntactic and lexical structures are typically (though not of course all the time) doing more than the language-system requires of them. Poetry makes use of the structures of language in a special way, saturating them with significances relevant to the individual poem. It makes use in language-acts of potentials which language-systems enable but do not enforce. This applies even to lines which, at first sight, may appear very simple, for example, these two lines from a haiku-based verse in my *Vaughan Variations*: 'The lily's petals ... begin to open'. As a result of having acquired distinctness in the system by distinguishing meanings (say, *pet* from *bet*), the English phoneme /p/ is recognizable when it occurs in a particular language act. The system also gives perceptual status to stress, syllabification and so on. *Petals* and *open* come here into a one-off framework created by both line and rhythm: they appear as the last two syllables of their respective five-syllable lines and as the last /+ of a repeated rhythm: + ^ /+ ^ /+ ... +/ ^ + ^ /+; ^ here indicates word-boundaries, important because they introduce variety in an otherwise regular pattern. (The tensioning of rhythm against word or phrase boundaries, so beautifully demonstrated in Robert Frost's *Stopping by Woods*, seems to be an essential feature of all rhythmic success, but its importance for regular metres could scarcely be over-emphasized.) The recurrence of /p/ in *petals* and *open* is 'offset' in relation to word-stress (*pet* initiates a stressed syllable, *pen* an unstressed syllable). But the rest of the framework should be regular enough to draw the reader's attention to /p/ (if only subliminally) especially as there is no other important sound-repetition between these lines. Such a repetition might of course have no significance – it is always for the perceiver to sense whether it has or not, in the given context. In this example, I hope that the sound-link established between these words may bring to mind the slight oddity of saying that *petals* open and so lead the perceiver's mind to the hidden reality of the bud, in which the future (both flower and pollen) lies. Stillness and attention to nature is also essential to this passage, as to the whole poem, so if the second /p/ evokes a sense of the tiny sound the petals must make when they first come apart, so much the better.

From the writer's point of view, setting up such effects (consciously or otherwise) is a means of delving into experience. The difficulty, slight or great, of creating them opposes easy solutions. They make one ransack dimensions of awareness that might otherwise be left undisturbed. The more difficult the demands, the deeper and more unexpectedly (within the limits of technical competence) they enable one to explore, and be explored. But the impression with which I began, of something beckoning from the right-hand corner of the mental eye, suggests yet another reason for the inspirational power of form. For while language in its ordinary uses is largely the business of the left hemisphere of the brain, the right hemisphere controls synthetic and holistic operations, especially those involving images, metaphor and (most relevant here) music. Perhaps the brain has a sense of its own workings? Creating poetry may be a matter of testing language against forms of ordering offered by the right hemisphere. The whole brain would then be fully engaged, explaining why awareness of outer events may be almost obliterated. And since these forms of ordering are too complex to control by merely conscious means, subconscious forces are brought automatically into play and are then perhaps more readily available for other purposes too.

For a listener or reader, though, the language of a poem may work only in ordinary ways, without any additional potential being realised. In other words, poetic functions are optional. Even structures too obvious to be perceptually missed (say, strict metre or the line-unit itself) may fail to achieve their semantic potential. Not only that, but once they *have* been noticed (perhaps through critical study) they may still not be integrated into perception on any given occasion. Moreover, Gestalt psychology has shown how certain perceptual features are the property only of wholes, not of the parts which make them up. Nevertheless, a poem remains *capable* of delivering its charge. It is in fact a uniquely individual, stable language-act, more resistant than most language-acts to linguistic and social change: aspects of its internal structure remain a reliable guide to its meaning.

When it is fully experienced, a poem is form-saturated to an unusual degree with significance. Poetic significance is itself, therefore, extraordinarily rich. Both hemispheres of the brain must work simultaneously for this potential to be realised. The complexity of such an experience intensely engages the perceiver's subconscious, as it did the maker's. For these reasons, the impact can be overwhelming. No matter how detailed and sensitive our critical tools, this is a matter of experience, inaccessible to explication. This is the area from which, as George Steiner has insisted, the sense of 'presence' cannot be banished. Just as one reads 'as if' communicating with the writer, so one composes 'as if' self-exploration were continuously doubled by a sense of communication with the potential reader. And surely this 'as if' has a firm basis in linguistic fact, since to perceive in full the intricate structures of a poem is necessarily to inhabit the distinctive traces of another human mind.

Never the twain shall meet in the flesh, of course, but there is something more to be said concerning the role of rhythm. I tried earlier to indicate what an important role rhythmic choice may play in the genetic phases of a poem. Since most poems have to be resurrected by the reader from a 'score' on a page, its maker's ability to control perception of rhythm *in text* is crucial. But if the transaction represented by a text is to be completed, it might be said that a reader too has one last task to fulfil. Certainly, I find that it is when I read *aloud* that I come closest to hearing the rhythmic-intonational pulse which brings a poem to life – closest, in fact, to feeling the voice of another person vibrate in my own body.

The prose poem

Robert Bly has, as one might expect, written a challenging essay on the inscaping of form in the prose poem, called 'The Prose Poem as an Evolving Form'. It was first published in his *Selected Poems* (1986) and is available in his book of prose poems, *What Have I Ever Lost By Dying?* (Bristol, Weatherlight Press, 1994).

Basil Bunting 1900–85:
a personal memoir

Connie Pickard[1]

Gateshead, Tyne and Wear
It is 26th April and ten days since the death of the poet Basil Bunting.
Sitting at the typewriter I can hear the wind in the back lane. The notes
on my table tell of a friendship between three unlikely people, bits of shared
experience, a few entries from a few diaries.

In the early days Basil, who was sixty-five before a book of his poetry
was published in Britain,[2] hated the idea of interviews, personal anecdotes,
letters – anything about the poet that took away attention from the work
itself. I didn't keep a continuous diary. There are not many entries, but I
am glad there are some notes to act as remembrancers. Forgive me, Basil.

Friday, 25 July 1969

Barry Scaum's house in Bensham, Gateshead
Sitting in the garden facing the sun – someone appears at the gate
– bronze face, hair flowing: Robert Bly, back from the Buddhist
monastery? No, it's Basil, looking incredibly young and large. He
is working on a new poem, about the Isabella pit in Throckley
which his father helped to sink – a poem about the life that takes
over when the pit is finished: the 'goaf' – waste, by-product – the
hole left after the seam has been cleared – the dark hole with ice-
cold spray – the dense foliage growing around the outside. Only
children visit the site, for the swimming, leaping in the air, half
a dozen at a time. A completely different country, and only a few
miles from Newcastle. Never-Never Land. My daughter Cath, playing with water, letting it flow through her toes. She is becoming a
big, fat, earthy lass; suddenly lays into Basil for some reason. Basil
busy with Chalmers Burns on Matthew Arnold's 'Scholar Gypsy'
for a memorial concert for Peter Ure [late Professor of English at the

1. Connie Pickard's memoir was first published in *Stand*, Vol. 26, No. 3 (1985).
2. See R.S. Woof, 'Basil Bunting's Poetry', *Stand*, Vol. 8, No. 2 (1966).

University of Newcastle]. Have got to get a copy of *Nature*, look out for Moon Dust coming to Wylam.

26 April 1975

Avenue Road, Bensham, Gateshead
Basil arrived. We talked and talked about John Collier, Spence Watson, Fox and Quakerism; about the split in Quakerism between pantheism and puritanism – the Bensham Settlement had been an attempt to harmonize the two; Whittaker and the Bach Choir; the Veitches and the People's Theatre. Basil's father and old Runciman had helped set up the first Labour candidate. It all happened here in a house in Jessy Dene.

On to Haughton Castle; we sit by the river, watch dippers. Great Whittingham. Narrow lanes and Bewick motifs. Batch of hens with very red combs; Taoist trees. Basil's face very lined now – lines of age, lineage like an ancient king, rattish laugh. Then talks of Abeize Coppe with the enthusiasm of a young man. Sweet Sips of Spiritual Wine . . . he wrote in a prose style quite unlike anyone else . . . all that has been lost.

Abeize Coppe would have got into Basil's good books on the strength of his name alone. One of the things I had noticed early on was the musical attachment Basil had to names. I was always 'Connie my dear' not because I was particularly nice at all but it had a better resonance and he would always give your name its full weight and measure . . . and I am not talking about the Domenico Scarlattis and Eric Bloodaxes, but about ordinary names. When he said my little daughter Catherine's name it was always with a full trill on the 'r'. It sounded like a small fountain. And all of the former Catherines were there too: the mystic, the great letter-writer, the king's wives. The length of the 'a' when he said 'Matthew' was pastoral. I could never say my son's name in the same way.

The notes from my diary are so sparse – they were not meant to be anything more than a jog to the memory. I had asked Basil about the Bensham Settlement because I wanted to know more about his relation to the North-East, though I was curious, too, about its history. I knew that Joseph Skipsey had visited the house, and we loved Basil's story how, as a baby, he had been dandled on the knee of the Pitman Poet. While attending Gaelic classes at Bensham Settlement I had found out that another North-East writer, Jack Common, had attended classes for the unemployed there in the Twenties. I wondered if Basil had ever met him, but he had not, neither in the North-East nor in London, where Jack Common had worked on *The Adelphi* – although Basil had been a friend of A.R. Orage and some *Adelphi* contributors had also written for *The New English Weekly*, Orage's paper.

Both Basil and Tom Pickard had been born in Scotswood. In 1900 this part of West Newcastle was still quite rural, still a residential area for well-known Quaker families. At the nearby pit Basil's father was the miners' doctor. By the time Tom was born forty-six years later, Scotswood had become a slum. About the time Tom's family were moving into their house on one of the new post-war estates on the outskirts of the town, Basil would have been returning to England after being expelled from Persia.

We all finally met in Wylam, further up the Tyne, in a beautiful and substantial house overlooking the river. We sat in the garden, in Sima's domain full of raspberries and other good things. Sima was Basil's second wife, whom he had met in Persia. On that day she had just been playing tennis; her long black hair was tied in a pink scarf and her eyes sparkled. The Bunting children were quite young: Tom very plump, and Maria an exquisite figure from a Persian miniature. In the background Basil's mother, then in her nineties, fussed over the poet, calling him 'Son' in a broad Northumberland accent. There were one or two Persian students and lots of animals in that big household. Sima cooked us a great spaghetti dinner and afterwards Basil made Turkish coffee.

On that first evening in Wylam, Basil, you read us some of your poems. We were amazed and delighted: 'Let them remember Samangan', 'Mesh cast for mackerel', but the revelation was 'Chomei at Toyama'. In 1931, when it was written, the story of the devastation of a city must have seemed something remote

> To appreciate present conditions
> collate them with those of antiquity.

Tom and I were a very odd couple. Tom was eighteen and had recently published a piece called 'Workless Teens' in *Anarchy*. I was older. I came from a pit village and had graduated from King's College [now the University of Newcastle upon Tyne] and then taught until I was expecting Matthew. I was living with Tom, but as I was not yet divorced from my first husband I was naturally asked to leave my job; in fact, it was suggested that I should go and live in another town – advice which people still tend to give me. Good advice, but impossible. When some superannuation money I had applied for miraculously turned up – a whole £180 – we decided we would start a bookshop. Crazy. I managed to persuade the City Fathers to let me rent a medieval tower in a very unsalubrious back lane in downtown Newcastle for ten bob a week. When publishers' reps used to call they suggested that a better idea would be to keep pigeons. Basil thought all this was a hoot, but he did not discourage us.

By chance Tom had met Pete Brown while hitch-hiking to London, and Pete had invited himself to read in the Tower when he was to pass through Newcastle in a few weeks' time. We asked Basil to come to Pete's reading and were amazed when he said he would. A few years before, poetry and jazz had come to the town, announced when the immortal words 'Bird Lives' started to appear on walls among the graffiti. Our friends Tony Jackson and Roy Robertson were reading Rexroth, Patchen and Snyder. At that time we had still read only one poem of Basil's, 'The Complaint of the Morpethshire Farmer', and had been expecting someone quite different, so that we were very pleased to find Basil shared our enthusiasm for Snyder. He introduced us to William Carlos Williams and Zukofsky.

When Basil himself read in the Morden Tower he had a great appeal for young people. He could not understand this. But just imagine him as he was then, his face quite thin, almost wolfish, or cadaverous, reading Villon with the intensity of his own experience; add the fact that many of the people who came to the Tower had faced arrest in peace demonstrations, and some were lads who themselves had seen the inside of prison because of trivial offences. Also, it could be quite chilly sitting on the floor of a medieval tower. One begins to understand that Basil's reading was an impressive experience.

But it was not always solemn. Basil had a strong sense of humour and sometimes reminded us of Groucho Marx. Someone was always requesting 'An arles, an arles for my hiring'. And we wondered who had been the original Margaret Dumont for whom it had been written. There was another occasion. During Allen Ginsberg's first reading in Newcastle he had dedicated to Basil the poem 'To an Old Poet in Peru'. After the reading Basil retaliated by out-singing 'The Howling King of the Beasts' (as Allen had ludicrously been described in the local evening paper). For every mantra that Allen performed Basil would sing a sweet Purcell aria or a lovely song of Campion's – the strong voice getting stronger and stronger in tone, the centuries rolling away, till after some very stern Victorian ballads we all collapsed laughing, and Allen fell with his head on Basil's knee.

Some years later there was another good day with Allen when he wanted to visit Durham Cathedral. Basil, I remember you both discussing prayer very learnedly in the cloisters, discussing the way Buddhist or medieval Christian monks dealt with wool-gathering. Allen was obviously never guilty of wool-gathering, because he quoted the inscription on Bede's tomb even before we reached it: *Hac sunt in fossa Baedae venerabilis ossa.* After we had also paid our respects to Cuthbert's bones, Allen noticed the little fossil remains of the sea lilies in the Frosterly marble pillars. Allen had a broken leg, and your eyes, Basil, were not too great, but in no time at all we were clambering into your jalopy, driving over hill and dale and walking through fields until we came to the old working of the quarries of Frosterly. It was a day of huge time-scales. Often it seemed that we had stepped into eternity with you.

There were other times like that – when, for instance, you were writing *Briggflatts* sitting in St John's churchyard and you read out some lines that you were really pleased with:

> You who can calculate the course
> of a biased bowl,
> shall I come near the jack?
> What twist can counter the force
> that holds back
> woods I roll?

Until then I had thought that when Pound had addressed you and Zukofsky as strugglers in the desert he was talking about the difficulties poets face in making a living or getting accepted. It was only then that I realised it was something quite different: it was about the seriousness of the work in itself.

I love *Briggflatts*, not only because it is a great poem but also because we were privileged to be around you while you were writing it, and I can see that it is only fitting that your ashes should be scattered over the meeting-house in Briggflatts. Indeed, that they should also go to America. However, it is Chomei that keeps coming into my mind. It could almost have been written for 1985.

Fathers fed their children and died,
babies died sucking the dead.
The priest Hoshi went about marking their foreheads
A, Amida, their requiem . . .

Anyone wishing to know what you were like in the last few years
need only read the last few verses of that poem.

> The moonshadow merges with darkness
> of the cliffpath,
> a tricky turn near ahead.
>
> Oh! There's nothing to complain about.
> Buddha says: 'None of the world is good.'
> I am fond of my hut . . .
>
> I have renounced the world;
> have a saintly
> appearance.
>
> I do not enjoy being poor,
> I've a passionate nature.
> My tongue
> clacked a few prayers.

Requiescat in Pace Basil Bunting, Great Northumbrian poet.

References

The references are listed in the order in which they are cited in the text.

CHAPTER 1

William Wordsworth, *The Poems* (two vols.), edited by John O. Hayden (Harmondsworth, Penguin Books, 1977).

Graham McMaster (ed.), *William Wordsworth*, Penguin Critical Anthologies (Harmondsworth, Penguin, 1972).

S.T. Coleridge, *Biographia Literaria*, edited by George Watson (London, Dent, 1956).

Walt Whitman, *The Complete Poems*, edited by Francis Murphy (Harmondsworth, Penguin, 1975).

Walt Whitman, *Leaves of Grass* (the first (1855) edition), edited by Malcolm Cowley (Harmondsworth, Penguin, 1986).

Walt Whitman, *Specimen Days in America* (London, George Routledge, nd).

Francis Murphy (ed.), *Walt Whitman*, Penguin Critical Anthologies (Harmondsworth, Penguin, 1969).

Gay Wilson Allen, *The Solitary Singer* (New York, Macmillan Co., 1955).

Gerard Manley Hopkins, *A Selection of His Poems and Prose*, edited by W.H. Gardner (London, Penguin, 1953).

Gerald Roberts (ed.), *Gerard Manley Hopkins: Selected Prose* (Oxford, Oxford University Press, 1980).

Claude Colleer Abbott (ed.), *The Letters of Gerard Manley Hopkins to Robert Bridges* (London, Oxford University Press, 1935).

F.R. Leavis, 'Gerard Manley Hopkins', in *New Bearings in English Poetry* (Harmondsworth, Penguin in association with Chatto and Windus, 1950 (1932), pp. 135–8 (pp. 119–42).

Herbert Read, 'Gerard Manley Hopkins', in *A Coat of Many Colours* (London, Routledge & Kegan Paul, 1956), pp. 160–3.

Charles O. Hartman, *Free Verse: An Essay on Prosody* (Princeton, Princeton University Press, 1980).

Harvey Gross, *Sound and Form in Modern Poetry* (Ann Arbor, Michigan University Press, 1968 (1964)).

Timothy Steele, *Missing Measures* (Fayetteville, The University of Arkansas Press, 1990).

G.N. Leech, *A Linguistic Guide to English Poetry* (Harlow, Longman, 1969).

G.S. Fraser, *Metre, Rhyme and Free Verse* (London, Methuen, 1970).

Bishop Robert Lowth, 'Of the Hebrew Metre', in *Lectures on the Sacred Poetry of the Hebrews*, translated from the Latin by G. Gregory (London, Thomas Tegg, 1835).

Terry Eagleton, *Literary Theory* (Oxford, Basil Blackwell, 1990 (1983)).

Geoffrey Hill, 'Redeeming the Time', in *The Lords of Limit* (London, André Deutsch, 1984).

CHAPTER 2

Maurice Evans (ed.), *Philip Sidney: The Countess of Pembroke's Arcadia* (Harmondsworth, Penguin, 1977).
Peter Jones (ed.), *Imagist Poetry* (Harmondsworth, Penguin, 1972).
H.D., *Selected Poems*, edited by Louis L. Martz (Manchester, Carcanet, 1988).
Wilfred Owen, *The War Poems*, edited by Jon Silkin (London, Sinclair-Stevenson, 1994).
Herbert Read, *Selected Poetry* (London, Sinclair-Stevenson, 1992).
Herbert Read, *The Contrary Experience: Autobiographies* (London, Faber and Faber, 1963).
Herbert Read, *Phases of English Poetry* (Norfolk, Connecticut, New Directions 19, 1951).
Herbert Read, *A Coat of Many Colours* (London, Routledge & Kegan Paul, 1956).
Charles O. Hartman, *Free Verse: An Essay on Prosody* (Princeton, Princeton University Press, 1980).
T.S. Eliot, *Collected Poems 1909–1962* (London, Faber and Faber, 1963).
Valerie Eliot (ed.), *The Waste Land: A Facsimile & Transcript of the Original Drafts* (London, Faber and Faber, 1971).
T.S. Eliot, *Inventions of the March Hare: Poems 1909–1917*, ed. Christopher Ricks (London, Faber and Faber, 1996).
T.S. Eliot, *Selected Prose of T.S. Eliot*, edited by Frank Kermode (London, Faber and Faber, 1975).
T.S. Eliot, *Selected Essays* (London, Faber and Faber, 1972 (1951)).
T.S. Eliot, *On Poetry and Poets* (London, Faber and Faber, 1971 (1957)).
T.S. Eliot, *After Strange Gods: A Primer of Modern Heresy* (London, Faber and Faber, 1934).
C.B. Cox and Arnold P. Hinchcliffe (eds.), *T.S. Eliot: The Waste Land*, Casebook Series (Basingstoke, Macmillan Press, 1992 (1986)).
Helen Gardner, *The Art of T.S. Eliot* (London, Faber and Faber, 1979 (1949)).
Raj Nath, 'The Waste Land: The Facsimile Edition', *The Literary Criterion*, pp. 69–74.
C.K. Stead, *Pound, Yeats, Eliot and The Modernist Movement* (Basingstoke, Macmillan Press, 1989 (1986)).
A. Walton Litz (ed.), *Eliot in His Time* (Princeton, Princeton University Press, 1973).
Angus Calder, *T.S. Eliot* (Brighton, Harvester Press, 1987).
Peter Ackroyd, *T.S. Eliot: A Life* (London, Hamish Hamilton, 1985).
Osamu Dazai, 'Thinking of Zero', in *Printed Matter*, Spring 1991 (Tokyo), p. 44.
The Norton Anthology of English Literature, 3rd edition, Vol. 2 (New York, Norton, 1974), p. 2164.
Adam Piette, *Imagination at War* (Basingstoke, Macmillan General Books, 1995).

CHAPTER 3

Ezra Pound: Collected Shorter Poems (London, Faber and Faber, 1968 (1952)).
The Cantos of Ezra Pound (London, Faber and Faber, 1975).
ABC of Reading (London, Faber and Faber, 1991 (1951)).
Ezra Pound, 'Affirmations: AS FOR IMAGISME', in *Ezra Pound: Selected Prose 1909–1965*, edited by William Cookson (London, Faber and Faber, 1978 (1973)), pp. 344–7.
Ezra Pound: Selected Letters 1907–1941, edited by D.D. Paige (London, Faber and Faber, 1982 (1950)).
John Speirs, 'Mr Pound's Propertius: *Homage to Sextus Propertius*' [1935]', in *A Selection from Scrutiny*, compiled by F.R. Leavis (Cambridge University Press, 1968), pp. 101–7.
R.P. Blackmur, 'Masks of Ezra Pound', 1933, pp. 78–112 and 'An Adjunct to the Muses' Diadem', 1946, pp. 113–20, both in *Form and Value in Modern Poetry* (New York, Doubleday & Company, 1957).
J.P. Sullivan, *Ezra Pound and Sextus Propertius* (Austin, The University of Texas Press, 1964).
John Esprey, *Ezra Pound's Mauberley: A Study in Composition* (London, Faber and Faber, 1955).
A. Alvarez, 'Craft and Morals' [Pound], in *The Shaping Spirit* (London, Hutchinson, 1963), pp. 48–72.
Wendy Stallard Flory, *Ezra Pound and The Cantos: A Record of Struggle* (New Haven, Yale University Press, 1980).
Leon Surette, *A Light from Eleusis: A Study of Ezra Pound's Cantos* (Oxford, Oxford University Press, 1979).
Peter Ackroyd, *Ezra Pound and his World* (Literary Lives) (London, Thames and Hudson, 1980).
Jon Silkin , *Out of Battle* (London, Routledge & Kegan Paul, 1987), pp. 202–6.

CHAPTER 4

The Complete Poems of D.H. Lawrence, edited by Vivian de Sola Pinto and F. Warren Roberts (Harmondsworth, Penguin, 1980 (1977)).
D.H. Lawrence, *Kangaroo* (Harmondsworth, Penguin, 1968 (1950)).
D.H. Lawrence, *Lady Chatterley's Lover* (Harmondsworth, Penguin, 1961).
D.H. Lawrence, *Selected Literary Criticism*, edited by Anthony Beal (London, Heinemann, 1969 (1967)).
The Letters of D.H. Lawrence, edited by Aldous Huxley (London, Heinemann, 1937), p. 515.
R.P. Blackmur, 'D.H. Lawrence and Expressive Form', 1935, in *Form and Value*, pp. 253–67.
Herbert Read, 'D.H. Lawrence', in *A Coat of Many Colours*, pp. 262–4.
A. Alvarez, 'D.H. Lawrence: The Single State of Man', in *The Shaping Spirit*, pp. 140–61.
F.R. Leavis, '"Thought" and Emotional Quality', 1945, in *A Selection from Scrutiny*, pp. 214–17 (pp. 211–31).

Keith Sagar, ' "Little Living Myths": A Note on Lawrence's Tortoises', in *D.H. Lawrence Review* III (1970), pp. 161–7.
Iain Crichton Smith, 'The Feeling Intelligence', in *Towards The Human* (Loanhead, Midlothian, Macdonald, 1986), pp. 149–53.
Sandra Gilbert, *Acts of Attention: The Poems of D.H. Lawrence* (2nd edition), (Carbondale, Southern Illinois Press, 1990).
A. Banerjee (ed.), *D.H. Lawrence's Poetry: Demon Liberated: A Collection of Primary and Secondary Material* (Basingstoke, Macmillan Press, 1990).
Benjamin Hrushovski, 'Note on the Systems of Hebrew Versification', in *The Penguin Book of Hebrew Verse*, edited by T. Carmi (Harmondsworth, Penguin, 1981), pp. 57–72.
Walt Whitman, *The Complete Poems*, edited by Francis Murphy (Harmondsworth, Penguin, 1975).
Richard Holmes, *Dr Johnson & Mr Savage* (London, Hodder & Stoughton, 1993).
Jon Silkin, 'Keith Douglas', in *Agenda*, Vol. 19, Nos 2–3 (Summer–Autumn 1981), pp. 49–58.
John Milton, *The Poetical Works*, edited by H.C. Beeching (London, Oxford University Press, 1912).
Donald Davie, 'A Doggy Demos: Hardy and Lawrence', in *Thomas Hardy and British Poetry* (London, Routledge & Kegan Paul, 1973), pp. 130–51.
Philip Hobsbaum, *A Reader's Guide to D.H. Lawrence* (London, Thames and Hudson, 1981).

CHAPTER 5

Dylan Thomas, *Collected Poems 1934–1952* (London, Dent, 1952).
Ralph N. Maud (ed.), *Poet in the Making* (London, Dent, 1968).
Ralph N. Maud (ed.), *The Notebook Poems 1930–1934* (London, Dent, 1989).
Dylan Thomas, *Under Milk Wood: A Play for Voices* (London, Dent, 1955 (1954)).
William Empson, *Argufying: Essays on Literature and Culture*, edited by John Haffenden (Iowa City, University of Iowa Press, 1987).
Walford Davies, *Dylan Thomas* (Cardiff, University of Wales Press and The Welsh Arts Council, 1990).
Constantine FitzGibbon, *The Life of Dylan Thomas* (London, Dent, 1975 (1965)).
Winifred Nowottny, *The Language Poets Use* (London, University of London, The Athlone Press, 1968), pp. 187–203.
Seamus Heaney, 'Dylan the Durable? on Dylan Thomas', in *The Redress of Poetry* (London, Faber and Faber, 1995), pp. 124–45.

CHAPTER 6

Basil Bunting, *Collected Poems* (Oxford, Oxford University Press, 1987 (1978)).
Basil Bunting, *A Note on Briggflatts* (Durham, Basil Bunting Archive, 1989).
Basil Bunting, *Three Essays*, edited and introduced by Richard Caddel (Durham, Basil Bunting Poetry Centre, 1994).

Descant on Rawthey's Madrigal: Conversations with Basil Bunting by Jonathan, Williams (Lexington, Kentucky, gnomon press, 1968).
Basil Bunting Special Issue, *Agenda*, Vol. 16, No. 1 (Spring 1978).
R.S. Woof, 'Basil Bunting's Poetry', *Stand*, Vol. 8, No. 2 (1966), pp. 28–34.
Peter Makin, *Basil Bunting: The Shaping of His Verse* (Oxford, Oxford University Press, 1992).
Donald Davie, 'Basil Bunting & His Masters', *Poetry Durham*, No. 27 (1991), pp. 27–36.
Donald Davie, 'God and Basil Bunting', *Poetry Review*, Vol. 83, No. 1 (1993), pp. 82–3.

CHAPTER 7

R.H. Mottram, *The Spanish Farm Trilogy 1914–1918* (Harmondsworth, Penguin, 1979).
Edmund Wilson, 'Is Verse a Dying Technique?', in *The Triple Thinkers* (Harmondsworth, Penguin, 1962 (1952)), pp. 22–39.
Merle E. Brown, *Double Lyric: Divisiveness and Communal Creativity in Recent English Poetry* (London, Routledge & Kegan Paul, 1980).
Brian Stone, 'False Friends and Strange Metres', in *The Translator's Art*, edited by William Radice and Barbara Reynolds (Harmondsworth, Penguin, 1987), pp. 175–86.
Peter Dale, 'The New Freedom of Rhyme', in *Outposts* 168 (Spring 1991), pp. 3–8.
Peter Dale, *An Introduction to Rhyme* (London, Agenda Editions/Bellew, 1995).
Primo Levi, *If This Be a Man* (London, Sphere, 1987).
Roy Fisher, *Poems 1955–1980* (Oxford, Oxford University Press, 1980).
Roy Fisher, *Furnace* (Oxford, Oxford University Press, 1986).
Roy Fisher, *Birmingham River* (Oxford, Oxford University Press, 1994).
Roy Fisher, unpublished letter to the author, 20 January 1988.
Donald Davie, 'Roy Fisher: An Appreciation', in *Thomas Hardy and British Poetry* (London, Routledge & Kegan Paul, 1973), pp. 152–72.
Lorna Tracy, *Amateur Passions* (London, Virago Press, 1981).
Charles Tomlinson, *Collected Poems* (Oxford, Oxford University Press, 1987).
Charles Tomlinson, *The Way In and Other Poems* (London, Oxford University Press, 1974).
Charles Tomlinson, *Isaac Rosenberg of Bristol* (Bristol, The University of Bristol, 1982).
A. Alvarez and Donald Davie, 'A Discussion', in *The Review*, No. 1 (April/May 1962), pp. 10–25.
Isaac Rosenberg, *Poems*, edited by Gordon Bottomley with a Memoir by Laurence Binyon (London, Heinemann, 1922).
Isaac Rosenberg, *The Collected Works*, edited by Ian Parsons (London, Chatto and Windus, 1979).
Merle E. Brown, 'Intuition vs. Perception: On Charles Tomlinson's "Under the Moon's Reign"', in *Double Lyric*, pp. 146–77.

Peter Redgrove, *Poems 1954–1987* (Harmondsworth, Penguin, 1989 (1987)).
Neil Roberts, *the lover the dreamer & the world* (Sheffield, Sheffield Academic Press, 1994).
Rodney Pybus, *Cicadas in Their Summers: New & Selected Poems 1965–1985* (Manchester, Carcanet, 1988).
Rodney Pybus, *Flying Blues* (Manchester, Carcanet, 1994).
Ted Hughes, *New Selected Poems 1957–1994* (London, Faber and Faber, 1995).
Ted Hughes, *Wolfwatching* (London, Faber and Faber, 1989).
Ted Hughes, *Winter Pollen: Occasional Prose*, edited by William Scammell (London, Faber and Faber, 1994).
Peter Levi, in *Poetry Review*, Vol 84, No. 4 (1994–5), p. 51.
Ken Smith, *Eleven Poems* (Leeds, Northern House, 1964).
Ken Smith, *Fox Running* (Crouch End, London, Rolling Moss Press, 1980).
Ken Smith, *The Poet Reclining: Selected Poems 1962–1980* (Newcastle upon Tyne, Bloodaxe Books, 1989 (1982)).
Geoffrey Chaucer, *The Complete Works*, edited by The Reverend Walter W. Skeat (London, Oxford: The Clarendon Press, 1903).
Elizabeth Jennings, *Collected Poems* (Manchester, Carcanet, 1987 (1986)).
Elizabeth Jennings, *Every Changing Shape* (London, André Deutsch, 1961).
Derek Mahon, *Selected Poems* (Harmondsworth, Dublin and Oxford, Penguin/Gallery in Association with Oxford University Press, 1990).
Paul Muldoon (ed.), *The Faber Book of Contemporary Irish Poetry* (London, Faber and Faber, 1986).
Geoffrey Hill, *Collected Poems* (London, Penguin, 1985).
Geoffrey Hill, *The Lords of Limit* (London, André Deutsch, 1984).
Jon Silkin, 'War and the Pity', in *Geoffrey Hill: Essays on his Work*, edited by Peter Robinson (Milton Keynes, Open University Press, 1985).
Merle E. Brown, Chapters 2, 3 and 4 on Geoffrey Hill's poetry, in *Double Lyric*, pp. 20–72.
Thom Gunn, *Collected Poems* (London, Faber and Faber, 1994 (1993)).
Thom Gunn, *Shelf Life: Essays, Memoirs and an Interview* (London, Faber and Faber, 1993).
Merle E. Brown, 'Inner Community in Thom Gunn's "Misanthropos"', in *Double Lyric*, pp. 126–45.
Allen Ginsberg, *Collected Poems 1947–1980* (London, Penguin, 1987 (1985)).
John Lucas, 'Gunning for Vendler', in *Poetry Review*, Vol. 84, No. 4 (1994–95), pp. 15–16.

Bibliography

Abbott, Claude Colleer (ed.), *The Letters of Gerard Manley Hopkins to Robert Bridges* (London, Oxford University Press, 1935).

Ackroyd, Peter, *Ezra Pound and his World* (London, Thames and Hudson, 1980).

Ackroyd, Peter, *T.S. Eliot: A Life* (London, Hamish Hamilton, 1985).

Aiken, Conrad, 'An Anatomy of Melancholy', in *T.S. Eliot: The Waste Land, A Casebook*, edited by C.B. Cox and Arnold P. Hinchcliffe (Basingstoke, Macmillan Press, 1992 (1968)).

Alexander, Michael (trans. and ed.), *The Earliest English Poems* (Harmondsworth, Penguin, 1966).

Allen, Donald M. (ed.), *The New American Poetry 1945–1960* (New York, Grove Press; London, Evergreen Books, 1960).

Allen, Gay Wilson, *The Solitary Singer* (New York, Macmillan Co., 1955).

Alvarez, A., 'A Discussion' (with Donald Davie), *The Review*, 1 (April/May 1962), pp. 10–25.

Alvarez, A., *The Shaping Spirit* (London, Hutchinson, 1963 (1958)).

Alvarez, A., *The New Poetry* (Harmondsworth, Penguin, 1966).

Auden, W.H., 'D.H. Lawrence' (from *The Dyer's Hand*), in *D.H. Lawrence's Poetry: Demon Liberated*, edited by A. Banerjee (Basingstoke, Macmillan Press, 1990).

Babel, Isaac, *Red Cavalry*, translated by John Harland (London, A. Knopf, 1929).

Banerjee, A. (ed.), *D.H. Lawrence's Poetry: Demon Liberated* (Basingstoke, Macmillan Press, 1990).

Bell, John and Owen, Harold (eds.), *Wilfred Owen: Collected Letters* (London, Oxford University Press, 1967).

Benjamin, Walter, *Illuminations* (London, Fontana/Collins, 1992).

Binyon, Laurence, Introductory Memoir to *Poems [by] Isaac Rosenberg* (London, Heinemann, 1922).

Blackmur, R.P., *Form and Value in Modern Poetry* (New York, Doubleday Anchor Books, 1957) (essays published at various dates).

Blok, Aleksandr, 'The Twelve', translated by Alex Miller, in *Stand*, 8 (1954).

Bloom, Harold, *The Western Canon* (Basingstoke, Macmillan Press, 1995), especially chapter 11, 'Walt Whitman as Center of the American Canon', pp. 264–90.

Bly, Robert, 'The Prose Poem as an Evolving Form', *What Have I Ever Lost by Dying?* (Bristol, Weatherlight Press, 1994 (1992)), pp. 79–83.

Bottomley, Gordon (ed.), *Poems [by] Isaac Rosenberg* (London, Heinemann, 1922).

Bottrall, Margaret (ed.), *Gerard Manley Hopkins: Poems, A Casebook* (Basingstoke, Macmillan Press, 1975).

Brambert, Victor, 'Mussolini and the Jews', Review of *Benevolence and Betrayal: Five Italian Jewish Families under Fascism*, Times Literary Supplement, (5 June 1992), p. 12.

Brooks, Cleanth, 'The Waste Land: Critique of the Myth', in *T.S. Eliot: The Waste Land*, pp. 128–61.

Brooks, Van Wyck (intr.), 'Eliot', *Paris Review Interview*, in *Writers at Work*, 2nd Series (New York, Viking, 1963), pp. 79–84.

Brown, Merle E., *Double Lyric: Divisiveness and Communal Creativity in Recent English Poetry* (London, Routledge & Kegan Paul, 1980).

Bunting, Basil, 'Mr T.S. Eliot', *The New English Weekly* (8 September 1932).

Bunting, Basil, *Collected Poems* (Oxford, Oxford University Press, 1987 (1977)).

Bunting, Basil, *A Note on Briggflatts* (Durham, Basil Bunting Poetry Archive, 1989).

Bunting, Basil, *Uncollected Poems*, edited by Richard Caddel (Oxford, Oxford University Press, 1991).

Bunting, Basil, *Three Essays*, edited and introduced by Richard Caddel (Durham, Basil Bunting Poetry Centre, 1994).

Caddel, Richard (see under Basil Bunting).

Caddel, Richard (ed.), 'Sharp Study and Long Toil: Basil Bunting Special Issue', A *Durham University Journal* Supplement (1995).

Calder, Angus, *T.S. Eliot* (Brighton, The Harvester Press, 1987).

Calderon, Nissim, 'Natan Zach in the 1960s: On "From Year to Year" and Rhythmic Dilemmas', *Modern Hebrew Literature*, New Series 14 (Spring–Summer 1995), pp. 22–5.

Carmi, T. (ed.), *The Penguin Book of Hebrew Verse* (Harmondsworth, Penguin, 1981).

Carpenter, Humphrey, *A Serious Character: The Life of Ezra Pound* (London, Faber and Faber, 1988).

Caudwell, Christopher, *Illusion and Reality* (London, Lawrence and Wishart, 1974).

Chatman, Seymour, *A Theory of Meter* (The Hague, Mouton, 1965).

Cluysenaar, Anne, *Introduction to Literary Stylistics* (London, Batsford, 1976).

Coleridge, S.T., *Poems*, edited by Derwent and Sara Coleridge (London, Moxon, 1852) (see also his Preface to 'Christabel' and Letter to Byron, 22 October 1815).

Coleridge, S.T., *Biographia Literaria*, edited by George Watson (London, Dent, 1956).

Conran, Tony (trans. and ed.), *Welsh Verse* (Bridgend, Mid-Glamorgan, Poetry Wales Press, 1986).

Cookson, William (ed.), *Ezra Pound: Selected Prose 1909–1965* (London, Faber and Faber, 1978 (1973)), pp. 344–7.

Cookson, William, *A Guide to the Cantos of Ezra Pound* (London, Croom Helm, 1985).

Craig, David, 'The Defeatism of *The Waste Land*', in *T.S. Eliot: The Waste Land*, pp. 200–15.

Dale, Peter, 'The New Freedom of Rhyme', *Outposts*, No. 168 (Spring 1991), pp. 3–8.

Dale, Peter, *An Introduction to Rhyme* (London, Agenda Editions/Bellew, 1995).

Daleski, H.M., *The Forked Flame: A Study of D.H. Lawrence* (Evanston, Illinois, Northwestern University Press, 1965).

Davenport, Guy, 'Whitman', in *The Geography of the Imagination* (London, Pan/Picador, 1984), pp. 68–79.

Davie, Donald, 'A Discussion' (with A. Alvarez), *The Review*, 1 (April/May 1962), pp. 10–25.

Davie, Donald, *Thomas Hardy and British Poetry* (London, Routledge and Kegan Paul, 1979 (1973)).

Davie, Donald, *Under Briggflatts: A History of Poetry in Great Britain 1960–1988* (Manchester, Carcanet, 1989), especially 'Prosody', pp. 120–6.

Davie, Donald, 'Basil Bunting & His Masters', *Poetry Durham*, No. 27 (1991), pp. 27–36.

Davie, Donald, 'God and Basil Bunting', *Poetry Review*, Vol. 83, No. 1 (1993), pp. 82–3.

Davies, Walford and Maud, Ralph (eds.), *Dylan Thomas: Collected Poems 1934–1953* (London, Dent, 1988).

Davies, Walford, *Dylan Thomas* (Cardiff, University of Wales Press and The Welsh Arts Council, 1990).

Davis, Dick, 'The Revolt against Metre' (a review of *Missing Measures* by Timothy Steele), *Poetry Durham*, No. 28 (1991).

Dazai, Osamu, 'Thinking of Zeno', quoted by Bobbi Hernandez in 'From Decadence to Romance', *Printed Matter* (Tokyo) (Spring 1991), p. 44.

Delany, Paul, *D.H. Lawrence's Nightmare: The Writer and His Circle in the Years of the Great War* (New York, Basic Books, 1978).

Dillard, Annie, 'Modernist Poetry', *Parnassus* (New York), Vol. II, No. 2 (1986).

Doren, Mark Van, 'John Dryden: The Lyric Poet', from *John Dryden: A Study of His Poetry* (Bloomington, The University of Indiana Press, 1960), in *Seventeenth Century English Poetry*, edited by William R. Keast, (New York, Oxford University Press, 1962).

Dorsch, T.S. (trans. and ed.), *Classical Literary Criticism: Aristotle, Horace, Longinus* (Harmondsworth, Penguin, 1981).

Draper, Ronald P., *D.H. Lawrence* (London, Macmillan Press, 1976 (1964)).

Eagleton, Terry, *Literary Theory: An Introduction* (Oxford, Basil Blackwell, 1983).

Eliot, T.S., *Collected Poems 1909–1962* (London, Faber and Faber, 1963).

Eliot, T.S., *The Waste Land: A Facsimile & Transcript*, edited by Valerie Eliot (London, Faber and Faber, 1971).

Eliot, T.S., *Selected Essays* (London, Faber and Faber, 1972 (1951)).

Eliot, T.S., *On Poetry and Poets* (London, Faber and Faber, 1971 (1957)).

Eliot, T.S., *Selected Prose of T.S. Eliot*, edited by Frank Kermode (London, Faber and Faber, 1975).

Ellman, Richard, 'The First *Waste Land*', in *Eliot in His Time*, edited by A. Walton Litz (Princeton, Princeton University Press, 1973), pp. 51–66.

Empson, William, *Seven Types of Ambiguity* (Harmondsworth, Penguin in Assocation with Chatto & Windus, 1961).

Empson, William, *Argufying*, edited by John Haffenden (Iowa City, University of Iowa Press, 1987).

Evans, Maurice (ed.), *Philip Sidney: Arcadia* (Harmondsworth, Penguin, 1977).

Ferris, Paul (ed.), *The Collected Letters of Dylan Thomas* (London, Dent, 1985).

Figgis, Sean (with Andrew McAllister), 'The Last Interview', An Interview with Basil Bunting, *Bête Noire*, 2/3 (Spring 1987), pp. 22–50.

Fisher, Roy, *The Memorial Fountain* (Newcastle upon Tyne, Northern House, 1966).

Fisher, Roy, *Poems 1955–1980* (Oxford, Oxford University Press, 1980).

Fisher, Roy, *Furnace* (Oxford, Oxford University Press, 1986).

Fisher, Roy, *Birmingham River* (Oxford, Oxford University Press, 1994).

Fitzgerald, Edward, [The] *Rubaiyat of Omar Khayyam*, translated by Edward Fitzgerald, edited by George F. Maine (London, Collins, 1953).

FitzGibbon, Constantine, *The Life of Dylan Thomas* (London, Dent, 1975 (1965)).

Flory, Wendy Stallard, *Ezra Pound and The Cantos: A Record of Struggle* (New Haven, Yale University Press, 1980).

Fraser, G.S., *Metre, Rhyme and Free Verse* (London, Methuen, 1980).

Frye, Northrop, *Anatomy of Criticism* (London, Penguin, 1990 (1957)).

Fussell, Paul, *Poetic Meter and Poetic Form* (New York, Random House, revised edition, 1979).

Gall, Sally M. and Rosenthal, M.L. (eds.), *The Modern Poetic Sequence: The Genius of Modern Poetry* (New York, Oxford University Press, 1983).

Gardinier, Suzanne, 'The Pitches Between the Keys', *Parnassus* (New York), Vol. 20, Nos 1–2 (1995), pp. 188–95.

Gardner, Helen, *The Art of T.S. Eliot* (London, Faber and Faber, 1979 (1949)).

Gardner, W.H. (ed.), *Gerard Manley Hopkins: A Selection of His Poems and Prose* (London, Penguin, 1953).

Gascoyne, David, *Collected Poems 1988* (Oxford, Oxford University Press, 1988).

Gilbert, Sandra, *Acts of Attention: The Poems of D.H. Lawrence* (2nd edition) (Carbondale, Southern Illinois University Press, 1990).

Gilboa, Amir, 'Five Poems', translated by Bat-Sheva Sheriff, Natan Zach and Jon Silkin, *Stand*, Vol. 6, No. 4 (1968), pp. 2–6.

Ginsberg, Allen, *Collected Poems 1947–1980* (London, Penguin, 1987).

Glover, Jon, see Appendix.

Gross, Harvey, *Sound and Form in Modern Poetry* (Ann Arbor, The University of Michigan Press, 1968).

Gunn, Thom, *Collected Poems* (London, Faber and Faber, 1994 (1993)).

Gunn, Thom, 'Syllabics', see Appendix.

Gunn, Thom, *Shelf Life: Essays, Memoirs and an Interview* (London, Faber and Faber, 1993).

Haffenden, John, (ed.), *William Empson: Argufying, Essays on Literature and Culture* (Iowa City, University of Iowa Press, 1987).

Hamilton, David, 'Postscript' (Review of *Missing Measures* by Timothy Steele), *The Iowa Review*, Vol. 21, No. 2 (1991), pp. 194–202.

Harding, Denys, 'Isaac Rosenberg', in *Experience into Words* (London, Chatto and Windus, 1963).

Harris, T.J.G., 'Halophilus living by these far northern seas', *Poetry Nation Review*, Vol. 19, No. 3 (January–February 1993), pp. 22–7.

Hartman, Charles O., *Free Verse: An Essay on Prosody* (Princeton, Princeton University Press, 1980).

Hartman, Geoffrey H., from *Wordsworth's Poetry 1787–1814* (1964), in *William Wordsworth*, edited by Graham McMaster (Harmondsworth, Penguin, 1972), pp. 463–91.

Hartman, Geoffrey H., 'The Voice of the Shuttle', in *Beyond Formalism* (New Haven, Yale University Press, 1970), pp. 337–55.

Hayden, John O. (ed.), *William Wordsworth: The Poems* (two volumes) (Harmondsworth, Penguin, 1977).

H.D. (Hilda Doolittle), *Selected Poems*, edited by Louis L. Martz (Manchester, Carcanet, 1988) (see also *Imagist Poetry*, edited by Peter Jones).

Heller, Michael, 'The Uncertainty of the Poet', *American Poetry Review*, Vol. 24, No. 3 (May/June 1995), pp. 11–15.

Hernandez, Bobbi, see Dazai, Osamu.

Hill, Geoffrey, *Collected Poems* (London, Penguin, 1985 (1983)).

Hill, Geoffrey, *The Lords of Limit: Essays on Literature and Ideas* (London, André Deutsch, 1984).

Hill, Geoffrey, 'Dividing Legacies', *Agenda*, Vol. 34, No. 2 (1996), pp. 9–28.

Hill, Geoffrey *Canaan* (London, Penguin, 1996).

Hobsbaum, Philip, *A Reader's Guide to D.H. Lawrence* (London, Thames and Hudson, 1981).

Hobsbaum, Philip, *Metre, Rhythm and Verse Form* (London, Routledge, (1996), 1995).

Hoggart, Richard, *The Uses of Literacy* (Harmondsworth, Penguin, 1958).

Hollander, John, *Rhyme's Reason* (New Haven, Yale University Press, 1989).

Holmes, Richard, *Dr Johnson & Richard Savage* (London, Hodder & Stoughton, 1983).

Hopkins, Gerard Manley, *A Selection of His Poems and Prose*, edited by W.H. Gardner (London, Penguin, 1953).

Hopkins, Gerard Manley, *The Letters of Gerard Manley Hopkins to Robert Bridges*, edited by Claude Colleer Abbott (London, Oxford University Press, 1935).

Hopkins, Gerard Manley, *Selected Prose*, edited by Gerald Roberts (Oxford, Oxford University Press, 1980).

Horvath, Brooke, 'The Prose Poem and the Secret Life of Poetry', *American Poetry Review*, Vol. 21, No. 5 (September/October 1992), pp. 11–14.

Hrushovski, Benjamin, 'A Note on Hebrew Prosody', in *The Modern Hebrew Poem Itself*, edited by Stanley Burnshaw, T. Carmi and Ezra Spicehandler (New York, Schocken Books, 1966).

Hrushovski, Benjamin, 'Note on the Systems of Hebrew Versification', in *Hebrew Verse*, edited and translated by T. Carmi (Harmondsworth, Penguin, 1981), pp. 57–72.

Hughes, Ted, *Wolfwatching* (London, Faber and Faber, 1989).

Hughes, Ted, *Winter Pollen: Occasional Prose*, edited by William Scammell (London, Faber and Faber, 1994).

Hughes, Ted, *New Selected Poems 1957–1994* (London, Faber and Faber, 1995).

Huxley, Aldous (ed.), *The Letters of D.H. Lawrence* (London, Heinemann, 1937).

Imagist Poetry, see Peter Jones (ed.).

Jennings, Elizabeth, *Every Changing Shape* (London, André Deutsch, 1961).

Jennings, Elizabeth, *Collected Poems* (Manchester, Carcanet, 1987 (1986)).

Jennings, Elizabeth, in departure Pamphlets I, *Six Women Poets* (Oxford, departure Pamphlets, n.d.).

Johnson, Samuel, *The Complete English Poems*, edited by J.D. Fleeman (Harmondsworth, Penguin, 1971).

Johnson, Samuel, *Lives of the English Poets* (two volumes) (London, Oxford University Press, 1956).

Jones, Daniel (ed.), *Dylan Thomas, A Prospect of the Sea* (London, Dent, 1972).

Jones, Peter (ed.), *Imagist Poetry* (Harmondsworth, Penguin, 1972).

Julius, Anthony, *T.S. Eliot, Anti-Semitism and Literary Form* (Cambridge, Cambridge University Press, 1995).

Kavanagh, Patrick, *Collected Poems* (New York, W.W. Norton, 1964).

Keast, William R. (ed.), *Seventeenth Century English Poetry: Modern Essays in Criticism* (New York, Oxford University Press, 1962).

Kell, Richard, 'The Poem and the World', *Poetry Nation Review*, No. 106 (1995), pp. 9–10.

Kenner, Hugh, from *The Invisible Poet* 1959, in *T.S. Eliot: The Waste Land*.

Kermode, Frank, 'A Babylonish Dialect', 1967, in *T.S. Eliot: The Waste Land*.

Kermode, Frank (ed.), *Selected Prose of T.S. Eliot* (London, Faber and Faber, 1975).

Kinnell, Galway, unpublished transcript of G.K.'s talk on Walt Whitman given at Macquarie University, Australia, 9 May 1979.

Lahey, Dr Philip A., 'Dylan Thomas: A Reappraisal' (unpublished article).

Lawrence, D.H., *The Letters*, edited with an introduction by Aldous Huxley (London, Heinemann, 1937).

Lawrence, D.H., *Lady Chatterley's Lover*, with an introduction by Richard Hoggart (Harmondsworth, Penguin, 1961).

Lawrence, D.H., *Kangaroo* (Harmondsworth, Penguin, 1968).

Lawrence, D.H., *Selected Literary Criticism*, edited by Anthony Beal (London, Heinemann, 1969).

Lawrence, D.H., *The Complete Poems*, edited with an introduction by Vivian de Sola Pinto and F. Warren Roberts (Harmondsworth, Penguin, 1980 (1971)).

Leamon, Warren, 'Hopkins in Dublin', in *English Literature and the Wider World*, Vol. IV: *The Ends of the Earth* (London, Ashfield Press, 1992).

Leavis, F.R., Three articles from *Scrutiny*, reprinted in *A Selection from Scrutiny*, Vol. 1 (Cambridge, Cambridge University Press, 1968), pp. 211–57: (1) '"Thought" and Emotional Quality', (2) 'Imagery and Movement', (3) 'Reality and Sincerity'.

Leavis, F.R., *New Bearings in English Poetry* (Harmondsworth, Penguin in Association with Chatto & Windus, 1972 (1932)).

Leech, Geoffrey N., *A Linguistic Guide to English Poetry* (Harlow, Longman, 1969).

Lefevre, Andre, *Translating Poetry: Seven Strategies and a Blueprint* (Amsterdam, Van Gorcum, 1975).

Levi, Primo, *If this be a Man* (London, Sphere, 1987).

Lindop, Grevel and Schmidt, Michael (eds.), *British Poetry since 1960* (Oxford, Carcanet, 1972).

Litz, A. Walton (ed.), *Eliot in His Time* (Princeton, Princeton University Press, 1973).

Lockwood, M.J., *A Study of the Poems of D.H. Lawrence* (Basingstoke, Macmillan Press, 1987).

Lowth, Right Reverend Robert, *Lectures on the Sacred Poetry of the Hebrews*, translated from the Latin by G. Gregory (Cheapside, London, Thomas Tegg, 1835).

Lucas, John, 'Gunning for Vendler' (Review of *Shelf Life*), *Poetry Review*, Vol. 84, No. 4 (1994–5), pp. 15–16.

McAllister, Andrew (with Sean Figgis) 'The Last Interview' (with Basil Bunting), *Bête Noire*, 2/3 (Spring 1987), pp. 22–50.

McAllister, Andrew, 'Today's Poets' ('Basil Bunting and Louis Zukofsky and Meaning'), *Bête Noire* 2/3 (Spring 1987), pp. 56–76.

McMaster, Graham (ed.), *William Wordsworth: A Critical Anthology* (Harmondsworth, Penguin, 1972).

Magnusson, Magnus and Palsson, Herman (transl.), *The Vinland Sagas* (Harmondsworth, Penguin, 1965).

Makin, Peter, *Basil Bunting: The Shaping of His Verse* (Oxford, Oxford University Press, 1992).

Mallarmé, Stephane, *The Poems, A Bilingual Edition*, translated by Keith Bosley, (Harmondsworth, Penguin, 1977).

Martz, Louis L. (ed.), *H.D. Selected Poems* (Manchester, Carcanet, 1988).

Matejka, Ladislaw and Pormorska, Krystyna (eds.), *Readings in Russian Poetics: Formalist and Structuralist Views* (Cambridge, Mass., MIT Press, 1971).

Matthiessen, F.O., from *The Achievement of T.S. Eliot*, in *T.S. Eliot: The Waste Land*, pp. 108–27.

Maud, Ralph N. (ed.), *Poet in the Making* (London, Dent, 1968).

Maud, Ralph and Davies, Walford (eds.), *Dylan Thomas: Collected Poems 1934 1953* (London, Dent, 1988).

Maud, Ralph N. (ed.), *Dylan Thomas: The Notebook Poems 1930–1934* (London, Dent, 1989).

Mayakovsky, Vladimir, *How are Verses Made?*, translated from the Russian by G.M. Hyde (London, Jonathan Cape, 1970).

Milton, John, *The Poetical Works*, edited by The Reverend H.C. Beeching (London, Oxford University Press, 1912).

Moore, Harry T., *The Priest of Love: A Life of D.H. Lawrence* (Harmondsworth, Penguin, 1976 (revised edition 1974)).

Morton, Leith, 'Foraging on Green Mountain: An Exploration of the Modern in Twentieth Century Japanese Poetry', *Ulitarra* (Australia) No. 4 (1993), pp. 35–53.

Muldoon, Paul, *The Faber Book of Contemporary Irish Poetry* (London, Faber and Faber, 1986).

Murphy, Francis (ed.), *Walt Whitman: A Critical Anthology* (Harmondsworth, Penguin, 1969).

Murphy, Francis (ed.), *Walt Whitman: The Complete Poems* (Harmondsworth, Penguin, 1975).

Nath, Raj, 'The Waste Land: The Facsimile Edition', from 'T.S. Eliot's *The Waste Land*', *The Literary Criterion*, pp. 69–74.

Nowottny, Winifred, *The Language Poets Use* (London, University of London, The Athlone Press, 1968).

An 'Objectivist' Anthology, see Louis Zukofsky.

O'Donoghue, Bernard, 'The Fascination of What's Difficult; Poetry and Complexity', *Stand*, Vol. 34, No. 2 (1993), pp. 14–19.

Owen, Harold with Bell, John (eds.), *Wilfred Owen: Collected Letters* (London, Oxford University Press, 1967).

Owen, Wilfred, *Collected Letters*, edited by Harold Owen and John Bell (London, Oxford University Press, 1967).

Owen, Wilfred, *The Complete Poems and Fragments* (two volumes), edited by Jon Stallworthy (London and Oxford, Chatto & Windus, The Hogarth Press and Oxford University Press, 1983).

Owen, Wilfred, *The War Poems*, edited by Jon Silkin (London, Sinclair-Stevenson, 1994).

Paige, D.D. (ed.), *Selected Letters 1907–1941 of Ezra Pound* (London, Faber and Faber, 1982).

Panofsky, Erwin, *Renaissance and Renascences in Western Art* (London, Granada Publishing/Paladin, 1970).

Parsons, Ian (ed.), *The Collected Works of Issac Rosenberg*, with a Foreword by Siegfried Sassoon (London, Chatto & Windus, 1979). See also Isaac Rosenberg.

Perloff, Marjorie, 'The Linear Fallacy', *The Georgia Review*, Vol. 35, No. 4 (1981), pp. 855–68.

Pickard, Connie, 'Basil Bunting 1900–1985: A Personal Memoir', *Stand*, Vol. 26, No. 3 (Summer 1985), pp. 8–11 (see Appendix).

Piette, Adam, *Imagination at War: British Fiction and Poetry 1939–1945* (Basingstoke, Macmillan General Books, 1995).

Pinto, Vivian de Sola and Roberts, F. Warren (eds.), *D.H. Lawrence: The Complete Poems* (Harmondsworth, Penguin, 1980 (1971)).

Poirier, Richard, *The Renewal of Literature* (New York, Random House, 1987).

Pomorska, Krystyna, and Matejka, Ladislaw (eds.), *Readings in Russian Poetics: Formalist and Structuralist Views* (Cambridge, Mass., MIT Press, 1971).

Pound, Ezra, *Active Anthology* (London, Faber and Faber, 1933).

Pound, Ezra, *Collected Shorter Poems* (London, Faber and Faber, 1968).

Pound, Ezra, *The Cantos of Ezra Pound* (London, Faber and Faber, 1975).

Pound, Ezra, *ABC of Reading* (London, Faber and Faber, 1991).

Pound, Ezra, 'Affirmations: AS FOR IMAGISME', in *Ezra Pound: Selected Prose 1909–1965*, ed. William Cookson (London, Faber and Faber, 1978 (1973)), pp. 344–7.

Pound, Ezra, *The Selected Letters 1907–1941* , edited by D.D. Paige (London, Faber and Faber, 1982).

Preminger, Alex (ed.), *Princeton Encyclopedia of Poetry and Poetics* (enlarged edition) (London, Macmillan Press, 1975).

Pybus, Rodney, *Cicadas in Their Summers: New & Selected Poems 1965–1985* (Manchester, Carcanet, 1988).

Pybus, Rodney, *Flying Blues* (Manchester, Carcanet, 1994).

Pybus, Rodney, see Appendix.

Radice, William with Reynolds, Barbara (eds.), *The Translator's Art* (Harmondsworth, Penguin, 1987).

Read, Herbert, *Phases of English Poetry* (Norfolk, Conn., Direction 19, 1951).

Read, Herbert, *A Coat of Many Colours* (London, Routledge & Kegan Paul, 1956).

Read, Herbert, *The Contrary Experience: Autobiographies* (London, Faber and Faber, 1963).

Read, Herbert, *Selected Poetry* (London, Sinclair-Stevenson, 1992).

Redgrove, Peter, *Poems 1954–1987* (London, Penguin, 1989 (1987)).

Redgrove, Peter, 'The Other Funeral', *Poetry Wales*, Vol. 30, No. 2 (1994), pp. 12–22.

Reynolds, Barbara and Radice, William (eds.), *The Translator's Art* (Harmondsworth, Penguin, 1987).

Rhys, Ernest (ed.), *The Prelude to Poetry* (London, Dent, 1951 (1927)).

Ricks, Christopher (ed.), *Inventions of the March Hare: Poems 1909–1917 [T.S. Eliot]* (London, Faber and Faber, 1996).

Roberts, F. Warren and de Sola Pinto, Vivian (eds.), *D.H. Lawrence: The Complete Poems*, (Harmondsworth, Penguin, 1980 (1971)).

Roberts, Neil, *the lover the dreamer & the world: The Poetry of Peter Redgrove* (Sheffield, Sheffield Academic Press, 1994).

Robinson, Peter (ed.), *Geoffrey Hill: Essays on His Work* (Milton Keynes, Open University Press, 1985).

Rosenberg, Isaac, *Poems*, selected and edited by Gordon Bottomley, with an introductory Memoir by Laurence Binyon (London, Heinemann, 1922).

Rosenberg, Issac, *The Collected Works*, edited by Ian Parsons with a Foreword by Siegfried Sassoon (London, Chatto & Windus, 1979).

Rosenthal, M.L. with Gall, Sally M., *The Modern Poetic Sequence* (New York, Oxford University Press, 1983).

Rudolf, Anthony: *At an Uncertain Hour: Primo Levi's War against Oblivion* (London, The Menard Press, 1990).

Sagar, Keith, ' "Little Living Myths": A Note on Lawrence's Tortoises', *D.H. Lawrence Review* III, (1970), pp. 161–7.

Saintsbury, George, *A History of English Prosody* (three volumes) (London, Macmillan and Co., 1923).

Sassoon, Siegfried, *Collected Poems* (London, Faber and Faber, 1947).

Sawa, Yuki and Shiffert, Edith, *Anthology of Modern Japanese Poetry* (Rutland, Vermont and Tokyo, Tuttle, 1972).

Scammell, William (ed.), *Winter Pollen by Ted Hughes* (London, Faber and Faber, 1994).

Schevill, James, 'The Chances of Poetry', *The Abiko Quarterly* (Abiko, Japan) (Spring 1994), pp. 207–14.

Schmidt, Michael and Lindop, Grevel (eds.), *British Poetry Since 1960* (Oxford, Carcanet, 1972).

Shakespeare, William, *The Complete Works*, edited by Charles Jasper Sisson (London, Odhams Press, 1960).

Shapiro, Karl, *In Defense of Ignorance* (New York, Random House, 1960).

Shaw, Bernard, 'Morris as I Knew Him', William Morris Society, 1966.

Shiffert, Edith and Sawa, Yuki (eds.), *Anthology of Modern Japanese Poetry* (Rutland, Vermont and Tokyo, Tuttle, 1972).

Sidney, Philip, *Arcadia*, edited by Maurice Evans (Harmondsworth, Penguin, 1977).

Silk, Dennis, see Appendix.

Silkin, Jon, *Out of Battle: The Poetry of The Great War* (London, Routledge & Kegan Paul, 1987 (1972)).

Silkin, Jon (ed.), *The Penguin Book of First World War Poetry* (Harmondsworth, Penguin, 1981).

Silkin, Jon, 'War and the Pity', in *Geoffrey Hill: Essays on his Work*, edited by Peter Robinson (Milton Keynes, Open University Press, 1985), pp. 114–28.

Silkin, Jon, *Selected Poems* (London, Sinclair-Stevenson, 1994).

Smart, Christopher, *Selected Poems*, edited by Karina Williamson and Marcus Walsh (Harmondsworth, Penguin, 1990).

Smith, Iain Crichton, *Towards the Human* (Loanfield, Midlothian, Macdonald, 1986).

Smith, Ken, *Eleven Poems* (Leeds, Northern House, 1964).

Smith, Ken, *Fox Running* (Crouch End, Rolling Moss Press, 1980).

Smith, Ken, *The Poet Reclining: Selected Poems 1962–1980* (Newcastle upon Tyne, Bloodaxe Books, 1989).

Smith, Reginald, 'The Quaternary Structure of Symbolism in Whitman's "Lilacs": A Synchronic Analysis', *Calamus* (Tokyo), No. 28 (December 1986), pp. 1–20.

Speirs, John, 'Mr Pound's Propertius' (Review of *Homage to Sextus Propertius*), in *A Selection from Scrutiny*, Vol. 1 (Cambridge, Cambridge University Press, 1968), pp. 101–7.

Spenser, Edmund, *The Works of Edmund Spenser*, edited by The Reverend Henry John Todd (London, Moxon, 1852).

Stead, C.K., *The New Poetic* (London, Hutchinson, 1964).

Stead, C.K., 'The Poem and its Substitutes' (1964), in *T.S. Eliot: The Waste Land*, pp. 216–23.

Stead, C.K., *Pound, Yeats, Eliot and the Modernist Movement* (Basingstoke, Macmillan Press, 1989).

Steele, Timothy, *Missing Measures* (Fayetteville, The University of Arkansas Press, 1990).

Steiner, George (ed.), *Poem into Poem: World Poetry in Modern Verse Translation* (Harmondsworth, Penguin, 1970).

Stock, Noel, *The Life of Ezra Pound* (New York, Random House, 1970).

Stone, Brian, 'False Friends and Strange Metres', in *The Translator's Art*, pp. 175–86.

Sullivan, J.P., *Ezra Pound and Sextus Propertius* (Austin, The University of Texas Press, 1964).

Sullivan, J.P., 'Pound's Homage to Sextus Propertius', *Agenda*, Vol. 4, No. 2 (October–November 1965), pp. 57–61.

Surette, Leon, *A Light from Eleusis / Study of Ezra Pound's Cantos* (Oxford, Oxford University Press, 1979).

Taguchi, Tetsuya, 'New Morning, New Man, and New Poetry – from Eliot and Lawrence to Rexroth', *The Literary Essays* (Second Series), No. 8 (September 1991).

Templin, Lawrence, 'The Quaker Influence on Walt Whitman', in *On Whitman: The Best from American Literature* (Durham, North Carolina, 1987), pp. 129–44.

Thomas, Dylan, *Portrait of the Artist as a Young Dog* (London, Dent, 1940).

Thomas, Dylan, *Collected Poems 1934–1952* (London, Dent, 1952).

Thomas, Dylan, *Quite Early One Morning* (broadcasts) (London, Dent, 1954).

Thomas, Dylan, *Under Milk Wood: A Play for Voices* (London, Dent, 1955).

Thomas, Dylan, *Adventures in the Skin Trade* (New York, New Directions, No. 183, 1964).

Thomas, Dylan, *Poet in the Making*, edited by Ralph N. Maud (London, Dent, 1968).

Thomas, Dylan, *A Prospect of the Sea*, edited by Daniel Jones (London, Dent, 1972).

Thomas, Dylan, *The Collected Letters*, edited by Paul Ferris (London, Dent, 1985).

Thomas, Dylan, *Collected Poems 1934–1953*, edited by Walford Davies and Ralph Maud (London, Dent, 1988).

Thomas, Dylan, *Dylan Thomas; The Notebook Poems 1930–1934*, edited by Ralph N. Maud (London, Dent, 1989).

Tolstoy, L.N., *Tolstoy on Art* (includes *What is Art?*), selected and translated by Aylmer Maude (London, Oxford University Press, 1924).

Tomlinson, Charles, 'Poetry Today', in *The Modern Age*, ed. Boris Ford (Harmondsworth, Penguin, 1961), pp. 458–72.

Tomlinson, Charles, *The Way In and Other Poems* (London, Oxford University Press, 1974).

Tomlinson, Charles, *Isaac Rosenberg of Bristol* (Bristol, Bristol Branch of the Historical Association, No. 52; The University, Bristol, 1982).

Tomlinson, Charles, *Collected Poems* (Oxford, Oxford University Press, 1987).

Tomlinson, Charles, unpublished essay on the plays of Isaac Rosenberg

Tracy, Lorna, *Amateur Passions: Love Stories?* (London, Virago, 1981).

Trilling, Lionel, *Sincerity and Authenticity* (Cambridge, Mass., Harvard University Press, 1972).

Trotsky, Leon, *Literature and Revolution*, translated by Rose Trunsky (Ann Arbor, Michigan, The University of Michigan Press, 1971).

Turco, Lewis, *The Book of Forms: A Handbook of Poetics* (New York, E.P. Dutton, 1968).

Ungaretti, Giuseppe, *Selected Poems*, translated by Patrick Creagh (Harmondsworth, Penguin, 1971).

Walsh, Marcus and Williamson, Karina (eds.), *Christopher Smart: Selected Poems* (Harmondsworth, Penguin, 1990).

Ward, J.P., 'The Relevance of Gerard Manley Hopkins for Welsh Poetry in English Today', *New Welsh Review*, Vol. II, No. 3 (Winter 1989–90), pp. 39–45.

Welland, D.S.R., *Wilfred Owen: A Critical Study* (London, Chatto & Windus, 1960; revised edition, 1978).

Whitman, Walt, *The Complete Poems*, edited by Francis Murphy (Harmondsworth, Penguin, 1975).

Whitman, Walt, *Leaves of Grass; The First (1855) Edition*, edited, with an introduction, by Malcolm Cowley (Harmondsworth, Penguin, 1986).

Whitman, Walt, *Specimen Days in America* (London, George Routledge, nd).

Williams, Jonathan, *Descant on Rawthey's Madrigal: Conversations with Basil Bunting by Jonathan Williams* (Lexington, Kentucky, gnomon press, 1968).

Williams, W.C., 'An Elegy for D.H. Lawrence', in *Collected Poems* (two volumes), edited by A. Walton Litz and Christopher MacGowan, in Vol. I, 1909–39 (London, Collins Paladin, 1991), pp. 392–5.

Willamson, Karina and Walsh, Marcus (eds.), *Christopher Smart: Selected Poems* (Harmondsworth, Penguin, 1990).

Wilson, Edmund, *The Triple Thinkers* (Harmondsworth, Penguin, 1962).

Wilson, Jean Moorcroft, *Isaac Rosenberg: Poet and Painter* (London, Cecil Woolf, 1975).

Woof, R.S., 'Basil Bunting's Poetry', *Stand*, Vol. 8, No. 2 (1966), pp. 28–34.

Woolf, Virginia, *Granite and Rainbow* (London, The Hogarth Press, 1958).

Wordsworth, William, *The Poems* (two volumes), edited by John O. Hayden (Harmondsworth, Penguin, 1977).

Worthen, John, *D.H. Lawrence: A Literary Life* (Basingstoke, Macmillan Press, 1989).

Zukofsky, Louis, *An 'Objectivist' Anthology* (France and New York, Le Beausset, Var, 1932).

Zweig, Paul, *Walt Whitman; The Making of the Poet* (Harmondsworth, Penguin, 1986).

Index

Academic readers, 55–6
Accentual verse, 271–3
Ackroyd, Peter, Eliot's anti-
    Semitism, 52–4; 68, 69, 161
Ahti, Risto, 321
Aidan, 279
Aiken, Conrad, The 'free verse of
    Prufrock', 45–6
Aldington, Richard, 181
Anglo-Saxon words, 311, 325
    (Pybus)
Auden, W.H., on Lawrence, 224,
    372; 378

Babel, Isaac, *Red Cavalry*, 105–6
Beake, Fred, 224
Bedient, Calvin, 311
Bell, Marvin, 4, 381–3
Bennett, Arnold, 'Mr Nixon', 123–4
Bergonzi, Bernard, 59
Berryman, John, 372
Blackmur, R.P., Pound, 108, 115;
    Lawrence, 182–3, 227
Blake, William, 244, 247, 272
Blok, Aleksandr, 'The Twelve', 338
Blunden, Edmund, 339
Bly, Robert, the prose poem, 389
Bradley, A.C., 256
Brambert, Victor, 55, 157
Bridges, Robert, Hopkins' letters
    to, 25–6, 28; 374–6
Brooks, Cleanth, 70–1
Brown, Merle E., 309, 313–14, 359
Brown, Pete, 393
Buffalo, University of, 257
Bunting, Basil, 271–99; Connie
    Pickard on Bunting, 390–5;
    prosody and the individual
    voice, 273–5; like Eliot's verse,
    near the ambit of metricality,
    273; music, 275; his pacifism in
    the First War, 279; his
    participation in the Second War,

279; the poet as outsider and
    visionary; traditional and
    modernist, 285–7; the question
    of Christianity in *Briggflatts*, 294;
    northern distrust of elaboration
    and luxury, 295; *Briggflatts*,
    273–99, 394; Love, 276, 280, 281,
    298–9; Bloodaxe, 276, 282, 287,
    his murder, 289; Pasiphae, 277,
    likely respect for, 290; Hell and
    the shit eaters, 277, 291;
    Alexander, 277, 282, 292–3;
    battle at Catterick, 278; the
    poets, Aneurin and Taliesin,
    278–9; the saints, Aidan and
    Cuthbert, 279, 282, 287, disgust,
    280; Northumberland, 280; Bede
    and Cuthbert, 294–5; Bunting's
    music, 298; 'Chomei at Toyama',
    273, 394–5; 'The Spoils', 273; 'To
    Mina Loy', 275; 'Villon', 273
Burns, Robert, 302
Byron, George Gordon, 256

Calder, Angus, opening of
    'Prufrock', 46–7
Chaucer, Geoffrey, 172, 271, 340
Christ, addressing his mother,
    215–16, 250
Clare, John, his nightingale
    compared with Keats's, 339; 373
Cluysenaar, Anne, 384–8; *Vaughan
    Variations*, 386
Coleridge, S.T., 2–3, 70; on
    Wordsworth's 'freshness', 102;
    'The Ancient Mariner', 104–5;
    202, 271, 302
Common, Jack, 391–2
Conran, Tony, 278
Conroy, T.F., 57
Craig, David, 70, 75, 93–4
Creeley, Robert, 363
Cuthbert, 279, 294, 295

Daleski, H.M., 188
Daryush, Elizabeth, 374
Davie, Donald, 212, 280, 294, 317
Dazai, Osamu, Ant, not authority, 101
Dixon, R.W., Hopkins' letter to, 3
Donne, John, 329, 376
Douglas, Keith, 213
Dunn, Douglas, 379
Durational (quantitative verse) 28, 179, 271, 272–3, 286–7; (relationship with) isometrics, 311

Eliot, T.S., 45–107, *After Strange Gods*, 55–6, 89, 227, 284, 385; 'Ulysses, Order and Myth', 61; 'Little Gidding' compared with Lawrence's 'Bavarian Gentians', 8; 'Little Gidding', 146–6, 189; the way a poem works, 31, 155; anti-Semitism, 52–7, 133, 349; 'The Use of Poetry', 71, 104; Eliot and the First War, 124; his plays, 271; A 'Cooking Egg', 53; 'Ash-Wednesday', 60, 69; 'Gerontion', 52–3, 60, 64, 67, 91, 133; 'Sweeney Agonistes', 90; 'Sweeney among the Nightingales, 53; 'The Love Song of J. Alfred Prufrock, 45–51, 60, 62, 63, 90, 91; metre, 45–6; etherizing, active and passive, 47–8; rhyme, 48; prosody, 49–51, Prufrock's tenacious vision, 51; *The Waste Land* (suppositional poem), 59–69; Pound's interventions, 61–8, 96; *The Waste Land*, 69–107, 241, 275, 302; Metre and syntax in the opening, 73–4; the Hyacinth girl, 51, 77–9, 88; and Dante, 77; Stetson, 80–1; 'A Game of Chess', 81–5; 'The Fire Sermon', 82–96, 307, 309; Babylon and spiritual exile, 87–8; Tiresias, inhibiting role of his authority, 89–92, 106; seduction scene, 91–3; Elizabeth and Leicester, 93–4; further

seduction', and aftermath, 94–6; St Augustine, 96; 'Death by Water', 96–7; 'What the Thunder said', 98–105; Wisdom, 100; Authority, 101–2, Coleridge's 'The Ancient Mariner', 104–5; Love without forgiveness, 104–5; *The Waste Land* as a type of drama, 106–7; *Four Quartets*, 8, 67, 241
Ellman, Richard, the 'free verse' of 'Prufrock', 45
Emerson, Ralph Waldo, 13, 188; Whitman's letter to ('gallantry'), 219
Empson, William, 81, 242; Thomas's complexity, 243, 250, 256, 261; preference for early poems, 265
Esprey, John, Sexuality in 'Mauberley', 118–20
Evans, Maurice, 30
Everyman, 355

Fainlight, Ruth, 330
Fisher, Roy, 303–9; 'After working', 304; *A Furnace*, 304; 'For Realism', 304, 305–7, 308, 313; The vitality of a working-class community, 306; the woman and the pissing man, 306; a conscience poised athwart bureaucratic authority, 307; punctuation, 307; flowing enigma of syntax, 307; 'Paraphrases', 304; 'Seven Attempted Moves', 304; 'Starting to Make a Tree', 204, 304–5, re-works imagism, 305; 'The thing about Joe Sullivan', 304; 'Wonders of obligation', 304, 305, 307–9, 313; its deliquescence, 304; lack of respect for water, 307; a mass war-time grave prepared, 305, 307; Old Lady Moth, 308
Fitzgerald, Edward, [The] Rubaiyat of Omar Khayyam, 165–6

FitzGibbon, Constantine, 245
Flint, F.S., 37
Flory, Wendy Stallard, on the
    Cantos, 139–40; Pound and his
    idea of pure art, 140, 152, 159,
    162, 165
Forche, Carolyn, 142
Fraser, G.S., 187, 369
Frost, Robert, 386
Fuller, Roy, 10

Gardner, Helen, 63, 66, 69–70, 72,
    74, 75–7, 80, 83, 84, 104, 105
Gilbert, Sandra, 183, 188,
    Lawrence's alleged 'hatred' of
    humanity, 192; 194, 197, 199,
    205, 211–12
Gilboa, Amir, 'Here I blow out',
    330
Ginsberg, Allen, 360, 381, 393–4
Glover, Jon, 369–71, Owen's
    'Strange Meeting' and Silkin's
    'Death of a Son', 369–70; *Our
    Photographs*, 371
Gourmont, Remy de, 120
Graves, Robert, 217
Gray, Thomas, 302
Gunn, Thom, 358–65, 374–6;
    metrical and free verse, 4;
    aggression, and the ego, 359;
    Bunting, 360; syllabics, 360,
    374–61, 382; *Shelf Life*, 358–60;
    Ginsberg and perception of
    'losing the succinctness', 360,
    362; 'Winters and the plain
    style', 360, 364; 'A Blank', 359;
    'All Do Not All Things Well',
    359; 'Considering the "Snail"',
    359; 'Flying Above California',
    359; 'Lament', 359, 363–5;
    function of metricality and
    rhyme, 364; 'plain style', 364;
    lightness of touch, 364, narrative
    economy, 365; 'Misanthropos',
    359, 361–2; variety of disciplined
    metrical and patterned forms,
    361–2, integrity of Anton
    Schmidt, 361–2; free verse, 363;
    'The Conversation of Old Men',

359, 363; 'The Geysers', 359;
    'The Old Woman', 359, 363;
    'The Wound', 359; 'Touch', 359,
    363; 'Waking in a Newly Built
    House', 359; 'Words', 359;
    'Wrestling', 359
Gurney, Ivor, 284

Haffenden, John, 242
Hall, Donald, 374–5
Harding, D.W., 5; The 'root' image
    in Rosenberg's poetry, 195
Hardy, Thomas, 202
Hartman, Charles O., relation
    between lineation and syntax in
    free verse, 7; prosody in W.C.
    Williams' 'Exercise', 45;
    unmetred verse's conversion to
    metricality, 281
H.D., 38–43; draws Lawrence into
    contributing to Imagist
    anthologies, 32; Wordsworth's
    'melting down of language', 41;
    Martz's description of her
    language, 41–2; 'Evening', 42;
    'Oread', 38–40; syntax in
    'Oread' compared with
    Whitman's 'Look Down Fair
    Moon', 38–40; 'Sitalkas', 42
Heaney, Seamus, *The Redress of
    Poetry*, 270, 339, 380
Hill, Geoffrey, ix, 352–8, 'cross-
    hatching' in Hopkins;
    irreconcilables and opposites
    held in interplay, 61; 'Funeral
    Music', 278, 347, 354; 'Funeral
    Music', 355–6; survivor, witness,
    356; armies' vanity and how
    they feed each other's;
    gorgonizing, 356; emblematic
    power and pride of the carrion
    birds, 356; metricality of the
    sonnet compared with free verse
    of 'September Song', 356–8;
    gravitas, 358; Sonnet form,
    argument, 358; 'September
    Song', 92, 349–50; 'September
    Song', 352–5; *Zeugma*, 252;
    sexual desire and racism, 352;

Hill, Geoffrey – continued
'proper', 353; syntax and
lineation, 353–4; ambiguity of
who elegy is for, 354; co-
ordinates of Keats and Hill
contrasting, 355
Hobsbaum, Philip, compares
Lawrence with Whitman, 182;
322
Holmes, Richard, 202
Hopkins, Gerard Manley, rhythms
in Wordsworth's 'Immortality
Ode', 3; God and Nature, 13–14;
his adjectives compared with
Whitman's nouns, 16–17; Hill
on 'cross-hatching' in Hopkins,
17–18; rhythm and metre, 21–2,
26–8, 179; letter to Bridges
concerning Whitman, 25–6;
Hopkins and his prosody, 26–9;
Nature, 30, 169; one rhythm
cross-currenting within another,
180; 'figure of grammar'
(parallelism), 181; Hopkins,
Welsh and Dylan Thomas,
245–6; possible influence on
Dylan Thomas, 262–3, 271;
'Spelt from Sibyl's Leaves', 15,
18–21; 'The Blessed Virgin
Compared to the Air we
Breathe', 14–15; Compared with
Whitman, 14; 'The Golden
Echo', 14; 'The Windhover',
rhythms in, 6; 'The Wreck of the
Deutschland', 28–9; the
difficulty of hearing metrical
congruence throughout, 28–9
Hrushovski, Benjamin, Hebrew
parallelism, 187
Hughes, Ted, 271, 330–8, his
language compared with Ken
Smith's, 339; 'An Otter', 330,
333; 'Crow Wakes', 330; Crow,
330, 335; 'Dust as we are', 336,
'Duration', 336, Child's
sensitivity to and knowledge of
father, 336; 'Full Moon and
Little Frieda', 330; Lupercal, 330;
'Sacrifice', 336; 'Source', 336;

'That Morning, 333–4, epiphany
rather than revelation, 334; 'The
Burnt Fox', 331, 334; 'The
Horses', 330, 332–3, 334, 339,
epiphany, 334; 'The Thought-
Fox', 330, 331–2, 334;
'uncollected poems', 334–8;
'Walt', 328, 337–8; slow halting
rhythms, 337–8; syntax, 337;
Woodwo, 330; Wolfwatching, 330,
334, 338
Hulme, T.E., 37

Imagism, 35–7, 38, 43, 360
Isherwood, Christopher, 358, 359

Jennings, Elizabeth, 343–8, her
metricality and enjambments,
343–5, 346, 348; 'confessional
poetry', 347; rhymes, 348; 'A
World of Light', 345, 346; Every
Changing Shape, 344–6, 348;
'Childhood in Lincolnshire', 345,
346–7; 'Heyday', 345, 347–8; 'I
Count the Moments', 345;
'Identity', 344; 'Lazarus', 345;
'Song for a Birth and Death',
345–6, 348
Johnson, Pamela Hansford, 257
Jonson, Ben, Volpone, 246
Joyce, James, 61

Kavanagh, Patrick, The Great
Hunger, 62; 270
Keats, John, 30, 189, 249, 315, his
nightingale compared with
Clare's, 339; 355
Kenner, Hugh, 67, 90, 99–101
('DA', TWL), 159, 374

Langland, William, 69, 271
Larkin, Philip, 380
Latinate words, 311, 325 (Pybus)
Lawrence D.H., ix, 179–241, Lady
Chatterley's Lover, 75; his poetry
compared with Rosenberg's, 180;
'hidden emotional pattern' in
poetry, 180, 213; 'skilled verse',
180; free verse ('Poetry of the

Lawrence D.H. – *continued*
Present'), 181; congruity in,
223–4; free verse (*BBF*), 181; his
iambic pentameter, 181; his
metricality, 224–6; parallelism,
32, 212–13, 226–8; his poetry
lacking form, 182–3; his poetry
ignored, 183; 'stable ego' v.
allotropic states', 196; teleology,
or the reverse, 196–201,
Kangaroo, 197, Lawrence and
Whitman; prose element in
verse (American and English
languages), 186–90; *The Rainbow*,
210; Lawrence on the novel, 211;
Lawrence as outsider, 284, 378;
Rhyming Poems, 'Piano' and
'Discord', 184–6, 'Hymn to
Priapus', 225; *Look! We have come
through*, 191; 'Frost Flowers',
191; 'Craving for Spring', 191;
Birds, Beasts and Flowers,
191–224; 'Pomegranates', 191,
193–4; 'Peach', 193; 'Medlars
and Sorb-apples', 194;
'Cypresses', 195–6, 201;
'Almond Blossom', 197–8, 202,
216; 'Sicilian Cyclamens', 198–9;
'Fish', 200; 'Man and Bat',
200–1, 205; metricality in *BBF*,
201–3; 'Snake', 206–9, 240; 'The
Peaceable Kingdom', 208–9, 211;
Lawrence as moralist, 209–13,
'Baby Tortoise', 33, 213–14;
'Tortoise Shell', 214–15; 'Tortoise
Family Connections', 215–17;
'Lui et Elle', 217–18, 219;
'Tortoise Gallantry', 218–19;
'Mountain Lion', 200, 212,
220–3; *Pansies*; 'Elephants in the
Circus', 212; 'Nottingham's New
University', 225; 'Desire is
Dead', 225–6; *More Pansies*;
'Flowers and Men', 195; Prayer,
229–30; *Last Poems*, 226–41;
'Phoenix', 213, 226–9; 'The
Greeks are coming', 229;
'Invocation to the Moon', 230–1,
235; 'Butterfly', 231; 'For the

heroes are dipped in scarlet',
232–3; 'The Man of Tyre', 233;
'Whales Weep Not!', 233–4;
'Bavarian Gentians', compared
with Eliot's 'Little Gidding', 8;
232, 233, 235–7; 'The Ship of
Death', 34–5, 196–7, 228–9,
236–41, 302, its metricality,
238–40; 'apples' and scale, 240,
Hamlet reference and
Renaissance diction, 240
Lawrence, Frieda, 215, 224, 284
Leavis, F.R., interpretation of a
passage in 'Spelt from Sibyl's
Leaves', 20, 210, 339
Lehmann, John, 164
Levertov, Denise, 381
Levi, Peter, 335
Levi, Primo, 11
Levine, Philip, 375
Lewis, C. Day, his narrative
poems, 267
Lewis, C.S., 1–2
Lindop, Grevel, 352
Lockwood, M.J., 198–9, 230, 235
Lomas, Herbert, 321
Lowell, Robert, 302, 382
Lowth, Right Reverend Robert,
Hebrew parallelism, 12

MacDiarmid, Hugh, 270, 380
Mahon, Derek, 348–52; 'A
Disused Shed in County
Wexford', 349–52; Comparison
with Hill's 'September Song',
350; syntax and prosody, 350;
generosity, 350; Nazi camps,
351; victims' response, 351;
openness of poem, 351; charity,
352; distinction between Pound's
res and *verba*, 352
Makin, Peter, 272, 277, 278, 286–7,
289, 294–5, 298
Mandelstam, Nadezdha, 275
Mandelstam, Osip, 275
Marlowe, Christopher, 270
Marsh, Edward, Lawrence letters
to, 180; Rosenberg letter to, 312
Martz, Louis, on H.D., 41–2

Matthiessen, F.O., conduct of
Eliot's couples, 85–6
Maud, Ralph N., 242, compassion
in 'The force that through', 248;
and chapter 5, passim
Maurras, Charles, 75
Melville, Herman, 13; Moby Dick
(Lawrence on), 233–4; 362
Metre, syntax and lineation, 7–8
Milton, John, 28; metres, 179, 235,
236
Monroe, Harriet, 125, 129
Moore Marianne, 374–5
Morrell, Lady Ottoline, 124, 131
Mottram, R.H., 300
Music, 27, 171–2, 275, 302–3

Nath, Raj, 59
Nims, John Frederick, 348
Nowottny, Winifred, 270

Olson, Charles, 381
Owen, Wilfred, 5, 21, his
treatment of war compared with
Pound's, 124; slant rhyme, 164;
compared with Rosenberg, 189,
284; 'Dulce et Decorum Est', 70,
212; 'Exposure', 40; 'Spring
Offensive', 336, 360; 'Strange
Meeting', 125, 369–70

Pater, Walter, 30–1, 36
Pickard, Connie, Basil Bunting
Memoir, 390–5
Pickard, Tom, 392
Piette, Adam, 54
Pinto, Vivian de Sola, 210
Poirier, Richard, 187
Pope, Alexander, 64, 68, 81; The
Dunciad, 128–9
Pound, Ezra, humour, 32, 110;
definition of the 'image', 33;
anti-Semitism, 55, 57–8, 141, 349;
Fascist art, 139–43; Continued
support for fascism, 144;
Pound's suffering in the DTC,
144, 146; The Fascist kingdom,
145; Sexuality and rhythm, 147;
Res and Verba, 352; Lustra,

348–9; 'Homage to Sextus
Propertius', 108–18; Blackmur's
perception of Pound's original
work and his translations (re.
'translation' see also 165–8), 108;
Love, not war, the better subject
for poetry, 109–10; Cynthia, 'his'
love, 110–13; persiflage, and
humour, 110–11; humour, wit,
112; and veracity, 114; rhythm,
and stepped lines, 115–18;
feeling and rhythm, 147; Pound
as outsider, 284; metronome and
musical phrase, 378; Hugh
Selwyn Mauberley, 118–39;
Esprey, his perception of the
poem's sexuality and aesthetics,
121; 'refined' English, 120–2,
126–8; relations of past to
present, 122; Pound's scorn for
democracy, 122; Lady Ottoline
Morrell, society women and
culture (see also Eliot's
'Prufrock', 49–50), 124, 131, 133;
inadequate treatment of war,
124–5; pure English, 126; pure
aesthetics, 126, 135; pure
morality, 126; pure culture,
126–7, 129–31; another
touchstone; Pope and The
Dunciad, 128–9; Ford, stylist and
pure conduct, 129–31; prose and
poetry (letter to Harriet
Monroe), 129; attenuation
through pursuit of purity,
132–3, 136–7; The Pisan Cantos,
pure art, crystalline art, fascist
loyalties, 142; re-espousal of
fascist loyalties, 150–7, 161–2;
instances of dislocation, 157–8;
individual kindness shown to
Pound in DTC, 158; Lynxes, and
the passage concluding with
atonement (?), 159–61, Hooo
Fasa and Fascism, 161; the ego,
163; veracity (Ford and Yeats),
164; Tudor, conflict expressed in
poetry, 164–70; 'translation' of
Omar Khayyam, 165–8; stoic

Pound, Ezra, humour – *continued*
wry humour, 170; 'Libretto' (and
its metres), 170–2; vanity/
humility, 173–8; moral
judgement expressed in scale,
174–6; modesty, 175–6; foreign
words, 177–8

Pybus, Rodney, 325–30, 378–80,
vii, 190, 317, 325 (letter);
'Admirable Wings', 327–8; 'Little
Girl Asleep', 325–30; grief for
unborn child and his wife,
325–6; comparison with
Redgrove on treatment of
reality, 327; child and nature,
327; speaking and lyric voices
(*cantare*), 328; guilt, 329; passage
of time, 329; Candle, 329–30

Quinn, John, 57

Ravagli, Angelo, 215
Raw, Colin, 330
Read, Herbert, criticism of linguist
practice, 37, 40; *The End of a War*
('Meditation of a Dying German
Officer'), 43–5
Redgrove, Peter, ix, 317–25;
rhythm and reality, 321;
comparison with Pybus on
treatment of reality, 327;
metaphoric abundance, 359; 'At
the Cosh Shop', 318; 'Living at
Falmouth', 321–5; mineral
exploitation and sexual
exploitation, 323–4; the
condition of the miners, 323–4;
'Renfield Before His Masters',
318–21; doubleness of vision,
319–20; problems of success
with rhythm, 320–1; 'The
Weddings at Nether Powers',
320
Reed, Henry, 'Chard Witlow', 60
Reeves, James, criticism of
Whitman, 179; 'iambic norm',
179, 202
Robinson, Peter, 352
Rosenberg, Isaac, ix, 5; Pound's

apparent encouragement to
enlist, 125–6; Pound's generosity
in having his work published,
125; Pound's characterization,
'horribly rough', 125; his poetry
compared with Lawrence's, 180;
on Whitman and Emerson, 187;
his poetry compared with
Owen's, 189; the 'root' image,
195; 'Emerson', 284; 'simple
poetry', 312; 'Break of Day in
the Trenches', 88, 125, 312, 315;
'Dead Man's Dump', 263;
'Daughters of War', 125; *Moses*,
284
Rota, Bertram, 257
Russian Formalist criticism, 238–9

Saintsbury, George, review of
Whitman, 26
Sassoon, Siegfried, 131, 337
Schmidt, Michael, 352
Shakespeare, William, 81–2, 240,
243–4, 248, 301–2, 323, 385
Shelley, P.B., 'The Triumph of
Life', 9, 152, 198
Sherriff, Bat-Sheva, 330
Sidney, Philip, 30
Silk, Dennis, 316, freer rhythms,
and mixing free and metrical
verse, 372–3
Silkin, Jon, on Owen, 125, 195,
213, 330, 369–70, 377
Silver, Keith, 371
Simic, Charles, 378
Skipsey, Joseph, 391
Smart, Christopher, *Jubilate Agno*,
13, 188, 272, 335, 373, 382
Smith, I.C., 185
Smith, James, 1–2
Smith, Ken, 338–43; valency of his
metricality, 342–3; 'Family
Group', 339, 'Fox Running':
Smith's outsidered, city
language, 338–9; hunted
haunted speech, 339; rhythm
and running ('on the run'), 340;
de-registering of language, 340;
marriage, 341–2; hallucination of

Smith, Ken – *continued*
London H-bombed, 341; Write
or die; re-affirms his
humanness, 342; desperation,
342
Speech, and speaking poetry,
179–80; centre of gravity of
spoken speech, 300–2; the
unknown person, 301
Spenser, Edmund, 'Prothalamion',
and Eliot's 'nymphs', 85–6
Speirs, John, 111
Stead, C.K., on Imagism, 38; on
Eliot's Rightism, 52; on Eliot's
anti-Semitism, 55; on Pound's
anti-Semitism, 59, 77, 93, 113,
161
Steele, Timothy, 13
Stein, Gertrude, 379, 381
Steiner, George, 388
Stephens, Alan, 375
Stramm, August, 43
Surette, Leon, 159–60, 172
Swift, Jonathan, 373
Syllabics, 374–6

Takahiro, Goto, 208
Tennyson, Alfred, 13, 204, 271,
283; *Maud*, 362
Thomas, Dylan, 242–70, Maud,
242, and passim; John
Haffenden, 242; William
Empson, *Argufying*, 242; 'free
verse', 242; metricality, 242–3;
Englyns and Cynghannedd,
245–6; Thomas's 'early' and
'later' poems, 256–7, 265–6; sale
of Thomas's four notebooks,
257; complicated and direct
poetry, 257; Heaney's criticism,
270; his traditional metricality
and his complex language, 284;
'And death shall have no
dominion', 251–2; doubleness of
'hammer' and defiance of death,
252; 'After the funeral', 252–6,
329; authentic mourning, 253–6;
bard, English and Welsh
conceptions, 254; 'Sculptured',

art and life, 255; possible abuse
of her, 255; 'A Refusal to
Mourn', 261–3; double
possibility of syntax, 262;
metricality and lineation, 262;
'one death is too many', 262;
'Hopkins-like' accumulation of
adjectives, 262–3; 'Fern Hill',
265–9; flowing rhythms and
lineation, 266; use of traditional
codes and their appeal, 267–8;
Time and childhood, 268–9; 'In
my Craft or Sullen Art', 263–5;
metricality and its possibilities,
264–5; perfect, modest poem,
265; 'I see the boys of summer',
246–8, 260, 261; the abuse of
sexual richness, 246–7; 'Over Sir
John's Hill', 269–70; 'Poem in
October', 265; 'Poem on his
birthday', 269; 'The force that
through', 248–51; compassion,
248; irony that is true, 249; life
and our destruction of it,
249–50; 'fuse' and Empson,
250; 'The Hunchback in the
Park', 257–61; Notebook version,
258; development of woman
figure, 258; and her creative,
restorative function, 260; dual
role of the children, 258–9;
'Lock', 260;
Tolstoy, Leo, *What is art?*, 194
Tomlinson, Charles, ix, 303,
309–17; arrogance in some
verse, 310–11; isometrics, 311; 'A
Meditation on John Constable',
309, 310–11; 'For Miriam', 309,
316; 'On the Hall at Stowey',
309, 312; council's collusion in
destruction of some buildings,
312; 'The Flood', 309, 316–17;
'The Ruin', 309, 312–13; 'Under
the Moon's Reign', 309, 313–16;
The dream under the dream,
314–5; moon's impartiality, 315;
Tomlinson's notable courage,
315–16
Tracy, Lorna, vii, 265, 308

Tudor: Tudor history in Pound's
Canto, 80, 164–70; Tudor poetry,
271

Ure, Peter, 390

Wales, 245
Weekley, Ernest, 215
Whitman, Walt, his nouns
compared with Hopkins'
adjectives, 15–16; his free verse
compared with Pound's, 34;
cited by Eliot, 36; the need for
an aerial character in poetry, 64;
under emotional pressure tends
towards metricality, 177;
compared with Lawrence
(Hobsbaum), 182; Whitman's
and Lawrence's poetry
compared, 186–92; few
enjambments, 190; letter to
Emerson ('gallantry'), 219;
earlier version of Lawrence's
'The Ship of Death', more
Whitmanesque, 237; 272, 283–4,
342; Ginsberg via Whitman, 382;
'Gods', 232; 'Look Down Fair
Moon', 38–40, compared with
H.D.'s 'Oread'; syntax and
lineation compared with H.D.'s
'Oread', 39–40; 'Out of the
Cradle', 17; quoted by Pound,
162, 269; 'Reconciliation', 24–5;
syntax, dynamic parallelism and
crux of 'For' mid-poem, 25;

'Song of Myself', Chant 24,
22–4, 322; the praise of the male
body culminating in a
declaration of love, 24; the
'envelope', 23; culminating form,
24; 'Song of the Broad-Axe', 187,
322; 'To a Locomotive in
Winter', compared with
Hopkins' 'The Blessed Virgin',
14
Williams, W.C., 45, 197, 370
Wilson, Edmund, 302–3
Wilson, Jean Moorcroft, Rosenberg
and Pound, 125
Winters, Yvor, 358, 359, 364
Woof, R.S., 275
Woolf, Leonard, quoted by
Ackroyd, 54
Woolf, Virginia, 68–9
Wordsworth, William, on
language in the 1815 Preface,
40–1, 272, 283, 302, 304; 'I
Travelled among Unknown
Men', 192; 'Immortality Ode', 3,
264; 'Michael', 1, 3, 264, 364–5;
'Resolution and Independence',
8; 'The Solitary Reaper', 8;
Wroth, Lady Mary, 373

Yeats, W.B., inclusions and
exclusions in his *The Oxford Book
of Modern Verse*, 43; delicate
expression of sexuality, 136, 207

Zach, Natan, 330